Great European Itineraries

THE GREAT WEEKEND ESCAPE BOOK
THE AMERICAN WAY OF WORKING
A STUDENT'S GUIDE TO JULIUS CAESAR

Great European Itineraries

EVERYTHING YOU NEED TO KNOW
TO PLAN YOUR OWN MEMORABLE VACATION

Michael Spring

Doubleday & Company, Inc., Garden City, New York
1987

Library of Congress Cataloging-in-Publication Data

Spring, Michael.
  Great European itineraries.

  Includes index.
  Contents: Ireland: the southwest—England: Bath,
the Cotswolds, and Stratford-upon-Avon—Germany:
Heidelberg and the Romantic Highway—[etc.]
    1. Europe—Description and travel—1971- —Tours.
I. Title.
D909.S67 1987   914'.04558   86–19858
ISBN 0-385-23336-1

For Marge and Bill Bauer,
who also know how to travel without leaving home

CONTENTS

INTRODUCTION

I wrote this guide for those of you who hate rubbing suitcases with strangers on guided tours, but who need help deciding where to go and how to organize your time.

I hope you'll see me as your travel agent and close friend, who sat down with you and helped you plan the vacation of your life. Since friends value honesty, I tried to sweep away the fluff and hyperbole of travel writing, and leave you with the truth. There are many places you won't hear about, because I wouldn't send friends there or wouldn't choose to go back myself.

I've chosen the most popular trips in each of eight European countries, and shown you how to make do with a little money and how to spoil yourself with a lot. Each trip can be made by car or by public transportation. If you're looking for a bargain on a car rental, try Inter-Rent (800/421-6878) or Kemwell (800/468-0468). If you're staying abroad more than three weeks, consider leasing a car from a company like Renault (800/221-1052). The itineraries are for 3–5 days, 5–7 days, and 7–14 days —but you can combine them into longer trips, or adjust them to meet your own schedules and needs.

To get you started, each itinerary begins (when appropriate) with the following sections:

Major Attractions
Introduction
The Main Route
Getting Around
Special Events
A Note on Shopping
Things to See and Do with Children

A Note on Sports
A Note on Art, Architecture, and History
A Note on Dining
A Note on Lodging
Emergencies
For Further Information
The Itinerary

I then take you on a day-by-day trip along the proposed route, suggesting things to do and places to stay and eat.

Here are some of the highlights:

Austria: Medieval towns along the Danube
Ireland: Slea Head, on the wild west coast of Dingle Peninsula
England: Salisbury Cathedral and the Cotswold countryside
France: Saint-Tropez at dawn and the perched village of Peillon
Italy: The Temple of Neptune in Paestum and the hill town of Ravello
Yugoslavia: The ancient stone city of Dubrovnik
Spain: The Alhambra and the White Villages of Andalusia
Germany: The Royal Castles and Heidelberg

The hotels I most highly recommend are:

Park Hotel, Kenmare, Ireland
Wyck Hill House, Stow-in-the-Wold, England
Sign of the Angel, Lacock, England
Il San Pietro di Positano, Positano, Italy
Parador Nacional San Francisco, Granada, Spain
Marbella Club, Marbella, Spain
Schloss Dürnstein, Dürnstein, Austria
Château du Domaine St. Martin, Vence, France
Hotel Negresco, Nice, France

Since I'm asking you to trust me, I had better say a word about my sensibilities. I have omitted many chain hotels because they could be anywhere in the world, and I'm partial to hotels that capture the spirit of a place; that are one of a kind; that could be nowhere other than where they are. On the other hand, I know that age is no guarantee of atmosphere or charm, and that many modern hotels have twice the character of so-called historic inns listed in the guides. I dislike yellow water glasses, all-weather carpeting, soft mattresses, and furnishings that are cute, over-decorated, or deliberately old-fashioned. I like to fall asleep in rooms softened with age. My favorite hotel organization is Relais & Châteaux (800/372-1323 or 212/696-1323), because the hotels it represents are historic buildings that are exquisitely furnished and maintained.

If you feel I've been too kind or too uncritical, or have overlooked interesting places, please let me know so that I can include the information in future editions. Write to Michael Spring, c/o *Great European Itineraries,* Doubleday & Company, Inc., 245 Park Avenue, New York, N.Y. 10017.

Many people have helped make this book possible. I'd like to thank Hedy Wuerz of the German National Tourist Office, Pilar Vico of the National Tourist Office of Spain, Josephine Inzerillo of the Italian Tourist Board, Bedford Pace of the British Tourist Authority, Simon O'Hanlin of the Irish Tourist Board, Gerhard Markus of the Austrian National Tourist Office, and Pavle Lukac of the Yugoslav National Tourist Office.

Material on Spain was prepared with the help of two very special guides, Angel López Macias and Julian Sarabia. Material on Austrian and German restaurants was prepared with the help of Konrad Sönnichsen.

I'd also like to thank Abe Pokrassa, Lucille Hosadjian, John Lampl, William Connors, Daphne Warner, Carol Forman, and my editor, Les Pockell.

Travel books which I found particularly helpful in formulating my own ideas are listed as Recommended Reading at the end of each itinerary.

IRELAND

❦ *The Southwest*

MAJOR ATTRACTIONS

• Seascapes and spectacular mountain passes on the Dingle Peninsula, where *Ryan's Daughter* was filmed.

• A wealth of outdoor sports—golf, tennis, boating, fishing, and hiking—along the Ring of Kerry and among the beautiful mountains and lakes of Killarney.

• The greatest collection of ancient monuments in Ireland, including the Rock of Cashel, where St. Patrick is said to have baptized Ireland's first Christian king.

• The Blarney Stone.

INTRODUCTION

Ireland is small enough that you can enjoy a wonderful range of scenery with a minimum amount of driving. Wild mountain passes, rich green farm country, romantic seascapes—the view changes from one moment to the next.

The weather changes, too, creating a sense of expectancy, as if you had stumbled on an unfinished bit of creation. If you're addicted to blue skies, stay away; Ireland is for those romantic fools who know that only on a misty day can you see forever.

The itinerary takes you around the south and southwest coasts of Ireland, primarily through Cork and Kerry. You can begin either at Shan-

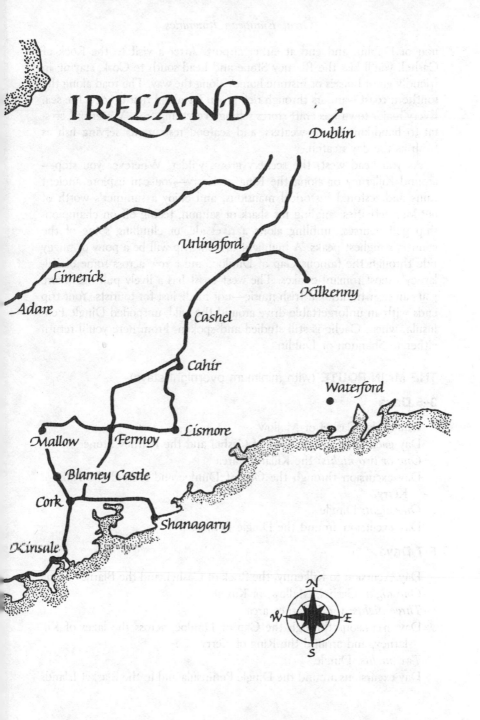

IRELAND

Dublin

Urlingford

Limerick

Kilkenny

Adare

Cashel

Cahír

Waterford

Lismore

Mallow   Fermoy

Blarney Castle

Cork

Shanagarry

Kinsale

N
W   E
S

non or Dublin, and end at either airport. After a visit to the Rock of Cashel, you'll kiss the Blarney Stone and head south to Cork, staying in friendly guest houses or historic homes along the way. The road along the southern coast wanders through rich green farmland that borders the sea. Every major town has craft stores selling everything from Waterford crystal to hand-knit Aran sweaters, and seafood restaurants serving fish as fresh as the day's catch.

As you head west, the scenery grows wilder. Wherever you stop—around Killarney or along the Ring of Kerry—you can explore ancient ruins and restored historical mansions, and enjoy a summer's worth of outdoor activities: angling for shark or salmon, teeing off on championship golf courses, ambling along a riverside, or climbing some of the country's highest peaks. A highlight of your trip will be a pony or buggy ride through the famous Gap of Dunloe, and a row across some of Killarney's most romantic lakes. The west coast has a lively pub life where you can hear traditional Irish music—not made just for tourists. Your trip ends with an unforgettable drive around the wild, unspoiled Dingle Peninsula, where Gaelic is still studied and spoken. From here you'll return either to Shannon or Dublin.

THE MAIN ROUTE (with minimum overnight stays)

3–5 Days

One night: Cashel or Mallow
Day excursions to the Rock of Cashel and the Blarney Stone
One or two nights: the Killarney area
Day excursion through the Gap of Dunloe and around the Ring of Kerry
One night: Dingle
Day excursion around the Dingle Peninsula

5–7 Days

Day excursion to Kilkenny, the Rock of Cashel, and the Blarney Stone
One night: Cashel, Mallow, or Kinsale
Three nights: the Killarney area
Day excursions through the Gap of Dunloe, across the lakes of Killarney, and around the Ring of Kerry
Two nights: Dingle
Day excursions around the Dingle Peninsula and to the Blasket Islands

7–14 Days

Day excursion to Kilkenny and the Rock of Cashel
One night: Mallow or Shanagarry
Day excursion to Cork and the Blarney Stone
One night: Kinsale
Day excursion: Beara Peninsula
One night: Ballylickey
One night: Kenmare
Five nights: The Killarney area
Day excursions through the Gap of Dunloe, across the lakes of Killarney, around the Ring of Kerry, and to the Skellig Islands
Three nights: Dingle
Day excursions around the Dingle Peninsula and to the Blasket Islands

GETTING AROUND

Getting to Ireland

Flying to Dublin and returning from Shannon will save you about 3½ hours of driving time and about $20 in gas. The scenery gets more beautiful as you head west (toward Shannon), so, on the principle that it's better to save the best for last, see Dublin first and fly home from Shannon.

Five airlines operate between Ireland and the United States: **Aer Lingus** (Tel. in New York State: 800/631-7917; elsewhere: 800/223-6537); **Northwest Orient, Delta, Pan American,** and **Transamerica** (c/o Sceptre Charters. Tel. in New York City: 718/624-7835; elsewhere, 800/221-0924).

Aer Lingus flies direct to Dublin and Shannon from New York, Boston, Chicago, Los Angeles, and San Francisco. Fares to Dublin are slightly higher. **Northwest** flies to Shannon from New York, Boston, and Chicago. **Delta** flies to Shannon direct from Atlanta. **Pan American** flies to Shannon from New York. **Transamerica** is a discount carrier with direct flights to Shannon from Los Angeles, San Francisco, and New York.

British Airways has frequent service between London and both Dublin and Shannon.

Traveling Through Ireland

By car:

Driving is on the left, as in Britain. Drivers and front-seat passengers must wear seat belts. Rented cars will not have automatic transmission unless you request it in advance.

While the country shifts from miles to kilometers, some signposts are in one, some in the other. Expect to be confused.

One of the most reasonably priced Irish car rental companies is **Dan Dooley**, which has desks at both Shannon and Dublin airports. The Dublin number is 01-787496. Arrangements can be made in the United States by calling Dan Dooley collect at 718/767-0524. Mention this guide for a 10 percent discount.

Aer Lingus has some attractive fly/drive packages. Some include prepaid vouchers for meals and/or accommodations.

By public transportation:

This is the one trip which you would be advised to make by car. Trains and buses do exist, but they won't get you to many of the most beautiful, out-of-the-way spots. Best bet is simply to skip the south coast and take the train directly from Dublin to Killarney. From here you can take local buses or sign up for daily excursions to all local points of interest, including the Ring of Kerry and Dingle Peninsula. Rented bikes will get you everywhere you want to go in the Killarney area.

Should you want to go from **Dublin** to **Cork**, the train takes 2 hours and 40 minutes. A bus goes from **Cork** to **Kinsale** in 50 minutes. The train from **Cork** to **Killarney**, via Mallow, takes 1 hour and 50 minutes. The train from **Dublin** to **Killarney** via Mallow takes 3 hours and 45 minutes. From **Killarney** there is regular bus service around the **Ring of Kerry** and to the town of **Dingle**. From **Dingle**, the bus to the **Tralee** train station takes 80 minutes. From **Tralee** the train back to Dublin takes 3 hours and 35 minutes.

If you plan to travel extensively, buy a **Rail-only Rover Ticket** or a **Rail-Road Rambler Ticket**. The latter is valid on all trains and buses. Both the **Eurailpass** and the **Eurail Youthpass** are valid in Ireland.

The 3–5 Day Trip

It will take most of a day, leaving from Dublin, to tour the Rock of Cashel and the Blarney Stone. After reading the itinerary below, decide whether you want to see these sights or drive directly to the west coast.

If you plan to visit the Rock of Cashel and the Blarney Stone: From Dublin take Route N7 southwest to Port Laoise and continue on Route N8 to Cashel and Cork. Drive north 5 miles to the Blarney Stone. Return to Cork and take Route N22 west to Killarney. Drive around the Ring of Kerry, seeing the south coast first: from Kenmare to Waterville, Cahirciveen and Killorglin. From Killorglin, drive around the Dingle Peninsula through the towns of Dingle, Dunquin, Ballyferriter, back to Dingle, and north across the Conor Pass to Tralee. Take Route N21 east to Castleisland, and north to Adare and Limerick. If you're returning to Shannon, drive northwest on Route N18 from Limerick to Shannon Airport. If you're returning to Dublin, take Route N7 from Limerick to Dublin.

If you don't plan to visit the Rock of Cashel or the Blarney Stone: From Dublin take Route N7 west to Limerick and Route N211 to Tralee. Following the itinerary in reverse, drive around the Dingle Peninsula, heading along the north coast, and crossing the Conor Pass to Dingle. From Dingle, follow a circular route west to Dunquin and Ballyferriter, and back to Dingle. From Dingle, head east to Castlemaine and south to Killorglin. Drive around the Ring of Kerry from north to south: from Cahirciveen to Waterville, Kenmare, and Killarney. From Killarney take Route N22 north and N21 northeast to Adare and Limerick. If you're returning to Shannon, drive northwest on Route N18 from Limerick to Shannon Airport. If you're returning to Dublin, take Route N7 from Limerick to Dublin.

The 5–7 Day Trip

From Dublin take Route N7 southwest to Port Laoise and continue on Route N8 to Cashel and Cork. The Blarney Stone is five miles north of Cork. From here you can take Route N22 direct to Killarney, which will give you more time to explore the beautiful west coast, or you can see more of the country by taking the slower but more scenic route along the south coast from Cork to Kinsale, Clonakilty, Skibbereen, Bantry, Ballylickey, Glengarriff, and Kenmare. Drive around the Ring of Kerry, through Waterville, Cahirciveen, and Killorglin to Killarney. Return to Killorglin and drive around the Dingle Peninsula through the towns of

Dingle, Dunquin, Ballyferriter, back to Dingle, and north across the
Conor Pass to Tralee. Take Route N21 east to Castleisland, and north
to Adare and Limerick. If you're returning to Shannon, drive northwest
on Route N18 from Limerick to Shannon Airport. If you're returning to
Dublin, take Route N7 from Limerick to Dublin.

The 7–14 Day Trip

From Dublin take Route N7 southwest to Nasse and Route N9 south
to Kilkenny. From Kilkenny, drive west to Urlingford and south on
Route N8 to Cashel and Cashir. Leave the main highway and follow
signs south to Clogheen and Lismore, then west along the Blackwater
River to Fermoy, and south on Route N8 to Cork. From Cork drive
south to Kinsale, and west through Skibbereen, Bantry, Ballylickey, and
Glengarriff. Drive around the Beara Peninsula to Castletown Bere and
Kenmare. Drive around the Ring of Kerry, through Waterville, Cahirciveen, and Killorglin to Killarney. Return to Killorglin and drive around
the Dingle Peninsula through the towns of Dingle, Dunquin, Ballyferriter, back to Dingle, and north across the Conor Pass to Tralee. Take
Route N21 east to Castleisland, and north to Adare and Limerick. If
you're returning to Shannon, drive northwest on Route N18 from Limerick to Shannon Airport. If you're returning to Dublin, take Route N7
from Limerick to Dublin.

A NOTE ON SHOPPING

It's not necessary to go to Waterford to buy Waterford glass; the price
is the same everywhere in Ireland, even at the factory store. The factory
may have a wider selection, but there are no "seconds" at reduced prices.
Part of what you're paying for is the name; consider buying other Irish
glass made in Kilkenny, Cork, Galway, and Dublin, at considerably lower
prices.

Almost every town has a shop or two selling handwoven tweeds, un-
dyed wool sweaters (the so-called Aran knitwear), and linen. Some of the
knitted goods are made by hand, others—the less expensive ones—by
machine. Some fabrics and knitwear are made locally, so goods vary from
shop to shop. Prices vary, too; Aran-style sweaters, for instance, cost up to
40 percent more at the airport. The rule is to buy what you like when you
see it, for you probably won't see one exactly like it again. You'll find the
largest selection (but not the lowest prices) at the Woolen Mills at the

entrance to **Blarney Castle**, and at the **Design Workshop** in Kilkenny. Irish **poplin** is woven only in Cork.

Ireland is famous for its hand-thrown **pottery**. Some of the best shops are in Kinsale, Dingle Town, and Dunquin (on the west coast of the Dingle Peninsula).

The tradition of Celtic ornamentation has inspired the jewelry and silverwork of present-day Irish craftsmen. Particularly popular are designs based on the Book of Kells.

THINGS TO SEE AND DO WITH CHILDREN

Ireland is geared to family travel, which makes it an ideal country to visit with children of any age. Most hotels and private homes can make arrangements for babysitters.

Almost every town along the route offers swimming, hiking, biking, fishing, and pony rides. Families can rent ponies or pony carts for trips through the Gap of Dunloe. They can also take boat trips on the lakes of Killarney. The grounds of **Muckross House**, on the shores of two of Killarney's most beautiful lakes, are a safe and scenic place for kids to bike. Killarney has several bike-rental shops.

Kids will love **Blarney Castle** and a walk through its **Rock Close**. They should also enjoy exploring **Muckross Abbey** near Killarney, and climbing to the dizzying heights of the **Great Blasket Island**, off the coast of Dingle.

A NOTE ON DINING

Your safest bet, as you travel along the coast, is fresh fish, particularly salmon (either poached or grilled). Other favorites are sea and brown trout, sole grilled on the bone, oysters, and lobster. For meat dishes, try Irish mutton, spring lamb, or steaks.

Simplicity is the keynote of native Irish cooking, with such unpretentious dishes as Irish stew, bacon and cabbage, spring chicken with fresh vegetables, roast pork with applesauce, or eggs with homemade wholemeal bread. The leading restaurants lean toward French cuisine—either classic or nouvelle, with an emphasis on fresh local produce. The more imaginative establishments try to blend French and Irish influences: a sauce made with Irish whiskey, say, or Bailey's Irish Cream.

The word *whiskey* is derived from the Irish *uisce beatha,* meaning "water of life." You'll want to try it in Irish coffee, topped with a thick layer of fresh cream.

For quick, inexpensive lunches, you can't go wrong with pub grub and a pint of cider, stout, or lager.

A 10–15 percent service charge is usually added to your bill; there's no need to add more unless the service is exceptional. Tipping is not expected at bars.

Restaurants are rated, for two, E (expensive, over $60); M (moderate, $25 to $60); I (inexpensive, under $25).

A NOTE ON LODGING

The choice is yours between hotels—some modern high-rises, others restored mansions—and private homes offering bed and breakfast. My vote would be to stay either in the best hotels or in private guest homes, or in a combination of the two. The exclusive hotels have the atmosphere and amenities that many travelers want. The second- and third-class hotels—many of them older hotels lacking the funds for renovations—are not in themselves objectionable, but the private homes are usually cleaner, friendlier, and more modern. The Irish Tourist Board publishes an indispensable guide to Irish bed-and-breakfast establishments, which shows you pictures of each home, and gives you information on prices and facilities, including availability of rooms with private bath. The Irish Tourist Board publishes a similar listing of hotels. Bed-and-breakfast reservations can be made through Tourist Information Offices in major Irish towns or by writing to the Central Reservations Service, 14 Upper O'Connell Street, Dublin 1. A fee of about $1.50 is added for each booking. Hotel reservations can, of course, also be made through your travel agent at home.

Irish hotels almost always charge per person rather than per room. Hotel rates start at about $22 per person, including a full American breakfast. The private homes cost $12–$18 per person, including breakfast. Lodgings listed below are rated per person: E (expensive, over $30), M (moderate, under $30), and I (inexpensive, under $23).

Published rates do not always include taxes and service charges; it pays to ask beforehand. The larger chain hotels that cater to the package-tour trade have gone the way of the world and begun charging extra for breakfast: tourists should boycott them on principle. It's not just a matter of dollars and cents: a breakfast "on the house" has always been part of the Irish (and British) experience, giving Americans the sense that they are guests in a foreign home.

EMERGENCIES

For the **police** or **medical help** dial 999 anywhere in Ireland.
The **American Embassy**, 42 Elgin Road, Ballsbridge, Dublin. Tel. 01-764061.

FOR FURTHER INFORMATION

Contact the **Irish Tourist Board**: 757 Third Avenue, New York, N.Y. 10017. Tel. 212/418-0800.

THE ITINERARY

EN ROUTE

Those of you with limited time will want to take **Routes N7 and N8** direct from **Dublin** to **Cashel**—a 2½-hour drive. Those with more time or with a keen interest in Irish history, will want to make a side trip to **Kilkenny** (2¼ hours), following **Route N7** southwest from **Dublin** to **Dorrow**, and **Route N77** south to **Kilkenny**.

⚜ KILKENNY *(Cill Chainnigh, Canice's Church)*

Kilkenny is billed as the best example of a medieval town in Ireland, but its historic roots are less than obvious to the casual visitor. Even with its narrow side streets with names like Collier's Lane, you'll have to use some imagination to envision its antiquity. What makes a side trip here worthwhile is **St. Canice's Cathedral**, with its ancient stone tower; the restored medieval **Black Abbey**; a restored sixteenth-century home, the Rothe House—a rare sight in a country whose past is so often glimpsed only in broken stone and rubble; and **Kilkenny Castle**.

Anyone who wants to understand Anglo-Irish relations has to go back at least to the infamous 1366 **Statutes of Kilkenny**, which were meant to strengthen English authority in Ireland, and to keep the Irish and the Anglo-Norman settlers apart. No Irish cattle could graze on English land. Marrying the Irish was punishable by death. Anglo-Norman settlers—many of whom went native—had their estates forfeited for speaking Gaelic, for giving their children Irish names, or for dressing in Irish clothes. Wearing Irish-made underwear was enough to get a person thrown in jail. The native Irish were not allowed within the town walls, but had to live in shanty Irishtowns—in their own country! The intermingling of Irish and Anglo-Norman elements was well under way when the Statutes of Kilkenny went into effect; if this fusion had been allowed to continue, who knows, there might be no civil war in Northern Ireland today.

By the early seventeenth century the Irish Catholics had had enough, and formed the **Confederation of Kilkenny**, which governed Ireland for six years and tried to bring about reforms. Pope Innocent X sent money and guns. Cromwell responded in 1650 by overrunning the town, sacking the cathedral, and using it to stable his horses.

• Begin your tour at **St. Canice's Cathedral**, one of the finest in Ireland, despite Cromwell's defacements. The **round tower** is all that's left of the sixth-century monastic settlement around which the town developed. The cathedral, mostly Early English, is thirteenth century (restored in 1866), with a twelfth-century marble font, a **library** you should ask to see, and a stone seat built into the north wall, said to be Saint Canice's. Within the massive walls is a Gothic structure with "all the exultant sensuality of the Provençal love poetry that the Normans brought to Ireland" (Tom Cahill). The knights in full armor stare upward at eternity. Their faces are more Irish than French—a reminder that the Irish influenced the Normans, too, at least in bed.

The **tower** is one of the few in Ireland you can climb.

• From the cathedral, return to the road, turn right, and make your first left past the hairdresser's shop to reach the **Black Abbey**, a recently restored thirteenth-century friary, named after the black capes of the Dominican friars. Note how the transept is longer than the nave—a good example of how the Irish played tricks with Gothic forms, which never suited them, and a sad reminder of what the Irish could have accomplished architecturally if they had been permitted to develop styles that reflected their own Celtic sensibilities.

• From the Black Abbey, turn left and follow narrow **Abbey Lane**—one of the town's more medieval-looking streets, to **Parliament Street**. Turn right. Two blocks down on your right is **Fitzpatrick's Pub**, a good bet for some pub grub. Across the street is the late-sixteenth-century **Rothe House**, the restored home of a Tudor merchant. Ask to see a small costume collection hidden away in an armoire. Open April through October from 10:30 to 12:30, and from 3 to 5; Sundays, from 3 to 5.

• Continue down Parliament Street. Where the road splits, bear left on **St. Kieran Street**. On your left is **Don Kyteler's Inn**, the fourteenth-century house of Dame Alice the witch. Perhaps because four husbands died on her, she was accused of holding witch's sabbaths, sacrificing black cocks, and mixing their innards with herbs, bugs, and the hair and nails of unbaptized children. She escaped without her maid, Petronilla, who was burned at the stake.

• Where the street ends, turn left to the bridge. Another left at the edge of the River Nore takes you to **Tynan's Bridge House**, one of the country's best and oldest pubs—a good bet for lunch. Across the river you can see **Kilkenny College**, the former **St. John's College**, where Swift, William Congreve, and Bishop George Berkeley were educated.

• Return to the bridge without crossing it, and continue along the path beneath **Kilkenny Castle**. A narrow break in the wall takes you up a flight of stairs to the castle. There's some lovely woodwork, an impressive Grand Hall, and a gallery of modern Irish art, but those of you with only a passing interest in the arts may want to pass by. Best bets are the extensive grounds and the **Kilkenny Design Workshop**, one of the best in the country, selling locally made woven textiles, silver and metal work, hand knits, crystal, etc. Open June through September from 10:30 to 7; off-season, open daily except Mondays from 10:30 to 5.

• **Dunmore Cave**, 7 miles north of Kilkenny, is modest in size, yet has some beautiful formations which children in particular will enjoy. The bones found here belonged to forty-four hapless individuals—twenty-five of them children—who were probably seeking refuge from a Viking attack. Scholars theorize that the coins found here fell from the armpit of a Viking: the Irish didn't use coins then, and the Vikings in those pocketless days wound them in a screw of cloth which they attached with beeswax to their armpit hair. A Viking probably dropped them in battle. "When you enter, a sudden Chilliness seizes all parts of the body," wrote an earlier visitor, "and a Dimness surrounded our lights, as if the Place were filled with a thick Fog. . . . Our Faces, through this Gloom, looked as if we were a Collection of Ghosts, and the Lights in our Hands seemed as if we were making a visit to the infernal Shades."

Dining

Tynan's Bridge House (I, see above) is your best bet for pub grub. **Fitzpatrick's** (I, see above) is another local favorite, particularly for salads. **Don Kyteler's Inn** (M, St. Kieran Street), features a Friday night Witch's Banquet, with mulled wine and traditional Irish music. Daily fare includes white dover sole filled with salmon and mushrooms, and cooked in champagne.

Lodging

The three main hotels are modern but charmless—no more than places to put your head for the night. All are too far from town center to walk. The best, though it smelled of disinfectant when I was there, is the **Kilkenny Hotel**, formerly Rose Hill House (M/E, College/Callan Road, Kilkenny. Tel. 056-62000). Though popular with tour buses, it has a lovely glassed-in porch, tennis, hot tubs, and a heated indoor pool.

Newpark (M, Castlecomer Road, Kilkenny. Tel. 056-22122), north of town, is second best, with a choice of lovely old rooms without baths in the main Victorian house, or charmless rooms with bath in the annex.

Springhill Court Hotel (M/E, Waterford Road South, Kilkenny, 2 miles south of town on Route N10. Tel. 056-21122) is a simple, basic, whitewashed brick motel next to a modern restaurant that looks like a fort made of whipped cream.

For a taste of old Ireland, best bet is the inexpensive, in-town **Club House Hotel** (M, Patrick Street. Tel. 056-21994).

❧ *HOLYCROSS*

Whether or not you visit Kilkenny, you'll be passing through **Urlingford** on the **Dublin–Cork Road** (N8), and then heading south to **Cashel**. It will add another 45 minutes to your trip to head west through **Thurles**, and stop at the **Abbey of Holycross** en route to **Cashel**. Whether it's worth the time depends on whether you want to join the faithful who since the late twelfth century have been making pilgrimages to this Cistercian Abbey to see a piece of the Cross.

❧ *CASHEL* (Causeal, stone fort)

For anyone who cares about the past, a visit to the **Rock of Cashel** is a high point of a trip to Ireland. The rock rises like a stone castle, 200 feet above the town, and contains the best examples of medieval architecture in Ireland. It was here, it is believed, that St. Patrick baptized the Irish King Aengus, who thus became Ireland's first Christian ruler; here that St. Patrick plucked the shamrock that he used to explain the doctrine of the Trinity, which gave Ireland its national emblem; here that you can glimpse that Gaelic Ireland which has survived in spite of the Normans, the Danes, the British, and the tourists. The Rock is open June through August, from 9 to 7:30; off-season, from 10 to about 4:30. You can explore the ruins on your own or on a 50-minute guided tour.

The most romantic route to the Rock is along the **Bishop's Walk**, a ten-minute hike from the **Cashel Palace Hotel**. Try to get Tom Wood as your guide.

The Rock dominates the surrounding landscape, which in the fifth century was covered with dense oak forests. Legend has it that the devil, flying back to England, took a bite from a nearby hillside and dropped it here in the Golden Vale. Ask a guide to point out the "bite" in the side of the Slieve Bloom Mountains.

As you enter this royal city, you'll see ahead of you a rough stone with an ancient cross, where Patrick is said to have baptized King Aengus. Patrick was old then and drove his staff into the earth to support himself. After the ceremony, it was discovered that the staff had passed through the king's foot, and that the grass was soaked with blood. Aengus never cried out because he thought that suffering was part of the Christian experience.

The stone is a replica; the actual one is on display in the museum across from the entrance. One piece is missing from the triple cross, which symbolizes the three crosses on Calvary. Carved on the back is the figure of a robed bishop. It is believed that the stone beneath the cross was once a Coronation Stone for pre-Christian Irish kings, and before that, a sacrificial altar. How emblematic of the blend of pagan/Celtic and Christian elements in the Irish character!

Behind the cross are **Cormac's Chapel**, which is the best preserved Romanesque ruin in the country, and the **cathedral**. When H. V. Morton calls the chapel "whimsical"—an example of "gay Norman"—he is referring to its individuality, to the refusal of its builders to submit to foreign influences. Built by well-traveled Irish monks a half century before the Normans came, it has a uniquely Irish double roof, high-pitched to keep the rain away without pushing the walls out. The eastern end is not pointed directly east, as in other Romanesque churches, because the chapel was dedicated to Our Lady and built so that on her feast day, May 1, the sun streamed through two windows (now blocked up), and fell directly on the altar below. Similarly, the cathedral was built a few degrees off so that the sun could shine through three lancet windows and illuminate the altar on another feast day, March 17. Notice how the chancel arch (the rounded arch that separates the body of the chapel from the "front") is lopsided, symbolizing the drooping of Christ's head on the cross. Each column in both chapel and cathedral has a different shape, as if each were carved by a different artist faithful to his own private vision. How contrary to European models, and how sad that these Celtic anomalies were eventually stuffed into an English form.

Compare the rough, simple chapel, built in the earliest days of Christianity, to the relatively grand, sophisticated Gothic cathedral, built in a later age when Christianity was more established, and faith more formalized. Ironically, it is the more modest chapel that has survived.

Dining

Cashel Palace Hotel (E, Main Street, Cashel. Tel. 062-61411) is a French restaurant with an Irish accent, serving such imaginative specialties as lamb stuffed with sweetbreads and mushrooms, roast quail in Bailey's Irish Cream, and poached lobster with Irish whiskey, cream, shallots, and spring onions.

Chez Hans (M, Rockside, Cashel. Tel. 062-61177) is a converted chapel on the side road leading to the Rock. The menu, which changes with the seasons, includes such local specialties as mussels with garlic and cream of mushroom soup, Dover sole, poached salmon, and spinach-stuffed lamb with fresh vegetables. For dessert, try the chocolate mousse or homemade ices.

Lodging

Cashel Palace Hotel (E, Main Street, Cashel. Tel. 062-61411) is a conversation piece. The eighteenth-century mansion was for 140 years the palace of the Archbishop of Cashel. The Palladian architect Sir Edward Pearce also designed Parliament House in Dublin, now the Bank of Ireland. One room has a 12- by 18-foot bathroom, with 16-foot ceilings. Running along the wall and across the mirror is a family of Beatrix Potter rabbits—the work of the Right Rev. Dr. Robert Wyse Jackson, Bishop of Limerick, who resided here as dean of Cashel from 1946 to 1961. When I made the mistake of lifting the heavy fabric from my night table, I discovered that it was made from two pieces of interlocking chipboard—which only added to the hotel's charm. I also had a fancy color TV with remote control, that let me switch between Ireland's two channels before they went off the air on Saturday night at 11:45. The staff here is friendly and accessible. The dining room has earned a Michelin star—one of the country's few. The taproom is a favorite with locals. Rooms are unequal in quality; avoid 8; try for 25, which enjoys a view of the Rock, or 21. Fielding likes 2 and 7.

Tipperary Inn, formerly the Cashel Kings (M/I, Tel. 062-61477) is now in the hands of some capable Americans, who have redone most of the rooms. The ambiance is Cinderblock Modern, but the price is right, and the view is breathtaking.

For Further Information

Tel. 062-61333.

❧ CAHIR

Cahir, 11 miles south of Cashel, has a fully restored fifteenth-century castle, with a massive keep, high enclosing walls, and spacious courtyards. The entrance fee includes a 12-minute audiovisual show.

Lodging

If you just need a place to stop overnight on the Dublin–Cork Road, you won't find anything nicer than the **Kilcoran Lodge Hotel** (M, Cahir. Tel. 052-41288), a few miles south of Cahir, on your right. Rooms are small and undistinguished, but very clean, cheerful, and homey; and the restaurant enjoys a loyal local following. A few rooms have antiques; ask for one that's quiet and in the original lodge, not in the wings. Facilities include tennis and an indoor pool.

EN ROUTE: From CAHIR to CORK

The fastest route is along the Dublin–Cork Highway (N8) to **Mitchelstown** and **Fermoy.** If you appreciate beautiful scenery, however, it's worth an extra half hour turning off N8 at **Clogheen,** driving over the mountains to **Lismore,** and then heading west to **Fermoy.** (About 30 miles northwest of Fermoy is the town of **Buttevant.** Cross-country horse racing is said to have began here in 1752 when Edward Blake challenged a neighbor to race to the church at **St. Leger** four miles away. The steeple gave them a point to head toward; hence, the term steeplechase.)

At Fermoy you have two choices: (1) To skip Cork and the south coast, and head directly west on Route N72 to **Killarney.** This makes sense if time is limited and you want to reach the west coast as soon as possible. The road takes you through **Mallow,** which has one of Ireland's better hotels (see below). (2) To head south to **Cork** and the south coast. It's the latter route we'll be following.

❧ CORK (Corcaigh, marsh)

Cork is so named because the area within the arms of the River Lee—the center and the oldest part of Cork—is filled-in marshland. If you're looking for a colorful old town with memorable walks, historic hotels, and first-class restaurants, Cork is *not* the place to visit, or at least not to stay. Those with a passing curiosity should plan to spend a morning or afternoon, and then overnight in **Shanagarry** (to the east), **Mallow** (to the north), or **Kinsale** (to the south). Visitors who spend more time in Cork should have a serious interest in its history as a center for the struggle for independence.

The Anglo-Normans invaded in 1172 and the native chieftain was forced to marry a Norman woman. The townspeople, led by merchants, won a good deal of independence over the years, but in 1492 they took up the cause of **Perkin Warbeck**, pretender to the throne, and the mayor and leading citizens were executed and Cork lost its charter. The city surrendered to Cromwell in 1649, and in 1690 had to surrender again to William III. The **Fenian** movement, the secret revolutionary society that sought independence from England by force, began here in 1858. These early terrorists played an important role in the War of Independence (1919–21), earning the city the name of Rebel Cork, which it kept until independence was won in 1922. The British burned down much of the city in 1920, so many of the buildings, including the City Hall, are relatively new.

It was here that **William Thackeray** composed *Vanity Fair* with the help of his mother-in-law, and here that the writers **Frank O'Connor** and **Sean O'Faolain** were born. It was nearby at Youghal that Edmund Spenser wrote the *Faerie Queene*, with financial help from the mayor, an Englishman named Sir Walter Raleigh. Raleigh may have been polite to women, but he recommended a ruthless policy against the Irish, helping to suppress rebellions and recommending assassination of their leaders.

• You can tour the city's high points in about two hours. Begin near **St. Patrick's Bridge**, beneath the statue of **Theobald Mathew** (1790–1861), who championed at least one side of the Irish character by leading a nationwide temperance campaign. He looks young and dashing, but his right hand is raised, either to bless you or to say "no."

• Follow **St. Patrick's Street**, the main street of town, toward the center of the island. Turn right on **Academy Street** to **Emmet's Place** and see the modern Irish landscapes on display in the **Crawford Municipal School of Art Gallery** (open daily from 9:30 to 5:30; Sundays, from 9 to 1).

• From the Gallery, follow **Paul Street**. On your right is the **City Park Shopping Centre**, where you can compare Waterford glass to less expensive Cork crystal. Turn right on **Cornmarket Street**, which has an outdoor market. Continue to the river. Turn left and walk to the bridge. Cross over and follow **Shandon Street** to **Church Street**. Turn right to St. **Ann's Shandon Church**. Sing "The Bells of Shandon" as you climb the 120-foot bell tower for a gull's-eye view of the town. "With deep affection/ And recollection," wrote Father Francis Sylvester Mahoney, "I often think of/ Those Shandon bells,/ Whose sounds so wild would/ In the days of childhood/ Fling around my cradle/ Their magic spells." Is it any wonder many locals prefer Father Francis to O'Connor or O'Faolain?

• Return down **Shandon Street**, recross the bridge, and continue along **North Main Street**. At the **Hilser Jewelry Store**, which is worth a visit, turn right on **Washington Street**, and then left on **Grand Parade**, past an enclosed vegetable and meat market, to the **Information Office**. Behind the office is an **Entertainment Centre**, where you can take in a one-act Irish play at lunch. If you plan to spend the evening in the area, find out what's happening at **Everyman Place**, where modern plays are performed, and at the **Opera House**.

Shopping

Best bet for Irish crafts, fabrics, and knitwear is the **Blarney Woolen Mills and Shop**, at the entrance to **Blarney Castle**, 5 miles north of Cork (see below). In Cork, try the **Savoy Centre** or the **Queen's Old Castle Shopping Centre** on St. Patrick's Street.

Egan's on St. Patrick's Street is famous for jewelry and silver. So is **James Mangen**. For antiques, try the **Antique Shop** on Academy Street, the **Antique Market** on Tuckey Street, and the side streets between St. Patrick's and South Mall. Many shops and department stores sell locally made **Glengarriff lace**.

Dining

Pubs

Pub collectors won't mind going a bit out of the way to **The Gateway** (follow South Main Street across the South Gate Bridge to Barrack Street), the oldest pub in town, dating back to the early 1600s. The Duke of Marlborough drank ale here.

Reardon's Cellar Bar on Washington Street dates back to the 1800s. Its pub grub is popular with the legal folks from the nearby Court House.

On St. Patrick's Street are **Le Château**, established in 1793, and the **Old Bridge Tavern**.

Restaurants

If you're spending the night in Cork, your best bet for dinner is the **Arbutus Lodge** (E, Middle Glanmire Road, Montenotte, Cork. Tel. 021-51237), a short walk uphill from the train station. The menu features nouvelle dishes with an Irish twist: chicken Hibernia in a sauce laced with Irish whiskey instead of Cognac, Irish nettle soup, sole fillets with a sea urchin sauce, noisettes of lamb with fresh pasta, sautéed lobster with fresh fennel sauce. The view from the open terrace is first-class.

Second choice, farther away from town, is **Lovett's** (E, Churchyard Lane, off Wells Road, Douglas. Tel. 021-294909), a Georgian-period house in the suburbs with such seafood specialties as mousseline of turbot and sea trout cooked in parchment.

If you're staying in **Shanagarry** (see Lodgings below), about 20 miles southeast of Cork, or willing to drive for a first-class meal, dine at the elegant **Ballymaloe House Restaurant** (E, Shanagarry, about 20 miles southeast of Cork. Tel. 021-652531). The five-course set dinner, which comes from the hotel's own working farm, includes a peasant soup made from home-grown vegetables, herbs, garlic, and smoked bacon; stuffed mussels; baked trout; quail with grapes; trout baked with watercress; calf's liver sautéed in whiskey; and steak.

It's also worth the 22-mile drive north to the **Longueville House** (M/E, Mallow, just west of town on T30, toward Killarney. Tel. 022-27156). This prestigious country restaurant (see Lodgings below) also features fresh produce from its working farm, and fish from the famous Blackwater River which runs through the property. Specialties include salmon mousse pâté, crisp duck, roast leg of lamb, black sole, trout baked in herbs, and veal kidney in a mustard sauce.

Lodging

Unless you have a special reason to sojourn in Cork, I recommend you spend the night in one of the lovely country hotels to the north, southeast, and south. In Cork itself, the two top hotels are **Jury's Hotel** (E, Western Road, Cork. Tel. 021-96637) and the **Imperial** (E, South Mall, Cork. Tel. 021-23304). Both are within walking distance of downtown Cork, but there the similarity ends. Jury's is the more modern of the two. Despite the lime-colored cinder-block walls, rooms are spacious and comfortable. The package-tour crowd is attracted to facilities that include a sauna, indoor and outdoor pools, tennis and squash. Style or class Jury's has not; but for amenities it leads the pack. In contrast is the sedate, old-fashioned **Imperial**. The spirit of an earlier age is captured in the public rooms, with their high ceilings, marble floors, and crystal chandeliers. Room 115 is a good bet.

For a smaller in-town hotel, try the **Arbutus Lodge** (E, Middle Glanmire Road, Montenotte, Cork. Tel. 021-51237). Nestled in a garden on a hill overlooking the city, it has small, friendly, traditional rooms in a very modernized Georgian house. The restaurant is considered one of the best in Ireland.

For an inexpensive guest house also in walking distance of downtown Cork, try the plain but friendly **Gabriel House** (I, Summerhill Street. Tel. 021-500333), which once belonged to the Irish Christian Brothers.

Your choice of hotels outside of Cork depends on your schedule. If you plan to tour Cork in the afternoon and to take the slower but more scenic drive along the south coast, it makes sense to spend the night in **Kinsale**, which has several decent hotels and restaurants (see the town listings below). In a class by themselves, however, are **Ballymaloe House** in **Shanagarry**, and **Longueville House** in **Mallow**.

Ballymaloe House (E, Shanagarry, about 20 miles southeast of Cork, on L35A, County Cork. Tel. 021-652531) is not directly on our proposed route. It would make sense staying here only if (1) you plan to spend a few days in the Cork area; (2) you arrive at the hotel in the evening, spend the night, and then continue to Cork the next morning on your way west; and/or (3) you're willing to go out of your way to stay in a family-run country hotel rich in charm (more than elegance) and character. The hotel, part of it dating back to the seventeenth century, sits on 400 acres of rolling farmland. William Penn, Oliver Cromwell, and Bishop Berkeley stayed here—in the days before it had a swimming pool, tennis courts, and nine holes of golf. The restaurant, lined with the paintings of Jack Yeats (William Butler's brother) is first-rate, particularly for Sunday dinner. To reach **Shanagarry**, leave the Dublin–Cork road at Cahir and drive south to **Lismore** and **Mallow**.

Longueville House (M/E, Mallow, just west of town on T30, toward Killarney. Tel. 022-27156) is 22 miles north of Cork, so you wouldn't want to stay here either unless (1) you plan to spend a few days in the area; (2) you arrive at the hotel in the evening, spend the night, and then, in the morning, continue south through Cork; or (3) you're willing to go out of your way for a night in one of Ireland's best-loved country hotels. The Georgian mansion sits on 500 acres overlooking the Blackwater River, which supplies one of the country's top restaurants with its fresh fish (see Dining above). In spite of the owner's efforts to modernize the hotel, it has managed to keep its Old World charm, with an elegant drawing room, a library bound in silence, and lots of molded plaster, Waterford chandeliers, and beautiful, inlaid mahogany doors. Ask for a bedroom with traditional furnishings overlooking the ruins of Dromineed Castle.

If you're looking for something more modest, Eileen O'Reilly's guide to Irish country inns recommends the Gables (I/M, Stoneview, Blarney, County Cork. Tel. 021-85330), a small, friendly, family hotel about 4 miles north of Cork, en route to Blarney Castle. The century-old house, the former home of the parish priest, has a tennis court and sits on two acres.

✤ *BLARNEY CASTLE*

The castle is open daily in May from 9 to 7; in June and July from 9 to 8:30; in August from 9 to 7:30; in September from 9 to 6:30; Sundays, from 9:30 to 5:30; off-season, from 9 to sundown.

Kissing the Blarney Stone is like standing for the Hallelujah Chorus of *The Messiah*—it's something you do. But the romantic ruins of Blarney Castle are also worth a visit, and so are the Woolen Mills—the largest emporium of Irish crafts in the country—located on the castle grounds. The castle is five miles (a ten-minute drive) north of Cork; just follow the signs. If you're staying in Mallow, stop off at the castle en route south to Cork.

Why is there so much blarney about a simple stone? As the story goes, an emissary named George Carew was sent by Queen Elizabeth I to get the Lord of Blarney Castle, Cormac McDermot MacCarthy, to transfer his allegiance from his clan to her; in other words, to surrender his fortress. Again and again MacCarthy agreed, but at the last moment he always found another reason to delay. His excuses were so frequent and so reasonable that Carew became a joke at Elizabeth's court. Elizabeth is reported to have told Carew in exasperation, "This is all Blarney talk; what he says he never means." And so the word blarney has come to stand for smooth talk—charming, basically harmless, but meant to deceive.

High up on the battlements of the ancient castle, embedded in the outside wall, is the Blarney Stone. Kissing it is said to give one the gift of eloquence, which makes men (and now women, I suppose) irresistible to the opposite sex. Of all visitors to the castle—Germans, Japanese, and so on—Americans, the manager tells me, are most likely to kiss the stone and be on their way, neglecting the romantic fifteenth-century castle itself, and the beautiful castle grounds.

Visitors, including the Irish, have been kissing the stone since the eighteenth century. No one knows exactly why. Some say MacCarthy rescued a drowning witch, who thanked him by telling him the secret of the magic stone. Others say the stone was brought from the Holy Land during the Crusades. The most palatable explanation is that the stone had some significance to the MacCarthy clan—perhaps as the stone on which the chieftain sat—and it was later incorporated into the battlements.

What will surprise you is the considerable effort you must make to kiss the stone. After climbing 127 very steep stone steps, you have to lie on your back and lean backward over the edge of the wall so that you're peering down more than 150 feet. Visitors were once dangled by their heels over the side of the castle, but in 1912 a hapless pilgrim fell ineloquently to the ground, and an iron guard rail was installed. Ninety-year-olds have kissed the stone, so there's no reason why you can't, too; and a photographer will take your picture to prove it.

The path leading to the castle veers left to the **Rock Close**, a grove of ancient yew trees—some of the oldest in the world—and weirdly shaped boulders. Don't miss it. The paths were probably laid out by an eighteenth-century owner of the castle, but when you see the witch's stone and wander through her kitchen, you'll agree with those who seriously believe that this was once a center of Druidic worship.

If you want to do all your shopping at once, the best place to go is the **Blarney Woolen Mills** at the entrance to the castle. Prices are not low, but the selection is impressive.

✤ KINSALE *(Ceann Saile,* head of the tide)

Kinsale, 18 miles southwest of Cork, is one of Europe's top deep sea fishing and sailing centers. It also holds an important place in Irish history, for it was here, in 1601, in the **Battle of Kinsale**, that the Irish, aided by some 4,000 Spaniards, held the town for 10 weeks, before surrendering to English forces. This was the final effort by the medieval chiefs to fight the British; after the battle, the Irish were outlawed from the town (as in Kilkenny) and not permitted to live within its walls until the late eighteenth century. It was from Kinsale that the *Cinque Ports* set sail in 1703 with a sailor named Alexander Selkirk. Selkirk was marooned on the lonely Pacific island of Juan Fernandez and became the model for Defoe's *Robinson Crusoe.*

Kinsale today is one of Ireland's most attractive, sophisticated harbor-front towns, with a reputation for good food. It is here that the annual Gourmet Food Festival is held in early October. Even if you don't plan to spend the night, it's worth stopping for lunch and a short walk around town.

The Museum in the seventeenth-century Market House has models of local ships and examples of Kinsale lace. The twelfth-century St. Multose Church has a Norman tower, and some stocks for unruly children.

You'll find several tasteful craft shops as you walk about town, notably the Craft Shop and Bill Godkin's Quayside Pottery (open 9 to 6 daily) near Actons Hotel. Bill is a frank, friendly fellow who will give you honest answers to your questions about Kinsale.

If you plan to spend time in the area, there's river and deep-sea fishing (Kinsale Angling Center, Tel. 021-72209); golf (Tel. 021-72197); tennis at the Kinsale Community Tennis Club; and windsurfing at the Oysterhaven Board-sailing Centre, Tel. 021-73738. Walking tours of historic Kinsale can be arranged by phoning 021-72044.

Dining

It would be a shame not to try one of Kinsale's first-rate seafood restaurants, but if you're searching for pub grub, best bet is the Spaniard on the edge of town. This popular hangout has a fishing-net-and-wooden-beam ambiance—a perfect setting for listening to Irish music.

The most popular seafood restaurant with visitors is Blue Haven (E, Pearse Street. Tel. 021-72209). The owner worked with Bloomingdale's in New York on its 1981 promotion of Irish cuisine. Popular dishes include seafood chowder; fillet of Dover sole with saffron sauce on a bed of chicory; duckling baked with honey, with a touch of gentian; seafood pancakes; smoked mackerel; boned chicken in Irish whiskey, mushrooms, and cream sauce; and homemade ice creams. In 1982 and 1983 the Blue Haven was winner of the Irish Tourist Board's Award of Excellence for medium-priced restaurants.

The top choice among locals is Man Friday (M, Scilly, Kinsale, County Cork. Tel. 021-72260), located near the Spaniard pub on the edge of town. Specialties include black sole stuffed with seafood, escargots with garlic, chicken Hawaii with pineapple and prawns, and homemade soups.

Bernard's, formerly Toucan (M, Milk Market, Kinsale, County Cork. Tel. 021-772233) is an Irish restaurant which had just opened when I visited. The owner is the former chef at Man Friday, so the dining should be first-class.

Another well-regarded restaurant is the **Vintage** (M/E, Main Street. Tel. 021-772502). There's a cottage feeling in this small, friendly, German-run restaurant that features smoked trout mousse, Norwegian hot smoked salmon steak, a brace of quail stuffed with five vegetables with a juniper-berry sauce, sweetbreads with oysters, veal with sausages, and monkfish in a blackberry butter sauce.

Lodging

Acton's Hotel (M/E, Cork Road, The Pier, Kinsale, County Cork. Tel. 021-772135), with 55 rooms, is the largest, most luxurious, most expensive hostelry in town. Rooms are spacious but functional; ceilings are high but walls are bare. Bathrooms are pleasantly old-fashioned. Best bet are the front rooms with private bathrooms, overlooking the harbor. Facilities include an outdoor pool.

The Old Presbytery (I, Cork Street. Tel. 021-72027), run by the former manager of Acton's, has five rooms and is your best bet for a guest house.

Blue Haven Hotel (M, Pearse Street, Kinsale, County Cork. Tel. 021-772209) has 12 clean, friendly rooms, 7 with showers.

Perryville House (M, Long Quay, Kinsale, County Kerry. Tel. 021-772731) has 10 rooms in a Regency townhouse. Rooms have bare orange walls and no-nonsense Sears-type furniture; but some are very spacious, with their own living rooms—ideal for families with children.

EN ROUTE: From KINSALE to SKIBBEREEN and BANTRY

The narrow road twists and turns through rich green farm country, cultivated to the very edge of the sea. The roller coastal ride drops you down into hollows among fat sheep and contented cows, then up over the crest of hills where you can look out over a patchwork quilt of sweet green meadows extending in every direction, each patch a different shade of green; and see beyond them the colorful fishing boats and the sea. There's a domestic beauty here—a sense of fullness—you won't find elsewhere in Ireland. When you reach **Ballydehob,** the landscape becomes starker, leaner, and suddenly you realize you're in the west. Gone are the prosperous farms and the happy, gentle landscapes; suddenly you're in a world of wild seascapes and stone. You're sure to prefer one world to the other; but the joy of this trip is that you'll have an opportunity to experience both. There's a shortcut from **Skibbereen** inland to **Bantry**, but it's not worth saving a few minutes and missing some splendid views of the coast.

❦ TIMOLEAGUE

Sixteen miles west of **Kinsale** is **Timoleague**. Be sure to stop and walk through the 600-year-old ruins of the largest Franciscan friary in Ireland. People are still being buried among the rough grasses of the roofless church. A more romantic setting at the edge of the bay would be hard to find. The reputable Egon Ronay guide recommends the **Racing Demon** (M, Maryboro, Timoleague. Tel. 023-46468) as a good nouvellish French restaurant specializing in fresh seafood such as salmon with a creamy sorrel sauce, and, for dessert, a serious homemade chocolate cake.

❦ CASTLETOWNSHEND

If you have time to visit only one seaside village off the main road, stop in Castletownshend. **Baltimore** would be a good choice, too, but getting there involves a 16-mile round trip from the coastal road, while Castletownshend is only a few miles away and requires no backtracking. Leave the coastal road at **Rosscarbery** and follow signs to **Glandore**, **Unionhall** and **Castletownshend**. The town has only one main street that slides steeply down to the sea, passing around an ancient sycamore that keeps the tour buses away.

Stop for a drink or lunch at **Mary Ann's** (Tel. 028-36146)—one of the noblest pubs in Ireland. Mary Ann, who never married, died in 1966, but the pub itself is some three hundred years old. Play snooker (a type of billiards) or darts, enjoy lunch under the trees in the garden, or climb upstairs to a small dining room for homemade soups, lobster, or pâté. One sighs at the bland and tasteless furnishings which destroy the atmosphere of so many venerable old Irish hotels and pubs; so drink a toast to Mary Ann, who understood the beauty that comes with age.

Lodging

If you want to build memories on your trip, consider spending a night in one of Castletownshend's two hotels. Both can arrange for fishing, riding, golf, and tennis.

Bow Hall (M, Castletownshend. Tel. 028-36114) is as close as you'll come in Ireland to an American country inn—not surprising, since it's run by a family of bright, eager Midwesterners who fell in love with Ireland in the 1970s and decided to stay. The seventeenth-century house has 5 guest rooms, one with bath, all bright and cheery, with American-made quilts and several summers' worth of books. Nowhere in Ireland will you be made to feel more of a welcome guest in a private home. Dinners are farm fresh, with vegetables from the garden. A typical meal includes vegetable soup, beef burgundy, new potatoes with parsley butter, and homemade bread.

Castle Townshend (Castletownshend, County Cork. Tel. 028-36100), the seat of the Townshend family that gave the town its name, is the sort of place a pair of glassy-eyed teenagers might find themselves trapped in —in a late-night horror movie. One guidebook refers to its torn carpets and peeling wallpaper as "seedy elegance," but this doesn't do justice to the ghostly presence of a bygone age. Anyone young at heart and/or in love should stay here—but probably only in the "Studio," with its fabulous antiques, or in a room called "Army."

➷ *BANTRY* (Beann traighe, the race of Beann)

Bantry is delightfully situated at the head of Bantry Bay, one of the most beautiful bays along the Irish coast. If you're only passing through, try to find time to tour **Bantry House**, one of the Great Houses of Ireland —one of the very few whose furnishings do justice to their surroundings. If you plan to spend more time, you can arrange to angle for trout and salmon (contact Justin McCarthy, Tel. 027-50053); to go sailing or wind-surfing, contact John Crowley (Tel. 027-50030); to go bike riding, contact Kramers (Tel. 027-50278); to play golf, contact the Bantry Golf Club (Tel. 027-50579 or 027-50488); to go horseback riding, contact O'Dono-ghue's Riding Stables (Tel. 027-63069); or to play tennis, contact the Bantry Community Tennis Club near Strand (Tel. 027-50447 or 027-50113).

Bantry House (Tel. 027-50047; open in the spring and summer daily from 9 to 8; off-season, from 9 to 6) has been the seat of the Earls of Bantry since 1765. The brick Georgian mansion was enlarged by the second Earl, who filled it with treasures from his travels around Europe— Flemish tapestries, fireplaces from Versailles, floor tiles from Pompeii, etc. In one small dressing room is a dollhouse that is kept safe for examination by young female visitors. Give my regards to the current earl and his attractive wife, who are actively involved in the community and in the running of the estate. If you can't spend the night here (see Lodgings below), consider staying for tea or homemade soups.

Lodging

Imagine having bed and breakfast among the treasures and sumptuous gardens of **Bantry House** (I, Bantry. Tel. 027-50047). Four plainly decorated rooms in the 1850 wing—the best of them is the family room—can now be rented overnight, and cost no more than any other B and B establishment. What a great bargain!

Vickery's (I, New Street. Tel. 027-50006) is a friendly, old-fashioned hotel with a basic boardinghouse ambiance. It has been in the same family since 1822. Two of the 15 rooms have a private bath.

✤ BALLYLICKEY

From **Bantry**, head north 3 miles around the head of the bay to **Ballylickey**, which has two lovely hotels.

Dining

Ballylickey House (E, Ballylickey, Route T65, Bantry Bay, County Cork. Tel. 027-50071) is a candlelit French-country restaurant with ice-blue tablecloths and an open fireplace. The traditional French cuisine has earned a Michelin star.

Lodging

Ballylickey House (E, Ballylickey, Route T65, Bantry Bay, County Cork. Tel. 027-50071) belongs to the famous Relais & Châteaux group of hotels, and has a sophistication not easy to find on the west coast of Ireland. The ambiance is more country French than Irish—which will be a plus or minus, depending on why you're here. The four rustic pine chalets around the pool seem out of place; best bet are the elegant rooms and suites in the recently rebuilt, 300-year-old main house. Furnishings are a blend of Cork and Provence—and, difficult as it is to believe, it works! The hotel is surrounded by gardens on a hillside overlooking the bay. The grounds include a pool and private streams for fishing. The restaurant is in itself a good reason to stay.

Sea View House Hotel (M, Ballylickey, County Cork. Tel. 027-50462) is a clean, well-run guest house, with very friendly owners who do their best to make you feel at home. Some rooms and bathrooms are more basic than others. Best is room 7. Here, as elsewhere along the coast, owners can arrange for riding, boating, fishing, and golf.

✤ GLENGARRIFF *(Gleann Garbh,* rugged glen)

From **Ballylickey,** head west around the island-studded bay to the tourist center of **Glengarriff,** which, because of its sheltered location, is famous for its semitropical vegetation.

The top attraction is **Garinish Island,** a 10-minute boat ride from town. Barren fifty years ago, it now has a lovely Italian garden with plants and shrubs from around the world. Shaded paths lead to Roman statues, Grecian temples, a miniature Japanese garden, and an old Martello tower. It's also called Bryce Island, after the family who gave it to the nation. Shaw was a frequent visitor when he was living in the neighborhood, writing *Saint Joan.*

If time permits, or if you're partial to seascapes, follow a 67-mile circular route around the **Beara Peninsula** from **Glengarriff** to **Castletownbere,** then north to **Kenmare.** The scenery is similar to but less spectacular than that of the Ring of Kerry and Dingle Peninsula, which you'll see later on, so you may prefer to head directly north from **Glengarriff** to **Kenmare.** This is a beautiful drive through wild mountain scenery, with cloud shadows racing across purple mountains, and pillars of golden gorse.

✤ KENMARE *(Ceann mara,* head of the sea)

Kenmare is a delightful tourist center at the head of the Kenmare River, 20 miles south of Killarney. If you want a single base from which to explore the entire west coast, you're better off closer to Killarney, which is central both to the Ring of Kerry and to the Dingle Peninsula. Kenmare, however, has the **Park Hotel,** which is the number one hotel on your itinerary. Kenmare is also much more sophisticated and uncommercial. If you want to enjoy some outdoor sports for a few days, or need a place to stop overnight before heading around the Ring of Kerry, Kenmare is ideal. At the very least, you should stop for lunch at one of its first-class restaurants, or have a deli make a picnic lunch for you. Sandwiches come on homemade brown bread—that's how sophisticated Kenmare is! If you're here on a Monday, the **Town Fair** on Main Street has some good buys on hand-knit sweaters.

Dining

Park Hotel Kenmare (E, Kenmare, County Kerry. Tel. 064-41200) is a stately old hotel with a very expensive nouvelle menu. Popular appetizers include salmon with champagne and basil sauce, and fresh mussels with white wine and a hint of curry. Main dishes include turbot baked with crabmeat and apples in a saffron sauce, and duck breast in a pastry with port and orange sauce. Ask for a window table overlooking lawns that sweep down to the bay.

Remy's House (M, Main Street, Kenmare. Tel. 064-41589) is a sweet, whitewashed building with blue trim—as country French as the owner. The menu includes French puff pastry with spinach and creamed mussels; poached prawns; turbot wrapped in lettuce with a mustard sauce; rack of lamb with green peppercorns; and, for dessert, a good assortment of local cheeses.

The Lime Tree (M/I) is a charming old stone house—a good bet for dinner for those who can't afford the Park Hotel next door. Entrées include mussels in garlic butter; smoked chicken with curried rice salad; and rack of lamb with red currant and almond sauce.

Dutch Bistro (M, Henry Street) is a popular spot for light, healthy lunches. It's run by the same couple who own the Lime Tree.

For picnic sandwiches, try **Mickey & Ned's** (6 Henry Street).

Lodging

Park Hotel Kenmare (E, Kenmare, County Kerry. Tel. 064-41200) is a 90-year-old, 50-room, former bishop's palace on 11 beautifully kept acres overlooking Kenmare Bay. Here at last is a historic Irish hotel with bedrooms as distinguished as its public areas. Some rooms have four-posters, Liberty fabrics, and antique furniture from stately mansions of England and Holland. Others are smaller and more modern, but also decorated with flawless taste. The hotel grounds are a natural garden of dracaena palms, gladiolus, rhododendrons, fuchsia bushes, and other flora typical of southwestern Ireland. In its first incarnation the Park Hotel belonged to the chain of Great Southern Hotels built at the turn of the century for the English gentry who wanted their comforts away from home. Facilities include a 9-hole golf course and tennis, but no pool. Fishing and riding can be arranged nearby.

Hawthorne House (I, Kenmare, County Kerry. Tel. 064-41035) is a newly renovated bed-and-breakfast house that also serves meals to guests.

The owners, Ann and Gerry Browne, are extremely efficient and friendly. A good bargain.

Remy's House (M, Main Street, Kenmare. Tel. 064-41589) is a charming cottage dripping with flowers in the center of town. The 3 rooms are simply decorated, with a chic, French-peasant ambiance that reflects the sensibilities of the French owners. The restaurant has a solid reputation.

EN ROUTE: From KENMARE to KILLARNEY

Kenmare is the starting point for drives around the **Ring of Kerry** to Killarney—a full day's trip. By taking this circular route, however, you'll miss the sensational drive north over the mountains from **Kenmare** to Killarney. Be sure to include this drive on an excursion from Killarney to Ladies' View (discussed on page 41).

✤ RING OF KERRY

The famous Ring is a road that skirts the coast of the Iveragh Peninsula, with dramatic seascapes, fine mountain scenery, and restaurants and hotels for every taste and budget. It's less wild than the Dingle Peninsula to the north, but it also has more amenities. If you have time for only one side trip from Killarney, tour the Dingle Peninsula instead; the Ring of Kerry is better suited for those who plan to stay in one of its resorts and take advantage of the outdoor activities—tennis, fishing, hiking, riding, and golf. The 110-mile drive around the Ring is a full-day trip. Start in Kenmare, since most daytrippers will be heading in the opposite direction. The most dramatic views are west of **Parknasilla** on the south coast, and west of **Glenbeigh** on the north coast—particularly around **Cahirciveen**.

✤ TAHILLA COVE (11 miles west of Kenmare, 3 miles east of Parknasilla)

Lodging

Tahilla Cove (M/I, Tahilla, Route N70, County Kerry. Tel. 064-45104) is a small, unpretentious guest house on 12 acres of undeveloped land along the bay. The nearby village consists of a Catholic church, a petrol pump, a post office, a school for 40 children, and lots of grazing cows and sheep. The travel writer Ashley Courtnay described his two nights here as the high point of his visit to western Ireland—probably not because of the physical layout (unmemorable), the furnishings (friendly in a sensible, boardinghouse sort of way), or the activities (there's almost nothing to do here but exist), but because of the secluded, out-of-the-way atmosphere, and the friendliness of the hosts. (The President of Ireland reportedly came here before taking office to recover from his campaign.) Don't stay here or anywhere on the Ring of Kerry if you want to explore the Killarney area in a limited time—hotels on the peninsula aren't central enough—but stay if you're passing through, or if you want to take a few days off to fish or simply to come to rest. Some rooms are plainer than others; of the 4 in the main house, room 6 is best. The tiny bar is popular with local fishermen. The popular Sunday menu includes scallops, salmon, and lobster.

❧ PARKNASILLA (15 miles west of Kenmare)

Parknasilla, located on the shores of the Kenmare River at the edge of the sea, is a center for sailing, fishing, tennis, pony trekking, and golf. Thanks to the Gulf Stream, the vegetation is tropical. The main attraction is the famous **Parknasilla Great Southern Hotel**, a perfect destination for families who want a full-service resort with a wealth of outdoor activities, and who can afford the giddy prices.

Lodging

Parknasilla Great Southern Hotel (E, Parknasilla, on the Ring of Kerry, County Kerry. Tel. 064-45122) is one of those great, elegant turn-of-the-century hotels which were built for the English upper classes so that they could brave the wilderness in comfort. The architect also designed the Park Hotel in Kenmare. (The Park seems to attract more Americans; the Parknasilla, more Europeans.) Among the most famous guests have been General de Gaulle, Princess Grace, the Dutch royal family, and George Bernard Shaw, who wrote much of *Saint Joan* while staying here in suite 216. The atmosphere has an institutional edge to it, but also conjures up the glamour of a bygone age. Rooms are a bit plain, but very tasteful, with soft pinks and blues. Guests, most of whom prefer to stay in the old section, are greeted by a porter in frock coat and striped gray pants. Extensive facilities include a heated indoor saltwater pool, sailing, golf (9 holes), sauna, tennis, windsurfing, riding, and 300 acres of trails and bridlepaths.

❧ SNEEM (17 miles west of Kenmare)

Buried in the Catholic church (1865) is Father O'Flynn of the famous song. The Protestant church, dating back to Elizabethan times, has a salmon as a weathervane. Along the main street are two stores selling hand-knit sweaters at attractive prices.

❧ STAIGUE FORT

Beyond Sneem, the road winds inland for a few miles through wild scenery, meeting the coast again at **Castlecove**. Just past Castlecove, on the right, is a sign leading you 1½ miles to **Staigue Fort**, one of the most remarkable prehistoric monuments in Kerry. Many of you will wonder what the fuss is all about, since there's nothing to see but a circular wall of dry masonry 18 feet high. But let your imagination lift you thousands of years back in time, to when the fort contained two thatched cottages and was used to shelter farmers and their animals from wolves. The walls, constructed without mortar, are 13 feet wide at the base. Along the interior of the walls are several well-constructed flights of stairs. Staigue Fort is one of the finest of some 35,000 surviving ring forts scattered throughout Ireland, dating from the Iron Age to early Christian times. In spite of their name, they were not used as military forts but as homesteads and cattle enclosures.

❧ CAHERDANIEL

Beyond Westcove is the village of **Caherdaniel**. In the vicinity, near the shores of **Derrynane Bay**, is the curious hermitage of **St. Crohane**, carved from solid rock. Slightly under 2 miles southwest of **Caherdaniel** is **Derrynane House**, the former home of **Daniel O'Connell** (1775–1847), one of the most famous and revered fathers of Irish independence. If you know nothing of O'Connell, and care little for Irish history, you'll have no reason to visit—just as an Irishman might not go out of his way to visit the birthplace of Martin Luther King on a tour of the United States. O'Connell, like King, was committed to nonviolence. While living here he defended the poor in court, helped win emancipation for Catholics (he was the first Catholic Irishman to sit in the British Parliament), demonstrated to the Irish the power of numbers, and helped win back for them a sense of pride and self-respect.

❧ THE SKELLIG ISLANDS (the road from Caherdaniel to Waterville)

The views become more spectacular as you head north around the western rim of the peninsula. The road climbs above the sea, beneath smooth brown hills and sheep-colored rocks. Neat white cottages stand like sentinels among the green fields, running down to the very edge of the sea. There's something noble about this effort to claim every inch of available soil—a human drama you're not aware of in the richer country to the east.

The islands rising offshore are the **Skelligs**. The government's efforts to close the Skelligs to the public so that restorations can be made have been met with outrage from locals, whose livelihoods are at stake. Call **Des Lavell** on Valencia Island (Tel. 0667-6124) for the latest word, and hope that he can take you. If you're young at heart and want a real adventure, this is the one trip you shouldn't miss; the memory will linger for a lifetime. The 9-mile voyage from Valencia Island (north of Waterville) is made only in calm weather, and even then the sea can be rough; be sure to take motion-sickness pills before you sail.

The **Great Skellig** or **Skellig Michael** (Michael is the patron saint of high places) is the largest of the three—an enormous mass of rock rising more than 700 feet above the sea. Steep and sometimes slippery steps lead up to the best-preserved early Christian monastic settlement in Europe. The ruins include a small, ancient church; a larger, tenth-century church; two oratories (similar to the Gallarus Oratory which you'll see on Dingle); six beehive cells rising up to 17 feet; several burial enclosures; crude crosses; and two wells. In former times Skellig Michael was a place of pilgrimage. Above "Christ's Saddle" is a projecting flake of rock inscribed with a cross which pilgrims kissed in an act of penance. En route to Skellig Michael you'll pass **Little Skellig**, home of 20,000 pairs of gannets—the second-largest gannetry in the North Atlantic.

❧ WATERVILLE (An Coirean, little waterfall)

The road from Derrynane House crosses the 700-foot **Pass of Coomakista**, and then winds down to **Waterville**. The popular angling center is on a strip of land between **Ballinskelligs Bay** and **Lough Currane**, one of the loveliest lakes in Ireland. Like Parknasilla, **Waterville** is a popular tourist destination with a few good restaurants and hotels. There's a summer's worth of outdoor activities, including sailing, tennis, hiking, and riding; but the main attractions are fishing and playing golf on an eighteen-hole championship course. You also have the exhilarating feeling of being on the ocean.

Dining

Locals agree that the best place to eat is the **Huntsman** (E/M, Waterville. Tel. 0667-4124), which features fresh, plainly cooked fish: lobsters from the tank (broiled, and served with roe), creamy seafood bisque, scampi Newburg, salmon with hollandaise, and delicious homemade bread. The color scheme, softened by candlelight, is Bordello Red: bright red carpets running up the side of the bar, red-colored chairs, and lamp-shades with red-tinted lights.

Lodging

Waterville Lake Hotel (E, Waterville, County Kelly. Tel. 0667-4133) is Waterville's deluxe hostelry—a smart, modern hotel particularly geared for fishermen and golfers. The 74-par course is one of the best in Europe. Fishing is in the ocean, on Lough Currane, or on mountain lakes with names like Derriana and Cloonaghlan, where the average size of spring salmon is fourteen pounds. Rooms are very decorated with modern, serviceable furniture and fabrics. Critics give the restaurant only a passing grade. Activities include pony trekking, tennis, and indoor swimming. Fielding gives the hotel its top score of five stars.

Butler Arms (M, Route N70, Waterville, County Cork. Tel. 0667-4144) has 43 rooms, half with bath. Charlie Chaplin stayed here with his daughter. It is a large, established, residential-type hotel, neither sophisticated nor elegant, but friendly and old-fashioned in a distant-aunt sort of way. Best bet are rooms facing the sea. Ask for 215, or something comparable.

The Huntsman (I, Waterville. Tel. 0667-4124), known primarily as a restaurant, also has some fairly basic but clean and reasonably priced rooms that sleep up to 4.

❖ *CAHIRCIVEEN*

Cahirciveen, located at the foot of 1,245-foot Mount Bentee, and overlooking **Valencia Harbor** (where boats leave for the **Skelligs**), is the shopping center of the western end of the Ring of Kerry. Of all the towns on the Ring, Cahirciveen has the most charm, in part because it enjoys a life independent of the tourists passing through. Take your camera with you as you walk past the old houses, each a different color, each with its own hand-painted sign. Stop for a pint at the Angel, one of the country's most famous pubs (but unknown to tourists), where writers and artists (Liam O'Flaherty was one of them) rub mugs with local farmers and fishermen. Down the street is the Iveragh Inn, a modest but friendly coffee shop for sandwiches or pies.

Lodging

One of the loveliest and friendliest guest houses on the Ring is Mount Rivers (I, Cahirciveen, County Kerry. Tel. 0667-2509). There are books everywhere in this late-nineteenth-century home at the far end of town. Of the 6 rooms, 2 share a bath; others have their own. Rooms 2, 3, and 6 are best, in that order. A very good bargain.

✤ GLENBEIGH

The road northeast from Cahirciveen to Glenbeigh is scenically the highlight of the drive around the Ring of Kerry. Across the wide bay is Dingle Peninsula, which you'll be exploring in future days. Glenbeigh is the starting point for some of the best hikes in western Ireland, particularly around the Glenbeigh Horsehoe, near Commasaharn Lake, and along the slopes of Drung Hill. Ask locally for details or consult the *Irish Walk Guides/1.*

A few minutes west of Glenbeigh is a 2-mile-long spit of land jutting into Dingle Bay, with soft yellow sand backed by high dunes, and breaking surf. Across the bay, on Dingle Peninsula, is a similar spit, perfect (at low tide) for walking, jogging, or swimming. If the weather is right, don't wait for Dingle; in Ireland you never know when you'll see the sun again.

✤ CARAGH LAKE

A few miles northeast of Glenbeigh, on the Ring Road toward Killorglin, you'll see signs on your right pointing to Caragh Lake. This is a beautiful expanse of water, set among broom- and heather-covered hills with majestic mountains in the background. Much of the lakeside property is privately owned—as is much of the Killarney area—by Germans. If you're making a quick tour of western Ireland and want to see as much as possible, it makes little sense to base yourself on Caragh Lake. Stay here either (a) as a starting or ending point for a trip around the Ring of Kerry, or (b) as a place to stay put for a day or two that's near a lake and off the beaten track.

Lodging

A hundred yards back from the lake are two lovely, secluded hotels surrounded by woods and gardens. Though both have access to the lake and their own boats for rowing and fishing, neither is close enough to enjoy lakeside views.

Ard na Sidhe, pronounced *sheen*, meaning "hill of the fairies" (M/E, Caragh Lake, near Killorglin, County Kerry. Tel. 066-69105) is a secluded and extremely peaceful Victorian mansion 3 miles from the Ring Road. Most of the 24 rooms have private baths. The hotel is now run by the same German group that manages Hotel Europe and Dunloe Castle Hotel in Killarney (see below). Rooms are a bit bare, but have nice, traditional furnishings. The main house is preferable to the annex.

Caragh Lodge (M, Caragh Lake, near Killorglin, County Kerry. Tel. 066-69115), only a mile from the Ring Road, is friendlier, more relaxed, and less expensive than **Ard na Sidhe**, but the facility is also less elegant. It is situated in 9 acres of parkland with rare and subtropical trees and shrubs that won the owner the National Garden Award in 1982. Facilities include tennis and a sauna.

❧ KILLORGLIN

After **Glenbeigh** the scenery becomes tamer, less spectacular. The best time to visit **Killorglin** is during the three-day **Puck Fair** in August, which is attended by thousands of people from all over Ireland. On the evening of the first day a procession assembles at the bridge and a large billy goat, his horns bedecked with ribbons and rosettes, is borne in triumph through the streets to a raised platform on a square in the center of town. Here Puck is enthroned for two days, presiding over a great cattle, horse, and sheep fair, with nonstop dancing and entertainment. The tradition is a holdover either from pagan times, or from colonial days, when the stampeding of goats gave warning of the approach of English forces.

Killorglin is a pleasant 14-mile drive from **Killarney**.

❧ KILLARNEY

There are two Killarney's—one, a spectacular region of mountains and island-studded lakes, wooded shores, and romantic glens; the other, a tourist-infested town, whose population more than triples in the summer months. The town—more a place of transit than a destination—is in the wrong place: on a flat plain more than a mile from the lakes. The only reason to come here is to satisfy a nostalgia for noise, traffic, and fast food; to mingle with the under-twenty-five crowd; to shop; or to dine at one of the two quality restaurants. Fortunately, there are hundreds of guest houses and hotels in the surrounding countryside, so you don't need to visit the town too often.

What makes the scenery around Killarney so breathtaking is that rare combination of lushness and grandeur, of wild mountain scenery and tropical vegetation. A climate warmer than anywhere else in the British Isles encourages the growth of Mediterranean strawberry trees, cedars of Lebanon, and wild fuchsia sprouting from gray stone walls. Happiness, you'll find, has very little to do with the mind here. There are historic buildings to check off as you tour the country, but most of your time will be spent getting back in touch with yourself: biking along the shores of Muckross Lake, hiking to some windswept peak, angling for salmon, or simply watching the morning mist uncurl from a mountain lake.

• Among the Things to Do, the most memorable is a full-day excursion that includes a pony or pony-cart ride through the **Gap of Dunloe** and a boat trip through the three lakes of Killarney. Hotels can make arrangements for you. If you can afford the price, arrange for your own private ponies and boat. The trip was the standard Killarney adventure in the nineteenth century; today most visitors haven't time for a full day of anything, and make do with the pony trip alone, which is the least rewarding part of the tour.

If you're crossing the Gap on your own, drive west 4 1/2 miles on **Route T67** to **Beaufort**, and follow the signs another 1 1/2 miles to the **Gap of Dunloe**. Men with pony carts will "assault" you along the way, but it's best to wait till you reach **Kate Kearney's Cottage** at the entrance, where the rates are regulated (but be sure to agree on a fee before you set off).

Have some ale or a cup of Irish coffee at **Kate Kearney's Cottage**, and toast the lady who was famous in her day for her moonshine and her beauty. Wrote Lady Morgan:

> Oh, did you ne'er hear of Kate Kearney,
> She lived on the banks of Killarney;
> From the glance of her eye
> Shun danger and fly
> For Fate's in the glance of Kate Kearney.
>
> For that eye is so modestly beaming,
> You'd ne'er think of mischief she's dreaming.

Yet, oh, I can tell
How fatal's the spell
That lurks in the eye of Kate Kearney.

Though she looks so bewitchingly simple,
Yet there's mischief in every dimple,
And who dares inhale
Her sigh's spicy gale
Must die by the breath of Kate Kearney.

Kate never married. When the law came after her, she disappeared—some say to Australia or New Zealand. The Irish loved her because she flouted the law, and the law was British; and they continue to love wild, voluptuous women who flout the codes by which they're told to live.

On any given summer day the pony carts make some three hundred 90-minute trips about halfway through the Gap and back, so don't expect to feel like Lewis and Clark. It's a scenic and romantic trip, though, past a series of clear mountain lakes through a rift in the great MacGillycuddy's Reeks—surely a great improvement over seeing the world framed through a car window. Since the ponies leave their own trailmarkers along what is essentially an unimproved dirt road, you'll want to think twice about squishing forth on foot. If you're traveling off-season or want, because of health or children, to take a pony cart, a trip through the Gap is a great treat; otherwise, I'd suggest you take your feet or your rented ponies and explore other, equally spectacular areas of this beautiful country, such as the **Horse's Glen** described in Charles Kidney's *Visitor's Guide to Killarney*. A trip through the Gap makes sense, too, if you're leaving the crowds behind and taking a boat ride through the lakes.

The most romantic of the three lakes, **Upper Lake,** is also the least accessible. A road runs along a section of it, so, for the right price, you may be able to arrange through your hotel or through a tour agency to have a boat put in the water for you, or to get one at **Lord Brandon's Cottage,** at the western end of the lake. Speak to **Henry Clifton** at Ross Castle.

• **Ross Castle,** a sixteenth-century stronghold of the O'Donoghue clan and the last castle to fall to Cromwell's army in 1652, will be closed until 1988 for restorations, but Henry Clifton runs a boat concession on the castle grounds, on the western shore of **Lower Lake.** You can row yourself around—a memorable experience, particularly at dawn or dusk—or allow yourself to be taken to **Innisfallen Island.** Those of you with an interest in antiquity or a fondness for romantic ruins will want to visit the remains of a seventh-century abbey on Innisfallen, which, like the Rock of Cashel, goes back to the earliest days of Christianity. Brian Boru, the last High King of Ireland, and St. Brendan, who probably "discovered" America centuries before Columbus, are said to have been educated here. H. V. Morton writes that "there was once a Frenchman who said that Ireland was the jewel of the west, that Kerry was the jewel of Ireland, that Killarney was the jewel of Kerry, and that the little uninhabited isle of Innisfallen was the jewel of Killarney. I have nothing to add to this."

• Another delightful, half-day excursion from Killarney is south on **Route N71** to **Muckross Abbey, Muckross House,** and **Torc Waterfall,** and around the southern shore of the three lakes to **Ladies' View** (20 miles round trip). This trip will take you along a section of the spectacular road between Killarney and Kenmare which you missed by driving from Kenmare around the Ring of Kerry. The **Abbey** and **House** are located in wooded parklands along the tranquil shores of Muckross and Lower Lakes —an idyllic spot for walks, bike rides, or pony-cart rides (cars are not permitted on the grounds). There are several bike-rental shops in Killarney.

You'll reach **Muckross Abbey** first—a quarter-mile walk from the parking lot, and 2½ miles from Killarney. You can rent a pony cart here to take you on a delightful 1- or 2-hour ride to Muckross House and Torc Waterfall. You can also arrange to ride to Muckross House, and then walk back. What the drivers won't tell you is that you can return to your car after seeing the abbey and then drive directly to Muckross House without their services.

The fifteenth-century Franciscan abbey, partially restored in the past twenty years, was wrecked by Cromwell's forces in 1652, but is still amazingly complete, though roofless. An ancient yew tree rises up through the cloister and branches out over the broken abbey walls. The lakefront walk called **Lovers' Lane,** which runs halfway from the abbey to Muckross House, is one of the most beautiful in the park. Look at the islands in the lake—the abbey's treasures were buried on one of them in 1589 to avoid pillage and have not yet been found.

Muckross House is a nineteenth-century mock-Elizabethan manor house which no one knew what to do with for thirty-two years. It is now a craft center where blacksmiths, weavers, basket makers, and potters demonstrate their skills. Also on display are exhibits of old tools and an assortment, more representational than exceptional, of nineteenth-century country furnishings. Muckross House is clearly not for everyone; what shouldn't be missed, however, are the **Muckross Gardens,** with its many tender and exotic shrubs, and a stroll along **Arthur Young Walk** to **Brickeen Bridge** on a narrow strip of parkland between the two lakes.

Unless you go by pony cart, return to **Route N71** and drive to Torc **Waterfall** (4½ miles from Killarney). The falls are a 10-minute walk from the parking lot. Visitors whip out their cameras as the falls roar into view; if you want more privacy, continue up a long flight of stone steps for about 10 minutes to the second clearing. There's a marvelous view from here of the lakes of Killarney. If you need more exercise, bear right where the path splits and continue walking through the 20,000-acre national park.

• Return to your car and continue west another 5 minutes or so to the **Ladies' View**. If I were Irish, I would feel a certain outrage at the fact that what is perhaps the region's most spectacular setting is named in honor of Queen Victoria's Ladies-in-Waiting—not even the Queen herself—who once upon a time expressed their pleasure at the view. Stop at the café if you need some refilling; but the best view is at another parking area 100 yards farther west. If you haven't had enough beautiful scenery, continue across the mountains to **Kenmare**; otherwise, return to Killarney.

• A delightful way to end the day is to drive at dusk to the ruined tower on **Aghadoe Heights**, only 2½ miles west of town, and watch the shadows creep over **Lough Leane** (Lower Lake).

Walks

• The easiest walk, but one of the most delightful, is along the paved paths through the wooded parklands surrounding Muckross House.

• Follow the steps past Torc Waterfall for a splendid view of the lakes of Killarney.

• The most satisfying short walk (5½ miles or 3 to 4 hours round trip) is to the top of 1,764-foot **Torc Mountain**, where you can enjoy breathtaking views of the entire region. Follow **Route N71** past the entrance to **Muckross House**. Where the Kenmare road veers right, an unsurfaced road (the Old Kenmare Road) runs straight ahead into the forest. Drive uphill till you reach a locked gate beside the water supply station. Walk straight (disregarding forest roads to the left) to the bridge across the Owengarriff River above Torc Waterfall. The steep east face of Torc Mountain should be ahead of you. Continue uphill (left) along the road to the open moorland, where the river runs down from a mountain lake called the Devil's Punch Bowl. Continue till you come to a weather recording station within a wire enclosure. When a bridle path joins the road on the right, begin your ascent, making your own way up to the summit. Be sure to return the same way you came; descent by the steep east side of Torc would be foolhardy.

• If you're partial to mountain lakes, take the 6-mile walk (3 to 4½ hours round trip) to the **Devil's Punch Bowl**, the lake that feeds Torc Waterfall. The lake is 300 feet below the summit of 2,300-foot **Mangerton Mountain**. You should be able to arrange in advance to make most of the trip by pony, but since the ascent is gradual, the summit is accessible on foot to all age groups. Take **Route N71** from Killarney toward **Muckross House**. Just past the **Muckross Hotel** (you might stop here for further details), take the road left to the **Mangerton Viewing Park**. At the upper end of the wood, swing right, past the car park, to the end of the surfaced road. Park by the concrete bridge. From here an old pony path leads up the mountain. The path swings right to an estate boundary fence, which runs left to the Punch Bowl. Just beside the outlet from the Punch Bowl is **Bachelor's Well**. Drink from its magic waters and you'll remain single all your life.

• Charles Kidney's *Visitor's Guide* highly recommends a walk to the **Horse's Glen**, which he considers the wildest in the country. There are three lakes here suitable for swimming and fishing: **Lough Garagarry**, **Lough Managh**, and **Lough Erhogh**. The starting point, near **Muckross Hotel**, is only 6 miles from Killarney, yet the lakes are seldom visited. This and other, more ambitious hikes—the most spectacular being the MacGillycuddy's Reeks Peak Walk, the finest ridge walk in the country— are described in Sean O'Suilleabhain's *Irish Walk Guides No. 1, Southwest*, which is available at local bookstores.

Ponies or pony carts are available at the entrance to the **Gap of Dunloe** and at the entrances to **Muckross Abbey** and **Muckross House**. Pony rides through other areas of the National Park can be arranged through the Ballydowney Riding School. Tel. 064-31686.

Fishing. Trout and salmon fishing are free on all Killarney lakes, except Kilbrean. Contact the Tourist Information Office for permits for river fishing. Sea angling can be arranged in Cahirciveen and Valentia.

Golf. The **Killarney Golf and Fishing Club** (Tel. 064-31034) has two championship courses, at **Mahoney's Point** 2½ miles from Killarney on the road to Killorglin, and at **Killeen**.

Tours. Counihan's Travel Agency, High Street, Killarney. Tel. 064-31874; Joe O'Donovan, Innisfallen Mall, Main Street. Tel. 064-33880. Also **Cronin's Tours**, College Street, and **Deros Bus Tours**, Main Street.

Boat hire and tours. Henry Clifton at Ross Castle; Dermit O'Donoghue, High Street. Tel. 064-31068.

Windsurfing. Killarney Windsurfing Centre, Lake Hotel, Killarney. Tel. 064-31105.

Bike rentals. Billy Hearne, Upper High Street; O'Neill's, Plunkett Street; O'Callaghan's, College Street.

Dining

Gaby's (E, 17 High Street, Killarney. Tel. 064-32519), with its crowded tables and wood-slat benches, gets low grades for atmosphere, but high honors for its menu of fresh fish: lobster bisque, sole, turbot, salmon, lobsters from the tank, an enormous shellfish platter, or smoked salmon. Reservations are not accepted, so come early.

Foley's Seafood and Steak Restaurant (M/E, High Street. Tel. 064-31217) is a smart pub/restaurant that is either gay and lively or crowded and smoky, depending on your preferences. In either case, it has lots of atmosphere, thanks in part to the colorful characters playing turn-of-the-century ballads.

The best hotel food is in the elegant (and expensive) Panorama Restaurant in the Europe Hotel (E, Tel. 064-31900). The menu features such local specialties as oxtail soup, Irish stew, Dingle Bay lobster, and sea trout with toasted almonds.

For a budget meal, try the Laurels (I/M, Main Street. Tel. 064-32771), a pub with good local food, such as cockle and mussel chowder, Irish stew, corned beef and cabbage, shepherd's pie, and Irish sole.

Lodging

Europe (E, Killorglin Road, Fossa, Killarney, County Kerry. Tel. 061-31900) is a very spacious, modern, 170-room hotel under the same German management as Dunloe Castle Hotel. Though a bit impersonal (banquet facilities for 600), it attracts a well-heeled, educated clientele, and has an old-fashioned elegance you won't find in hotels that cater exclusively to the package-tour trade. Ask for an upstairs room facing the lake. Facilities include bowling, an indoor pool, snooker, sauna, gym, boating and riding.

Dunloe Castle, just south of Beaufort, on the road to the Gap of Dunloe, 4½ miles west of Killarney (E, Tel. 064-32118) is not a castle, but a modern hotel built in the 1960s, under the same German management as the larger, more expensive and somewhat more elegant Hotel Europe. Public areas have classical statues and lovely terra cotta floors, but rooms are Butcher-block Modern. Still, the Castle is much classier than Killarney's mass-market hotels, such as Aghadoe Heights. Facilities include a pool, sauna, tennis courts, and a putting-and-driving range.

The B and B set, or those with limited budgets, can take Don Fullington's advice in *An American's Ireland* and stay at **Tullig House,** near Dunloe Castle (I, Beaufort. Tel. 064-44183). He describes it as a very basic but romantic and peaceful farmhouse where kids can help feed the chickens and milk the cows. The owner, Mrs. Joy, serves hearty, honest Irish fare.

Killarney Great Southern Hotel (E, Railway Station, Killarney, County Kerry. Tel. 064-31262) is a good chain hotel that hasn't entirely lost that old world feeling it had at the turn of the century when the British came by train and talked of Empire over their afternoon tea. The rambling, in-town Victorian hotel has 180 spacious rooms, conference facilities, garden, sauna, indoor pool, tennis, and golf. Guests have included Caroline Kennedy and Pat Nixon.

Aghadoe Heights Hotel (M/E, Killarney, County Kerry. Tel. 064-31766) is a modern hilltop hotel 2 miles northwest of Killarney, whose main attraction is its exquisite view over Lower Lake. Be sure to ask for a room with a lake view. Geared for the package-tour trade, it is part of a new breed of mass-market Irish hotels that charge extra for everything from ice to room service and have little time to deal with the problems of individual travelers. Still, it's a very clean, comfortable hotel that meets high international standards. Facilities include indoor pool, squash, riding, tennis, and dancing nightly in season.

Cahernane (E, Muckross Road, Killarney, County Kerry. Tel. 064-31895) is an 1877 Victorian mansion, the former home of the Earls of Pembroke. If you're looking for a small, peaceful hotel (35 rooms) with a certain amount of character, this is the place to stay. Public areas have rich wood paneling and a sense of the past. Rooms in the main building vary considerably in furnishings and size. Best bet is 26, where the owner, a German lawyer, stays when he visits. Ask for a room with a lake view. Avoid rooms in the modern wing, which are very undistinguished. Facilities include a putting green, tennis, riding, boats, fishing, sauna, and bikes.

Castlerosse (M, Killarney, County Kerry. Tel. 064-31144) is a 42-room Best Western hotel in a peaceful setting with lovely views, and lower prices than many other of Killarney's modern hotels. The ambiance is Turnpike Modern—each room with its own parking place. Rooms are clean, charmless, functional, ample. Facilities include a swimming pool, tennis, and piped music.

Carriglea (I/M, Killarney, Route N71, 1½ miles from Killarney. Tel. 064-31116) is a clean, friendly, reasonably priced guest house on a farm set back from a main road. The 5 rooms in the main house are generally preferable to those in the annex. More amusing than offensive is the extraordinary collection of clashing colors, as if one person were responsible for curtains, another for bedspreads, etc. Rooms 1 and 8 are a bit more color-coordinated. The public areas are fussy in a delightfully proper Victorian way.

Arbutus Lodge (M, College Street. Tel. 064-31037), a former shelter for monks, is a small, unpretentious hotel—the best budget hotel for those who want to stay in town. Another inexpensive in-town hotel is the quieter, 16-room **East Avenue House** (I, Kenmare Place. Tel. 064-32522). Rooms are basic but clean.

✤ DINGLE PENINSULA

Dingle Peninsula is the true wild west of Ireland—visually, because it has the grandest scenery; historically, because it has the most impressive number of Iron Age and early Christian monuments; and spiritually, because it was never tamed by the English (as the Ring of Kerry was), and has kept alive those Gaelic traditions that have all but disappeared from the rest of the country. The circular route around the peninsula from Killarney to Tralee is 104 miles, and should take the better part of a day. On a day's outing you'll drive through magnificent coastal scenery and cross the most spectacular mountain pass in Ireland. You'll walk or swim along soft, sandy beaches, visit quality craft shops, dine in first-rate restaurants and pubs. Should you want to spend more than a day here, you can base yourself in any number of charming guest houses and explore the Blasket Islands, play golf, go fishing, and hike some of the most dramatic trails in Ireland. The best places to stay are in the far west, around the towns of **Dingle, Ventry, Dunquin,** and **Ballyferriter.**

✤ INCH STRAND

From **Killorglin,** head north to **Castlemaine,** and then west along the southern coast of Dingle about 10 miles to the town of **Inch,** where Synge's *The Playboy of the Western World* was filmed. If the weather is behaving, and the tide is low (check the tides the night before), park your car, take off your shoes and socks, and let the wind blow through your hair as you wander out along **Inch Strand**, a wide, sandy beach stretching 2 miles into the bay. (When you leave your hotel in the morning, bring towels and wear bathing suits under your clothes.)

From **Inch** continue west along the road to **Annascaul**. A right turn off the coastal road takes you to the **South Pole Inn**, named in honor of the local sailor who went to rescue Robert Scott and found him dead in his tent, having failed in his mission to reach the South Pole in 1912. Could anything be more wonderfully incongruous, and more appropriate, than a South Pole Inn in a tiny fishing village in western Ireland?

✤ DINGLE *(Daungean,* stronghold)

The road west from **Annascaul** is pleasant, but the real adventure begins in **Dingle**, the chief town and touring center of the district. Dingle was a Norman administrative center, a walled city in Elizabethan times, and chief port of Kerry in the old Spanish trading days. Today it's a center of Gaelic studies that attracts students from around the world—its existence does not depend solely on tourists. You'll want to walk around town, visiting **An Café Liteartha**, a café/bookstore with a marvelous collection of Irish books and records, many of them in Gaelic; shopping for knitted goods, pottery, and yarn in several sophisticated craft shops such as **Commodum** (Green Street); and photographing many of the colorful old houses. You'll also want to dine in one of its first-rate restaurants.

From Dingle you can arrange for a boat trip from **Dunquin** (10 miles west) to the **Blasket Islands** (see Dunquin, page 49). There's pony trekking in **Ventry**, four miles to the west; golf at **Sybil Head**, near **Ballyferriter**; beaches at **Ventry** and **Dunquin**; deep-sea fishing off the coast of **Dingle**; trips to ancient monuments (see below), spectacular drives around **Slea Head** and over the **Conor Pass**, and an endless variety of hikes to mountain ridges and lakes.

The high point of my visit to Dingle was an evening at **O'Flaherty's Pub**, drinking bitters with strangers and listening to some very local, traditional music played with guitars, flutes, accordions, and spoons. This is a place of great character where locals and tourists join together in the fun.

Dining

An Café Liteartha (M, Dykegate Street) is a bookstore that doubles as a café-restaurant. Food is simply prepared and wholesome (fresh mussels and prawns, poached salmon, sandwiches, and salads), but it is the atmosphere that makes this such a special place for lunch or for a reasonably priced dinner.

Doyle's (M/E, John Street, Dingle. Tel. 066-51174) is the best, most sophisticated seafood restaurant in town. At the table across from mine was a Canadian couple who had come here on their twentieth anniversary, and were back again for their thirtieth. The menu depends on the day's catch, but usually features cockle and mussel soup with garlic, grilled black sole, salmon cooked in parchment, and salmon poached with a sharp sorrel sauce.

Half Door (M/E, John Street), next door to Doyle's, is considered the second-best seafood restaurant. Popular dishes include crab quiche, trout in oatmeal, mussels in garlic, seafood au gratin, and a variety of meat dishes.

The Armada (M, Strand Street) is a less expensive, popular seafood restaurant near the pier, with homemade chowders, fresh Dingle cod, and seafood curries.

Whelan's (M, Main Street) hasn't a great deal of atmosphere, but no one faults its seafood pancakes, rainbow trout, crab salads, or Irish specialties, such as shepherd's pie or homemade soups and stews.

Lodging

The Tourist Office has a complete list of hotels and guest houses. When we went to press, the town's one modern, first-class hotel, the **Sceilig**, had been shut down because of tax irregularities; check to see if it's opened again. **The Sceilig** (E/M, Dingle, County Kerry. Tel. 066-51144) has 80 rooms at the edge of the sea. Facilities include an outdoor pool, riding, and floodlit tennis. Most guide books have kind words for the Sceilig; outside, however, it has an uninteresting modern façade and is bordered by a large macadam parking lot. If you're looking for amenities, this is the place to stay; but to capture the spirit of western Ireland, consider a guest house instead.

Cleevaun (I, Dingle, about 1 mile west of town, County Kerry. Tel. 066-51108) is a B and B guest house that's more comfortable and modern than many of Ireland's aging hotels. Rooms are spotlessly clean and cheery. The living room has a helpful collection of books on the Dingle area. A second choice of B and B's is the friendly **Ballymore House** (Dingle, County Kerry. Tel. 066-59050), 1½ miles beyond Cleevaun.

Benner's Hotel (I, Main Street, Dingle, County Kerry. Tel. 066-51638) is run by a group of Americans who seem to have more interest in tax deductions than in offering comfortable accommodations for guests. The atmosphere is either funky or down-and-out, depending on how close you are to college life. Restorations are planned, however, so hope for the best.

If you're on a budget and want to stay in town, try **Leonard's** (I, Dykegate Street. Tel. 066-51549). Five rooms share two baths. Rooms are very boardinghouse-basic, but clean and pleasant. Room 5 is best.

✤ *VENTRY*

There's a magnificent horseshoe of soft sand here; follow signs to the beach. Ventry Harbor was the scene of the ancient romantic tale, "The Battle of Ventry Strand," which, as told in a fifteenth-century manuscript now in the Bodleian Library at Oxford, describes how the King of the World, Daire Doon, landed at Ventry in an attempt to invade Ireland, and was defeated in a battle that lasted a year and a day. One of the loveliest walks in the region is to the lake on **Eagle Mountain**, to the west of Ventry. Inquire about the route in Ventry.

✤ *DUNBEG*

Past Ventry, about 2 miles before Slea Head, look carefully for a small sign on the left pointing to a fort called **Dunbeg**, which is romantically situated on a promontory 90 feet above the sea. This is the country's most notable example of an Iron Age promontory defense fort—a refuge of last resort. Note the underground tunnel, called a souterrain, leading from the center of the fort to an escape hatch in front of the entrance; when the enemy entered the fortification, the people inside could crawl out and trap the invaders within. Notice, too, the drainage system to stop the water coming down the mountain, and the guard rooms with spy holes on either side of the entrance. Because of sea erosion, the fort will probably disappear by the end of the century.

✤ *SLEA HEAD*

The road is cut from the slopes of Mount Eagle, and the views, if the weather is right, are as spectacular as any in Ireland. Where the land juts into the sea you'll see the rusted hulk of a Spanish freighter, sunk in a storm in 1982. Beneath the black cliffs is a magnificent beach, perhaps 100 yards deep at low tide. Slea Head points to a group of islands and rocks known as the **Blaskets**. The largest, **Inishmore** or the **Great Blas-**

ket, has an abandoned village which you can explore on a day trip from **Dunquin** (contact Michael O'Connor, Tel. 066-56146). The island was the home of a remote and self-contained Irish-speaking community with a rich oral literature. In time, the younger islanders married into an easier life on the mainland, and in 1954 the remaining people were resettled near Dunquin. A walk along the high cliffs of the Great Blasket, above the crying gulls, is a memory to cherish for a lifetime.

The Blaskets acquired a new importance at the turn of the century when there was a revival of interest in Irish culture; the playwright J. M. Synge spent two weeks here in 1905, and it is believed that the character of Pegeen Mike in *The Playboy of the Western World* was inspired by his hostess. What is extraordinary is the literary outpouring from such a small, remote settlement: Maurice O'Sullivan's *Twenty Years A-Growing*, Thomas O'Criffan's *The Islander*, and Peig Sayers's *Peig*. Synge also wrote about the Blaskets, and so did the Englishman Robin Flower. What fun you can have reading their books (available in American libraries and in many Irish tourist shops), and then visiting the Blaskets and trying to identify the homes!

✤ DUNQUIN

If it interests you, ask at the public house for directions to the *Ryan's Daughter* schoolhouse, which is on a nearby cliff. The film was shot nearby.

Of all the pottery stores on Dingle Peninsula, the finest is in **Clothar**, 1½ miles past Dunquin. In addition to pottery, you can buy beautiful handwoven blankets, coveralls, wallhangings, and scarves.

✤ BALLYFERRITER

From Ballyferriter you can look down on **Smerwick Harbour** where the old fortress of **Dún an Óir** (Fort of Gold) stands on a rock promontory. It was here in 1580 that some six hundred Italian, Spanish, and Irish, supported by the Pope, held out against English Protestant forces, and were butchered by Lord Grey's troops. Grey's secretary was none other than the poet Edmund Spenser, who loved Ireland but not the Catholics, and who advocated starvation and genocide to bring the Irish under the sway of the Faerie Queene (Elizabeth I). Unsuccessful in its efforts to conquer England through the back door (Ireland), Spain made a frontal attack eight years later, with a 130-ship Armada. The force was routed in the English Channel. The ships that were not destroyed fled around the top of Scotland and down the west coast of Ireland. Twenty-five Spanish ships were lost off the Irish coast, including two wrecked near the Blasket Islands. (Ironically, there's a modern Spanish ship aground there today.)

Lodging

Not to be confused with the Fort of Gold is the modern **Dun an Oir Hotel** (M, Ballyferriter. Tel. 066-56133). The only thing Gaelic about this Best Western hostelry is its name. The hotel is essentially a complex of small white buildings squeezed together on a grassy field in the middle of the countryside, with virtually no trees or landscaping; how it ended up in the *Country Inns of Ireland* guide is a mystery. In its favor, however, is the fact that it's the only modern resort on the western end of the peninsula; its motelish rooms are softened by tasteful fabrics; it has a golf course; and the setting is as peaceful as anyone could wish. There are 20 cottages and 20 rooms, 8 with private bath. Facilities include a nine-hole golf course, tennis, deep-sea fishing, and riding.

❖ *GALLARUS ORATORY* and *KILMALKEDAR CHURCH*

Don't take the road south from Ballyferriter back to Ventry; follow signs toward the village of **Ballydavid** and two important historical monuments, **Kilmalkedar** and **Gallarus Oratory**. The seventh- or eighth-century **Gallarus Oratory** is one of the best preserved early Christian churches in the country, and an unrivaled example of the use of corbeling —successive levels of stone projecting inward from both side walls until they meet at the top. Though made of unmortared stone, it is still watertight after more than a thousand years. The two stones with holes in them on either side of the entrance were probably meant to hold the ends of wooden doorposts.

Kilmalkedar Church, 2 miles north of Gallarus, is one of the finest examples of Romanesque (Early Irish) architecture in the country. Churches such as this replaced the more modest beehive huts in the thirteenth century, when a local and decentralized church developed into a formal system of dioceses and parishes. Kilmalkedar Church was founded in the seventh century, but the present structure, standing in a graveyard, dates from the twelfth century. Note how—as at Cormac's Chapel at Cashel, by which it was inspired—the native craftsmen integrated foreign influences with their own local traditions: keeping the blank arcades and round-headed windows, for instance, but using stone roofs, sloping doorway jambs, and weirdly sculptured heads.

In the immediate vicinity you can "sample" a great variety of ancient Irish monuments. Just to the right of the entrance to the churchyard, beside a tomb, is a stone with mysterious decorations. It is usually regarded as a sundial, but could also be an early cross or even a pre-Christian monument. Nearby is an **ogham stone** with a hole in it. The writing on these stones, which date from the Late Stone Age and early Christian periods, consists of up to five strokes on either side of an imaginary vertical guideline. It begins on the bottom, continues upward and, if necessary, down the other side. The lines represent letters in the Roman alphabet, but the language itself is an early form of Irish. Most inscriptions commemorate the deceased and give details of their ancestry.

Near the church is **Caherdorgan Stone Fort**, which contains five almost complete beehive huts; **St. Brendan's House**, a two-story fifteenth-century building, now roofless but otherwise well preserved, where the local clergy probably lived; and the **Chancellor's House**, a two-room medieval building. The Chancellor was a cathedral dignitary who occasionally resided there.

◈ *THE CONOR PASS*

From **Gallarus Oratory** return to the town of **Dingle**, and then head north across the **Conor Pass**, the most spectacular high-level crossing in Ireland. The parking area at the head of the pass is a good starting point for the ascent of **Ballysitteragh** (2,050 feet) to the west or **Slievanea** (2,020) to the east. Neither walk should take more than an hour round trip. You don't need a marked path on these treeless slopes; just head for the summit. The climb is gradual, so anyone with perseverance can make it to the top.

From the top of Conor Pass you can look down and see **Brandon Bay**. It was from here that St. Brendan the Navigator (484–577) is believed to have set sail at age fifty-nine in a boat of skins and wood for "the Land of Promise." He got as far as Iceland, landing once on the back of a whale, which he thought was an island. On his second trip he may have reached either Newfoundland or Labrador, and "discovered" America more than nine hundred years before Columbus. In 1977 three men sailed 3,000 miles to Newfoundland in a replica of Brendan's boat, proving that it could be done.

St. Brendan was a Kerryman from Tralee who founded an important monastery at Clonfert, in County Galway, and later became the patron saint of Dingle Peninsula. The town of **Ballybrack**, 6 miles north of Dingle, is the starting point for a grueling 3½-hour (one-way) hike to Brendan's hermitage (**St. Brendan's Oratory**) on the top of the peninsula's most famous landmark, **Brandon Mountain**. Don't go if the summit is shrouded in mist—which it usually is. The route follows an ancient pilgrim route, the **Saint's Road**, to the high point of an enormous 4-mile ridge. Brandon was a sacred mountain in pagan times, when there was an annual pilgrimage to the summit to celebrate the festival of the Celtic god Lugh. After Christianity was introduced, the event was transformed into a pilgrimage in honor of Brendan.

✪ CAMP

Head down the **Conor Pass** to **Kilcummin**, and right (east) to **Tralee**. If you want one final hike, visit a great prehistoric stone fort, one of the country's highest, on a 2,050-foot spur of the 2,712 **Cahercontree Mountain**. The fort can be reached from **Camp**, following signs to the **Promontory Fort**. Ask locally for details.

From **Tralee** take **Route N21** east to **Limerick**, and then head either north to **Shannon Airport** or east to **Dublin**. If you need to spend the night near Shannon, consider staying in **Adare**, 10 miles southwest of **Limerick**. Voted the tidiest town in Ireland, it has some lovely thatched cottages on the banks of the Mai River, three medieval abbeys, a thirteenth-century castle, and a popular inn with good food (**Dunraven Arms**, M, Main Street, Route N21, Killarney Road. Tel. 061-94209).

RECOMMENDED READING

A Motorist's Guide to the Dingle Peninsula (a small useful guide sold in local shops).

Don Fullington, *An American's Ireland* (Panafast, New York).

ENGLAND

❦ Bath, the Cotswolds, and Stratford-upon-Avon

MAJOR ATTRACTIONS

- Three of England's greatest cathedrals—at Salisbury, Winchester, and Wells.
- Some of Britain's greatest palaces, parish churches, and castles.
- The Roman city of Bath—a fashionable eighteenth-century spa; today a sophisticated tourist center with elegant shops, music festivals, and first-class hotels and restaurants.
- The mysterious standing stones of Stonehenge.
- Stratford-upon-Avon—the Bard's birthplace and home of the Royal Shakespeare Theatre.
- The picturesque stone villages of the Cotswolds.
- Dining and lodging in restored manor houses and Elizabethan inns.

INTRODUCTION

Nothing is far away in England. Your trip will never take you more than 2 hours from London, but you'll be seeing an extraordinary variety of sights—with a minimum of driving.

From London you'll head southwest to Salisbury, to visit what many consider the most perfect cathedral in the country. Not far away are the mysterious standing stones at Stonehenge. After a night in a Tudor inn or

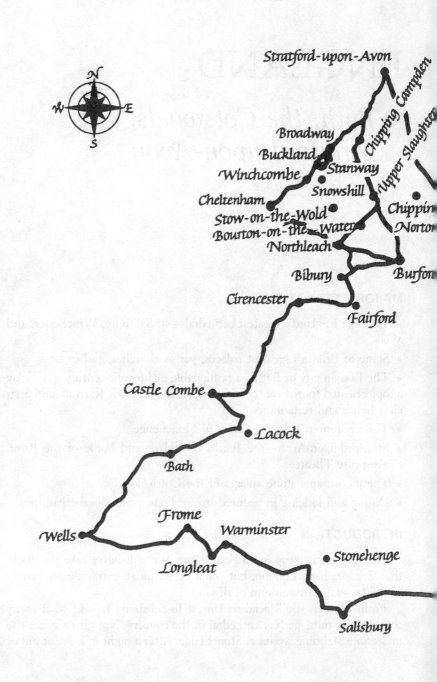

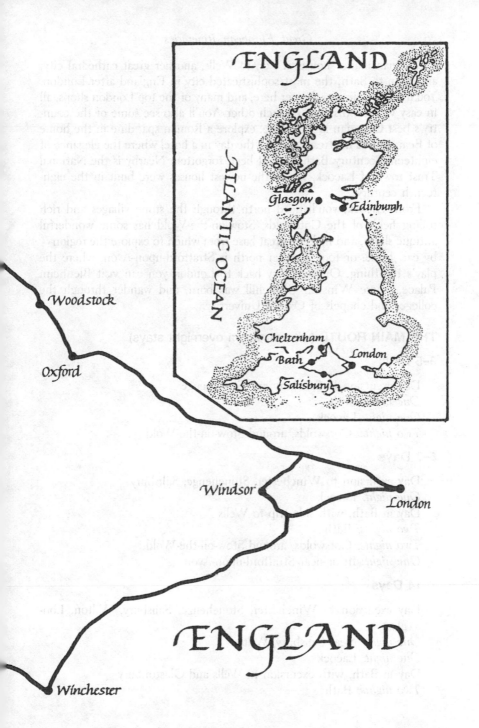

a Georgian manor house, it's on to Wells, another great cathedral city; and then to Bath, the most sophisticated city in England after London. You'll find music and theater here, and many of the top London shops, all in easy walking distance of each other. You'll also see some of the country's best Georgian architecture, explore a Roman spa, dine in the home of Beau Nash's mistress, and end the day in a hotel where the elegance of eighteenth-century Bath has not been forgotten. Nearby is the National Trust town of Lacock, where the newest houses were built in the eighteenth century.

From Lacock, you'll head north through the stone villages and rich rolling fields of the Cotswolds. Stow-on-the-Wold has some wonderful antique shops, and makes a great base from which to explore the region— by car, horse, or foot. Farther north is Stratford-upon-Avon, where the play's the thing. On your way back to London you can visit Blenheim Palace, where Winston Churchill was born, and wander through the colleges and chapels of Oxford University.

THE MAIN ROUTE (with minimum overnight stays)

3–5 Days

Day excursion to Salisbury and Stonehenge
One night: Bath
One night: Lacock
Two nights: Cotswolds, around Stow-on-the-Wold

5–7 Days

Day excursion to Winchester, Stonehenge, Salisbury
One night: Lacock
Day in Bath, with side trip to Wells
Two nights: Bath
Two nights: Cotswolds, around Stow-on-the-Wold
One night: In or near Stratford-upon-Avon

7–14 Days

Day excursion to Winchester, Stonehenge, Salisbury, Wilton, Longleat
One night: Near Salisbury/Wilton
One night: Lacock
Day in Bath, with excursion to Wells and Glastonbury
Two nights: Bath

Day excursion to Castle Combe, Cirencester, Fairford, Bibury, Burford, Northleach

Three nights: Cotswolds, around Stow-on-the-Wold

One night: Near Stratford-upon-Avon

Excursions to Warwick Castle

One night: Woodstock

Excursion to Blenheim Palace and Oxford

GETTING AROUND

Getting to London

British Airways (Tel. 800-AIRWAYS) flies to London from more American cities than any other airline: from Boston, New York, Philadelphia, Baltimore, Washington, D.C., Miami, Orlando, Tampa, Detroit, Chicago, Los Angeles, San Francisco, Seattle, and Anchorage. It's also the only airline that flies the Concorde—from New York to London in three hours.

Traveling through England

By car:

Driving on the left sounds frightening if you've never done it before; but when your life is on the line it's amazing how quickly it becomes second nature. The most important rule to remember is that the driver *inside* a roundabout has the right of way.

British Airways has a fly-and-drive package that saves about 20 percent on car rentals. BritRail Travel (Tel. 212/599-5400) has a BritRail/Drive pass that lets you take the train and pick up a car at or near your destination. You can then leave the car at another station with no drop-off costs. (The BritRail/Drive pass won't make much sense if your trip is limited to our itinerary, since distances are short and you will probably want to travel the entire route either by car or by public transportation.)

Most visitors to London will want to rent a car only when it's time to leave on this trip. If you're flying to and from London, arrange both to pick up and return your car at Heathrow Airport *after* your stay in London.

Don't be satisfied with a general road map of England. The Ordnance Survey 1:50,000 maps indicate all back roads and footpaths, and allow you to discover the beauty of the countryside and avoid heavy traffic. These maps are sold in map stores in large American cities, and in gift shops throughout England.

By public transportation:

You should follow this itinerary by car if possible, since otherwise you will miss many of the small, out-of-the-way places. Still, it is possible to see most of the major sites by train and bus.

There's good train service between **London** and **Winchester** (from Waterloo Station) and between **London** and **Salisbury** (also from Waterloo Station), but *not* between **Winchester** and **Salisbury**. To get from **Winchester** to **Salisbury**, you need either to backtrack to **Basingstoke** or ride to **Southampton**. Unless Winchester Cathedral is high on your list of musts, consider skipping Winchester and taking the train directly to Salisbury. From here there's regular bus service in season to **Stonehenge**, and direct train service to **Bath**. From **Bath** there's regular bus service to **Wells** and frequent bus tours to **Longleat House**.

From **Bath**, take a train to **Stratford-upon-Avon** via Bristol and Birmingham. From **Stratford-upon-Avon**, ride to **Moreton-in-Marsh**, which is as close as you can get by train to the center of the Cotswolds. From **Moreton-in-Marsh** rent a car or bike to tour the countryside. Trains go from **Moreton-in-Marsh** to **Oxford**, and back to Paddington Station in **London**.

Give a list of towns you want to visit to the **BritRail** office, and they will work out an itinerary for you and issue either a single-journey ticket or a **BritRail Pass**, depending on which is cheaper. Apply to **BritRail Travel International**. *New York:* 630 Third Avenue, New York, N.Y. 10017. *Los Angeles:* 510 West Sixth Street, Los Angeles, Cal. 90014. *Chicago:* 333 N. Michigan Avenue, Chicago, Ill. 60601. *Dallas:* Cedar Maple Plaza, 2305 Cedar Springs Road, Dallas, Tex. 75219.

The **BritRail Pass**, which you need to purchase before leaving home, allows unlimited rail travel through the entire British rail system for periods of 7, 14, 21, or 30 days, and is available for both first- and economy-class travel. Even if you don't make full use of the pass, it saves time waiting on ticket lines. Passes are available through travel agencies or through offices of the **BritRail Travel International** in New York, Los Angeles, Chicago, and Dallas (addresses above). Children get a 50 percent reduction. There are also **BritRail Youth Passes** for youths from fourteen through twenty-two.

The least expensive way to travel is by coach (as opposed to local buses). The **Britexpress Card** gives you a third off on all National Express coaches for a 30-day period. It can be purchased from travel agencies in the States or from National Express at Victoria Coach Station in London. Unfortunately, there is no single pass good for both trains *and* buses.

BritRail also sells **Open to View Tickets**, good for one month to hundreds of castles, historic homes, and sites.

By bike:

Flat or rolling countryside, short distances between towns, plenty of traffic-free back roads—all add up to a perfect landscape for biking. Bring bikes from home or rent them in London or in towns along the route, and, when you've had enough exercise, put them on the train with you at little or no cost. Penguin Books publishes a *CTC Route Guide to Cycling in Britain and Ireland* by Christa Gausden and Nicolas Crane. If you want to join a bike tour or organize your own, having your luggage carried ahead, contact **Bike Tours**, P.O. Box 75, Bath, Avon, England.

SPECIAL EVENTS

April–December: Royal Shakespeare Theatre season at Stratford-upon-Avon

April: English Bach Festival, Oxford

May: Bath International Festival of Music

May: Royal Windsor Horse Show

July 13–28: Cheltenham International Festival of Music

August 6–17: British Craft Fair, Stratford-upon-Avon (craftspeople sell and demonstrate their wares)

A NOTE ON SHOPPING

If you're making large purchases, ask for forms to exempt you from payment of a 15 percent Value Added Tax (VAT). Not all stores have this service.

Almost anything you could buy in London you can find in Bath—and at similar prices.

Stop at any of the National Trust shops for potpourri, woolen ties, pottery, Beatrix Potter books, and dozens of other tasteful gifts.

Best antiques are in Bath and Stow-on-the-Wold.

THINGS TO SEE AND DO WITH CHILDREN

The effigies of medieval knights in armor in various churches and cathedrals, particularly in Winchester, Wells, and Salisbury.

King Arthur's Round Table in Winchester.

Most of the cathedrals and parish churches along the route have memorial brasses which children (and adults) can rub for a small fee. The process is as simple as putting a coin beneath a piece of thin paper and rubbing with a pencil until the image comes through. Many churches sell equipment, but any art store will sell you (a) masking tape (b) drafting paper, and (c) a wax lumber crayon, and explain how to get started.

A back-road bike ride through the Cotswolds.

The caverns, antique pinball machines, and wax figures at Wookey Hole, near Wells.

The costume and carriage museums at Bath.

The wildlife park at Longleat.

A NOTE ON SPORTS

Golf

Courses near or along the itinerary include: *In Gloucestershire:* **Broadway Golf Club** (18 holes), Willersey Hill, Broadway, Tel. 0386-853683; **Cotswolds Hills Golf Club** (18 holes), Ullenwood, Cheltenham, Tel. 0242-522421; **Tewkesbury Park Golf and Country Club** (18 holes), Lincoln Green Lane, Tewkesbury, 12 miles north of Cheltenham, Tel. 0684-295405; **Gloucester Golf and Country Club** (18 holes), Matson Lane, Gloucester, Tel. 0452-411331 or 25653. *In Oxfordshire:* **Burford Golf Course** (18 holes), Burford, Tel. 099 382-2149; **Chipping Norton Golf Course** (9 holes), Southcombe, Chipping Norton, Tel. 0608-2383.

Fishing

The most famous streams for trout fishing are near **Bibury** and **Fairford**. All are privately owned. Your best bet is to stay in a hotel that caters to anglers: **Bibury Court Hotel**, Bibury GL7 5NT. Tel. 028-574-337. **Swan Hotel**, Bibury GL7 5NW. Tel. 028 574-204; or **Wroxton House Hotel**, Wroxton St. Mary, Wroxton OX15 6PZ. Tel. 0869-244731.

Riding

Beginners and experts can both saddle up for rides through the Cotswold countryside from the town of Stanton (see the Itinerary below). Riding centers in or near towns on the itinerary include: *In Gloucestershire:* **The Talland School of Equitation** (Church Farm, Siddington, Cirencester, Tel. 0285-2318. *In Hampshire:* **Arniss Riding Stables** (Godshill, Fordingbridge, 17 miles south of Salisbury, Tel. 0425-53042. **Harroway House Riding School**, Penton Mewsey, Andover SP11 ORA, just west of Andover, 20 miles northeast of Salisbury, Tel. 026 477-2295.

Walking

For free brochures describing paths and trails, contact the **Cotswold Wardens**, c/o County Planning Dept., Shire Hall, Gloucester. Tel. 0452-21444, ext. 7542. Also useful are the *Cotswold Way Handbook* from the **Rambler's Association**, c/o R. A. Long, 27 Lambert Avenue, Shurdington, Cheltenham. Tel. 0242-862594; *The Cotswold Way, a Walker's Guide* by Mark Richards (Thornhill Press), and *A Guide to the Cotswold Way* by Richard Sale (Constable).

A NOTE ON ARCHITECTURE

Most English churches were built and expanded over a period of hundreds of years—each restoration reflecting the styles and values of a new age. Nothing could be more satisfying than walking through these buildings and identifying the different periods of construction. **Norman** (1066–1189) is the British term for Romanesque. It is named for the Normans, who brought their Romanesque style with them when they conquered Britain in 1066, and grafted it onto the existing English Saxon Romanesque style already begun by Edward the Confessor (1044–66). **Early English** (1189–1307) is, in effect, Early Gothic. **Decorated** (1307–77) is mature Gothic. **Perpendicular** (1377–1485/1546) is Late Gothic. In Europe, the flamboyance of Late Gothic marked its decline; in England, it was the most original and distinctive of all British styles. In contrast to the Decorated style, the Perpendicular is marked by (a) a stress on straight verticals and horizontals, (b) window tracery with simple designs, and (c) fan vaulting (ceiling ribs that fan outward).

A NOTE ON DINING

The myth of pale, overboiled vegetables and tough, overdone meats fades slowly. The emphasis today is on local produce, prepared simply to enhance natural flavors. Traditional English fare is beginning to disappear, but you can still find game soups; roast beef with Yorkshire pudding; roast lamb with mint sauce; and shepherd's pie (so-called because the shepherds took something similar with them to the fields) filled with a mixture of meats—veal and ham, steak and kidneys, beef, and oysters. Your most reasonably priced lunches are in pubs, which now serve both hot and cold food, including "banger" sausages with mashed potatoes, and Cornish pasties (crescent-moon-shaped pies filled with meat, onions, and vegetables).

Even towns in the Cotswolds have reasonably priced Indian restaurants. The curries are usually not very hot. Fish and chips are a staple for travelers on the run; an ordinance has forbidden the sale of fish and chips wrapped in newspapers, so you can no longer read about the IRA while chewing on some limp fries.

Restaurants are rated for two: E (expensive, over $45); M (moderate, from $25–$45); I (inexpensive, under $25).

Imported liquor is heavily taxed and therefore quite expensive. Drinks are cheaper in pubs than in restaurants. Drinkers of Scotch will want to sample the great variety of Scotch whiskies—light or heavy; made with malt, grain, or blended. Try sweet or dry cider, too—but remember, it's not as innocent as it tastes.

The most popular drink is beer—bitter, brown ale, light ale, stout, and lager. Bitter is the standard draft beer. Ale is served at room temperature to bring out its flavor; the brown ale is sweet; the light ale is similar to many American beers. The most popular beer among American visitors is lager, which is similar to German beer and is served chilled.

Most, but not all, hotels add a 12 1/2–15 percent service charge to the bill.

Wine is heavily taxed and can therefore be very expensive; a decent vintage could double the cost of your meal. Visitors on tight budgets should check prices before they buy.

A NOTE ON LODGING

Those of you who haven't been to England for a while may be dismayed by the high price of a night's lodgings. Despite the inroads that the dollar has made against the pound, expect to pay about $14 per person for bed and breakfast in a private home, and a minimum of $45 for a double with breakfast at a modest hotel.

Rates, particularly at the more expensive hotels that cater to the package-tour trade, no longer routinely include breakfast, service charges, and taxes. This seems terribly shortsighted of the British—what American, after all, wants to cross an ocean to be treated the way he is at home? In any case, ask before you leap. Rates are usually given per person rather than per room.

Visitors have an opportunity to stay in private homes offering bed and breakfast (B and B), restored mansions, and old inns with creaky stairs and low-beamed ceilings. Why not experience all three? You could, for instance, stay in a Georgian town house in Bath, a 350-year-old country inn in Lacock (near Bath), and both a B and B and a great manor house in the Cotswolds.

The private homes usually have only a few rooms—sometimes with private bath, and almost always with large English breakfasts. They are usually spotless, and offer guests a great opportunity to make new friends. You can take your chances with B and B signs along the road, or make reservations through regional tourist offices. As in Ireland, you'll find that luxury hotels are in a class by themselves, but that for comfort, private homes are often light years ahead of fading second-class hotels.

Accommodations for two are listed below in three categories: E (expensive, over $70); M (moderate, from $35–$70); I (inexpensive, under $35).

EMERGENCIES

Call 999 throughout the country.
U.S. Embassy, 24–31 Grosvenor Square, London W1. Tel. 499-9000.

FOR FURTHER INFORMATION

British Tourist Authority. *New York:* 40 West 57th Street, New York, N.Y. 10019. *Los Angeles:* 612 Flower Street, Los Angeles, Cal. 90017. *Dallas:* Cedar Maple Plaza, 2305 Cedar Springs Road, Dallas, Tex. 75219. *Chicago:* 875 North Michigan Ave., Chicago, Ill. 60611.

THE ITINERARY

⚜ *WINCHESTER*

How to Get There. By car: 65 miles from London on M3 and A33. By rail: 63 minutes from London's Waterloo Station.

The Anglo-Saxons—Germanic-speaking peoples who settled in England after the Romans left—made Winchester the capital of their kingdom of Wessex. Threats from the Danes forced rulers from all over England to unite under the Wessex King, Egbert (802–39), and Winchester became, in effect, the capital of all England. The town flourished under Alfred the Great (871–99), and was later the seat of Canute (1016–35) and Edward the Confessor (1042–66). When the Normans conquered England in 1066, William the Conqueror (1066–87) made Winchester his capital, too, and power did not shift to London for another hundred years.

Winchester Cathedral—the longest Gothic church in England—is what draws most visitors to Winchester today. As you enter, you'll see long avenues of Norman columns encased in Gothic shells.

Walk down the left aisle. In the fourth bay is **Jane Austen's gravestone**. It makes no mention of her talents as a writer, since her fame followed her death. Farther down the aisle is a dark marble twelfth-century **baptismal font**, where children were being baptized at the time of the Battle of Hastings.

The **choir stalls** are among the oldest in England. Stand in the transepts (the arms of a cross-shaped church) and compare the rough stone pillars and ceiling to those of the rest of the church. What you're looking at is all that remains of the original Norman cathedral.

Look along the north aisle for the tomb of **Stephen Gardiner**. When the Protestants under Cromwell ransacked the cathedral they gave Gardiner's effigy the same rough treatment Gardiner gave the "heretics" during his lifetime. The Protestants were kinder to the blind and universally loved Bishop Richard Fox (1448–1528), whose effigy you'll find along the south aisle. Fox commissioned his own tortured effigy while he was still a young man—perhaps to remind himself that no one, not even a bishop, is free from corruption. How unlike the effigy of **Cardinal Beaufort**, all decked out in red, placidly awaiting his call to paradise.

As you walk through the chancel, look up at the painted chests holding the bones of several Saxon kings: Egbert (802–39); Ethelwulf (839–58), who was father of Alfred the Great; and Canute. The bones were scattered during the Civil War against Cromwell, so Egbert's head may be spending eternity with Ethelwulf's arms and Canute's legs.

A door on the south side leads to the library (open 10:30 to 12:30 and 2:30 to 4:30), which contains a tenth-century copy of the Venerable Bede's *Ecclesiastical History* and a twelfth-century painted Bible.

Make a sharp left as you leave the cathedral, and another left along a path beneath the buttresses. Notice how these buttresses, a Gothic invention, keep the walls from splaying out beneath the force of the roof, and thus permit the building of churches with higher, thinner walls, using glass instead of solid masonry. Bear right. Ahead of you is a red brick building. Walk around it to the left, following a sign to the **College/ Water Meadows**. Leave the cathedral close (where the clergy lived) and pass through the fourteenth-century town gate. To the right of the gate is the **Parish Church of St. Swithun upon Kingsgate**, founded in 1263. It seems odd that a tiny parish church would be built so close to a cathedral until you realize that cathedrals were used primarily by the clergy; that they had no seats or pulpits; that the naves were used primarily for processions; and that the laymen were encouraged by the clergy to build churches of their own.

Ahead of you, as you pass through the gate, is **Wykeham Arms** (1755), a good pub for an inexpensive plowman's lunch. Turn left on **College Street**. A plaque indicates the house, now privately owned, where Jane Austen died from Addison's disease at age forty-two. She was born and spent most of her life elsewhere, but she was often in ill health and in 1817 put herself in the care of a Winchester doctor.

On the right side of College Street, at the end of a long, unbroken stone wall, is the arched entranceway to **Winchester College**. Founded in 1382, it is the oldest public school—an English "public" school is the equivalent of an American "private" school—in England. The college was established as a training ground for applicants to New College in Oxford. Both schools were founded by the same man.

Continue down College Street. On your left is **Wolvesey Castle**, which Cromwell's forces destroyed in 1646. Directly across from the castle is a sign to **St. Cross via Water Meadows**. If you have time, take this pleasant one-mile walk through the meadows and school playing fields. At the lock, cross the road, and continue along the river. **The Hospital of St. Cross**, founded in 1133 by a grandson of William the Conqueror, may be the oldest functioning almshouse in the country. Guidebooks tell you that the gatekeeper maintains an ancient tradition of doling out beer and bread to all visitors—but you have to ask. The twenty-five brothers (old-age pensioners) wear gowns and live in fifteenth-century quarters. Visitors can tour a fifteenth-century kitchen and a twelfth-century Norman chapel with a bell tower you can get permission to climb.

From the Hospital, take a mile walk or a bus ride back to town. **St. Cross Road** turns into **Southgate Street**. At **High Street**, turn left to the **Great Hall**, which is all that's left of a Norman castle. Hanging here is the legendary **Round Table of King Arthur**, now known to be from the fourteenth century, and looking very much like a giant dart board. Was there really a King Arthur? Of course. When the Romans left Britain in 410, towns decayed and the country was plunged into a Dark Age of lawlessness and civil unrest. Into this vacuum swept a number of military leaders and kings. One of them was Arthur. In the mid-sixth century, the invasion of German-speaking Anglo-Saxons began. Arthur defended the Romanized Britains against the advancing Saxons in southwest England. Fighting like Roman cavalrymen against the Saxon foot soldiers—wearing helmets and chain mail against Saxon infantrymen with nothing but swords and spears—Arthur was able to keep them at bay for fifty years. He was probably Christian. Later English kings played up the Arthur legend to unite the country. Stories of Arthur and his Round Table were creations of the Age of Chivalry, and have no known basis in fact.

Dining

Old Chesil Rectory (M/I, 1 Chesil Street. Tel. 0962-53177) is the oldest house in town, with the requisite low-beamed ceilings and creaky floors. It's a 10- to 15-minute walk from the cathedral. The former owners have taken their Egon Ronay recommendation and moved to Paris; the new owner is now serving Old English cuisine, featuring steak and kidney pudding, sweetbreads, and boiled beef and carrots.

For a quick, convenient lunch, stop at **Wyckeham Arms Pub** on College Street (described above) or at any number of small restaurants on and around the pedestrian mall on **High Street**. Best bet on the mall is probably the **Eclipse**, around the corner from **Laura Ashley**, and a half-block from the cathedral. For a budget meal, try **Little Minstrels** (18 Little Minstrel Street), which serves vegetarian lasagna or prawn-and-avocado salad for under $4.

Lodging

Hotels in Winchester offer no more than convenience. The poshest is the **Wessex Hotel** (E, Paternoster Row, Winchester S021 9LQ. Tel. 0962-61611), a Trusthouse Forte property only seconds from the cathedral. The mood is defined by the backlit, "medieval" Plexiglas in the lobby. Rooms are clean and adequate. Somewhat less expensive is the **Royal Hotel** (M, St. Peter Street, Winchester S023 8BS. Tel. 0962-53468), located about five minutes from the cathedral. The hotel has a restful, glassed-in restaurant against an old brick wall, but the rooms themselves are Faded Motel Modern.

For those who can afford the price, the best bet is **Lainston House** (E, Sparsholt S021 2LT. Tel. 0962-63588), about 2 miles northwest of Winchester, off Route 272. A three-quarter-mile driveway, lined with lime trees, winds through parklands to an ivy-covered seventeenth-century manor house built by staunch supporters of Cromwell. There's an ancient dovecote, the ruins of a twelfth-century chapel, bird songs, and peace. Inside, there are some beautifully turned moldings, a mahogany staircase, and a wonderful cedar-paneled bar. It should be added that recent, extensive renovations were made by a consortium and that the hotel, which caters to business groups, has something of a consortium atmosphere. The furnishings, while tasteful, fall short of a seventeenth-century manor house. Rooms are comfortable but plain; ask for one in the main building.

For Further Information

The Tourist Information Centre is in the **Guildhall** (Tel. 0962-65406) on Broadway, near the cathedral.

❧ STOCKBRIDGE

How to Get There. By car: Take A272 7 miles northwest from Winchester.

As you drive to **Salisbury**, stop to look at the craft and antique shops on either side of the road. There's also a famous restaurant, and several small, friendly, medium-priced hotels.

Dining

The atmosphere at the **Sheriff House** (E, Stockbridge. Tel. 0264-10677)—the former jail—is as unprepossessing as can be, yet it's one of a select group to win a star rating from Egon Ronay. Dining is by reservation only—and tables are booked weeks in advance. Tables are in several small, homey rooms of a private house. The style of the cuisine is French Burgundian, with an emphasis on farm-fresh local produce. The menu changes daily and may include fresh Dorset lobster, salmon, sole, roast pork Dijonnaise, local cheeses, and homemade ice creams. Bread is baked daily with wheat brought from the Isle of Wight. Even the butter is home-churned.

Lodging

Sheriff House (M, Stockbridge. Tel. 0264-10677) has several rooms above the restaurant. The atmosphere is very, very homey, and will appeal to the extremely sophisticated and the extremely unsophisticated.

Old Three Cups (M, Tel. 0264-810527) is a fifteenth-century inn with 7 cheerful, serviceable rooms.

✤ SALISBURY

How to Get There. By car: From **Stockbridge**, drive 14½ miles west on A30. From London, bypassing Winchester, drive 83 miles on M3 and A30. By train: From Winchester, backtrack to **Basingstoke**, and catch another train to Salisbury. From London, it's a 90-minute ride from Waterloo Station.

• Salisbury is the Melchester of Hardy's novels, and the Barchester of Trollope's. It is also the home of what many consider the most perfect English cathedral ever built. It owes its unity to the fact that it was constructed in thirty-eight years (1220–58)—which was unheard of in those times—and therefore stands exactly as its designers conceived it more than seven hundred years ago. Winchester Cathedral, which you just saw, is typical of most cathedrals in that it is an amalgam of styles, from Norman/Romanesque to Perpendicular/Late Gothic. Salisbury, in contrast, is in a single style, Early English—the purest expression of Early English in Britain.

Take your time walking around the cathedral grounds and looking up at the cathedral from different angles, appreciating its confidence, its restrained dignity, and its strength. Walk around on summer nights, too, when the cathedral is floodlit. The masons had trouble securing the weighty spire, which was added a century later, and it still leans slightly, despite the use of heavy arches to support it. At 404 feet, it's the tallest medieval spire ever built.

It has been said that the outside is all decoration, and the inside, all lines. You may find the uncluttered interior disappointing, in comparison: all ribs without flesh, appealing more to the mind than to the senses. This was due to an eighteenth-century housecleaning by some ill-advised ecclesiastical schoolmarms.

Near the west end of the north aisle—the aisle on your left as you face the front—is the oldest clock mechanism (1326) in England, perhaps in the world. As you walk down the aisles, you'll see the tombs of knights who went on the Crusades or who died at Agincourt, where Henry V routed the French in 1415. In Salisbury, as in other English cathedrals, you'll notice that the aisles are lined with small chapels enclosing an altar and an effigy. These are called **chantries**. Wealthy laymen endowed these chapels, paying priests to say daily masses for their souls and for the souls of their families, in perpetuity or for a fixed number of years.

Climb the tower, open 10:30 to 12 and 2:30 to 7.

In the **Trinity Chapel** is a sheet of blue stained glass, the *Prisoner of Conscience*, glazed in 1980. Turn and compare it to the medieval shields and figures in the west window.

• Leave by the **cloisters**, the earliest and longest in any English cathedral, and visit the adjoining **chapter house** (the room in a cathedral where business was conducted). You'll find here one of four extant copies of the **Magna Carta**, the foundation of English, and American, liberty. The Barons prepared it, and King John put his seal to it at Runnymede in 1215. In an effort to circumscribe the arbitrary powers of the king, Article 39 states that "no free man shall be seized or imprisoned, or stripped of his rights or possessions, or outlawed or exiled, or deprived of his standing in any other way, nor will we [the king] proceed with force against him, or send others to do so, except by the lawful judgment of his equals or by the law of the land."

• Salisbury has the best **cathedral close** in the country, with houses from the thirteenth to the eighteenth century. It was in these stone and brick buildings surrounding the cathedral that the clergy lived. The clergy of **monastic cathedrals** consisted of monks who lived around a cloister. The clergy of Salisbury Cathedral were **secular canons**—clergymen who went out into the community and were not bound by monastic vows. These canons could live where they wanted, but usually chose to stay in houses near the cathedral, called a **close**. The secular cathedrals had cloisters, too, but they were often merely decorative.

Of particular note in the close are (1) **King's House**, home of the **Salisbury and South Wiltshire Museum**, which has some models of Stonehenge that will make your visit there more meaningful; (2) the

College of Matrons (built in 1682 for the widows of canons); (3) the Military Museum; and, above all, (4) the beautifully furnished Mompesson House (1701), with an exquisite Queen Anne interior.

• Exit through the north door of the cathedral and cross the lawn to where North Walk intersects with High Street. If you have only a few minutes, follow High Street past Mompesson House, and beneath North Gate. There's a National Trust Gift Shop here. Turn left on Crane Street. Just after the bridge, cut left through the Queen Elizabeth Gardens to another bridge over the River Nadder. It was from here that Constable painted his famous portrait of the cathedral. If time permits, follow a footpath from this bridge through open countryside, and enjoy changing views of the cathedral.

• If you have an extra half-hour, *don't* go up High Street; rather, turn right on North Walk to St. Ann's Gate. Handel is said to have given his first public concert in the room above. Turn left on St. John Street, which turns into Catherine Street and then into Queen Street. On your left is Market Square, where outdoor markets (Tuesdays and Saturdays) have been held since 1361. Cross through the market to St. Thomas' Church, founded about 1220 in honor of Thomas à Becket. It was rebuilt in the fifteenth century in the Perpendicular style, and has a notable fresco (1475) of the Last Judgment above the chancel arch (the arch separating the nave from the front of the church). From St. Thomas', take High Street back toward the cathedral, turn right on Crane Street and take the abbreviated walking tour listed above.

Tours

Guided Walking Tours begin outside the Tourist Information Centre, Fish Row, daily except Sunday, at 10:30 and 2:30 in August, and at 2:30 from late April to mid-October.

Dining

There are several good restaurants around Silver Street, including Manuel's, formerly Provençal (M, 14 Ox Row. Tel. 0722-28923).

Lodging

Salisbury's hotels are adequate/pleasant but not outstanding. The main reason to spend the night is to see the floodlit cathedral.

White Hart Hotel (E, St. John's Street, Salisbury SP1, 2SD. Tel. 0722-27476) is a 72-room Georgian hotel not far from the cathedral. Best bet are the larger, more traditional rooms in the original building. Newer rooms are pricey for what they offer.

Old Bell Inn (M, 2 St. Ann Street, Salisbury SP1 2DN. Tel. 0722-27958) is a converted fourteenth-century inn which has managed to keep some charm despite its functional carpets and other modern refurbishings. Try for a room with a four-poster.

Rose and Crown Hotel (M, in Harnham, Harnham Road, Salisbury SP2 8JQ. Tel. 0722-27908) is a half-timbered, old country inn not far from town. Rooms are uneven; a few in the original building have four-posters and some Old World charm; others need refurbishing. Modern rooms are functional.

Red Lion Hotel (M, Milford Street, Salisbury. Tel. 0722-23334) is a seventeenth-century inn that is now a Best Western with a Ye Olde atmosphere, complete with sagging floors and low-beamed ceilings. Not all rooms have private baths. Those in the newer wing are smaller. Try for room 36.

❖ WILTON HOUSE

How to Get There. By car: From **Salisbury**, go 4 miles west on A30.

Open late March through mid-October, Tuesday through Saturday from 11 to 6; Sunday from 1 to 5:15.

Wilton House is one of England's greatest, most opulent mansions, designed by Inigo Jones and his son-in-law, James Wyatt. The home of the earls of Pembroke for over four hundred years, it contains a world-famous collection of paintings, furniture, and sculpture; an exhibit of 7,000 model soldiers; a palace dollhouse; a working model railroad; even a lock of Queen Elizabeth I's hair. John Webb's staterooms are among the most palatial seventeenth-century rooms left in England.

In about 1530, a Welshman named **William Herbert** married the sister of Catherine Parr, who became Henry VIII's last wife. When Henry confiscated the Church's lands, he abolished Wilton Abbey and gave the property to his brother-in-law. Herbert's eldest son later married **Mary Sidney**, sister of the poet **Philip Sidney**, who wrote *Arcadia* while staying here. Scenes from this famous poem are painted on the walls of the **Single Cube** room. There's also a painting of the seventh earl's wife in the buff—one wonders what the earl thought of it.

The famous **double cube** and **single cube** rooms, built to show off the paintings of Van Dyke, follow the rules of proportion that Jones learned from the Renaissance architect Palladio (1508–80); namely, that beauty consists of fixed, mathematical relationships between parts, none of which can be changed without destroying the harmony of the whole. The assumption is that God ordered the universe according to immutable mathematical laws, and that beauty comes from creating a similar order here on Earth.

♥ STONEHENGE

How to Get There. By car: From Salisbury take A360 north 8 miles and turn right about 2 miles on A303. From Wilton House, take A36 north to Stapleford, B3083 north, and then turn right on A303. Buses leave from the Salisbury Train Station a few times daily except Sunday from mid-April to mid-December. There's more frequent service from Salisbury Bus Station near Market Place, a few blocks from the cathedral.

The best time to visit Stonehenge (open from 9:30 to 6:30) is early in the morning, or just before closing, when the shadows are longer than the lines. A fence keeps you from wandering among the stones, so you may want to avoid the entrance fee and watch from the road. Even if the site is officially closed, you can see it quite well from the embankment, so also consider visiting at sunrise or sunset, when the dim light creates an even greater sense of mystery.

What was this circular group of standing stones? An astronomical observatory? A Druidic temple? A navigational aid for flying saucers? Evidence seems to point to its being an open-air temple dedicated to sky gods. It was built from about 2200 to 1550 B.C.—later than the Great Pyramid, contemporary with the Minoan civilization on Crete, and a thousand years earlier than the Great Wall of China. The Druids, a Celtic priesthood, did not get here until 250 B.C.

The stones were shaped with hammers, and upended in holes dug with antler picks and spades made from the shoulder bones of cattle. The lintel stones ("henges") were set in place with the help of log platforms. The bluestones, which weigh up to four tons each, were brought some 240 miles on logrollers and sledges, or lashed to the sides of rafts. The other stones weigh up to 50 tons each and were brought mostly uphill from 20 miles away. At the time, only nomadic hunters lived on Salisbury Plain, so whoever built Stonehenge must have come from another, more sophisticated civilization.

The most important clue is the blue beads called *faience* which have been found in many parts of Britain and which could only have come from workshops in Egypt and Mycenae. The Egyptians and Greeks made these beads for trade with Europe. If you look where they've been discovered over the years, you find that they follow a trail along the southern coasts of France and Spain, up to Brittany, up the Dorset coast of England, to the greatest concentration—around Stonehenge. It was here that these beads were traded for Irish gold; here that Mycenaean civilization, through the medium of these traders, was introduced in Britain; and here that one of the traders or his associates must have been commissioned to build Stonehenge. It may seem farfetched, but how else do you explain the Mycenaean-type dagger carved into one of the Stonehenge stones, or the fact that the very same technique used to fasten the stone lintels to the uprights was used to construct the stone gateways at Mycenae?

Stonehenge—a temple dedicated to the sun—was needed by a people who were moving from a female-dominated society that worshiped earth goddesses, to a male-dominated society that worshiped gods of the sky. The same transition went on in Greece, when the old Achaean earth gods were replaced by Zeus and his cronies on Olympus. The transition took place in Greece about 1600 B.C.—the very same time that the Beaker Folk were engineering the final remodeling of Stonehenge.

By standing at the center, the sun can still be seen rising over the Heel Stone on the summer solstice. So sophisticated were the techniques of these early astronomers that posts were placed to indicate where the moon rises over the horizon, as it shifts every two weeks in 18.61-year cycles. Yet Stonehenge was probably not an early version of Palomar Observatory, but a temple where the movement of the planets was observed for religious reasons.

❧ WARMINSTER

How to Get There. From Stonehenge, drive 18 miles west on A303 and A36.

Lodging

Bishopstrow House (E, Boreham Road, Warminster BA12 9HH. Tel. 0985-212312) is the best hotel between London and Bath. The 15-room Georgian mansion is located about two miles outside of Warminster and belongs to the prestigious Relais et Châteaux group of hotels. The formal lounge has Persian carpets, jade green upholstery, antiques, and French windows overlooking the extensive grounds. Furnishings have a formal, decorated look, but are comfortable and in good taste. Whether you stay in the converted stables or the main house, furnishings are traditional, with soft, subdued pastels. The small rooms aren't quite worth the price; but the suites are wonderfully luxurious, some with Jacuzzis made for two. Facilities include tennis and indoor and outdoor pools. The tiled indoor pool, surrounded by classical pillars, is as elegant as the pool at the Palace Hotel in St. Moritz.

✤ STOURHEAD HOUSE and GARDENS

How to Get There. From Stonehenge take A303 about 25 miles, then turn north on B3092 for about 2 miles.

A trip to **Stourhead House and Gardens** will add about 15 miles to your drive, but anyone who loves gardens will find the trip worthwhile. These are among the finest eighteenth-century gardens in England. A river was dammed to create a three-part lake, whose shores are surrounded by various Italian temples and grottoes. The gardens are open daily from 8 A.M. to dusk. The eighteenth-century house with Chippendale furniture is open May through September, daily except Friday, from 2 to 6; and on fall and spring weekends from 2 to 6.

✤ LONGLEAT HOUSE

How to Get There. From Stourhead House and Gardens, take B3092 north about 6 miles and follow signs. From Stonehenge, drive 18 miles west on A303 and A36 to Warminster, and follow signs.

What I remember most about Longleat House is the guide shaking the change in his pocket so we wouldn't forget to tip him at the end of the tour. The house itself is an exercise in wowmanship, with busloads of tourists tramping through the gilded halls among the priceless antiques, some more tasteful than others. Longleat is the only surviving sixteenth-century example of a Renaissance-style house in England. It was redecorated in the Italian Renaissance style during the nineteenth century, and stuffed with a dizzying collection of artifacts which the fourth marquess gathered on a grand tour of Europe. Chinese vases, Venetian ceilings lifted from the Doge's palace, Sicilian clocks, nineteenth-century salt-shakers—Longleat has them all. Highlighting the tour are the erotic murals—apples hanging from phallic trees, etc.—painted in 1973 by the good Lord Weymouth, who is said to have had an unhappy childhood.

For children, the highlight of the trip to Longleat is a visit to the **Dolls' Houses** and a drive through **Safari Park** among the not-very-wild animals. There's also a **maze**, a 15-inch narrow-gauge **railway**, and **safari-boat rides** through a lake full of hippos and sea lions.

Tickets for all attractions cost about $10 per person. The house is open daily in season from 10 to 6; off-season, from 10 to 4. The Safari Park is closed in winter.

Dining

A good bet for lunch near Longleat is the **Bath Arms** (Horningsham. Tel. 09853-308), en route to Frome. Lord Christopher from Longleat likes to come here for a pint with the locals.

♦ FROME

How to Get There. From **Longleat House**, take A362 about 3½ miles north.

Frome (pronounced *froom*) isn't directly on the route from **Stonehenge** to **Bath**; you'll pass through only if you're visiting **Longleat House** or **Wells**. There's no need to make a special trip, but if you're passing through at lunch- or teatime, stop at **The Settle** (Tel. 0373-65975) on Cheap Street. The food and pastries are as memorable as the atmosphere. The lunch menu includes Somerset gammon (ham) with Damson sauce, pork in rough cider, and rabbit pie.

♦ WELLS

How to Get There. By car: From **Frome** take A361 east 11 miles. From **Bath**, take A39 south 21 miles. By bus from Bath: The 21-mile trip takes 80 minutes. Buses leave hourly during the week, less frequently on Sunday, from the bus terminal one block from the train station.

If you're spending several days in Bath, it makes sense to settle in and make a side trip to Wells. If time is limited, however, save time by visiting Wells en route to Bath.

• Wells is the smallest cathedral city in England, but its cathedral, built by secular canons, is said to be the most graceful in the country. Because the complex of church buildings is so well preserved, it makes a great introduction to life in the Middle Ages. Come if you can on market days —Wednesday and Saturday.

The cathedral took three centuries to plan and build (1175–1508) and therefore offers a lesson in the history of architectural styles.

As you enter, look up at the famous west façade and try to imagine the statues colored and gilded, as they were in the thirteenth century. The

Puritans destroyed some of the 400 statues, but 297 remain—the greatest and richest display of thirteenth-century sculpture in England.

Ahead of you is a pair of strangely inverted scissor arches that were added to support the new tower, which was so heavy that it threatened to tumble into the nave. The arches look modern but were built six hundred years ago. Some think them gross, others graceful, but all agree that they're unique, and that they worked.

Follow the left (north aisle) to the transept and look up at the clock. Knights rush out every quarter hour and fight with lances. One has been knocked down each time—since 1390. On the hour Jack Blandiver kicks the bells with his heels, and hammers one in front of him. No one knows how he got his name. Below the clock is a modern, life-size carving of Christ rising from the tomb (1955).

Continue toward the front, east end of the church and look for the door leading to the **Chapter House**—the finest in the country. In the octagonal room, thirty-two ribs fan out from the central pier like fronds on a giant palm tree. Don't miss it!

Look at the capitals (the heads of columns) in the south transept—on your right as you face the front of the church—and find the heads and animal masks hidden among the leaves. One has a toothache and seems to be waiting for a dentist to pass by.

The cathedral has some wonderful chantry chapels. Look especially for **Bishop Thomas Bekynton's**. The two views of him, in this life and the next, say more about mortality than a hundred sermons. Look, too, for chantries of **Nicholas Bubworth**, Bishop of Bath, and **John Drokensford**, who is waiting for Judgment Day with his feet on a lion and his head on a pillow.

• From the cathedral walk through the fifteenth-century **cloisters** to the grounds of the **Bishop's Palace**, the only medieval bishop's palace still occupied. It's open from Easter through October, on Sunday and Thursday from 2 to 6. Since the bishop still lives here, the rooms we'd all like to see—bedrooms, bathrooms, etc.—are closed to the public. The 15-foot-thick walls and moat were added in the fourteenth century to protect the bishop from town riots. Guidebooks tell you that swans in the moat ring a bell for dinner; but the swans find it easier to be fed by tourists, and the bell, alas, hasn't tolled for years.

• **Wookey Hole** is a cave and paper mill two miles from Wells. If you dismiss it as a tourist trap run by Madame Tussaud's, you're making a mistake. It *is* commercial, but it's great fun, too, and families in particular shouldn't miss it. What makes a tour worthwhile is the fact that prehistoric folks once lived here, and it's fun imagining their lifestyle. Watercolorists can buy handmade paper here, and children of all ages can play prehistoric penny-arcade games and tour a room filled with Madame Tussaud's retired wax figures. Open from mid-March to mid-October daily from 9:30 to 5:30; off-season, from 10:30 to 4:30.

✤ BATH

How to Get There. By car: From Wells, take A39 21 miles northeast. From Salisbury, take A36 40 miles northwest.

Bath is England's most elegant city, famous for its history, its architecture, and its hot springs. It's also a clean, comfortable town with sophisticated restaurants and first-class hotels. The shopping, along traffic-free pedestrian malls, is in some ways the equal of London's, minus the logistical headaches of getting around. The major sights are the **Roman Baths**, a **costume museum** (the finest in England), and the **Georgian buildings** where British society stayed in the eighteenth century. None of this will mean much, however, unless you know something about Bath's history.

A Brief History of Bath

The Romans knew about the springs and their restorative powers when they began moving west in the first century A.D. to mine lead. They built the baths around them—nothing as grand or elegant as the baths in Rome, but luxurious for such a distant outpost; and here they remained for nearly four hundred years. The baths are still well preserved, and are today the best Roman ruins in Britain.

The fame of Bath disappeared with the Romans in the fifth century. Medieval chroniclers knew about the health-giving properties of the waters, but the spa was neglected until the seventeenth century. The diarist Samuel Pepys wrote in 1668, "Methinks it cannot be clean to go so many bodies together in the same water." Among those who disagreed was Charles II, who brought his Queen Catherine here to make her fertile and give the crown a legitimate heir. It didn't work; but others followed, including Queen Anne, who, suffering from dropsy and gout, came twice, in 1702 and 1703, bringing the rest of English society in her fashionable wake.

In 1704 a thirty-one-year-old gambler, **Richard "Beau" Nash**, was chosen to oversee the spa's restoration. In the next forty years this obscure Welshman virtually invented the resort business, and became the

Arbiter of Elegance. His famous Code of Behavior, posted in the Pump
Room for all to see, included the following rules:

1. That ladies coming to the ball appoint a time for their footmen
coming to wait on them home, to prevent disturbance and inconvenience
to themselves and others.

2. That no gentleman give his ticket for the balls to any but gen-
tlewomen. —N.B.: Unless he has none of his acquaintance.

3. That the elder ladies and children be content with a second bench
at the ball, as being past or not come to perfection.

On three points Nash was particularly insistent: that there should be
no dueling and wearing of swords; that women should never appear at
assemblies in white aprons, and that men should never appear at fashionable gatherings in riding boots. The fight against white aprons was particularly severe. The climax came when the Duchess of Queensberry arrived
at the Assembly Room in an apron which the Beau ruthlessly stripped
from her and threw among the ladies-in-waiting. The duchess took the
insult in stride, and meekly submitted to the uncrowned King of Bath.

Once Nash freed Bath from its rustic associations, the *beau monde*
began to flock here, certain that dignity and decorum would prevail. In
the first four decades of the eighteenth century, Bath became the center
of Fashion and Polite Society during the long summer months. **Richard
Sheridan** wrote *The Rivals* here in the 1770s while living on Terrace
Walk; **Charles Dickens** hung out in the card rooms (now the **Assembly
Rooms**) and put the city in several chapters of *The Pickwick Papers.* **Jane
Austen**, who was often sick, came for the cures in the early nineteenth
century. When you visit the Assembly Rooms you can imagine Catherine
Morland, heroine of *Northanger Abbey*, and a projection of Jane herself
as a young girl, being snubbed by fashionable visitors till she finds a
suitable gentleman to show her around.

While Nash organized concerts and gambling, and lit the streets to
make them safe, the architect **John Wood** (1700–54) was busy transform-
ing Bath into a town suitable for the upper classes. A classicist inspired by
the town's Roman past, he conceived of a plan to unite all houses in a
larger structure with a common façade. The most noble of these Palladian-style groupings were the **King's Circus** and the **Royal Crescent**, the
latter designed by Wood's son in 1767. Not only can you still see these
buildings today, you can stay in some of them, in hotels with appoint-
ments as splendid as the buildings themselves.

• Begin your tour at the **Abbey**, a good example of late Perpendicular
Style—one of the last great achievements of Catholic England. Do you

see the angels climbing ladders on the west façade? The sculpture was inspired by a dream of Bishop Oliver King, in which he saw angels climbing to heaven and heard voices commanding a king (his own name) to restore the church. The designers were very anxious to have the church well lit, and so they built the large clerestory windows (in the walls above the nave).

• Cross the Abbey Church Yard, past the **Tourist Information Centre**, to the **Roman Baths and Pump Room**. The Pump Room—named for the reservoir below that provides 280,000 gallons a day of hot, sulfurous water at a constant temperature of 116 degrees Fahrenheit—is in fact a Georgian assembly hall. For a taste of eighteenth-century Bath, be sure to come from 9 A.M. to noon, for coffee, a sip of the evil-tasting waters, and the sounds of violins. Be on your best behavior, for Nash—at least a painting and statue of him—are looking down on you. The Pump Room was actually built in 1789–99, after Nash's death, when the middle classes had begun to gate-crash, and the high-born and low-born were engaged in a frantic round of pleasure and diversion, both an easy prey to sharks and fortune-hunters. Close your eyes and think of the Pump Room as described by the novelist Tobias Smollett through the eyes of one of his heroines, Lydia Melford:

"All is gaiety, good-humour, and diversion. The eye is continually entertained with the splendour of dress and equipage; and the ear with the sound of coaches, chaises, chairs, and other carriages. We have music in the Pump-room every morning, cotillions every fore-noon in the rooms, balls twice a week, and concerts every night, besides private assemblies and parties without number. The Squares and the Circus put you in mind of the sumptuous palaces represented in prints and pictures. At eight in the morning we go déshabillé to the Pump-room, which is crowded like a Welsh fair; and there you see the highest quality and the lowest tradesfolks, jostling each other, without ceremony. Hard by the Pump-room is a coffee-house for the ladies; but my aunt says young girls are not admitted, inasmuch as the conversation turns upon politics, scandal, philosophy, and other subjects above our capacity. . . ."

Descend to the **Roman Baths**. Most of the excavations were made in the late nineteenth century, long after Nash's reign. The **Great Bath**—in essence, a warm swimming pool—is still unroofed, and has the original Roman lead plumbing; the columns and statues above are Victorian. There were no luxurious changing rooms in the eighteenth century; visitors arrived in carriages, wrapped in robes; after wallowing in the rather scuzzy waters, they wrapped themselves up, returned to their carriages, and niddlenoddled home.

• Next to the Great Bath is a **museum** of Roman remains. Leave the Baths and turn right on **Stall Street.** You'll find many fashionable shops on this pedestrian mall, and along the side streets. On your right is the **Octagon,** an eighteenth-century hall housing the **National Centre for Photography** (open 9:30 to 5:30 daily; off-season, closed Sundays), which has quality exhibits and a 20-minute **Bathorama** audiovisual show that takes you through the history of the city from pre-Roman times to the present. Shows begin every 30 minutes, daily except Sunday, from 10 to 5.

• **Stall Street** turns into **Milson Street,** which runs into **George Street.** Bear right on **Bartlett Street,** which has several antique shops, and continue to **Alfred Street.** Turn left. On your right are the famous **Assembly Rooms,** built by John Wood's son in 1769–71 so that visitors didn't have to go all the way to the baths to socialize. The Assembly Rooms soon became the center of the town's social life, with balls, card playing, tea drinking, entertainments, and an endless stream of gossip and scandal. The rooms were gutted during the war and reconstructed a bit too perfectly in the mid-sixties, but they still have their original chandeliers and fireplaces.

Below the Assembly is the **Museum of Costumes,** the largest of its kind in the world, with costumes dating back to the sixteenth century, some of them in period rooms. Don't miss it!

• From the **Assembly Rooms,** turn right on **Circus Mews** to the **Carriage Museum,** which has the best collection of carriages in England. Your kids will thank you for taking them to see them.

• Backtrack down **Circus Mews** and turn right into the **Circus,** a circle of identical Georgian houses which many consider John Wood's finest work. (A "circus" is a circle or ring.) Wood designed it, and it was completed by his son, who also designed the Royal Crescent (see page 81).

In order to appreciate the Georgian architecture of John Wood and his son, keep in mind that it was based largely on the concepts of the Italian Renaissance architect Palladio. If Wood's buildings seem cold to you, it's because they are meant not to overwhelm your senses, as, say, a Gothic or Baroque building would, but to appeal to your mind—to your sense of order and harmony and proportion. Every part has a fixed size and shape in relation to every other, and to the whole. This harmony, in the rationally conceived universe of the eighteenth century, was thought to be an echo of the harmony of the universe—a universe which, like a clock, was set in motion by a rational God. As you walk around the Circus, try to appreciate these harmonic ratios, and think fondly of an age when people could believe that Truth was known, and that the world was ruled by reason.

• Leave the **Circus** and walk down **Brock Street**, which was built by John Wood the Younger in 1767. The street was conceived as an avenue connecting the town's two architectural masterpieces, the **Circus** and the **Royal Crescent**. You won't know what's in store for you until the moment you turn into the Crescent—which is exactly as Wood planned it more than two hundred years ago.

• The **Royal Crescent** is the severest expression of the Palladian style in England. Designed in 1767–74, it consists of thirty houses with a continuous façade of 114 Ionic columns. Ask yourself: would you rather live here or in the Circus? I'd prefer the Circus; it seems more human. Yet Smollett seems unfair when he dismisses the Royal Crescent as "a pretty bauble, contrived for show, [that] looks like Vespasian's amphitheater turned inside out." Note that though the façade gives the buildings a uniform face, the interiors were all designed differently, by various contractors, and that the back sides, which no one was supposed to see, are, in comparison, rather shabby. How eighteenth century, this distinction between a person's private life and the face he presents to the world!

The **Georgian House Museum** at 1 Royal Crescent is now a museum where you can capture a sense of life in eighteenth-century Bath. In the very center of this noble arc is the **Royal Crescent Hotel**. Note the fashionably understated hotel sign beside the door.

• From the **Royal Crescent**, return to the **Circus**. Turn right (counterclockwise) in the **Circus**, past the hotel at number 6, and make your first right down **Gay Street**, which turns into **Barton Street**. On your right is the most popular restaurant in town, **Popjoy's**, where Nash once lived with his mistress, Juliana Popjoy. Beside the restaurant is the beautifully restored **Theatre Royal**, where you should get seats for an upcoming performance.

• Cross the open square and turn left on **Westgate Street**, which will take you back to **Stall Street**, the **Baths**, and the **Abbey**. Between the **Abbey** and the **River Avon** are the lovely **Parade Gardens**, where you can rest your feet. To the right of the gardens (facing the river) is a bridge. Cross over, and turn immediately left on a path along the river bank. There's a place here to catch a boat for a peaceful 60-minute cruise on the Avon. Continue along the river to the next bridge, which has shops on it, inspired by the Ponte Vecchio in Florence. Cross the bridge, which leads into **Bridge Street**. Turn right on **High Street**. On your right is the **Guildhall**, the banquet room of which is one of best interiors in Bath. Next door is the **covered market**. Continue down High Street and you're back at the **Abbey**.

Tours

For current tours, contact the **Tourist Information Centre** in the Abbey Church Yard, daily from 9:30 to 5; Sunday from 10 to 4. Tel. 0225-62831.

There are free, 1³/4-hour **conducted walking tours** in season, weekdays at 10:30 A.M. and Sundays at 10:30 and 2:30. They begin outside the Pump Room, in the Abbey Church Yard.

Jane Austen Tours take you in the footsteps of the author and her characters. The 60-minute tour begins at the Beau Nash Gallery, York Street, 100 yards from the Tourist Information Centre.

For those who want to tour Bath by bus, there are at least four bus tour companies, some with open-top buses that leave both from near the Tourist Information Centre and from the bus terminal. Contact the Tourist Information Centre for schedules and prices.

For personal tours, contact **Beau Nash Guides**, Tel. 0225-63030; or **The Red Guild of Tour Guides**, Tel. 0225-312757.

The Arts

Nothing could be more pleasant than an opera or play at the historic **Theatre Royal** (Tel. 0225-65065). Try to get seats while you're in London, or before you leave home. A good ticket agency is **Tickets**, Kingston House, Pierrepont Street. Tel. 0225-66541.

The internationally famous **Bath Festival** runs from late May through early June and features everything from choral music to opera and jazz. Get tickets when you're reserving your hotel room.

Boating

Punts and canoes can be rented on the Avon, just northeast of town, from the **Bath Boating Station**, Forester Road. Tel. 0225-66407. Call this same number for canal boat cruises.

Biking

For bike rentals, contact **Avon Valley Cyclery**. Tel. 0225-61880. The Avon Valley Cycle Path is a peaceful, 4-mile stretch of abandoned railroad line between Bath and Bitton.

Golf

Bath Golf Club (18 holes), Sham Castle. Tel. 0225-63834. **Lansdown Golf Club** (18 holes), Lansdown. Tel. 0225-22138. **Entry Hill Golf Course** (9 holes). Tel. 0225-834248.

Riding

Call 0225-66375.

Tennis

Royal Victoria Park, Sydney Gardens, and Alice Park. Tel. 0225-23915. Recreation Ground (grass courts). Tel. 0225-62563.

Dining

Popjoy's Beau Nash House (E, Sawclose, Bath. Tel. 0225-60494) is the place to dine if you have only one evening in Bath. It's conveniently located next door to the theater, and comes closer than any restaurant in town to capturing the elegant atmosphere of eighteenth-century Bath. The limited, fixed menu features local fish and game, with such specialties as goat cheese profiterole, duck livers in pepper and sherry jelly, char-grilled duck with grapefruit and peppercorn sauce, and quail stuffed with pine nuts and raisins. Coffee is served upstairs. Reservations are essential. Nash lived here with his mistress; when he died she vowed never to sleep in a bed again, and ended her life in a hollow tree in Wiltshire.

A mile outside of town, in a 160-year-old Georgian country house, is the **Priory Hotel Restaurant** (E, Weston Road, Bath, BA1 2XT Avon. Tel. 0225-331922). The Royal Crescent is historically a place not to miss, but the food at the Priory enjoys a slightly better reputation. The cuisine leans toward traditional French, but you can ask to have your meal prepared without sauces. Main dishes include medallions of venison with black currant sauce and chestnut purée; and veal kidneys with white wine, juniper berries, and mushrooms.

Royal Crescent Hotel (E, 16 Royal Crescent, Bath. Tel. 0225-319090) has the most formal restaurant in town—the sort of tie-and-jacket place where Americans worry about making too much noise putting their butter knives down on their plates. If you're not staying at the Royal Crescent and can afford the dizzying prices, this is a great opportunity for you to tour John Wood's masterpiece and learn what eighteenth-century elegance was all about. The nouvellish menu includes chilled crab and lobster terrine; lightly curried mussel soup; salmon steak topped with salmon mousse and steamed in fresh spinach leaves; and roast pigeon with turnips and mushrooms in a rich wine sauce.

Downstairs Restaurant (M, 32 Milsom Street. Tel. 0225-27758) isn't much for atmosphere, but it enjoys a sound reputation for home-cooked French meals at reasonable prices. Specialties include salmon baked in pastry with tarragon, and escalope of veal cordon bleu.

Lodging

The **Tourist Information Centre** (Tel. 0225-62831), located near the Abbey and the Baths, can make reservations for you. Also call the **Accommodations Service** at 0225-60521.

Royal Crescent Hotel (E, 16 Royal Crescent, Bath BA1 2LS. Tel. 0225-319090) was the best address in Bath two hundred years ago—and still is today. Staying in one of these lovingly restored townhouses is as close as you'll come to recapturing the grandeur of Georgian Bath. Rooms in the renovated building behind the crescent are tastefully decorated in hushed pastels, but those who know the history of Bath will probably feel cheated unless they stay in the original building designed by John Wood. The atmosphere is formal and discreet, with most guests on the far side of thirty-five. The larger rooms and suites are exquisite; the smaller, least expensive rooms are a bit worn. If you can't afford the best, you may be better off paying the same price as the cheaper rooms to stay in the best rooms at **Number 6 Kings Circus Hotel**.

Number 6 Kings Circus (E, Bath BA1 2EW. Tel. 0225-28288) is a real find, not known by many tourists: a lovingly restored, family-run town house in John Wood's famous Circus. The house was built in 1756 for Lady Lucy Stanhope, and reflects the lifestyle of the nobility of the time. Highly recommended!

Number 9 (E/M, Miles Buildings, Bath BA1 2QS. Tel. 0225-25462) is another find, not far from the Circus: a lovingly renovated early-eighteenth-century town house built by John Wood the Elder. Furnishings are not as grand or formal as at Number 6, but prices are considerably lower. Rooms are individually decorated, most with canopied beds. Rooms 8 and 4 are particularly lovely. As with Number 6, Number 9 is run by an intelligent, enthusiastic young couple who make it possible for guests to enjoy both the formality of an eighteenth-century home and the hospitality of a country inn.

The Priory Hotel (E, Weston Road, Bath, BA1 2XT Avon. Tel. 0296-331922) is a rambling 160-year-old Georgian house about 1 mile from town. The Royal Crescent has the atmosphere of a city hotel; the Priory, of a country estate. The atmosphere here is refined, but much more relaxed than at the Royal Crescent. There are rooms to curl up in here— one would never curl up at the Royal Crescent, at least not in public! Pay the extra price for the suites; they're worth it. The best standard rooms are in the older wing. Facilities include a heated outdoor pool. The restaurant has a first-class reputation.

Apsley House Hotel (E/M, Newbridge Hill, Bath BA1 3PT. Tel. 0225-336966) is a great stone mansion set back from a busy road, A431, a mile west of Bath. The recently converted William IV-style house has 7 rooms, all with double beds. Rooms are immaculately clean, and guests are given a sense of being in a home rather than a hotel. Still, a bit expensive for what it has to offer.

Ston Easton Park (E, Ston Easton, 12 miles from Bath, BA3 4DF. Tel. 076 121-631) is one of England's most elegant country houses, with period antiques, a formal grand salon with ornate plaster ceiling and other Palladian-style details. Best bedrooms have four-posters.

Other recommended hotels include **Lansdown Grove** (M, Lansdown Road, Bath BA1 5EH. Tel. 0225-315891), a recently renovated hotel above the city; **Francis Hotel** (E, Queen Square, Bath BA1 2HH. Tel. 0225-24257), 90 rooms in six eighteenth-century houses on one of Bath's most famous squares; and **Ladbroke Beaufort Hotel** (E, Walcott Street. Tel. 0225-63411), a large, modern hotel popular with business folks.

❧ LACOCK

How to Get There. Take A4 about 12 miles east of Bath, then turn left (south) on A350.

If you want to see an eighteenth-century village that hasn't been prettified or overwhelmed with tourist shops, visit Lacock. It can be overwhelmed on summer days by tourists stalking the Real England, so stay overnight—before or after your trip to Bath—and explore the town when the daytrippers are gone. In the Middle Ages Lacock was a weaving community on an important Bath–London route. Prosperity continued through the eighteenth century, when—as with other towns you'll be visiting—the Industrial Revolution put the cottage weaving industry out of business. Unlike other towns, however, Lacock was owned largely by a single family, the Talbots, who preserved its heritage, and in 1944 put it safely in the hands of the National Trust. Thanks to the preservationists, the newest houses are eighteenth century, and the town remains one of the most homogeneous in England.

The main street, leading to the Abbey, is **High Street**, lined with moss-covered stone houses spanning at least four centuries. **Church Street**, which parallels High Street, leads to **St. Cyriac Church**. This is a Perpendicular-style wool church—so-called because it was built by prosperous wool merchants during the fourteenth to seventeenth centuries. Note the memorial brass in the south transept to Robert Raynard and his eighteen children. Note, too, the weird faces in the arches of the **Lady Chapel** (on the left, facing frontward).

Lacock Abbey was the last religious house in England to be suppressed at the Dissolution—when Henry VIII established the Church of England and appropriated church lands to fill his coffers. It is a good example of a medieval Augustinian priory that was converted into a private home, incorporating both the chapter house and the cloister. Open April through October from 2 to 5:30; closed Tuesdays.

Visit the **Fox Talbot Museum**, which contains photos by Fox Talbot, who made the first photographic prints in 1833. Open March through October from 11 to 5:30.

Dining

Sign of the Angel (M, Tel. 024 973-230) is a beautifully maintained old inn with an unbeatable sense of the past. Traditional English fare includes roasts with fresh vegetables; braised kidneys in Madeira sauce, salmon mousse, and homemade pies, cheeses, and ice cream.

Lodging

If you're going to experience southwestern England, you should spend at least one night in a Georgian town house, another in a restored manor house, and a third in an old inn. The best of the inns is **Sign of the Angel** (M, Wiltshire SN15 2LA. Tel. 024 973-230). This fifteenth-century wool merchant's house has low oak-beamed ceilings, even in the bathrooms, and whitewashed, stenciled bedroom walls. What makes the inn unique is that it hasn't been mucked up with tasteless modern furnishings, and has avoided the annex-expansion that has turned so many cozy English inns into tour-bus destinations. Each room is different. Number 3 is more spacious than some; if noise bothers you, avoid number 1. The breakfast omelets, with ham, mushrooms, and tomatoes, should see you through the day.

If you want to experience an old Tudor inn, you can't do better than Sign of the Angel, but if you prefer the more polished atmosphere of an English country house, drive two miles to **Beechfield House** (E, Route

A350, Beanacre, Wiltshire SN12 7PU. Tel. 0225-703700). The stone Victorian mansion has 16 rooms, half in the main house, half in the restored coach house. Facilities include a pool and tennis.

King John's Hunting Lodge (M, Tel. 024 973-313) has only two rooms, one of them with a four-poster. The lodge is run by a young, intelligent couple who turn guests into friends. If you don't stay here, stop in for tea.

The Old Rectory (M, Cantax Hill, Lacock, Wiltshire SN15 2JZ. Tel. 024 973-335) is a large, friendly guest house on the edge of town. A bit pricey for what it offers, but less expensive than the Angel. Try for the four-poster room, or the Laura Ashley room—if you're into Laura Ashley.

❧ THE COTSWOLDS

The Cotswolds are England's "green and pleasant land"—a region of soft stone villages and rich, rolling pastureland, where nothing seems to change, or matter, but the seasons. Americans love these picturesque villages because they have everything America lacks: tradition, homogeneity, local color, and a sense of place. The towns seem to spring organically from the soil, and no one needs an advanced degree to appreciate their timelessness, their beauty and their strength.

A "wold" is an upland common—in other words, a stretch of high land or plateau that's owned in common, usually as pastureland. The Cotswold Hills are about 100 miles long and 40 miles wide, and rise to about 1,000 feet; but the surrounding countryside, extending northeast roughly from Bath to Stow-on-the-Wold, is often considered part of the Cotswolds, too.

From the thirteenth to the fifteenth century, the wool raised here was England's main export. The wool trade created great wealth and much of the money went into the construction of cottages, manor houses, and the so-called wool churches—buildings that give the Cotswold villages their unique architectural charm.

The cotton mills of Lancashire unraveled the wool trade. The commons were enclosed and turned into private farms by the Enclosure Acts (1795–1812). The drystone walls put an end to the small farmer and the great sheep runs; and when the bottom fell out of the wool trade in the seventeenth and eighteenth centuries, construction stopped and the towns remained suspended in time—until the tourists arrived and put the Cotswolds back on the map.

The challenge is to find some way to enter this world—not merely to pass through. It's not an easy task when you're one of hundreds of Americans sniffing around a tiny stone village, all searching for the Elusive Past.

Rule One is to avoid the main roads whenever possible. Get yourself a 1:50,000 map and drive down the backest of the back roads. Rule Two is to pick your towns carefully. The itinerary below should give you some sense of which ones to visit or avoid. The area around **Stow-on-the-Wold** makes a great base, since it's centrally located, has restaurants, hotels, and shops for every taste and budget, and is large enough to absorb the crowds.

Rule Three is to leave the pavement at least once and walk from one town to another, following a footpath through the meadows. One popular walk is from **Stow-on-the-Wold** to **Lower Swell, Upper Slaughter,** and **Lower Slaughter;** but wherever you are, ask a policeman or desk clerk to suggest a route, or pick up one of the hiking guides sold throughout the region. Among the best are *Along the Cotswolds Ways* by G. R. Crosher (Pan) and *A Visitor's Guide to the Cotswolds* by Richard Sale (Moorland).

There are some 1,600 miles of pathways in the Cotswolds—along country lanes, footpaths, and ancient sheep tracks as old as Stonehenge. Most are marked with signposts and indicated on 1:50,000 maps. Villages are so close together that you rarely need more than an hour or two to hike between them. If a circular route is unfeasible, walk from A to B and arrange for a taxi to take you home.

☙ CASTLE COMBE

How to Get There. From Bath: take A46 north 6 miles to A420. Turn right (east) to **Ford,** and follow signs north to **Castle Combe.** From **Lacock:** Take A350 north to **Chippenham,** A420 west, and follow signs on your right to **Castle Combe.**

The film *Dr. Doolittle* was a financial disaster, but it seems to have brought a lot of attention to **Castle Combe,** where it was filmed, and which subsequently won a national poll as the prettiest town in England. The old wool weaver's village hasn't changed much in the past 250 years, except for the sea of tourists in which, each summer, it threatens to drown. The problem with Castle Combe is that it's a one-street town jammed with traffic; there are no side streets to get lost in, no alleyways to discover. If you're collecting lovely Cotswold villages, don't miss it; but don't expect to be overwhelmed by local color.

Dining

The **Manor House Hotel** (see below) is more famous for its atmosphere than its food—a decent resting place for lunch, if you can cope with the crowds. The **Castle Hotel** in town is where the locals go for lunch; it doesn't have the panache of the **Manor House**, but there are times when a quiet meal means more than panache.

Lodging

The **Manor House Hotel** (E, Castle Combe SN14 7HR, Wiltshire. Tel. 0249-782206) can be a madhouse during the day; but if you spend your afternoons exploring, you'll return at night to one of the most romantically situated manor house hotels in England. The 34 rooms sit on 26 acres with a trout-stocked lake, Italian gardens, wooded trails, swimming pool and tennis. The public areas are filled with heirlooms and rich wood paneling. Furnishings are old-fashioned. If there's anything wrong with the Manor House it's that it's so Discovered—a place one does as part of the Cotswold Experience. It's also expanding at an alarming rate. Be sure to get a room in the main house; the workmen's cottages look lovely from without but are in fact charmless, with worn carpets and small basic bathrooms. Two rooms have four-posters.

Castle Hotel (M, Castle Combe SN14 7HN, Wiltshire. Tel. 0249-782461) is plainer, quieter, cheaper and more informal than the Manor House. Not even the red industrial carpet destroys its age-old charm. Best bet is room 1. Young couples will appreciate room 9.

✤ *CIRENCESTER*

How to Get There. From Castle Combe: The fastest route is to Malmesbury and then north on A429 and A433. The more scenic route is via **Tetbury**.

Cirencester (pronounced *Sisiter*, but known locally as "Ciren") is a busy district center, with markets and shops. It was once the second largest Roman town in Britain after London. During the Middle Ages it was the largest wool market town in the country.

The main reason to stop here is to visit **St. John the Baptist Church**, the finest of all the wool churches, and one of the largest parish churches in England. Because of its unusual length (180 feet), it looks more like a small cathedral. The aisles are wide to accommodate the faithful, and give the church a sense of being of and for the people—an impression you don't always get in English cathedrals. The church was begun in the twelfth century, but the **Tower,** the **Trinity Chapel,** and the **Lady Chapel** were built in the early fifteenth. The Norman nave was raised 15 feet a century later in the new Perpendicular style. The fifteenth-century wineglass pulpit is one of a few left in the region from before the Reformation. To the right of the chancel arch is the **Boleyn Cup,** which Henry VIII gave to Anne two years before her execution. The **Trinity Chapel** has some great fifteenth-century brasses, which you can rub (contact Rev. Lewis. Tel. 0285-3142).

From the church turn right and go down **Castle Street.** Bear right on **Silver Street,** which turns into **Park Street.** On your right is the **Corinium Museum** (open 10 to 5:30; Sundays, 2 to 5:30), the finest museum of Roman remains in the country, with reconstructions of a Roman kitchen, dining room, and workshop. It also houses well-preserved mosaic pavements in replicas of rooms where they once stood.

Continue down **Park Street.** Bear right on **Thomas Street** and make your first right on **Coxwell Street,** which has many lovely old houses. At the end of **Coxwell Street,** turn right and return to the church.

A five-minute walk from the church takes you to the **Cirencester Workshops** (open daily except Sunday from 10 to 5:30), where you can buy hand-printed textiles (number 7) and other crafts. To get there from the church, turn right to the light; turn left on **Cricklade,** then make your first right.

For Further Information

Tel. 0285-4180.

⚓ THE WOOL CHURCHES

Cirencester has the best of the wool churches. If you want to see some of the others, drive east on A417 to Fairford; north on A361 to Burford, and east on A40 to Northleach. From here take A429 north to Stow-on-the-Wold. If you've seen enough churches, take A429 direct from Cirencester to Stow-on-the-Wold.

⚓ FAIRFORD

How to Get There. From Cirencester drive east 9 miles on A417.

The main attraction of Fairford is **St. Mary's Church,** and the main attraction of St. Mary's is the stained glass windows. No other parish church in England has retained its complete set of medieval glass. The 28 windows serve as a picture book meant to teach the story of the Bible, beginning with Adam (the green glass which you'll see when you stand with your back to the organ), and ending with the Last Judgment. The "Short Guide," sold at the entrance, gives a brief description of each panel. Except for the base of the tower, the wool church was completely rebuilt in the Perpendicular style by John Tame (1470–1534), a rich wool merchant, and his son Edmund. Below the carpet in the **Lady Chapel** are commemorative brasses to Edmund and his two wives. His second wife commissioned it.

For examples of medieval humor, don't miss the misericords—the seat projections on the choir stalls. You'll see carvings of a woman giving grief to her husband, a couple draining a cider barrel, and so on.

Lodging

Bull Hotel (M, Market Place, Cirencester, GL7 4AA. Tel. 0285-712535) is a traditional Cotswold inn with old beams and exposed stonework. Fine for overnighting.

❧ *BIBURY*

How to Get There. From Cirencester take A433 northeast for 7 miles. From Fairford, follow back-road signs.

Bibury is the town most often used on British Tourist Board posters—minus the crowds. In season, you'll find yourself among a gaggle of tourists on what is essentially a tiny, one-street village—much like Castle Combe. Yet Bibury is worth a stop because it's so pretty a town—William Morris thought it the most beautiful in England—and the **Parish Church, Arlington Row,** and **Country Museum** are all worth seeing. Here, as elsewhere in the Cotswolds, the ideal time to visit is in the early spring or fall.

About 300 yards before the museum is a left turn leading to **St. Mary's Parish Church,** in an area of the town which many visitors miss. At Bibury the wool merchants did not completely rebuild the original Romanesque church, as they did at Cirencester, Fairford, and Northleach, so you'll be able to identify features that go back to Saxon times. There's a great Norman north door, and Saxon capitals. The north aisle is the earlier of the two—you can tell by the massive columns. The large windows of the north aisle are fourteenth-century work in the Decorated style. You won't see this in many Cotswold churches, since by the time the wool merchants had money for restorations, the Perpendicular style was in. The wall-cupboards (ambries) indicate that the church must once have had a great collection of plate or relics.

Arlington Row is a group of old Cotswold cottages that date back to the fourteenth century. Once the homes of shepherds, they were converted into houses in the seventeenth century to accommodate weavers from **Arlington Mill**. Don't peer into the windows; people are still living here. If you're ready for a walk, take the path uphill from Arlington Row to the gate, and follow the sign.

The **Cotswold Country Museum**, located in the former mill, has a fine collection of old carts and machines, and rooms showing how people lived and worked.

Lodging

Swan Inn (M, Bibury, GL7 5NW. Tel. 028 574-204) is a former coaching inn on the banks of the river, with spacious bedrooms and lots of beams and paneling. It's on the busy main street that quiets down when the daytrippers depart. Okay for overnighting.

Bibury Court Hotel (M, Bibury, GL7 5NT. Tel. 028 574-337) is a 16-room manor house from Tudor times on the outskirts of the village. Furnishings are a mix of Faded Modern, Art Deco, and Victorian. Try room 11, or the "Sackville Suite."

✤ BURFORD

How to Get There. From Bibury, take A433 northeast 9 miles.

Burford is not directly on the route from **Bibury** to **Stow-on-the-Wold**; to get there you have to swing east. The extra miles are worthwhile, however, if you want to see one of the most beautiful wool churches and visit a half-dozen quality antique shops strung along the main street of town.

The **Church of St. John the Baptist** is a late-twelfth-century Norman church that was transformed over the next three hundred years into the Perpendicular building you see today. That's why the chapels and aisles are all at different levels.

There's a lovely 2½-mile country walk east along the Windrush River to **Asthall**, where you can stop at the **Maytime Inn** for lunch. Ask locally for directions.

❧ *NORTHLEACH*

How to Get There. From Burford take A40 west for 9 miles. From Bibury, take A433 northeast to **Aldsworth**, and turn left about 3.5 miles, following back-road signs.

Northleach was a medieval wool-trading center on high ground between the valleys of the Coln and Windrush. The wool church is one of the grandest—and a favorite among brass rubbers.

The Church of St. Peter and St. Paul was built by God-fearing wool merchants, and looks as though it were made to last forever. Like most other wool churches, it is a Norman building that was rebuilt in the fifteenth century in the Perpendicular style. There's lots to see here: a fifteenth-century pulpit, a fourteenth-century carved baptismal font, and wonderful brasses of wool staplers, their feet resting on wool packs or sheep. For permission to rub brasses, contact the post office or the Tudor house on the Green.

Dining

Old Woolhouse (E, The Square, Northleach. Tel. 045 16-366) has only a few tables, so make reservations. A typical set meal begins with scallop mousse, moves on to veal kidneys with sweetbreads or roast rib of beef, and ends with French cheeses and tarts.

❧ *STOW-ON-THE-WOLD*

How to Get There. From Northleach take A429 9 miles north.

Stow-on-the-Wold is an ancient hilltop market town. At 700 feet, it's the highest town in the Cotswolds. It sits at the junction of seven important roads, but—and this is what makes Stow unique—none runs through the town itself. The seventeenth-century stone buildings are clustered around a market square as a defense against the wind; if you squint you can imagine yourself back in the Middle Ages, when the town was famous for its fairs. Stow makes a great base for exploring the Cotswolds because it's so centrally located and has all the facilities you would want, including some 22 sophisticated antique shops—even one for antique dolls. Day excursions from Stow are listed below.

St. Edward's Church, in the town center, is Norman with many additions, including a Perpendicular tower dominating the square. The nave has a notable seventeenth-century Belgian painting of the Crucifixion.

Dining

The emphasis is French nouvelle at the elegant **Wyck Hill House** (E, Stow-on-the-Wold, Gloucestershire GL54 1HY. Tel. 0451-31936), about 2 miles from town on A424. A favorite appetizer is mousseline of chicken with Roquefort served on a bed of celeriac with a walnut-flavored cream sauce. Entrees include rolled fillets of Dover sole with smoked salmon served in a vermouth-and-wine sauce and garnished with caviar; and medallions of venison served with a pistachio-and-game mousse on a Port wine sauce.

Candlesticks, formerly Rafters (Park Street, Stow-on-the-Wold. Tel. 0451-30200) had just changed management when I arrived; ask at your hotel about its reputation. Specialties include tenderloin pork with apricot and walnut mousse, and salmon steak with Béarnaise sauce.

Old Farmhouse (Lower Swell, 1½ miles from Stow on B4068. Tel. 0451-30232) has a sound reputation. For an inexpensive Indian meal, try **Prince of India Restaurant,** a short walk from the market place.

Lodging

Wyck Hill House (E, Stow-on-the-Wold, Gloucestershire GL54 1HY. Tel. 0451-31936, about 2 miles from town on A424) has had some management problems; let's hope it stays open, because it's one of the most tastefully restored grand manor houses in the country. The cedar-paneled library, high French windows, oriental lamps, plants, and thick carpets show a fine attention to detail, which is matched by the attentive service. The hilltop view of the Windrush Valley is glorious.

Unicorn Hotel (M, Sheep Street, Stow-on-the-Wold, Gloucestershire GL54 1HQ. Tel. 0451-30257) is a friendly, informal seventeenth-century stone hotel with an unpretentious, almost boardinghouse feeling to it. Steep stairs lead to beamed rooms with old-fashioned furnishings.

Royalist Hotel (M, Digbeth Street, Gloucestershire GL54 1BN. Tel. 0451-30670) is a step below the Unicorn, but probably not for long. The building has lots of character, with stone walls and ancient beams. The new owners inherited some unattractive red carpets and undistinguished furnishings, but they plan extensive renovations, and the work they've already done shows a good deal of taste. Try for the four-poster room, or one that's been recently restored.

For an inexpensive B and B in a bucolic setting, try the home of **Mrs. Berry** (I, Tel. 0451-30141), next door to the Wyck Hill House on A424, 2 miles from town on the road to Burford. Another good B and B is Mrs.

Buffery's (I, Evesham Road. Tel. 0451-30841), just out of town on the road to Broadway.

Fosse Manor House (M, Stow-on-the-Wold, Gloucestershire GL54 1BN. Tel. 0451-30354) was built in 1900 and served in turn as a private home, vicarage, nursing home, and hotel. It still has somewhat of a homey, nursing home ambiance, which some will love more than others. The contrast between the red floral carpets and the flowery William Morris-type wallpaper is, well, very country English. Best bet are the rural views, the bird songs, and the ebullient personality of the owner. Try for room 42, which, like many of the rooms, has no private bath.

For Further Information

Tel. 0451-30352.

The following towns can all be reached on a one-day excursion from Stow-on-the-Wold. They are listed in the order in which you would reach them on a circular tour.

✤ BOURTON-ON-THE-WATER

Kids and grownups who want Things to Do will love Bourton-on-the-Water.

Birdland (open March through November daily from 10 to 6; off-season, daily from 10:30 to 4) is a world-famous seventeenth-century manor house with more than 600 species of birds from around the world. The owner also runs a Motor Museum in an eighteenth-century water mill; the Cotswold Perfumery; and a Model Railway.

Fish for trout on the Windrush Trout Farm (open April through October daily from 10:30 to 5:30; off-season, daily from 11 to 4).

The Model Village is an exact scale replica (1:9) of the village before World War II, made from local stone.

Dining

Rose Tree (M, Riverside, Bourton-on-the-Water. Tel. 0451-20635) is a pretty cottage bordering the river. Home-style meals include baked local trout, pot-roasted venison, chicken and vegetable terrine, and puddings.

✤ LOWER AND UPPER SLAUGHTER

These are two delightful back-road villages—completely unspoiled except for the tourists searching for an unspoiled village. If you're here in summer, visit in the early morning or evening, when the daytrippers are gone. The half mile between the villages makes an ideal walk. Lower Slaughter is neater and prettier, with lovely stone bridges—which is why some people prefer Upper Slaughter.

Lodging

Lords of the Manor Hotel (M/E, Upper Slaughter, Gloucestershire GL54 2JD. Tel. 0451-20243) is a former rectory set in 7 acres of gardens, with a lake for fishing. Furnishings are old-fashioned, which is to say pleasant but undistinguished—not at all up to the character of the house. The absence of room TVs sets the mood for a peaceful, ivy-clad manor house with comfortable sofas and a relaxed, friendly atmosphere. Try for a four-poster room.

The Manor Hotel (M, Lower Slaughter. Tel. 0451-20456) was a Best Western until taken over by a new owner, who hopes to turn it into another Wyck Hill House. Rooms now are large and bright, with modern furnishings—some a bit faded, though still preferable to those at, say, Fosse Manor, outside Stow. Facilities include an indoor pool. The setting is idyllic.

✤ *NAUNTON*

For being less picturesque than other Cotswold villages, and for committing the unpardonable sin of permitting modern buildings, Naunton is blessed with an absence of tourists. The village won the 1981 Bledisloc Cup as Best Kept Village in England. "Most pleasant looking petrol station seen anywhere on the judge's rounds," says the award. "The telephone kiosk [behind the sign to the petrol station] adjoining the bus shelter cut into the face of the old building is ingenious." **Ye Olde Inn** is, despite its name, a good place for pub grub and a pint of anything.

✤ *COTSWOLD FARM PARK* (3 miles northeast of Guiting Power)

Kids will love the rare breeds of farm animals, including the breed of sheep that brought prosperity to the region, and some Iron Age pigs. You're 900 feet up—a great setting for walks among the enclosed animals.

♦ SUDELEY CASTLE (1/2 mile southeast of Winchcombe)

If your schedule is crowded, go directly from **Naunton** or the **Cotswold Game Park** to **Stanton** (see page 98). But if time permits, spend an hour in **Winchcombe**, stopping at **Sudeley Castle** on the way.

The fortified fourteenth-century manor house contains the tomb of Catherine Parr (1512–48), the sixth queen of Henry VIII. The king was Catherine's third husband—her second having died only months before the royal wedding. In the same year that Henry died, Catherine married a former lover, Thomas Seymour, who owned Sudeley Castle—and a year later she herself died in childbirth. Catherine of Aragon stayed here; so did Anne Boleyn. Elizabeth I lived here as a child. The modern **Queen's Garden** is laid out in authentic Tudor style. Inside, you'll find a wonderful collection of toys and dolls; the eighteenth-century Aubusson tapestries which belonged to Marie Antoinette; and paintings by Constable, Turner, Rubens, and Van Dyke. Open March through October, daily from 12 to 5:30; gardens open daily from 11 to 6.

♦ WINCHCOMBE

St. Peter's Church is a fine Perpendicular-style church, built in 1465, with a great gilded weathercock on top of the tower, and some 40 grotesque gargoyle waterspouts around the façade. The bullet marks are from the Civil War. The framed altar cloth behind blue curtains on the north wall is said to have been made by Catherine of Aragon. Look for the kneeling effigy of Thomas Williams of Corndean (d. 1636) in the chancel —he's staring at a space where his wife used to be: she remarried and is spending eternity with her second husband.

The church is on Queen Square. Opposite is the **Jacobean House** (1619) attributed to Inigo Jones, restored in 1876. Exit the church, turn left, then right on **Vineyard Street**, which has some lovely old cottages running down to the river. It's also called Duck Street because of the witches who had their heads held under the water. If instead of turning right on **Vineyard**, you continue straight, you'll come to the Town Hall, where you can put your kids in the stocks. The **Tourist Information Centre** is here.

Kids will also enjoy the **Railway Museum**, open Sunday and Monday from 2:30 to 6; 1st week in August, daily from 2:30 to 6.

The **Cotswold Way** runs south from **Winchcombe** to **Belas Knap** and then circles back to **Cleeve Hill** on A46, two miles south of

Winchcombe. You'll need an extra day for this, but if you like walking, this is one of the most memorable hikes you can make. After passing a Stone Age burial mound—the finest in the Cotswolds—you'll continue to **Cleeve Common**, the highest point in the Cotswolds, which has breathtaking views. The bleak open wolds give you a wonderful sense of what the Cotswolds were like before the Enclosure Acts.

One mile north of **Winchcombe**, on A46, turn left to **Greet** and greet the potters who sell their wares at **Winchcombe Pottery**.

❧ STANTON (off A46, north of Stanway, and west of Snowshill)

How to Get There. From **Winchcombe**, take A46 north about 5 miles, and look for signs on the right.

With a terrain of steep pastures and much unclaimed marshland, there was nothing at Stanton to attract speculators and profiteers. Any move to commercialize the village was stopped in 1908, when Philip Sidney Stott, a builder of cotton mills, bought virtually the entire village. The restoration work that followed his arrival was tastefully done, and the village today seems unchanged from the seventeenth century. The result is a village that has kept its integrity, and that wins the Mike Spring award as the most perfect, unspoiled village in the Cotswolds. It's likely to stay that way, too.

Above the town is **Mount Inn**, a newish stone building with not much atmosphere, but some outdoor tables with a splendid view. A good bet for drinks or lunch.

Arrange with the owners of the **Vine** (see Lodging below) to saddle up for a ride through the surrounding countryside.

The **Church of Saint Michael and All Angels'** is a fifteenth-century version of a Norman church, with a rare Decorated (1375) pulpit and a splendid font decorated with hares. The poppyheads on the medieval benches at the back of the nave are deeply ringed with marks of the chains of obedient sheepdogs, who sat through sermons with their masters.

Lodging

There's only one place to stay, the **Vine** (I, c/o Jill Gabb, Stanton, near Broadway, WR12 7NE. Tel. 0386-73250). This friendly B and B has 5 rooms, 2 with four-posters, three with showers. The owners have their own horses and can take you on rides through the glorious countryside.

❧ BUCKLAND

Two miles south of the bustle of Broadway is the small, quiet village of Buckland. St. Michael's Church is Early English, with three panels of fifteenth-century glass releaded by William Morris, and some humorous gargoyles. Buckland Rectory, still in use, is the oldest, best-preserved parsonage in England. The main reason to visit Buckland, however, is to dine or lodge at the Manor.

Dining

Buckland Manor (E, Buckland, WR12 7LY. Tel. 0386-852626) is an elegant setting for a traditional English lunch of roast beef with Yorkshire pudding, fresh local trout, or roast leg of lamb. The dinner menu is French with an emphasis on fresh local produce: boned roast pigeon cooked in parchment with wild mushrooms, red mullet with fresh rosemary sauce, or veal sweetbreads braised with Madeira and Port.

Lodging

Buckland Manor (E, Buckland, WR12 7LY. Tel. 0386-852626) has a staff of 45 for some 22 guests. The grand manor house, filled with antiques, fine china and crystal, sits among 10 acres of gardens and fields, with a putting green, tennis court, heated pool, and grazing horses which you can rent. The Manor is more formal than Lygon Arms in Broadway, but much smaller and therefore more personal. Staying here gives you the advantage of proximity to the busy town of Broadway, plus a bucolic setting in which to spend the night. The less expensive rooms are much smaller than the suites, but decorated with equal taste, and with great attention to detail.

❧ BROADWAY

Two miles north of Buckland is the popular resort town of Broadway, so named for its single main street. Most houses were built in the seventeenth and eighteenth centuries, when Broadway was an important staging post. The coming of the railway led to its decline. It was rediscovered in the late nineteenth century by William Morris and restored under his influence. It became an artists' colony before it was discovered by people like you and me.

What you will do in Broadway is walk down one side—at a faster pace, probably, than the traffic—and then back up the other, browsing in antique stores and gift shops, and stopping for lunch or drinks in any of several restaurants and pubs. The quality of goods is geared more to the package-tour trade than it is, say, in Stow-on-the-Wold, but there's something to buy—Paddington dolls, lady mice, model Cotswold cottages, woolens, cashmeres—for every budget and taste.

If you've had enough sightseeing for a day, take A44 directly back to **Stow-on-the-Wold**. Just west of Broadway, A44 climbs to **Broadway Tower**, the second highest point in the Cotswolds. There's a park here for lovely walks and a twelve-county view.

Dining

If you're not staying at the **Lygon Arms** (E, High Street, Broadway WR12 7DU. Tel. 0386-852255) and want a serious lunch, stop in the hotel's Great Hall Restaurant, and nibble on quail eggs in a royal hunting lodge atmosphere, complete with rich wood paneling and red barrel-vault ceiling. A real conversation piece.

Hunter's Lodge (M, North Street. Tel. 0386-853247) is a French-style restaurant with such dishes as grilled lamb cutlets with Madeira sauce; and guinea hen with cider, sage, apple, and Calvados.

Buckland Manor is only two miles away (see Buckland—Dining, page 99).

Lodging

Lygon Arms (E, High Street, Broadway WR12 7DU. Tel. 0386-852255) is a distinguished old hotel, as famous as the town. Both Charles I and Oliver Cromwell stayed here during the Civil War. Every year hundreds of groomed riders use the courtyard as the starting point for the North Cotswold Hunt. With so much expansion—there's a new wing and a very new wing—the Lygon Arms is less an inn than a 67-room luxury hotel on an inn-theme. Rooms in the modern wing are tasteful but conventional, some with unattractive views. Ask for room 17 or something similar. Room 8 is nice, and so are rooms with four-posters. Best bet are the very expensive rooms in the old section; the smaller rooms are disappointing for the price. As for staying in Broadway: after a diet of stone cottages and sheep, an hour of window shopping can be fun—but not everyone will want to spend the night.

Broadway Hotel (M, The Green, Broadway. Tel. 0386-852401) is a 150-year-old half-timbered and stone house with cheerful modern furnishings and more character than a motel. Stick to rooms in the old inn.

❧ SNOWSHILL

The most scenic route back to Stow-on-the-Wold—indeed, one of the loveliest drives in the Cotswolds—is along a narrow country road from Broadway to Snowshill, Taddington, and Ford, then east on B4077.

The main attraction of this secluded village is **Snowshill Manor**, a sixteenth- and seventeenth-century manor house. Charles Wade bought it in 1919 and filled it with everything from toys to musical instruments, old clocks, farm carts, dead beetles, and butterflies. He gave it to the National Trust, which left it just as they found it. Open May through September, Wednesday through Sunday from 11 to 1, and 2 to 6; April and October, open weekends only from 11 to 1 and 2 to 6.

❧ CHIPPING CAMPDEN

Chipping Campden is not directly on our route, but it's too lovely to miss, should you have time to visit en route from Broadway or Stow-on-the-Wold to Stratford-upon-Avon.

"Chipping" means "market"—and by 1247 Chipping Campden had them every week. In the fourteenth century it was a major wool-market center, whose wealthy merchants built the Perpendicular church (**St. James**) and houses that make the town so special. The church has a handsome tower and some outstanding brasses.

High Street has several interesting craft and antique shops, and a vitality that doesn't diminish at the end of the tourist season. G. M. Trevelyan called it "the most beautiful village street in England."

Kids will want to see the **Campden Car Collection** in **Sherborn House**. Open May through September daily from 11 to 6.

If you care about gardens, stop at **Hidcote Manor Garden**, a National Trust Property north of town en route to Stratford-upon-Avon. These world-famous gardens were one of the first to group plants in "rooms," using hedges as walls—each room devoted to a particular color, species or combination of species. Open April through October daily except Tuesday and Friday from 11 to 8.

Lodging

Best bet is **Noel Arms Hotel** (M, High Street, Chipping Campden, Gloucestershire GL55 6AT. Tel. 0386-840317), the oldest inn in town. Furnishings are friendly and old-fashioned, particularly in the older wing. Try room 14.

For Further Information

Tel. 0386-840289.

❧ STRATFORD-UPON-AVON

How to Get There. From **Stow-on-the-Wold** take A429 north 13 miles, then take A34 8 miles.

Stratford-upon-Avon is the most popular destination in Britain after London; more than a half-million tourists parade through its streets every year, visiting the Bard's birthplace and taking in a play at the Royal Shakespeare Theatre. Many Americans come prepared to sacrifice an evening in the name of Culture—as they would at home—and come away surprised at the wonderful fun a good Shakespeare production can be. It's only a half-hour drive from Stratford to Broadway, or 40 minutes to Stow-on-the-Wold, so you don't have to spend the night in Bardland; but should you decide to stay, you have a whole folio of hotels to choose from.

Mid-sixteenth-century Stratford was a prosperous market town. People who wanted to rise in the world came here from the surrounding farms. One was John Shakespeare, who succeeded beyond his dreams, first as a maker of gloves, and then as a justice of peace, and mayor. He also had a son named William who did quite well for himself, too. John's wife, Mary, came from one of the oldest families in the region, so the image of Will as an untutored country lad is just not true.

• Begin your tour where Shakespeare began his life, in a half-timbered house (1564) on Henley Street. The houses on either side were destroyed to reduce the chances of fire.

• Turn left from the house and continue down **Henley Street**. The Information Centre is at the major crossing. Turn left on **Bridge Street**. You'll pass some lovely Shakespeare-period houses as you approach **Clopton Bridge** over the **River Avon**.

• Turn right on **Waterside Street** (before the bridge). On your right is **Heritage Theatre**, where you can submit to a continuous, 30-minute multimedia introduction to Elizabethan England. Walk through the **Bancroft Gardens** (lit at night), watched over by a statue of the Bard surrounded by Hamlet, Lady Macbeth, Falstaff, and Prince Hal; and walk over to the **Royal Shakespeare Theatre**. No, this was not the Globe—that was in London, and burned down. The original Stratford theater was built in 1874. It was destroyed in a 1926 fire and rebuilt in 1932. You should have reserved seats, but it's sometimes possible to get them on the day of a performance.

• Take the river path to the **Brass Rubbing Centre**, where you can make your own souvenirs, and continue to **Holy Trinity Church**. It was here that Shakespeare was baptized and buried. The twelve trees, as you approach from the north, are said to represent the twelve tribes of Israel; the eleven on the right, the eleven faithful apostles; and the one slightly back, Mathias, who took the place of Judas. The slab covering Shakespeare's grave was replaced a century ago, after the footsteps of tourists had almost obliterated the words on it. Look for the bust of Shakespeare in a monument in the north chancel wall (on your left as you face the front)—it's believed to be the most authentic known portrait of the Bard. The **charnel house**—did it inspire the one in *Romeo and Juliet?*—is behind the north wall. Old bones were moved to make room for new ones —which is probably why Shakespeare wrote on his tomb, "And curst be he that moves my bones." Of course, he may also have wanted to prevent his wife, Anne—who lived seven years after his death—from spending eternity beside him.

• Leave by the north door and bear left on **Old Town Road** to **Hall's Croft**, on the right. It was here that Dr. John Hall lived with Shakespeare's daughter Suzanna. He had no medical degree, but that wasn't expected then. The timber-framed, late-sixteenth-century house is carefully restored and gives you a good sense of life in a middle-class Tudor home. The enclosed gardens are authentic, too, though replanted during restorations in 1950.

• Continue down **Old Town Road**, and turn right on **Church Street**. On your right, behind a row of almshouses, is the **King's New Grammar School**, closed to the public, where Shakespeare learned "small Latin and less Greek." The sons of the most prominent men went to the same free grammar school as everyone else. The curriculum bore no relation to life after school; it was meant to turn out clerks for church positions, and little was taught but Latin. Every weekday, summer and winter, Shakespeare went here from 7 in the morning—6 in summer—to 5 at night, with a two-hour midday break to go home for dinner.

• Continue down **Church Street**. On your right, on the corner of **Chapel Lane**, is the fifteenth-century **Guild Chapel**, which has a famous fresco of the *Last Judgment* above the chancel arch.

• **Church Street** turns into **Chapel Street**. On your right is **New Place**. Shakespeare, now rich and famous, bought the house in 1597 and realized his father's dream of becoming a gentleman. If your name is Gastrell, don't tell anyone: in 1759 a neighboring clergyman named **Francis Gastrell** was so furious at the tourists trooping through, that he had New House torn down. The town fathers were so angry, they ordered that no one with that name could ever live there again. Only the cellar steps remain. The foundations are planted with an Elizabethan-style garden containing all the plants and shrubs mentioned in Shakespeare's plays.

• Continue down **Chapel Street**, which turns into **High Street**. Families with children may want to turn left on **Ely Street** and visit the **Arms and Armour Museum**. Back on **High Street**, on the left, is the **Harvard House**. It was built in 1576 by a butcher and alderman (local magistrate) named **Thomas Rogers**. His daughter Katherine was the mother of John Harvard, one of the founders of Harvard College.

• You can drive to **Anne Hathaway's Cottage**, or take the lovely one-mile walk that the eighteen-year-old Shakespeare took to woo (or be wooed by) the twenty-five-year-old Anne. From **Harvard House**, turn right on **High Street**, and a quick right again on **Ely Street**. Where the street ends, turn right on **Rother Street**. Where **Rother** intersects with **Grove Road**, there's a marked path leading to the cottage. Anne lived in this thatched cottage until Will married her in 1582. She was pregnant at the time, and some iconoclasts, like Anthony Burgess, delight in the notion that Anne did hath-her-way, and that Shakespeare was forced to act against his Will. Controversy still rages over the meaning of the rushed marriage. It was customary for couples to proclaim banns on three Sundays so that anyone who objected could be heard. The alternative was to get a special license and to post a bond to indemnify the court if objections were made later. Two farmer friends of Anne's father posted such a bond—were they also holding a shotgun to young Will? Anne may have been a Puritan, who viewed actors not just with contempt but as threats to salvation. If that's the case, it's no wonder that Will skipped town and lived alone in London for twenty years in hired lodgings. Perhaps, though, he simply left because Stratford was too small for him, as the village of Shottery had been too small for his ambitious father.

Theater

The **Royal Shakespeare Theatre** season runs from mid-April through December. Tickets are on sale from late March through **Keith Prowse & Co. Ltd.** (234 West 44th Street, New York, N.Y. 10036. Tel. 212/398-1430 or 800/223-4446); and **Edwards and Edwards** (1 Times Square, New York, N.Y. 10036. Tel. 212/944-0290 or 800/223-6108). For ticket information in Stratford, call 0789-69191; for reservations, Tel. 0789-292271.

The Royal Shakespeare Company also performs at The Other Place (Southern Lane. Tel. for information: 0789-69191; for reservations: 0789-292271). Plays include new musicals and dramas on their way to London's West End.

Tours

Guide Friday, 13 Waterside. Tel. 0789-294466.

Things to Do near Stratford-upon-Avon

1. **Mary Arden's House** (Wilmcote, north of Stratford on A34) is where Shakespeare's mother lived before her marriage. It was still used as a farmhouse until the 1930s, and so has seen little modernization. Mary was the youngest of eight. Before marrying John she would have slept on the kitchen or living-room floor with the servants. Getting married meant, among other things, having a bed.

2. **Warwick Castle** (9 miles north on A46) is a great fourteenth-century castle, the most impressive in England after Windsor, with great towers and turrets on a steep rock over the Avon. You'll need a good 2 hours to tour some 30 state rooms; visit the armory; and explore the gardens. Kids will love the **Doll Museum** in **Oaken House** near the castle walls.

3. **Charlecote Park** (4 miles east of Stratford off B4086) is an Elizabethan mansion in a 228-acre park. It was here, it is said, that Shakespeare poached deer, for which he was fined by the owner and local magistrate, Sir Thomas Lucy. Shakespeare got even by turning Lucy into Justice Shallow in *Henry IV, Part II,* and *The Merry Wives of Windsor.* The main buildings were greatly altered in the mid-nineteenth century. The gardens were laid out by Lancelot Brown, nicknamed "Capability," in 1760. Brown (1716–83) designed some Palladian country houses but won lasting fame as a landscape gardener who broke away from formal, classical restraints, and created wide expanses of lawns, clumps of trees, and serpentine lakes. Kids will love the collection of carriages in the coach house.

Dining

Billesley Manor Restaurant (E, 4 miles west, off A422. Tel. 0789-763737) has a French nouvelle menu with such favorites as avocado with strawberry vinegar, turbot mousseline, and medallions of filet mignon with wild mushrooms.

Ettington Park Hotel Restaurant (E, off A34. Tel. 0789-740740) is a Victorian Gothic mansion with a French-English menu that includes terrine of wild salmon, and roulade of guinea fowl with red cabbage and creamy herb sauce.

Da Giovanni (M, 8 Ely Street. Tel. 0789-297999) is elegant but friendly, with Italian specialties at reasonable prices.

Welcombe Hotel Restaurant (M/E, Warwick Road, 1½ miles from town on A46. Tel. 0789-295252) is a French restaurant in an elegant Jacobean-style mansion.

Marlowe's Elizabethan Room (M, 18 High Street. Tel. 0789-204999) is upstairs in a private house, with a Tudorish atmosphere that includes candlelight and an open hearth.

Lodging

Stratford has no legendary hotels; what it does have are several comfortable properties that are perfectly adequate for a night or two. The better hotels are a few miles out of town.

Ettington Park Hotel (E, Stratford-upon-Avon, off A34, Alderminster, B49 6NF. Tel. 0789-740740) is a 49-room Victorian Gothic mansion with many antiques, sumptuous bathrooms (some with Jacuzzis), sauna, indoor pool, tennis, fishing, riding, and house movies.

The 85-room **Welcombe Hotel** (E, Warwick Road. Tel. 0789-295252) is an extensively refurbished Jacobean-style mansion with a Victorian atmosphere. Rooms in the main building have traditional furnishings. The new wing is on grounds surrounded by an 18-hole golf course.

Billesley Manor (E, 4 miles west, off A422. Tel. 0789-763737) is a peaceful, gabled, sixteenth-century manor house on splendid grounds. Best bet are the large rooms in the main house, some with four-posters. Facilities include a sauna, tennis, and indoor pool.

White Swan (M, Rother Street, Stratford-upon-Avon CV37 6NH. Tel. 0789-297022) is a pleasant, popular, Tudor-style hotel conveniently located in town. An inn since Shakespeare's time, it has the requisite black timbers and rich wood paneling.

The modern, comfortable 249-room **Moat House International** (E, Bridgefoot. Tel. 0789-67511) is a former Hilton at the water's edge.

The 112-room **Alveston Manor Hotel** (E/M, Clopton Bridge, Stratford-upon-Avon CV37 7HP. Tel. 0789-204581) is a converted Elizabethan manor house with beamed bedrooms and original oak paneling in the bar. The 7-acre garden was the scene of the first production of *Midsummer's Night Dream.* Avoid rooms in the annex.

Other adequate hotels include **Shakespeare Hotel** (E, Chapel Street, Stratford-upon-Avon CV37 6ER. Tel. 0789-294771), a modernized Tudor inn with old and new sections; the 9-room **Stratford House Hotel** (M, Sheep Street, Stratford-upon-Avon CV37 6EF, Warwickshire. Tel. 0789-68288), a friendly, family-run Georgian townhouse with modern furnishings, only minutes from the theater; the 73-room **Falcon Hotel** (M, Chapel Street, Stratford-upon-Avon CV37 6NH. Tel. 0789-205777) in town-center, with a half-timbered old wing, a functional modern wing, and a reputation for good food.

For Further Information

The **Tourist Information Centre** (1 High Street. Tel. 0789-293127) can make reservations. Open summers, Monday through Saturday from 9 to 5:30; Sundays from 2 to 5; off-season, daily except Sunday from 11 to 4.

EN ROUTE: From STRATFORD-UPON-AVON to LONDON

Your tour ends at Stratford-upon-Avon, a 2½ hour drive to London. If you want to extend your trip by another day, drive to **Woodstock** and visit **Blenheim Palace**, one of England's greatest stately mansions, where Winston Churchill was born, and where you can visit his modest grave. Two of England's most famous inns are in Woodstock, the **Bear** (E, Woodstock, Oxfordshire OX7 2SZ. Tel. 0993-811511); and **Feathers** (Market Street, Woodstock, Oxfordshire OX7 2SZ. Tel. 0993-812291).

From **Woodstock**, it's only a short drive to **Oxford**, where you can tour the venerable colleges and chapels of one of the world's most famous universities. If time permits, stop at **Windsor Castle** en route back to London, and send our regards to the Queen.

RECOMMENDED READING

Philip A. Crowl, *The Intelligent Traveller's Guide to Historic Britain* (Congdon & Weed).

GERMANY

❦ *Heidelberg, the Romantic Highway, Munich, and the Alps*

MAJOR ATTRACTIONS

• Heidelberg—the heart of German romanticism.

• The Romantic Road, with two of Europe's most perfect medieval towns—Rothenburg and Dinkelsbühl.

• Munich, capital of Bavaria.

• The fantastic castles of mad King Ludwig II.

• The breathtaking scenery of the German Alps, including the country's highest peak, the Zugspitze.

INTRODUCTION

People who speak of romantic Germany are usually thinking of the places you're about to visit. From Frankfurt, you head south to the ancient university town of Heidelberg. A drive through the peaceful Neckar Valley takes you to the Romantic Road and the fortified medieval town of Rothenburg, with its gabled houses and narrow, cobbled streets. Give a model of a medieval town to a child, and it will look exactly like Rothenburg.

Munich is a cosmopolitan city with the feel of a small town. You'll explore the past in palaces and museums, shop along convenient pedestrian malls, and then succumb to elegant restaurants, pastry shops, and beer halls. From Munich it's only an hour's drive to Germany's most complete four-season resort, Garmisch-Partenkirchen. Here, beneath the grand peaks of the Bavarian Alps, you can ski from December through May, go for mountain walks, ride cable cars to dramatic heights, visit the Passion Play town of Oberammergau, and tour the fairyland castles of Ludwig II. From Garmisch, you'll head home, or continue south to Austria or Switzerland.

THE MAIN ROUTE (with minimum overnight stays)

3–5 Days

One night: Heidelberg
Excursion along the Romantic Road
One night: Munich
One night: Garmisch-Partenkirchen
Tour of the Alps and the Royal Castles

5–7 Days

One night: Heidelberg
Excursion through the Neckar Valley and along the Romantic Road
One night: Rothenburg
Two nights: Munich
Two nights: Garmisch-Partenkirchen
Tour of the Alps and the Royal Castles

7–14 Days

Two nights: Heidelberg
Excursion through the Neckar Valley and the Romantic Road
One night: Rothenburg
Three nights: Munich
Four nights: Garmisch-Partenkirchen
Tour of the Alps and the Royal Castles

GETTING AROUND

Getting to Germany

The most reliable of all airlines, **Lufthansa**, has direct flights to Frankfurt from the greatest number of American cities: New York, Boston,

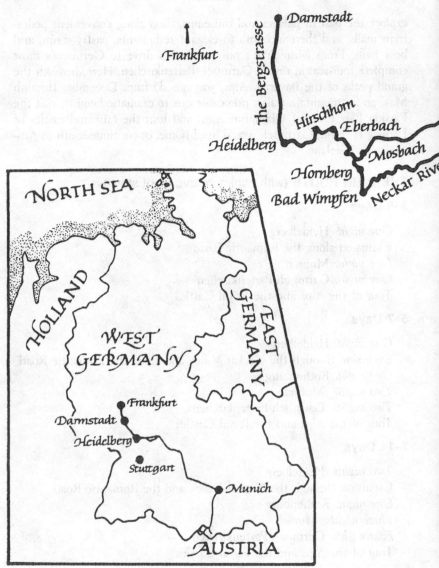

Darmstadt

Frankfurt

The Bergstrasse

Hirschhorn

Eberbach

Heidelberg

Mosbach

Hornberg

Bad Wimpfen

Neckar River

NORTH SEA

HOLLAND

WEST GERMANY

EAST GERMANY

Frankfurt

Darmstadt

Heidelberg

Stuttgart

Munich

AUSTRIA

WEST GERMANY

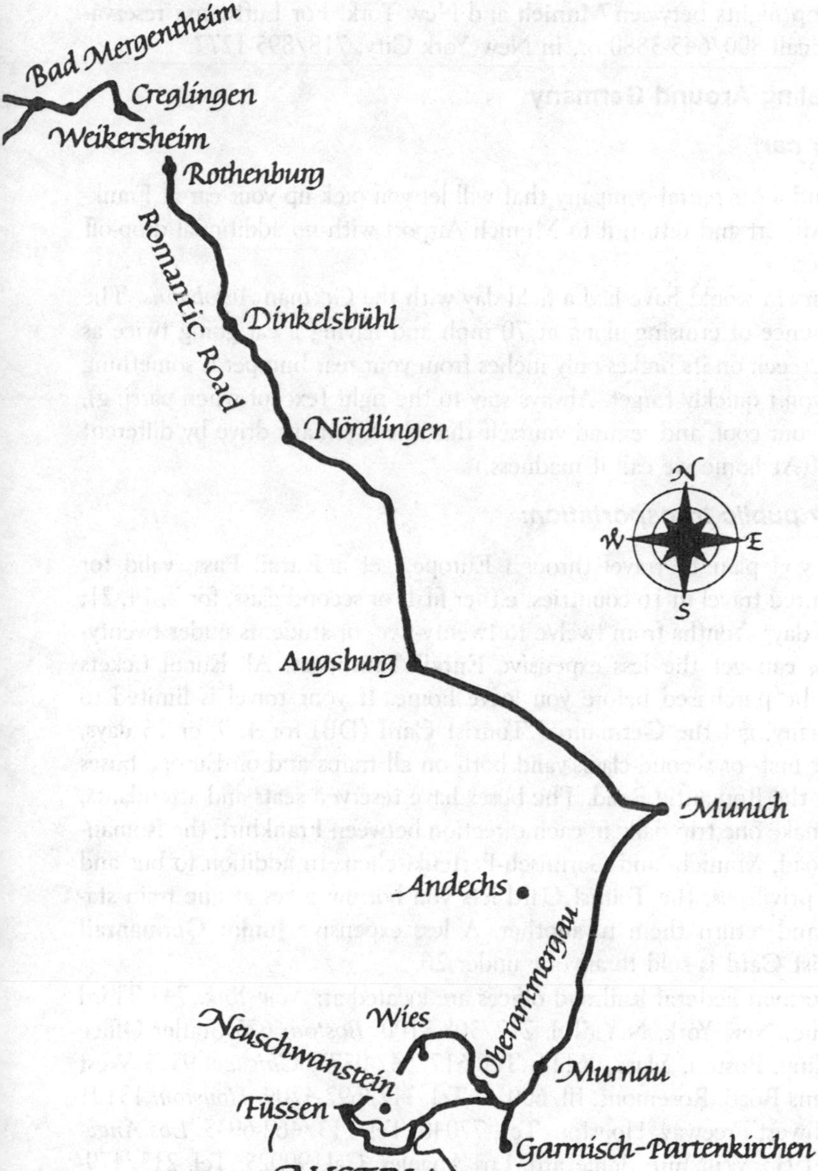
Bad Mergentheim
Creglingen
Weikersheim
Rothenburg
Romantic Road
Dinkelsbühl
Nördlingen
N
W
E
S
Augsburg
Munich
Andechs
Oberammergau
Wies
Neuschwanstein
Murnau
Füssen
Garmisch-Partenkirchen
AUSTRIA

Houston, Philadelphia, Chicago, Atlanta, Dallas, Miami, Houston, Los
Angeles, San Francisco, and San Juan. Both **Lufthansa** and **TWA** have
nonstop flights between **Munich** and **New York.** For Lufthansa reservations, call 800/645-3880 or, in New York City, 718/895-1277.

Traveling Around Germany

By car:

Find a car rental company that will let you pick up your car at Frankfurt Airport and return it to Munich Airport with *no* additional drop-off
charges.

Darwin would have had a field day with the German *Autobahns.* The
experience of cruising along at 70 mph and having a car going twice as
fast screech on its brakes only inches from your rear bumper is something
you won't quickly forget. Always stay to the right (except when passing),
keep your cool, and remind yourself that the Germans drive by different
rules. (At home we call it madness.)

By public transportation:

If you plan to travel through Europe, get a **Eurail Pass,** valid for
unlimited travel in 16 countries, either first- or second-class, for 7, 14, 21,
or 30 days. Youths from twelve to twenty-two, or students under twenty-
seven, can get the less expensive **Eurail Youthpass.** All Eurail tickets
must be purchased before you leave home. If your travel is limited to
Germany, get the **Germanrail Tourist Card** (DB) for 4, 9, or 16 days,
either first- or second-class, valid both on all trains and on Europa buses
along the Romantic Road. The buses have reserved seats and attendants,
and make one trip daily in each direction between Frankfurt, the Romantic Road, Munich, and Garmisch-Partenkirchen. In addition to bus and
train privileges, the Tourist Card lets you borrow bikes at one train station and return them to another. A less expensive **Junior Germanrail
Tourist Card** is sold to anyone under 26.

German Federal Railroad offices are located at: *New York:* 747 Third
Avenue, New York, N.Y. Tel. 212/308-3100. *Boston:* 625 Statler Office
Building, Boston, Mass. 06116. Tel. 617/542-0577. *Chicago:* 9575 West
Higgins Road, Rosemont, Ill. 60018. Tel. 312/692-4209. *Houston:* 13101
Northwest Freeway, Houston, Tex. 77040. Tel. 713/462-6935. *Los Ange-
les:* 11933 Wiltshire Boulevard, Los Angeles, Cal. 90025. Tel. 213/479-
2772. *San Francisco:* 442 Post Street, San Francisco, Cal. 94102. Tel.

415/981-5517. *Denver:* 8000 Gerard Street, Suite 518 South, Denver, Col. 80231. Tel. 303/695-7715.

All major towns on the itinerary can be reached by public transportation. Trains leave almost every hour from **Frankfurt** to **Heidelberg**. The trip takes about 60 minutes. A train goes from **Heidelberg** to **Rothenburg** (along the Romantic Road), but the **Romantic Road Bus** is faster and more direct. By train, you need to change at **Würzburg** and **Steinach**. The train trip takes about 3¹/2 hours. The bus ride direct from **Heidelberg** to **Rothenburg** takes 3 hours. Again, you could take the train or the Romantic Road Bus from **Rothenburg** to **Munich**, but the bus is preferable. Both train and bus take about 4¹/2 hours. By train, however, you need to change at **Ansbach**. From **Munich** to **Garmisch-Partenkirchen** there's train service almost every hour. The trip takes about 90 minutes. Tour buses leave daily in summer from **Garmisch** to the **Royal Castles**.

SPECIAL EVENTS

January: International Winter Sports Week, Garmisch-Partenkirchen
March (early): International Fashion Fair, Munich
Mid-June to mid-September: Augsburg Opera and Operetta Festival
June: Munich Film Festival
July: Munich Opera Festival
August: Heidelberg Open-air Theater
Late September to early October: Munich *Oktoberfest* (two weeks of beer drinking, dancing, and entertainment)

A NOTE ON SHOPPING

Popular items include **cameras, binoculars,** and **optical lenses;** Rosenthal **crystal, china,** and **cutlery;** Nymphenburg **porcelains** (Munich); leather goods; gourmet delicacies; handicrafts; and antiques. See the itinerary below for details.

THINGS TO SEE AND DO WITH CHILDREN

In **Heidelberg:** boat trips, bike rides, a visit to the castle. In **Regensburg:** the whole medieval town is a child's dream come true. In **Munich:** the largest science and technology museum in the world; the famous glockenspiel at the New Town Hall; bike riding, boating, and buggy rides in the English Gardens; ice skating at the Olympia Tower; numerous church towers; Hellabrunn Zoo. **In Garmisch-Partenkirchen**: four seasons' worth of outdoor sports, including skiing (December through May) and hiking, cable car and cog railway rides, and a stagecoach ride from Garmisch to Grainau. The former site of the Winter Olympics has seven indoor pools, including one with waves and man-made surf; indoor tennis; and three indoor skating rinks.

A NOTE ON DINING

Good Bavarian food isn't Bavarian: it's nouvelle with Bavarian touches. In all but the best restaurants the emphasis is on heavy, homecooked meals, hearty rather than sophisticated—meals that make up in wholesomeness what they lack in subtlety. Starch is the main ingredient: dumplings (knödel) in gravy, thick soups, pastas, cakes, pastries, and beer.

There may be no Bavarian cuisine—as, say, there is a French or Italian cuisine—but there *are* Bavarian specialties, mostly variations on a theme of sausages and dumplings. The varieties are endless. In Munich the sausages, called Weisswurst, are made from veal, calves brains and spleen. The dumplings are made from boiled and raw potatoes (Kartoffelknödel), liver, or dough, and are often served with roast pork (Schweinebraten), pork knuckle (Schweinshax'n) or veal shank (Kalbshax'n). Roast pork liver loaf (Leberkäs) is a specialty of Munich.

The main meal is at midday. The fixed-price menu *(Tageskarte)* is the best bargain and includes soup, a main dish, and usually a dessert. Go to a café for coffee. All restaurants display menus outside. Though prices include taxes and service, it's customary in lower-priced restaurants to round out the bill to the nearest mark, and in expensive restaurants to add another 5 percent.

Prices for two are indicated by I (inexpensive, under $20); M (moderate, $20 to $45), and E (expensive, over $45).

Department stores *(Kaufhäuser)* are a good bet for inexpensive lunches. Butcher shops, such as the Vincenz-Murr chain in Munich, often serve hot snacks, such as Warmer Leberkäs mit Kartoffelsalat (baked meat loaf with mustard and potato salad).

Germany has some 1,300 breweries, more than the rest of Europe combined. The average German consumes 29½ gallons of beer each year —in Bavaria, he drinks 47. (The Belgians and Czechs drink even more!) Even the tiniest villages have breweries serving beer comparable to the best in the world, but drunk only locally: ask for the local brew as you're passing through. Bavarian beer gardens, hung with lanterns, are the center of Bavarian life in summer, particularly in Munich. Types of beer include light (Helles, Export or "Ex"); light-colored but stronger (Pilsner); darker (Dunkles), and extra light (Weisse).

Most German wines come from the midwest. The exception is around Lake Constance and along the Neckar River. Ask for Lake Constance wines when you're touring the Garmisch area, and for Neckar (Württemberg) wines when you're in Heidelberg or driving through the Neckar Valley between Heidelberg and Rothenburg. If you're uncertain what wine to order, remember that all German wines are grouped in one of three categories, *Tafelwein* (table wines), *Qualitatswein* (quality wines) and *Qualitatswein mit Pradikat,* award-winning wines.

A NOTE ON LODGING

If you're looking for Laura Ashleyland, you're in trouble. Furnishings, even in many first-class hotels, tend to be functional and as subtle as Weisswurst and beer. On the positive side, rooms tend to be cheerful, at least in an open-eyed, red-cheeked sort of way, and always immaculately clean.

There's no official grading system for German hotels. For convenience sake, I have graded hotels, for two people: E (expensive, over $70), M (moderate, from $30–$70), and I (inexpensive, under $30).

Taxes, service charges, and Continental breakfast are usually but not always included in quoted rates. Ask before you sign.

You can't go terribly wrong staying in one of some 70 **Romantik Hotels,** many of them old postal inns along medieval trade routes. To belong to this association a hotel has to be privately owned and at least 100 years old, and more than 85 percent of the rooms must have private baths or showers. Prices range from moderate to expensive. A brochure with photos and descriptions of each property is available for $6.50 from **Romantik Hotels,** P.O. Box 7038, Bellevue, WA 98007. Tel. 206/885-5805. For reservations: 800/826-0015. A free list of Romantik Hotels is available both from the association and from the German National Tourist Board. Check into the Romantik Hotel **Open Voucher** program, which entitles you to a car and six nights' accommodations, which don't have to be booked in advance.

Germanrail sells a **Romantik Hotel** package that includes lodging in Romantik Hotels, unlimited rail travel, sightseeing trips and bike rentals.

Castle Hotels is an association of privately owned historic castles in attractive locations. Prices run from moderate to expensive. The German National Tourist Board has a free Castle Hotels brochure and information about Castle Hotels packages.

Lufthansa has several fly/drive packages, some of them including lodging in Romantik Hotels, Castle Hotels, and other properties.

FOR FURTHER INFORMATION

German National Tourist Board. *New York:* 747 Third Avenue, New York, N.Y. 10017. Tel. 212/308-3300. *Los Angeles:* 444 South Flower Street, Suite 2230, Los Angeles, Cal. 90017. Tel. 213/688-7332.

THE ITINERARY

EN ROUTE: From FRANKFURT to HEIDELBERG

Take the Autobahn (A5) south from Frankfurt to Darmstadt. From here you can either continue south on A5 down the center of the Rhine Valley, through flat agricultural country; or you can turn off on the slower but more scenic Bergstrasse (Route 3). The drive along the Bergstrasse, the old main road on the east side of the valley, is a pleasant rather than dramatic trip through wine-producing villages at the foot of gently sloping hills crowned with ruined medieval castles—some of them converted into restaurants and hotels.

About 12 miles south of Darmstadt, between the towns of Zwingenberg and Auerbach, look for signs to Auerbach Schloss (Auerbach Castle). A 10-minute drive takes you through a wooded *Naturpark*, with lovely hillside trails, to the romantic ruins. Though the castle is losing its battle against nature, the ramparts are still intact, and children of all ages will love scurrying in and out of its broken battlements. The castle is open from 10 to 6 in season; off-season, from 10 to 5.

If you're partial to apple strudel and lovely parks, turn left at the Hotel Krone in the center of Auerbach, and drive to Fürstenlager Park. Leave your car at the Park Hotel Herrenhaus, spend an hour walking among the tropical trees and pavilions, and then reward yourself with some strudel and a glass of the hotel's own white Auerbach Fürstenlager wine.

About 5 miles south of Auerbach, still on Route 3, is the town of Heppenheim. Stop at least long enough to appreciate the sixteenth-century town hall and pharmacy.

Lodging

The **Park Hotel Herrenhaus** (M, 6140 Bensheim 3. Auerbach. Tel. 06251-72274) is the former summer residence of the Grand Dukes of Something-or-Other. The mansion is somewhat worse for wear—the high ceilings and imposing façades suggesting a grandeur unequaled by the hand-me-down furniture in the rooms; but it's a one-of-a-kind place for those who enjoy the romance of faded charm, or who want to feel like impoverished royalty. The owners are very friendly, and you couldn't ask for a more peaceful setting within a lovely 125-acre park.

✤ HEPPENHEIM (2 miles south of Auerbach)

Park where you see the brown marker with the words HISTORISCHER MARKTPLATZ on your left, and spend a few minutes soaking up the atmosphere of the historic **Market Place** *(Marktplatz),* surrounded by sixteenth-century buildings and a Gothic church, the so-called **Bergstrasse Cathedral.** Heppenheim offers only a taste of what you'll see in Rothenburg, but it's virtually tourist-free, with a sense of reality you won't find in the postcard towns along the Romantic Road.

✤ HEIDELBERG

Heidelberg has the mellow flavor of old Germany. The country's oldest university town, it nestles along the banks of the fast-flowing Neckar River, beneath an imposing red sandstone castle. In the early evening the sun turns the red to gold; a deep radiance lies upon the town and prints itself upon the inner eye. It's a vision to cherish for a lifetime.

The students transform what could be just another pretty tourist town into a place of youthful vitality. You'll mingle with them as you walk among the fashionable shops and cafés along the half-mile pedestrian mall, or wander down narrow alleyways in search of Heidelberg's past.

The city was the political center of a German state called the Rhineland Palatinate—the name deriving from the title "palatines," which was given to the highest officers in the Holy Roman Empire. After the Thirty Years' War (1618–48) the Protestant Elector (hereditary ruler) Karl Ludwig married his daughter to the brother of Louis XIV in the hope of bringing peace to the Rhineland. But when the Elector's son died without an heir, Louis XIV used the marriage alliance as an excuse to claim Heidelberg, and, in 1689, the town was sacked and laid to waste. From the ashes of a devastating fire four years later arose what you see today: a

Baroque town built on Gothic foundations, with narrow, twisting streets and alleyways. The new Heidelberg is changing under the influence of U.S. Army barracks and industrial development stretching into the suburbs; but the old heart of the city remains unchanged, and continues to exude the spirit of romantic Germany.

Things to See and Do

• **The Castle** (open 9 to 12 and 1 to 5:30; off-season, closes at 5) should be seen early in the morning since it's the town's leading attraction, and afternoon lines for the 60-minute guided tour can be 30-minutes long.

Longfellow wrote that, "Next to the Alhambra of Granada, the castle of Heidelberg is the most magnificent ruin of the Middle Ages." The imposing ruin is at its romantic best from a distance. You can drive up **Neue Schlosstrasse,** but parking can be a problem, so leave your car at your hotel and take the funicular.

The castle, dominating the town, should remind you of the time when Heidelberg was the capital of the Palatinate. There was a fortress here since the thirteenth century, but it did not become the principal residence for the electors for another three hundred years. Construction began about 1300 and continued for the next four hundred years; the courtyard through which you enter is thus like the public square of a medieval town, surrounded by buildings representing four centuries of changing architectural styles. The best wings were built during the Renaissance and show a fine balance of strength and refinement, of might and grace. The late-Renaissance **Heinrichs Wing,** on the right side of the courtyard as you face the river, was built by Elector Otto-Heinrich in the mid-sixteenth century. It is pure Italian Renaissance, made of warm red sandstone from the Neckar Valley, and has a dignity and a simplicity that stand in marked contrast to the riot of Baroque ornamentation that flourishes elsewhere. Otto's son Friedrich IV (1592–1610) added the **Friedrichs Wing,** also in late-Renaissance style. In 1693, less than 100 years later, the castle was badly damaged by the French and in 1764 it was struck by lightning and left in ruins until the end of the nineteenth century, when the shell and interior of the **Friedrichs Wing** were restored.

Do you see, over the entrance, the relief of two angels holding a wreath of five roses enclosing a pair of compasses? The story goes that the twins of the masterbuilder fell from the scaffolding, and appeared as angels in the father's troubled dreams, holding the wreath of roses that covered their grave.

The interiors are filled with a modest number of artifacts, arranged museum fashion, and do not breath much living history; for most of you the rooms will be much less impressive than the façades. What you're not supposed to miss is the mid-eighteenth-century 49,000-gallon **Great Vat**. This is not a joke. It was built at a time when the Elector's subjects paid him one tenth of their wine in taxes. No one sent his best tenth, so it was customary to pour the whole amount in one cask and make a table wine for public celebrations or for payments to officials. The vat is made from 130 oak trees. The guardian was the jester dwarf **Perkeo**, known for his capacity to drink.

The one sight you truly shouldn't miss inside the castle is the **Pharmaceutical Museum**, the largest in the world. In a setting worthy of *The Sorcerer's Apprentice*, you'll see all the paraphernalia of medieval doctors. Kids in particular will love the dried beetles and toads, and the mummy with a full head of hair.

If you haven't time or patience to wait on line, don't leave without standing on one of the balconies and enjoying the magnificent view of the town below, with its spires and orange roof tiles spread along the river, and, stretching beyond them, the wooded mountains of the Palatinate.

• Walk or take the funicular back into town. From the funicular station, walk one block toward the river to the **Kornmarkt**, which has a statue of the Madonna. To your left is the oldest quarter of town, with narrow passageways leading to cozy wine taverns and pubs. You'll return here later. For now, make a short side trip to the right, to a square called **Karlsplatz**. On the far right corner (as you face the river) are two historic student pubs, the **Seppl** and the **Roter Ochsen** (Red Ox).

• Return to the **Kornmarkt**. On the river side is the **Town Hall** (Rathaus). Next to it is another square, the **Marktplatz**, which has an outdoor flower market and good views of the castle.

• Across from the Rathaus is the late Gothic **Church of the Holy Spirit** (Heilig-Geist-Kirche). Note how the aisles, though divided into galleys, are as high as the main body (the nave) of the church. This is the hallmark of the **Hall Style**. Slim pillars force your eyes upward toward God. In 1705 a wall was raised between choir and nave so that rival Christian sects could enjoy separate places of worship. The Roman Catholics fell heir to the choir and the Protestants were awarded the nave. Climb the tower for a view.

• Leave by the west end of the church. On your left is the **Ritter Hotel**.

When the armies of Louis XIV destroyed the town and castle in 1693, the only Renaissance building to survive was the Ritter.

• Continue down **Hauptstrasse**, a pedestrian street and the commercial center of town, which has many stores and restaurants. Here and on side streets you'll find some first-rate antique shops.

• Continue to a large open square, the **Universitätsplatz**. This is the entrance to the **Old University**. It was founded in 1386 by Paris professors and students who were offered asylum when they refused to recognize the opposition Pope the French king had installed in Avignon. It was the first university in Germany, and, after the Reformation had swept Europe, the chief Protestant center of learning in the country. In the back of the Old University is the **Students' Jail** (Studentenkarzer). Ancient tradition dictated that students couldn't be thrown in the town clinker, so from 1712 to the early twentieth century the Studentenkarzer was filled with unruly undergraduates who spent their leisure time carving inscriptions commemorating their imprisonment—a distinction of which they were proud. Students could be confined for up to fourteen days for such offenses as drunkenness, playing practical jokes, or disturbing the peace at night. After three days of bread and water they could accept food from outside, attend lectures, and receive visits from fellow prisoners. The walls are covered with cartoons, drawings, ribald verse—anyone who takes the time to examine signatures can probably find names of many who have achieved distinction in the arts, business, and politics.

• Nearby is the **University Library** (Universitätsbibliothek), in which you'll find some illustrated (illuminated) medieval books on display.

• Return to **Hauptstrasse**, turn left, and continue to the **Electoral Palatinate Museum** (Kurpfälzisches Museum)—open daily from 10 to 5; closed Mondays—and see the **Altarpiece of the 12 Apostles** (1509) by **Tilman Riemenschneider**. Riemenschneider is the greatest late-Gothic German wood carver, and this is his finest work. Compare the spiritual faces of the Apostles closest to Christ to the more worldly, worn faces of those farther away from Him. During the Peasants' War Riemenschneider sneaked the peasants of Würzburg into town by a secret path, and the Bishop of Würzburg punished him by mutilating his hands.

• Now cross **Hauptstrasse** and head toward the river on **Grosse Mantelgasse** (Big Coat Lane). When you can't go any farther, turn right. From here to the **Old Bridge** (Alt Brücke) there are several small side streets to explore. Cross the bridge and enjoy an unforgettable view of the town.

• Go for a walk along the far side of the river, on **Neuenheimer Landstrasse** and **Ziegelhäuser Landstrasse**. You'll get your best views of the castle from here—preferably in the late afternoon, when the sun turns the town to gold.

• A more challenging and rewarding walk is along **Philosopher's Walk** (Philosophenweg), on the slopes above the riverside path. After you cross the Old Bridge, take the street called Schlangenweg that zigzags up the mountain.

Shopping

Hauptstrasse is a pedestrian mall with many gift shops. For **antiques** try **Winnikes Antiquitäten**, Hauptstrasse 138 (eighteenth-century porcelain and furniture); **B & B Antiques**, Plöck 58 (old silver and glass), and several shops on **Haspelgasse**.

The Arts

There are summer performances in the Castle (the *Schlosspiele)*, including *The Student Prince*. Check for frequent organ recitals in the **Church of the Holy Ghost** (Heiliggeistkirche).

Boating

Boat trips along the river valley leave from the Stadthalle (Congress House. Tel. 06221-20181). Boats can be rented at Theodor-Heuss Bridge and at the Stadthalle (Congress House. Tel. 06221-20181).

Biking

Rentals are at the parcel counter in the main train station, from April through September.

Tours

Contact the Tourist Office or **Heidelberg Service**, Neckarmünzplatz, near the Town Hall. Tel. 06221-29641. Two-hour tours begin from Bismarckplatz and the train station, April through October at 10 and 2; off-season, Saturdays only at 2.

Dining

Weinstube zum Kurfürsten in the Hotel Europa (E, Friedrich-Ebert-Anlage 1. Tel. 06221-27101) is Heidelberg dining at its best—either in a wood-paneled tavern or on the terrace.

Hirschgasse (M/E, Hirschgasse 3. Tel. 06221-49921/2) is a hotel across the river on the edge of town. Gaudeamus Igitur (Let's be happy . . .) is the name of the small, unpretentious hotel restaurant serving regional specialties.

Kurpfälzisches Museum Restaurant (M, Hauptstrasse 97. Tel. 06221-24050) is a peaceful garden restaurant back from the main street—a peaceful oasis for a piña colada, a milk shake, or lunch.

Inexpensive student restaurants include **Zum Roten Ochsen** (Hauptstrasse 217. Tel. 06221-20977); the 580-year-old **Schnookeloch** (Haspelgasse 8. Tel. 06221-22733); and the more touristy **Zum Seppl** (Hauptstrasse 213. Tel. 06221-23085).

The best-known of the wine restaurants *(Weinstube)*, serving decent, inexpensive regional food, is **Schnitzelbank** (Bauamtsgasse 7. Tel. 06221-21189).

Lodging

Before you leave home, check with the German National Tourist Board for budget holiday packages that include three nights' accommodations, meals in student restaurants, entry fees, and guided tours.

Hotel Europa (E, Friedrich-Ebert-Anlage 1, Tel. 06221-27101) is a family-owned luxury hotel—the sort of place where an educated, well-heeled German would stay on frequent trips to Salzburg. The Red Baron would find himself outclassed in this classy hostelry, which has a marble entranceway flanked by carpeted lounges with wooden newspaper racks, leather chairs, and crystal chandeliers. Celebrated guests include Richard Strauss, King Edward VIII, and Maria Callas. Muhammed Ali signed the guest book, "Love is the net where hearts are caught like fish. Peace." Rooms vary significantly in size and decor, and many are decorated with money rather than taste; if you're unhappy, ask to see more. Room 205 is a good bet.

Romantic Hotel Zum Ritter (M, Hauptstrasse 178. Tel. 06221-24272 or 20203) occupies the only surviving Renaissance house in town. The Red Baron would feel right at home in the dining room, complete with suit of armor, rough plaster walls, arched doorways and ceiling beams. Rooms are clean and comfortable. Each is different, though—some modernish, some traditional—many with hideous orange carpets. Try room 34 on the top floor. The honeymoon suite has a mirror on the armoire at the foot of the bed. You'll love it here if it's your first trip to Europe. A Romantik Hotel.

Hotel Holländer (M/E, An der Alten Brücke. Tel. 06221-12091) is a renovated, centrally located, seventeenth-century house with lovely river views. Rooms are clean and friendly, but fitted with undistinguished orange-and-brown Sears Modern furnishings—headboards covered with an orangy velour. Room 452 has a skylight.

Hackteufel Hotel (M/I, Steingasse 7. Tel. 06221-25589) is a block behind the Holländer. It doesn't have the same character, but it's quiet and clean, and prices are lower.

Perkeo (M/E, Hauptstrasse 75. Tel. 06221-22255) was recently renovated, so all rooms have the same decor. The ambiance is a bit motelish, but with some homey, old-fashioned touches that you may find more agreeable than the deliberate Lederhosen Look of other hostelries. It's on a busy pedestrian street, so ask for a quiet room. Try for room 25.

Prinzhotel (E, Neuenheimer Landstrasse 5. Tel. 06221-40320) is a well-known, seventy-five-year-old luxury hotel across the river from the old town. It reopened in 1985 after extensive renovations. Perhaps because the owner's wife is Italian, the atmosphere is Trendy European, with some very smart, un-Teutonic colors—pink and gray. What the hotel lacks in warmth it makes up for in sophistication. Fight for a room with a river view.

Hirschgasse (E, Hirschgasse 3. Tel. 06221-49921/2) is across the river on the edge of town—a bit inconvenient if you want to go back and forth more than once a day. The atmosphere is young and yodely; but it's the least hokey, most friendly hotel in town. Rooms have painted armoires, beds with red tattersall covers, ceilings with new old beams. Room 18 has a four-poster with a red-fringed canopy. The original house was here when Columbus was crossing the Atlantic. Downstairs is a friendly, rustic restaurant called Gaudeamus Igitur.

Emergencies

Police: Tel. 112. *Ambulance:* Tel. 13013. *Doctor:* Tel. 27172.

For Further Information

The main Tourist Information Office (Verkehrsverein) is in the train station *(Hauptbahnhof).* Tel. 06221-21341. Open daily from 9 to 7; Sundays from 2 to 7. Branches are located in the funicular station halfway to the castle (Tel. 06221-29641) and at Neckarmüzplatz, near the City Hall (Tel. 06221-29641).

Train information: Tel. 06221-27156 or 525345.

✤ *THE NECKAR VALLEY*

Take Route 37 southwest through the Neckar Valley from Heidelberg toward Bad Wimpfen. The road passes through a gentle, rural landscape of orchards and vineyards. Wooded hills crowned with castles rise above the soft-flowing river. When your reach Neckarelz, you have a choice of continuing to Bad Wimpfen or turning left on Route 27 to Mosbach.

1. Route 27 is the most direct route to the Romantic Road. Turn left on Route 27 through Mosbach to Route 292. Turn right to Bad Mergentheim. Drive east to Weikersheim and head south along the Romantic Road.

2. If you have time, are enjoying the scenery, and are partial to castles and medieval towns, continue south from Neckarelz to Bad Wimpfen. This is the route described below.

✤ *NECKARGEMÜND* (8 miles east of Heidelberg)

Lodging

Hotel zum Rössl in Neckargemünd (I, Heidelberger Strasse 15. Tel. 06223-2665) is a bed-and-breakfast-style hotel with a restaurant that enjoys a fine reputation. During the busy tourist season you may want to leave Heidelberg and spend the night in these quiet surroundings in order to get an early start to the Romantic Road.

✤ *HIRSCHHORN* (7.5 miles east of Neckargemünd)

Dining and Lodging

Hirschhorn Castle Hotel (Schloss Hotel, M, Hirschhorn am Neckar. Tel. 06272-1373) is not so much a castle hotel as a pleasant if undistinguished modern hotel inside an old castle. Hallways have that medieval rough-plaster look, lest you forget you're in a castle, and some rooms have double sinks, carved oak beds, green velvet swag curtains, and canopied four-posters. The Grünes Zimmer and Hochzeitzimmer are the best rooms, but all have river views. Student Prince furnishings tend at times to confuse ornateness with class. Best bet may be to come for a meal (breakfast perhaps, after leaving Heidelberg), on a porch overlooking the river. The view is splendid, and the restaurant enjoys a good reputation for lunch or dinner.

⚘ NECKARZIMMERN

Dining and Lodging

Follow signs one mile to the left to **Hornberg Castle**, part of which has been converted into a hotel, the **Burghotel Hornberg** (M, Neckarzimmern. Tel. 06261-2758/4064). Best bet is lunch or dinner on the porch overlooking the Neckar Valley. Specialties include fresh fish and venison at reasonable prices. Rooms are comfortable, but haven't much panache for an eleventh-century castle. Ask for a room with a view and try for room 26. In the castle museum is the armor of Götz von Berlichingen (1480–1562), who was immortalized in Goethe's drama.

⚘ GUNDELSHEIM

A bridge beyond the town takes you 2 miles out of your way to the romantic, fortified **Guttenberg Castle**. Sights worth stopping for include a wooden library and an eighteenth-century herbarium, with plants grown in trick wooden boxes. Return to the main road and drive about 4.5 miles south to **Bad Wimpfen**.

⚘ BAD WIMPFEN

The old fortified quarter of Bad Wimpfen was, in the thirteenth century, an imperial residence. The network of picturesque streets such as **Klostergasse** are lined with timber-framed houses, and are well worth an hour of your time. The thirteenth-century Gothic church, **St. Peter's** (Stiftskirche), has a lovely cloister. For an impressive view, climb the tower of the **Imperial Palace**. Wander down **Schwibbogengasse**, a street of broken cobbles, full of warmth and character. The four-story house beside the Hotel Sonne belongs in a fairy tale.

EN ROUTE: From BAD WIMPFEN to the ROMANTIC ROAD

From Bad Wimpfen take country roads to **Domeneck**, **Schöntal**, and **Krautheim**, then turn north on **Route 19** to **Bad Mergentheim**. The best restaurants in Bad Mergentheim are **Zirbelstube** in the **Hotel Viktoria** (M, Tel. 07931-5930) and the less expensive **Alte Jagdstube** (M, Tel. 07931-2526). Drive to **Weikersheim** and head south along the **Romantic Road**.

✤ THE ROMANTIC ROAD

The road follows a medieval trade route through peaceful, rolling countryside, past vineyards and fields planted with sugar beets, potatoes, and wheat. This is not ooh-and-ah country, but a rural, daytime world of tractors and butterflies. The real romance is in the medieval towns along the route—the best preserved in Germany—particularly **Rothenburg**, **Dinkelsbühl** and **Nördlingen**.

✤ WEIKERSHEIM

The town developed around a **castle** (1580–1680) which has a first-rate collection of sixteenth- to eighteenth-century furniture and a marvelous **Great Hall** (Rittersaal) which is part Renaissance, part Baroque. (Open April to October from 8 to 6; off-season, from 10 to 12 and 2 to 4; closed Mondays in winter.) Huntsmen track their prey on the ceiling, and carved deer and bear seem poised to spring from the walls. Visitors pass beneath the unblinking gaze of local royalty, each in his own regal frame, each one uglier than the next.

Dining

For a quick lunch, try **Hotel-Restaurant Deutschherren-Stuben** (M, Tel. 07934-376), which is known for its fresh regional cuisine and its reasonable prices.

✤ CREGLINGEN

A mile side trip takes you to the **Chapel of Our Lord** (Herrgottskirche), which has a famous carved wooden altarpiece of the Virgin (1505–10) by **Riemenschneider**.

Dining

Gasthof Krone (M, Hauptstrasse 12. Tel. 07933-558) shares with the restaurant in Weikersheim a sound reputation for regional cuisine at reasonable prices.

✤ ROTHENBURG

In spite of the museumlike atmosphere and the spate of tourists (2,000 tourist beds, 90 restaurants), Rothenburg is one of the most colorful medieval towns in Europe. Every street has its own arrangement of beautiful churches, gateways, fountains, and wrought-iron signs. No roof is like its neighbor. The gabled houses are half-timbered or plastered, and dripping with flowers and vines. In America a street is an open road that could, it seems, go on forever; but in medieval Rothenburg the streets turn in on themselves, and seem to shelter you from the world outside.

The town developed around two twelfth-century castles that were destroyed in a mid-fourteenth-century earthquake. From the ruins, the wealthy burghers built public monuments, such as St. James's Church (St-Jakobskirche), the Town Hall, and the gabled houses in the Herrngasse. The town turned Protestant and then never recovered from the depression brought on by the Thirty Years' War (1618–48). It languished through the seventeenth and eighteenth centuries—a sleepy, forgotten, regional market town, too poor to expand beyond its medieval walls. It was this neglect, ironically, that preserved the town—keeping it the perfect gem of a sixteenth-century village that tourists enjoy today.

Things to See and Do

• Begin at the main square *(Marktplatz)*. Notice how all main streets converge here, in the geographic and spiritual heart of town—and that wherever you go within the medieval walls, you're always moving in relation to this central space. It must have been very satisfying, psychologically, always moving toward or away from a defined point; and it says something about our spiritual pilgrimage over the centuries that cities today no longer have this common center, these protective walls.

• Look up at the Town Hall, off this main square, and see if you can distinguish between the fourteenth-century Gothic section, with a gable topped by a belfry; and the newer, Renaissance section facing the Marktplatz, that was built after a fire in 1501. Standing in the Marktplatz, you can appreciate the contrast between the horizontal lines of Renaissance architecture, and the soaring, vertical lines of the earlier, Gothic building. (The arcade in front was added in 1681.) Inside the Town Hall is a museum and a tower with striking views. (Open April through October, daily from 9:30 to 12:30 and 1 to 5; weekends, closes at 4.)

• Also on the Marktplatz is the City Councillor's Tavern (Ratsherrntrinkstube), which you can recognize by the three clocks on its Baroque gable. If you're here at 11, 12, 1, 2, 9, or 10, you'll see the principal figures appear in what is referred to as the Drinking Feat of the Thirty Years' War. Regensburg, a Protestant town, lay in the path of Catholic forces under General Cserklas Tilly, and was taken on October 30, 1631. The following day it was to be destroyed and its officers executed; but during the night the victorious general was offered a 3¼-litre tankard of heavy Franconian ale, which, to his embarrassment, he was unable to empty in a single draft. With his manhood at stake—so the story goes— he offered to pardon the town if one of its officials could down it in one go. A former mayor named Nusch succeeded in ten minutes. It took him three days to recover, but the town was saved. The story is a bit hard to swallow, but who wants to question it? Skeptics can see the tankard in the museum, and draw their own conclusions.

• Cross the Marktplatz and walk down **Obere Schmiedgasse** (Upper Smithy's Lane). The second house (the **Master Builder's House**)—the one with the dragons on the gables—is the finest in town. The supporting figures at the upper windows represent alternately the seven vices and virtues; in the lower row Compassion, Gluttony, and Motherly Love stand side by side. The inner courtyard, unchanged for centuries, is today a café.

• On the right, where **Obere Schmiedgasse** turns into **Untere Schmiedgasse**, is the Gothic **St. John's Church** (Johanniskirche). Adjoining it is the **Medieval Crime Museum**, where kids can unlock their imaginations among the instruments of torture. (Open April through October, daily from 9:30 to 6; off-season, from 2 to 4; closed January and February.)

• Continue down **Untere Schmiedgasse** to **Plönlein**, a picturesque corner where two streets meet, both ending at gateways. If you have time, bear left and continue down **Spitalgasse** to the **Hospital** (Spital), a colorful group of sixteenth- and seventeenth-century buildings, including a notable Gothic chapel (Spitalkirche). Retrace your steps down **Spitalgasse**, back through the gate. Turn left and pass beneath the **Koboldzell Gate**.

• If you skip the Hospital, bear right to the **Koboldzell Gate**, make a sharp right turn, and follow the path along the outside of the wall, above the river. Pass through the arched entranceway into the **Burggarten**. Flowers bloom here now where the two fortified castles used to be.

• Follow the path through the public gardens. Pass through the fortified gateway *(Burgtor)*, which was part of one of the original castles, and head back toward the center of town. Bear right on **Herrngasse**, a commercial street lined with mansions of the medieval burghers, and peer into some of the courtyards. Soon you'll be back to the Marktplatz. Behind the well —which supplied the town's water needs 550 years ago—is a half-timbered house where artists display and sell their wares. To the left is the picturesque **Hofbronnengasse** (Court Well Lane), leading to the Dolls' Museum.

• Turn left on **Kirchgasse** and right on **Klostergasse** to St. James's Church. In the south aisle (on your right, facing front) is the famous 1504 Riemenschneider **altarpiece**, called the Holy Blood Altar because three drops of Christ's blood are said to be contained within a capsule of rock crystal in the gold-plated cross. Look closely at the facial expressions, particularly of Judas, in *The Last Supper*. Only John remains unperturbed.

Biking

Enquire at the train station.

Tours

Guided tours leave from the Tourist Office on the Marktplatz at 2 and 9 P.M. Also beginning at the central square are horse-drawn carriage rides.

Dining

Eisenhut (E, Herrngasse 3. Tel. 09861-2041), the number one hotel in town, has an attractive terrace restaurant overlooking the Tauber River. Popular dishes include "Franconian wedding" soup; saddle of venison with fresh mushrooms; and walnut ice cream with blackberries. Try the wines made from the hotel's own grapes.

Take a peek at the pastries on display in the sixteenth-century **Baumeisterhaus** (M, Obere Schmiedgasse 3. Tel. 09861-3404), and I'll bet you can't pass it by. Stop, too, for a lunch of regional specialties, such as dumplings in consommé, turkey schnitzel, and sauerbraten.

Lodging

Eisenhut (E, Herrngasse 3. Tel. 09861-2041) is considered the top hotel in town, so be sure to reserve rooms in advance. Former guests include Winston Churchill, William Randolph Hearst and the Shah of Iran. The century-old hotel was stitched together from four patrician houses. Old Bavarian furnishings are colorful in a busy, undisciplined sort of way; state your preference for modern or traditional decor. Smaller rooms are in back, facing the garden. Some of the marbleized bathrooms have twin sinks. Try for room 102, 108, or something comparable. The restaurant is excellent. What a lovely way to start the day, eating breakfast in the courtyard!

   Adam Hotel (M, Burggasse 29. Tel. 09861-2364) has the friendly, homey atmosphere of a wine house. It has a good kitchen, and its best rooms have carved wooden beds with canopies—equal to those at the Eisenhut at half the price. Be careful, though, about your choice of rooms. Room 2 is nice but tiny; room 1 has a small bathroom; room 4 had, at last look, a purple Dayglo-ish bedspread. Several other rooms have antique beds that are lovely to look at but not to sleep in—unless you're partial to the fetal position. Room 11 has a small but beautiful Bavarian farmer's bed. The Heart Room upstairs overlooking the garden has carved beds and stained-glass windows.

   The better rooms at the **Goldener Hirsh** (E, Untere Schmiedgasse 16. Tel. 09861-5061) are comparable in price to those at the Eisenhut, but the standard rooms are considerably cheaper—and just as nice. The hotel has a delightful Louis XVI-style restaurant on a blue terrace overlooking the town. Not all units have baths.

   Burg Hotel (M, Klostergasse 1-3. Tel. 09861-5037) is a bit flairless, but clean and comfortable, and fine for the price.

   Hotel Roter Hahn (M, Obere Schmiedgasse 21. Tel. 09861-5088) is more expensive than the Adam, with less character. The painted reproduction furniture lends a certain stolid cheerfulness to the rooms. The newly renovated units are best. Rooms are clean and comfortable, but each is different, so tell the management what you have in mind.

   Romantik Hotel Markusturm (E, Rödergasse 1. Tel. 09861-2370) is a family-type hotel just outside the walls, but only a few minutes' walk from town center. Some rooms have canopied four-posters. Most are small and unpretentious, and not without a certain character. Room 17 is as nice as any.

For Further Information

   The Tourist Information Office is at Marktplatz 2. Tel. 09861-2038. The office can help with accommodations.

   Train information: Tel. 09861-2330 or 2707.

♣ DINKELSBÜHL

   Dinkelsbühl offers a smaller, less perfect portrait of the Middle Ages than Regensburg—but it's also less precious. Regensburg exists to be looked at, Dinkelsbühl to be lived in. There are fewer tourists here— more people getting on with the business of life. If you have time for only one town along the Romantic Road, it should be Regensburg; but try to find time to see Dinkelsbühl, too. It's small enough that you can "do" it in under an hour. On any street you can glance back through the centuries at fifteenth- and sixteenth-century houses—both gabled and frescoed —and at great half-timber structures up to six stories high. Don't miss the houses with rich Renaissance decoration on **Martin-Luther Strasse**. Particularly notable is the fifteenth-century **Deutsches Haus**, which now has a small seventeenth-century Virgin over the entrance. Two other streets not to miss are **Segringer Strasse**, its houses adorned with flowers and picturesque signs, and **Nördlingen Strasse**, where the houses are out of line.

St. George's is one of the finest Gothic churches of its type in southern Germany. The Romanesque tower rises nearly two hundred feet, and affords fine views. (It may still be closed for restorations.) The interior is a Gothic hall with wonderful fan vaulting, and a notable fifteenth-century Franciscan altar in the south aisle (on your right, facing front).

Lodging

Deutsches Haus (M, Weinmarkt 3. Tel. 09851-2346), a 500-year-old half-timbered beauty, is the first choice of most visitors. The small, privately owned hotel has some rooms with private bath, and a good kitchen.

Gasthof Weisses Ross (I, Steingasde 12. Tel. 09851-2274) is an inexpensive guesthouse that has long been popular with artists. Rooms have old-fashioned family furniture. The kitchen has a sound reputation for fresh local food: asparagus with spicy ham; trout or carp from local ponds with melted butter and potatoes—and a glass of Frankenwein Bocksbeutel.

Goldene Rose (M, Marktplatz 4. Tel. 09851-831) is as venerable as the Deutsches Haus—Queen Victoria stayed here in 1891—but hasn't as much atmosphere. Recent furbishings, however, have helped.

Biking

Inquire at the Tourist Office.

Tours

Escorted tours run from April through October from St. George's Church. Tel. 09851-3013.

For Further Information

The **Tourist Office** (Verkehrsamt) is on the main square (**Marktplatz**). Tel. 09851-3013.

✤ NÖRDLINGEN

Nördlingen is a less perfect medieval town than Rothenburg or Dinkelsbühl, and its buildings, made from a grayer stone, don't have the same ruddy glow. But the town does have some venerable buildings, and visitors will enjoy walking along the crumbling fourteenth- and fifteenth-century ramparts, punctuated by five huge gate towers.

Like every self-respecting German town, Nördlingen has a mighty church near the center, thrusting its stately tower hundreds of feet into the sky. The late fifteenth-century **St. George's Church** is near the Marktplatz. A late Gothic hall-style building, it has attractive fan vaulting, a Baroque organ gallery decorated with hanging keys, a late-fifteenth-century pulpit, and a notable statue of Mary Magdalene which belonged to the original Baroque altarpiece. Climb the church steeple for a grand view.

The **Museum** (open 9 to 12 and 2 to 5; Sundays from 10 to 12 and 2 to 4; closed Mondays) has the original altarpiece from St. George's.

Dining

Hotel Sonne (M, 8860 Nördlingen, Marktplatz 3. Tel. 09081-51749), in the center of town, is a good bet for a reasonably priced lunch. Try roast pork or grilled knuckle of veal with a fresh salad.

For Further Information

The **Tourist Office** (Stätisches Verkehrsamt) is off the central square. Tel. 09081-84115.

✤ MUNICH

If you arrive here from Hamburg or Berlin you realize how much more easygoing the Bavarians are than their neighbors to the north. There, you have a sense that life is a serious business; here, that life is short and should be enjoyed.

Munich is the capital of Bavaria and the third-largest city in Germany. It's an industrial center—producing BMWs, helicopters, and beer—but also a cultural center with many art galleries, museums, and historic buildings restored since the war. Half the Münchners are immigrants, which helps explain the town's openness and diversity—its wonderful mix of corn and class.

Why visit Munich? To shop and dine along its pedestrian malls, to wander among the dizzying smells and colors of the outdoor market, to bang mugs in a funky beer hall or dine in an elegant three-star restaurant. You'll also want to ride bikes or row boats through the beautiful English Gardens; visit two of Europe's most important museums—one for art, the other for science; and go to the opera. Above all you'll want to soak up the atmosphere of a city impressed with the stamp of royalty—a city that has made an extraordinary recovery from the devastation of World War II, and that still, somehow, retains the unhurried, good-humored atmosphere of Bavaria.

The monk on the city's coat of arms recalls the city's origin as a monastic settlement *(Müchen* comes from Mönch, which means "monk") around 1100. Eighty years later Bavaria was given to **Otto of Wittelsbach**—an underling of Holy Roman Emperor Friedrich Barbarossa—and for the next seven centuries, till 1918, the history of Bavaria and that of this family were intertwined. Munich became the ducal residence in 1255, and in 1503, the capital of Bavaria.

People say that the medieval **Church of Our Lady** (Frauenkirche) captures the essence of Munich today, but the city is basically modern and owes its beauty to the taste of Ludwig I of Bavaria (1825–48). Soon after he was crowned, Ludwig proclaimed, "I shall make Munich such an honor to Germany that no one who has not seen it can pretend to know the country"; and he proceeded to lay out avenues and found galleries, libraries, and churches. Through his love of Italy and Greece, he attracted architects and artists who built the **Pinakotheks** (art museums), enlarged the **Palace** (Residenz), and constructed **Ludwigstrasse**.

Ludwig was forced to abdicate as the result of an eighteen-month affair, at the age of sixty, with a Spanish dancer named Lola Montez, the daughter of an Irish officer in India. She had burst into his quarters one day to protest her being banned from the stage.

Following the rule of Ludwig's son **Maximilian II** (1848–64), mad King **Ludwig II** (1864–86) assumed the throne, and built the castles you'll see during your stay in Garmisch-Partenkirchen. It says much about the people of Munich that they still love Ludwig, and protect his memory as a person would protect his dreams.

When Ludwig II died without an heir, **Prince Luitpold**, son of Ludwig I, assumed the Regency. It was he who laid out the great thoroughfare that bears his name (Prinzregentenstrasse), built the **German Museum** (Deutsches Museum), and completed the **New City Hall** (Neues Rathaus).

Things to See and Do

• Begin at **Karlstor**, one of the old city gates on **Karlsplatz Square**. Ahead of you is the **Richard Strauss Fountain**, which was named for the famous Munich-born composer (1864–1949). The fountain's central column is decorated with scenes from Strauss's opera *Salome*. Beneath the square is an **underground shopping arcade** that goes all the way to the train station *(Hauptbahnhof)*.

• Pass through the **Karlstor** and enter the old part of the city, largely destroyed in the war, now the pedestrian street **Neuhauserstrasse**. On your left is **Bürgersaal Chapel**, which has a Rococo interior with some notable frescoes.

• Just past the chapel, on your left, is the **Church of St. Michael** (Michaelskirche), 1583–97, the first large Renaissance church in South Germany, and the inspiration for many others. Don't be surprised if you think you're in Rome, for this spacious, white stucco building was modeled on the Gesù. It was built for the Jesuits and restored after war. In the crypt is the tomb of **Ludwig II** of Bavaria (see pages 149–54, under Excursions from Garmisch-Partenkirchen, for notes on Ludwig).

• Keep this church in mind as you visit (a) the **Church of Our Lady**, 1468–88; (b) the **Church of the Theatines** (Theatinerkirche), 1663–75; and (c) the **Church of the Asam Brothers** (Asamkirche), 1733. In these four churches you can trace the history of German architecture from Gothic to Baroque. The Frauenkirche is Bavarian Late Gothic; Michaelskirche is Renaissance; the Theatinerkirche is late Renaissance, but with the rich designs of the Italian Baroque; and the Asamkirche shows the full, riotous flowering of South German Baroque.

Neuhauserstrasse turns into **Kaufingerstrasse**. On your left, a block past St. Michael's, is a street leading to the **Church of Our Lady**, also known as Munich Cathedral. This late Gothic hall church has more character than originality, but its onion-shaped domes have been symbols of Munich since they were added in 1525. One of them, purists will be glad to note, is three feet higher than the other. Notice, too, the absence of buttresses, and the walls running smoothly up to the roof. The red brick exterior is strikingly plain but massive and has a strength and integrity missing from many of the more ostentatious, imitative churches around town.

The purity of line is unbroken inside, too. Largely restored since the war, the nave has twenty-two powerful pillars dividing it into three parts, and simple white walls that frame the light from the stained-glass windows. The interior is memorable for its stark whiteness, its height, and the way in which the pillars seem to hide the aisles. The ancient art and furnishings—hidden away during the war—stand out dramatically against the modern decor. In the south nave (on your right, facing front) is the black marble tomb (1622) of **Ludwig the Bavarian**. Not to be confused with his namesake, Ludwig II, Ludwig the Bavarian was one of the first Wittelsbachs, who went on to become king of Germany in 1314 and Emperor in 1328.

• Continue along **Kaufingerstrasse** to the square known as **Marienplatz** —the heart of the city. You'll find luxury shops, cafés, and restaurants here. Marienplatz was the central market until 1853, and is still a lively meeting place for people from all walks of life.

• To the left of the square is the **New Town Hall** (Neues Rathaus), 1867–1908. One of Ludwig's more fanciful creations, it looks back on the golden age of the city during the Middle Ages, when the Wittelsbach realm included both North and South Germany and the Low Countries. Built in Flemish Gothic, it was also meant to recall the rich autonomous towns of Flanders and thus the emancipation of Bavaria from the royal house. The Rathaus is nothing but a pastiche of styles, but is fun and impressive, nonetheless. On clear days the view from the **tower** (open weekdays from 8 to 3:45) extends as far south as the Alps. Come at 11, 5, or 9 and watch the knights and coopers (makers of wooden casks) perform on the early-twentieth-century **Glockenspiel** (carillon). Two knights joust in honor of a celebrated sixteenth-century marriage, ending in victory for the Bavarian nobleman. The coopers dance in gratitude for the town's escape from a sixteenth-century plague. If you arrive too early, find a window table in a third-floor café across the square.

• South of the Marienplatz is **St. Peter's** (Peterskirche), an old Gothic basilica in a Rococo dress. The archways seem to squeeze the walls together, forcing the worshiper's eyes upward to God. At the same time, the twelve gilded apostles direct your gaze forward to the golden altar. The 300-foot tower ("Old Peter") offers another view of the Alps.

• From Marienplatz take a short side trip down **Sendlingerstrasse** (a good shopping street) to the **Church of the Asam Brothers** on the right. This jewel box, this spiritual ballroom, was built by the brothers Asam from 1733 to 1746 and is the best example of late German Baroque architecture in town. The brothers built it at their own expense in a narrow space confined between two buildings—which is why the usual east-west axis (the entrance to the west, the altar to the east) has been reversed. Making a virtue of necessity, the brothers installed windows

above the door. The light filtering through them forces your eyes from
the altar to the suspended figure of Christ, and upward to the picture of
the Ascension.

The Asam brothers would have understood what Descartes, that master of reason, meant when he said, "The nature of men is such that they
value only those things which arouse their admiration, and which they
cannot entirely grasp." Note how the walls are molded as if of wax or
clay. Form, the essence of Renaissance art, dissolves. Everything moves,
undulates, flows. Nothing *is;* everything *becomes.*

Some of you will dislike the Asamkirche because it is the art of the
façade. In friends as in furnishings, you don't like to be fooled by surface
charm, but want things to be what they seem. To the Asam brothers,
however, as to all Baroque artists, the essence was revealed through appearances. The façade was not an escape from or a distortion of reality,
but proof of God's kingdom here on Earth.

• From the Asamkirche, walk to the busy, colorful outdoor **Food Market**
(Viktualienmarkt), which moved here from *Marienplatz* in the last century. Cheese, wine, flowers, vegetables—all are for sale here under striped
awnings. If the scene brings on hunger pangs, stop for a Schweinswürstl
or a Weisswurst; a bowl of hot soup at the **Münchner Suppenküche**, or
an order of fish (Fischsemmel) at the **Nordseefischhalle.**

• Return to **St. Peter's Church**, near Marienplatz. On the northeast side
is a street called the **Burgstrasse**. At number 5 is the **Weinstadel** (1552),
the oldest house in town. At number 10, take the passage right to the
Lederstrasse. Turn left on the **Orlandostrasse** to the **Platzl.**

Here you'll find the **Hofbräuhaus**, the most famous of Munich's beer
halls. The atmosphere is as heady as the ale, which is drunk from large
blue-glazed mugs in various rooms and courtyards. Music fills the air,
mixed with the thick, heavy smell of sausages and stale tobacco. Don't
miss it!

• Take the **Pfisterstrasse** to the **Old Castle** (Alter Hof) on your left, and
turn right on the **Hofgraben** to **Maximilianstrasse.** Cross over, to the
square **Max Joseph Platz.** On your right is the **National Theater**, which
houses the Bavarian State Opera. Ahead of you, across the square, is the
entrance to the **Palace**—the home of the Dukes of Wittelsbach for over
650 years.

Restored since the war, the **Palace** contains a **Treasury** with beautiful
crucifixes, diadems, and illuminated books; and a **Palace Museum** with
both gilded **State Rooms** and **Porcelain Rooms** displaying masterpieces
from Nymphenburg and Sèvres.

• The Palace is bordered on the west by **Residenzstrasse**, which takes you to the **Odeonsplatz** (another square) overlooked by the lofty **Church of the Theatines**, 1663–75. The elaborate stucco work in the chancel and dome are indicative of the Baroque at its best.

• From Theatinerkirche, head back down **Residenzstrasse to Maximilianstrasse**. Many of Munich's best shops are along this street.

• Most of you will find the following places too far to reach by foot. If you're taking public transportation, save money with either **strip tickets**, good for five journeys—red ones for the inner city, blue ones for longer distances—or the **24-Stunden Ticket**, valid on all buses, subways, and trams for 24 hours.

• **Schwabing**, a ten-minute ride from center city, is a fashionable suburb bordering the **English Gardens** (**Englischer Garten**). The Greenwich Village or Soho of the 1950s, Schwabing is now the place to be. Come here to dine, to escape the other tourists, and to wander among the smart, trendy boutiques. While visiting Schwabing, stroll through the lovely Englischer Garten—Munich's most famous park, and the largest city park in Europe. You can jog, ride rented bikes, go for buggy rides, row boats on lakes, and dine at the beer garden beneath a Chinese pagoda.

• Anyone with even a passing interest in art will want to visit the **Old Pinakothek** (Alte Pinakothek), the "old picture gallery," which houses the painting collections of several centuries of Wittelsbachs, beginning in the early sixteenth century. Under Ludwig I, the Alte Pinakothek became one of the top art museums in Europe. The collection includes notable works by Dürer, Albrecht Altdorfer, Raphael, Titian, Leonardo da Vinci, Van Dyck, Rubens, Rembrandt, and El Greco.

Nearby is the **New Pinakothek** (Neue Pinakothek), featuring works by the French Impressionists (Monet, Degas, etc.), and modern German painting, beginning with the wonderfully tasteless, oversentimental works of the German Romantics.

• Straddling an island in the Isar River is the **German Museum** (Deutsches Museum), one of the world's outstanding museums of science and technology. You can travel from prehistory into the space age in an hour; but the scale models and hands-on exhibits could keep you and your children happy for days.

• **Breweries** can be visited by appointment. Contact *Löwenbräu* (Tel. 089-52001) or Paulaner-Salvator-Thomasbräu. Tel. 089-41151.

• **Nymphenburg**—located in the northwest suburbs off Route 7, 4 miles from town center—is the former summer residence of the Bavarian rulers. The oldest part dates from 1664, with buildings and arcades added over the next century. The Rococo **Hall of Mirrors** is an exercise in wowmanship. In the **Gallery of Beauty** (Schönheits Galerie) Ludwig I collected portraits of beautiful women, both rich and poor, including his beloved Lola, for whom he forfeited his kingdom; see if you share his taste. It's not surprising that a back room upstairs was Ludwig II's favorite—it's so remote. Be sure to stroll through the park and formal gardens. The high point is a visit to the **Amalienburg hunting lodge,** a Rococo masterpiece, where no one seems to have hunted for anything but pleasure. Animals, birds, leaves—all join in a Rococo dance that captures the joy and movement of the chase. Kids in particular will love the **Museum of Royal Carriages,** where a mermaid holds the lamp on Ludwig II's carriage. Could anything be less appropriate!

• "Those who cannot remember the past are condemned to repeat it," says the brochure for the 4-hour morning tours to the Concentration Camp Memorial at **Dachau.** In this ultimate symbol of Nazi atrocities, 20 miles northwest of Munich, you can see cell-block interiors and the Krematorium where more than 206,000 prisoners lost their lives (see Tours, page 140).

Shopping

The most elegant shops are on **Theatinerstrasse, Maximilianstrasse,** and **Briennerstrasse.** The pedestrian shopping mall runs from **Karlsplatz** to **Marienplatz.** Many of the trendiest boutiques are in the suburb of **Schwabing,** a 10-minute ride from center city.

For two floors of **mugs, folk costumes,** and **antiques,** try **Wallach,** Residenzstrasse 3. **Loden-Frey** at Maffeistrasse 7-9 is well known for **Bavarian fashions.** To see what contemporary artisans are up to, visit the **Bavarian Association of Artisans** (Bayerischer Kunstgewerbeverein), Pacellistrasse 7.

The famous **porcelain factory Nymphenburger Porzellanmanufaktur** is on the grounds of the castle, 5 miles northwest of the city. Open weekdays from 8 to 12 and 1 to 5. For **gourmet food specialties,** don't miss **Alois Dallmayr,** Dienerstrasse 14-15. For **clocks,** go to **Andreas Huber,** Weinstrasse 8; or **Hauser,** Marienplatz 28. For **cameras,** best bet is **Kohlroser,** Maffeistrasse 14, near the Hotel Bayerischer Hof. For **optical goods, Sohnges,** at both Briennerstrasse 7 and Kaufingerstrasse 34.

For **china, crystal,** and **cutlery,** try **Rosenthal Porzellanhaus Zoellner,** Theatinerstrasse 8; or **Henckels,** at Weinstrasse 12. For **suitcases** and **leather goods, Plaschke,** at Briennerstrasse 11.

The most expensive **antiques** are on Ottostrasse. **Herbert M. Ritter,**

at Prannerstrasse 5, is one of the best. The **Antic Haus,** Neuturmstrasse
1, near the Hofbräuhaus, has fifty dealers on three floors. Also try the side
streets in the northern suburb of **Schwabing.** The antique market in
Haidhausen at Kirchenstrasse 15 is fun for browsing.

For fine **chocolates,** go to **Elly Seidl,** Maximilianstrasse 14, opposite
the opera house. Germany's largest **secondhand market** is at Kirchenstrasse 15 in Haidhausen, a southeast suburb not far from the Deutsches
Museum.

Biking

Free biking trail maps are available at all branches of the Bayerische
Vereinsbank. Bikes can be rented from May through October at the
English Gardens at the corner of Königinstrasse and Veterinärstrasse.
Tel. 089-397016. They can also be rented at **Lothar Borucki,** Hans Sachs
Strasse 7, near Sendlinger Tor Platz. Tel. 089-266506; and at stations of
the electric suburban railway (S-Bahn).

The Arts

The tourist office publishes a list of monthly offerings.

Munich has a fairytale **Opera House** (Bayerisches Nationaltheater) on
Max Joseph Platz. The renowned company, which goes back 450 years,
performed two premieres by Mozart and no fewer than five by Wagner.
Richard Strauss conducted the opera orchestra for seven years. Tickets
are sold at agencies and at the Opera Ticket Office at Maximilianstrasse
11 (open weekdays from 10 to 1 and 4 to 6; weekends, from 10 to 1).
Tickets are in great demand, so arrange to buy them when you make your
hotel reservations.

Agencies specializing in **concert tickets** for the Bavarian State Orchestra, the famous Bach Choir, etc. include: **Otto Bauer Musikalienhand-
lung,** in the Rathaus, Tel. 089-221757; **Residenz Bücherstube,** Residenzstrasse 1. Tel. 089-220868; and **Buchhandlung Lehmkuhl,** Leopoldstrasse
45. Tel. 089-398042. The most important concerts are held in the rococo
concert hall inside the Palace.

Check with the Tourist Office for upcoming **church concerts** in St.
Michael's, St. Matthew's, and the Frauenkirche.

There's a **summer concert series** from mid-June to mid-July in
Nymphenburg Castle.

Tours

Most tour buses leave near the main entrance of the train station. There are 1- and 2½-hour daytime tours, and a 4-hour "Munich by Night" tour. Contact your hotel, the tourist office (Tel. 089-239171), or Munich Sightseeing Tours (Tel. 089-5904314 or 5904248).

Also departing from the train station are excursion buses to the Royal Castles (described on pages 150–54), Dachau, and towns along the Romantic Road. Contact your hotel or the following travel agencies: Autobus Oberbayern, Sophienstrasse 2. Tel. 089-558061; Autobus Isaria Reisen, Neuhauserstrasse 47. Tel. 089-226622; or ABR, The Official Bavarian Travel Office, located at the train station. Tel. 089-591315.

Dining

Specialty snacks include Leberkäs: minced beef and pork liver baked with spices such as marjoram and nutmeg; Radi: white radishes sliced thin and salted; Steckerfisch: skewered fish roasted or grilled; Obatztler: cheese, mostly Camembert, with minced onions, pepper, salt, paprika, caraway, egg yolk, and butter; Weisswürst: a white sausage made with veal, bacon, and parsley spiced with sweet mustard and eaten with white crusty bread. The Bavarians like to have Weisswürst for their second breakfast *(Brotzeit)* before noon. Don't ask for less than two, or someone will think you're a tourist. The best are served in the Poststube of the Franzikaner Restaurant on Residenzstrasse, opposite the National Theater.

Gourmets from around the world come to feast on meals prepared by Munich's two top chefs, Eckart Witzigmann and Heinz Winkler.

The uncrowned king, Chef Eckart Witzigmann, gets 3 Michelin stars and 19 of 20 points from Gault Millau for his nouvelle-with-a-Bavarian-touch cuisine at Aubergine (E, Maximiliansplatz 5. Tel. 089-598171). The decor is white and modernistic, with brushed aluminum paneling.

Heinz Winkler reigns at the modular-modern Tantris (E, Johnann-Fichte Strasse 7. Tel. 089-362061) in the suburb of Schwabing. Regional specialties are cooked à la nouvelle with Teutonic touches. Specialties include calf's kidney with parsley, medallions of venison with cherries, and mousseline of hake with sorrel sauce.

Königshof (E, Karlsplatz 25. Tel. 089-558412), serves the best hotel food in town. The Belle Époque terrace restaurant has picture windows overlooking the busy Karlsplatz. The cuisine is a mix of nouvelle and classical, with such favorites as crab bisque, filet of Angus beef, and grilled fresh trout. Expensive, but impeccable service.

You shouldn't leave Munich without trying some Bavarian specialties, such as roast pork knuckles (Haxen) or sausages and sauerkraut. The best of the regional dishes are served at **Haxnbauer** (M, Münzstrasse 5. Tel. 089-221922). Next door is the **Hofbräuhaus**, which is great for beer but not for food.

For a reasonably priced Bavarian-style meal in a fun, unsophisticated atmosphere, join the 1,000 diners in the **Ratskeller** (M, Marienplatz 8. Tel. 089-220313) for a Knöedelsuppe (clear soup with liver dumplings) or Schlachtplatte (roast pork or sausages on sauerkraut). Almost every German city has its own Ratskeller, usually in the cellar of the town hall, where in the Middle Ages the officers received guests.

Alois Dallmayr's (E, Dienerstrasse 14. Tel. 089-2135100) is Munich's answer to London's Fortnum and Mason: a black-tie gourmet food shop with a busy, sophisticated upstairs restaurant. An ideal trysting place for a hot lunch or salad, or a gooey dessert you'll be talking about for years.

If you're going to the **National Museum**, cross the river for lunch at **Käfer Schänke** (E, Schumannstrasse 1. Tel. 089-41681) off Prinzregentstrasse. This is another food delicacy store with such staples as Caspian caviar and Hungarian goose-liver. When you've had enough looking, dine in the charcuterie or in the upstairs Italian/French restaurant with a Bavarian flair. The ambiance is gay and informal.

When you're visiting the Outdoor Market (Viktualienmarkt) go to **Straubinger Hof** (M, Blumenstrasse 5. Tel. 089-260844, near St. Peter's Church) for hard-to-find Bavarian specialties, such as baked udder and pudding, and pork with root vegetables. If you can pronounce it, try kälberne Briesmilzwurst in aufgeschmelzter Brotsuppe—a soup that will keep you strong for the rest of the day. Other popular dishes include roast suckling pig with potato dumplings, and Kaiserschmarren, a pancake with eggs and apples. One portion per family, please!

If you go to the **Deutsches Museum**, cross the River Isar and, in the same building as the Penta Hotel, enjoy lunch in the **Île de France** (M, Rosenheimerstrasse 32. Tel. 089-4481366), a nice French bistro with French specialties at reasonable prices.

The Four Seasons (Vier Jahreszeiten Kempinski, E, Maximilianstrasse 17. Tel. 089-230390) now belongs to the Kempinski Company and, as we all know, the kitchen of a company-minded restaurant is not as good as it could be. A few steps away is **Chesa Rüegg** (M, Wurzerstrasse 18. Tel. 089-297114), an excellent Swiss restaurant with a yodelly, Engadine look, complete with copper pans and beamed ceilings. Popular dishes include fresh lobster, terrine of fish, and the best Geschnetzeltes (shredded veal) you've ever had.

Montgelas-Keller in the **Bayerischer Hof Hotel** (M, Promenadeplatz 6. Tel. 089-21200) is a reasonably priced Bavarian-style restaurant in one of Munich's best hotels.

Schwarzwälder (M, Hartmannstrasse 14, across from the Bayerischer Hof Hotel) is a friendly restaurant in Bavarian-wine-cellar dress, with a familiar, international menu that's popular with American tourists.

Each of the major breweries has its own **beer hall** or **beer garden**, usually in a huge, cavernous space with a Medieval Cellar look, complete with red checkered tablecloths and arched entranceways. Beer drinkers can stagger from one hall to the next, comparing brews. The young at heart will want to go at least once: wholesome-heavy Bavarian-style meals are served, too. The best is the early fifteenth-century **Franziskaner** (Perusastrasse 5. Tel. 225002), not far from the Rathaus.

Munich is also famous for its **wine taverns**, where the emphasis is on drinking rather than eating. The cellars cultivate a Harvest Time look, with trellises and plastic grapevines. Among the most popular are **Weinkrüger** (Maximilianstrasse 21. Tel. 089-229295), a favorite meeting place for operagoers; and the atmospheric **Weinstadl** (Burgstrasse 5. Tel. 089-221047).

Lodging

For a clean, comfortable room, you can't go wrong with any of the 13 moderately priced hotels in a syndicate called **Münchner Hotel Verbund** (Arnulfstrasse 20. 8000 München 2. Tel. 089-554075). If you arrive in high season without a reservation, they should be able to help you. Most are modern and undistinctive—but small enough to be friendly, and quite adequate for a few nights in town. The most popular is **Hotel Uhland** (M, Uhlandstrasse 1. Tel. 089-539277), a 100-year-old private home that was turned into a hotel by the present owner's grandmother. Bathrooms are smallish. Connecting rooms are good for families. Room 11 has that orange all-weather carpet the Bavarians seem to love. Room 33 is a good bet, despite the green carpet and the requisite Alpine painting.

The **Four Seasons** (Vier Jahreszeiten Kempinski) (E, Maximilianstrasse 17. Tel. 089-230390) used to be the number one choice in town. It's still first-class, and attracts the same prominent clientele, but gone is much of its individual charm now that it's become part of a chain. A quiet dignity pervades the public rooms, with their rich mahogany paneling and leather couches. Many visitors love, others hate, the orange stained-glass ceiling that covers the lounge like a huge reproduction Tiffany-glass lampshade. Rooms have a friendly, residential hotel feeling to them—more Teutonic than Bavarian, with old-fashioned couches and framed botanicals. The less expensive rooms are smaller but thoughtfully furnished with upholstered chairs and ottomans.

As you walk down Maximilianstrasse, past Munich's best and most expensive shops, you'll come to **Hotel Splendid** (M/E, Maximilianstrasse 54. Tel. 089-296606), a pleasant, smaller hotel, a short walk from center city.

Across the river is the **Hotel Prinzregent** (M/E, Ismaninger Strasse 42. Tel. 089-4702081)—a bit out of the way, but friendly, with some unobtrusive Bavarian touches, such as a breakfast room paneled with wood from an old farmhouse.

Excelsior (M/E, Schützenstrasse 11. Tel. 089-557906) is a modern, postwar hotel with a smart Bavarian/Bloomingdales look, including brass bathroom fittings, muted pastel colors, and antiqued chandeliers and wall sconces. It's conveniently located on the pedestrian mall not far from the train station, and is a favorite with business people.

Königshof (E, Karlsplatz 25. Tel. 089-558412) is ideally located at the west end of the mall, and has a first-class restaurant overlooking Karlsplatz. The lobby is more hushed and elegant than at its sister hotel, the Excelsior. Rooms are decorated with soft, salmon-colored walls, swag curtains, and quality antique reproduction furniture. Corner rooms are best. Ask for a hard mattress.

Most critics consider the **Continental** (E, Max-Joseph Strasse 5. Tel. 089-557971) the leading downtown hotel. Rooms I saw had more character than those at a Hilton or Sheraton, but were plainly decorated and had no overwhelming character or charm. Public areas do have fine tapestries, impressive moldings, and antique furnishings.

The best thing about the 31-room **Biederstein** (M, Keferstrasse 18. Tel. 089-395072) is the birdsongs from the nearby English Gardens. The modern hotel is a rather undistinguished yellow ferro-concrete building with balconies and early-twentieth-century furniture, in the residential suburb of Schwabing, a 10-minute train ride from center city. Prices are reasonable for visitors who want to escape the more frenetic life downtown.

Hotel Gästehaus Englischer Garten (M, Liebergesellstrasse 8. Tel. 089-3920341) is a converted, ivy-covered nineteenth-century mill only steps from Munich's largest and loveliest park. Though preferable to the

Biederstein, rooms are still student-basic; and there's no reason to commute to Schwabing unless you want to be in a young, fashionable neighborhood bordering a park, or in-town hotels are full. Rooms in the main house are best.

Bayerischer Hof (E, Promenadeplatz 6. Tel. 089-21200) is a very large, traditional hotel with 725 beds and a clientele that's well heeled but less polished than at the Four Seasons or Excelsior. The renovated lobby has Italian marble floors, painted marble columns, and raw wood—an interesting blend of Caesar and Ludwig. The new rooms have a motelly, Sears-Bavarian feel to them, with an emphasis on orange. Best bets are the sliding-roof swimming pool—a real plus in summer—and the sauna-gym.

Eden Wolff Hotel (M, Arnulfstrasse 4. Tel. 089-558281) is a large old hotel—the best of the moderate-priced hotels near the train station.

For Further Information

The main **Tourist Information Office** is at Rindermarkt 5, near Marienplatz. Tel. 089-239171. The third-floor office can make room reservations but is open during working hours only. Other offices are at the airport; at the Bayerstrasse exit of the main train station; and in the underground shopping center at Karlsplatz. Tel. 089-2338242 or 554459.

For information on travel outside of Munich, contact the **Upper Bavarian Regional Tourist Office** (Fremdenverkehrsverband München-Oberbayern) at Sonnenstrasse 20, near the Karlsplatz. Tel. 089-597347.

American Consulate General: Königinstrasse 5–7. Tel. 089-23011. *American Express:* Promenadeplatz 3. Tel. 089-21990. *Train Information:* 089-592991 or 593321. *English bookstore:* Anglia, Schellingstrasse 3.

Emergencies

Police: Tel. 110. *Ambulance:* Tel. 222266. *Medical Emergency:* Tel. 558661.

EN ROUTE: From MUNICH to GARMISCH-PARTENKIRCHEN

The Autostrasse (A95) whirls you from Munich to Garmisch-Partenkirchen in only an hour. A slower, more scenic route is described below.

✤ ANDECHS

How to Get There. Take A96 west of Munich and follow exit signs to the Ammersee.

Beer drinkers will want to take a somewhat roundabout route to Garmisch in order to taste what many Bavarians consider the best beer in Germany. It's made at the Abbey at Andechs, 4 miles south of **Herrsching**, and sold at the beer garden overlooking the delightful **Ammersee** (Ammer Lake). The Gothic **Abbey Church** (Klosterkirche), now in Rococo dress, is in itself well worth a visit.

❧ *MURNAU*

How to Get There. The fast route is south from **Munich** on A95 for about 45 minutes to the **Murnau** exit. The more scenic route is via **Andechs** and **Route 2**.

Lodging

Alpenhof Murnau (E, Ramsachstrasse 8. Tel. 08841-1045) is a tasteful, comfortable, modern hotel with traditional furnishings and the best nouvelle dining in the area. The hotel is in a peaceful, rural setting with a distant view of the Alps: a sensible place to stay if you leave Munich in the afternoon and don't want to deal with Garmisch till the following day.

❧ *GARMISCH-PARTENKIRCHEN*

This is the largest winter sports complex in Germany, built almost entirely since World War I. The two towns—the hyphen is the stream that flows between them—sit in a valley ringed by the Bavarian Alps, including Germany's highest peak, the Zugspitze. Though originally a ski resort—the host for the 1936 Olympic Games—Garmisch-Partenkirchen has become a town for all seasons—the base for year-round sports and excursions into the countryside.

What Garmisch-Partenkirchen is not is a quaint Alpine village like Zermatt, huddled beneath towering peaks. It also lacks the panache of a St. Moritz, and seems to insinuate itself, rather than grow out of the Alpine setting. On the positive side, it can give you all the pampering you want after a day in the Great Outdoors, and has hotels and restaurants for all tastes and budgets. It makes a great base for hikes, scenic drives, cable car rides, and visits both to the Royal Castles of Ludwig II and to the Passion Play village of Oberammergau. If that's not enough to keep you busy, the town has six Olympic-size pools and three indoor skating rinks that seat 12,000! Furthermore, despite its success, Garmisch-Partenkirchen has remained small in scale, with nothing higher than an Alpine roof. Garmisch itself is the more fashionable and expensive part of town —more central to the cafés and nighttime activities; Partenkirchen is more low-keyed and family-oriented. But should both Garmisch and Partenkirchen be too commercial for your tastes, you can stay in dozens of charming, family-run chalets on the roads up to the mountains, and, like the American troops stationed nearby, come into town for R & R.

The ski slopes are open from December through May, but the cog railway and cable car to the highest peak, the **Zugspitze** (9,717 feet), are open year round, and a trip to the top is a must. For two different experiences, take the train one way and the cable car the other. It's a 7,000-foot climb from Garmisch to the summit, a trip that can be rough on the heart if made too quickly, so take the train up, and the faster cable car down. Trains leave almost hourly from 8 to 4 from **Zugspitzbahn station** in Garmisch and stop at **Lake Eibsee** on their way to the top. It's a 40-minute train ride just to the lake, so you may want to drive there—a 20-minute trip—and catch the train before it begins its ascent. The train bores through a 2½-mile tunnel to the **Hotel Schneefernerhaus** at 8,691 feet. From here you board a cable car to the summit—a trip as scenic as flying over the Alps in a plane. The hotel, despite breathtaking views, is more for serious skiers than for lovers or tourists, since it has only single beds; and when the last train or cable car descends, there is nowhere to go. (The hotel does serve dinner, which is included in the rate.)

Another popular cable car ride for those with less time is a 20-minute trip direct from Partenkirchen to the 5,840-summit of the **Wank**.

At the **casino** at the **Spielbank Garmisch-Partenkirchen**, 13 Marienplatz, you can try your luck at roulette, baccarat, or blackjack from 3 P.M.

Hiking

The most dramatic high-altitude hike for the casual traveler in good condition, is to take the cable car to the top of the Wank, and walk along the ridge.

More serious hikers can take overnight trips, staying in mountain huts belonging to the **German Alpine Association** (Deutscher Alpenverein). Some huts are supervised and serve meals. At other, unsupervised huts, you'll need to get a key. For information, inquire at the local tourist office or write to the German Alpine Association at Praterinsel 5, 8000 Munich 22. Tel. 089-293086—preferably before you leave home.

Another dramatic walk—one anyone can make both in winter and after the snow has melted—is through **Partnachklamm** Gorge, following a trail gouged from a ledge of rock above the frothing or frozen water.

Park near the Partenkirchen Sports Stadium and walk or take a horse-drawn carriage to the **Graseck cable car** (the road is closed to cars). Take the cable car to the lower station. There's a modern hotel here, the **Forsthaus Graseck Inn**, where you can stop for lunch or drinks. From the inn, a path leads up one slope of the valley. Don't take the first right, which descends into the valley; continue past the **Wetterstein-Alm Inn** (a much friendlier place for a snack), and then turn right, to the bottom of the gorge, which you follow downstream. It's an easy walk, all downhill, back to your car.

The various excursions from Garmisch-Partenkirchen are described on pages 149–54.

Dining

If you're willing to drive 9 miles, **Tonihof** (E, Walchenseestrasse 42, in Eschenlohe. Tel. 08824-1021) is one of the best restaurants south of Munich. A nouvelle menu features fresh fish, poultry, vegetables, and fruit. The restaurant also has 9 rooms with balconies overlooking the mountains.

Reindl-Grill in the Hotel **Partenkirchner Hof** (M, Bahnhofstrasse 15. Tel. 08821-58025) focuses more on food than on decor. It's not just a grill, it's an above-average restaurant serving the very freshest fish, veal, venison, and seasonal vegetables. Popular favorites include Lady Curzon soup, bouillabaisse, and Swiss *Bündnerfleisch*. For dessert, try peach Melba or a Salzburger Nockerl for two.

Restaurant Alpenhof im Casino (M/E, Bahnhofstrasse 74. Tel. 08821-59055) is run by the same owners as the Tonihof. There's an adequate restaurant with local dishes at moderate prices, and a smaller "Casino Stube" for people who are willing to pay for a top French meal.

Neither the international cuisine nor the service in the main dining room of the **Hotel Obermühle** (M, Mühlstrasse 22. Tel. 08821-7040) is exceptional, but in the same building is a small, plain, inexpensive restaurant called **Zum Mühlradl**, where you can go for pork and *Knödl*, and a local beer.

While driving to or from Lake Eibsee, stop for lunch or pastry at the terrace restaurant of **Haus Ingeborg** (Loisachstrasse 38, Granau. Tel. 08821-81856). For a more ambitious meal, try such local specialties as rainbow trout, roe deer with pears and cranberries, or roast wild boar with homemade dumplings.

Garmisch has many pleasant outdoor cafés where you can people-watch under a crowd of stars. In Garmisch, try the moderately priced Café-Konditorei Kronner on Achenfeldstrasse.

Lodging

Almost all hotels are low-roofed Alpine chalets with carved wood balconies. Ask for a room with a view.

There's some real cachet—no yodel stuff—at the century-old **Hotel Sonnenbichl** (E, Burgstrasse 97, Tel. 08821-7020) at the edge of town. If you want the Alpine Look, pack your lederhosen and move on; the Sonnenbichl is for those sophisticated international folks who feel at home in an Italianate marble foyer, and who appreciate an Old World hotel fed by new Arab money. The hotel's symbol is the peacock—could anything be more unBavarian? Facilities include a sauna, solarium, heated pool, tennis, and golf. The only drawbacks are the hotel's lack of privacy (it's close to the road), and the necessity of looking out over the traffic to see the distant mountains. Be sure to get an upstairs room with a mountain view; at these prices, you don't want to stare out at the parking lot.

Posthotel Partenkirchen (M/E, Ludwigstrasse 49. Tel. 08821-51067) is for those who want luxury Bavarian style. The eighteenth-century house was once a stopping place for postal carriages. Despite some allweather carpeting, it has managed to keep—and not overdo—its natural charm. There's lovely paneling and stuccowork, and some colorful antiques, including old painted chests and carved armoires. Ask for a room with a mountain view.

Obermühle (E, Mühlstrasse 22. Tel. 088821-7040) attracts a Best Western crowd. An old waterwheel turns outside to remind you of the hotel's antiquity—just in case you missed it in your traditionally furnished but standardized room. You need a car here, since you're on the edge of town, surrounded by lovely gardens.

Almenrausch-Edelweiss (M, 81 Garmisch-Partenkirchen, Kreuzstrasse 7. Tel. 08821-2527) is a family-run chalet guarded by a friendly dog named Toki. A kind of hairy industrial carpet sets the mood for the hallways, but rooms are cheerful in a grandmotherly sort of way.

Bernriederhof (M, von-Müller Strasse 12. Tel. 08821-71074) is a large old farmhouse with regional furnishings. A Romantik Hotel.

Gasthaus am Zierwald (8104 Grainau. Tel. 08821-8840) is a typical roadside chalet en route to Eibsee for those who want to be outside of town and closer to the mountains.

Roter Hahn (M, Bahnhofstrasse 44. Tel. 08821-54065) is a clean, adequate hotel for those who want to be near the train station and need a place to sleep.

Among the guesthouses, all relatively inexpensive, are **Haus Kornmül-ler** (Höllentalstrasse 36. Tel. 08821-3557); **Wilma Schwinghammer** (Münchner Strasse 8. Tel. 08821-56632) and **Gasthof Fraundorfer** (Ludwigstrasse 24. Tel. 08821-2176). **Haus Lilly** (Fran Maria Lechner, Zugspitzstrasse 20a. Tel. 08821-52600) is pretty basic, but Lilly is delight-ful. A good bet for couples with children, particularly room 3.

For Further Information

The **Tourist Office** (Verkehrsamt der Kurverwaltung) is at Bahnhof-strasse 34, near the train station. Tel. 08821-2570.

EXCURSIONS FROM GARMISCH-PARTENKIRCHEN

A must trip from Garmisch is to the three Royal Castles identified with Ludwig II: **Neuschwanstein, Hohenschwangau,** and **Linderhof.** You have a choice of two routes: a northern route through **Oberammergau,** and a southern route past **Linderhof.** The mountainous southern route is considerably more dramatic, and has the added perk of a trip to another country (Austria). Best bet is to take one route going, and the other back. If you plan to visit Linderhof, begin with the southern route so that you reach the castle early in the day; otherwise, you won't get there until after it's closed. The following itinerary takes you to the castles by this south-ern route, and returns you by the northern route. It's going to be a long day, so leave early in the morning, and don't expect to return to Garmisch till dark.

✤ ETTAL

Take **Route 23** north from **Garmisch-Partenkirchen** to Oberau, and continue about 3 miles to **Ettal.** The size of the abbey—now a boarding school—is extraordinary. It was founded by **Ludwig the Bavarian** in 1330, but wears an eighteenth-century Baroque dress.

The road splits past Ettal. The right fork (**Route 23**) continues north to Oberammergau. Take the left fork to **Linderhof.**

Dining

Ludwig der Bayer (M, Kaiser Ludwig Platz 10, Ettal. Tel. 08822-4637) is a hotel-restaurant in the center of town, not far from the abbey.

Stop for some yellow or green **Kloster Liqueur** produced by the monks—a liquid souvenir.

✤ *THE ROYAL CASTLES (Königsschlösser)*

Of the three castles, **Neuschwanstein** is the most impressive, **Linderhof** the least. But whether you have time to see one castle or three, it helps to know about the man whose life was intimately entwined with all of them—Ludwig II. It's important, too, to understand the symbolism of the swan, which you'll see so often as you tour the castles.

A Note on Ludwig II

Ludwig II was born in 1845 in **Nymphenburg Castle** (which you saw in Munich) but spent almost all his youth at his father's (Maximilian II's) castle, **Hohenschwangau**, in the Bavarian Alps. This was a fairy fortress, capturing the spirit of the Middle Ages, where Maximilian could escape the pressures of official life in Munich. The walls of Hohenschwangau were covered with paintings of the swan knight Lohengrin, and the young, impressionable Ludwig fell under their spell. Maximilian gave his son a Spartan education, seldom allowing him to see the real world of Munich. The boy turned his back on his stern father, and played not with soldiers but with puppets and dolls. His mother—one of the few women he ever saw—read him the Greek myths, including the story of how Zeus created swans from the waves.

When news came that his father was dying, Ludwig was absorbed in the text of Wagner's *Lohengrin*. The opera is based on a medieval German story of the knight Lohengrin, son of Parsifal, who sets off from the Castle of the Grail on the back of a swan to rescue the Princess Elsa. In the German legend, he saves her and is given her hand in marriage; but when she asks his name, in violation of a pledge, he must return to his castle, and the swan turns into Elsa's brother.

In 1864, at the age of eighteen, Ludwig became the king of Bavaria. One of his first royal wishes was to meet with the German composer Richard Wagner, who was at the time living at the Bayerischer Hof in Munich, in flight from his creditors. Ludwig had seen *Lohengrin* four years earlier and lived for the moment when he could meet its creator and help produce his plays. The fifty-one-year-old composer met the nineteen-year-old king at Hohenschwangau and thereafter became his soul mate, his confidant, his adviser.

Three years after assuming the throne, Ludwig became engaged to his cousin, **Princess Sophie of Bavaria,** a sister of the Austrian empress, Elizabeth. He is said never to have kissed her on the lips, only on the forehead, but he was wildly in love with her—why else would he spend his days rowing with her in a swan-shaped boat? And why else would he call her Elsa?

As the wedding day approached, Ludwig ordered his trousseau brocaded with scenes from *Lohengrin.* But then, at a ball for the royal couple, he rushed off to catch the last act of an opera without saying good-bye to anyone, including Sophie, and everyone knew the engagement was in trouble. Sophie, he had discovered, was only human. "When I marry, I want a Queen, a Mother for my country, not an imperious mistress," he explained later. But he never married. Instead, he flew back to Wagner. And on the ruins of an ancient castle near his father's, he decided to build an even grander castle of his own.

Neuschwanstein is a child's idea of a medieval knight's castle. It took seventeen years to build, but was never finished. As Ludwig got embroiled in hopeless wars, he withdrew more into himself and emptied his country's treasury to satisfy his fantasies. He began **Linderhof,** a Rococo pleasure palace with an artificial Blue Grotto in imitation of the one at Capri. He built **Herrenchiemsee** (which you won't be seeing), modeled on Versailles, on an island in the Chiemsee.

Eventually Ludwig was declared insane. When a commission came to take him away, he locked them up. Bismarck advised him to go to Munich and state his case before Parliament, but he was spiritually exhausted. All he could do was wait. Finally, in 1886, he was driven from Neuschwanstein to Berg Castle on Starnberg Lake. One of his favorite residences was turned into a prison, with barred windows and doors that opened only from without. On June 13, Ludwig and a Dr. von Gujdden took a stroll around the castle grounds followed by two guards. The deposed king returned, dined alone, then went to the window and surveyed the lake with a telescope. Later, he went for a second walk with the doctor, and dismissed the guards with a wave of his hand. Why they agreed to go, no one knows. When Ludwig and the doctor failed to return by seven, the entire staff went in search of them. Shortly after eleven the two men were found floating in the water, dead.

Did Ludwig commit suicide? Was he poisoned? In the stables of a nearby friend there were ten horses instead of two—was he trying to escape? Most important of all, was he truly insane, or merely the victim of a plot? After all, he was judged by physicians who never examined him. What was taken for madness may have been merely hypersensitivity. "If

I were a poet I might be able to reap praise by putting [my thoughts] into verse," Ludwig told an interviewer. "But the talent of expression was not given me, and so I must bear being laughed at, scorned at, and slandered. I am called a fool. Will God call me a fool when I am summoned before Him?"

The Bavarian people have always loved Ludwig, and if they could play God, even today, they would redeem him, or at least forgive him. An affront to him is an affront to their fierce sense of regional pride. In a workaday world, here was a man who played. In a land of beer and sausages, here was a man who dreamed. The Bavarians know that the final laugh is on those who condemned Ludwig, for the castles which almost bankrupted the royal treasury now bring fortunes in tourist revenues; and the money taken from the public coffers to support Wagner gave the world some of its most treasured music.

❧ LINDERHOF

The royal villa of Linderhof (1869–79) was once an annex of Ludwig's father's hunting lodge. It is said to have been inspired by the Petit Trianon—though, as one critic points out, it looks more like a small casino in southern France. Ludwig reportedly spent hours in the **Moorish Pavilion** —bought at the Paris Exhibition of 1867—playing the oriental potentate dressed in a bearskin. The **grotto** is a modern version of Aladdin's cave, where a rock moves back at the touch of a button. On an illuminated pond is a conch-shaped boat recalling the Venusberg episode in Wagner's opera *Tannhäuser.* More attractive than the house is the surrounding parkland—once the royal hunting grounds—with pools, Italian-villa-style waterfalls, and formal gardens with pyramid-shaped hedges.

The influence of the Bourbons is seen in the royal sun—symbol of Louis XIV—on the ceiling. In the ornate **Gobelin** or **Music Room,** notice how the Rococo wall paintings are meant to simulate tapestries. The **Hall of Mirrors** is a stage set for Ludwig's fantasies, in which nothing is what it seems. The **bedchamber** is a child's dream of luxury and opulence. Royal insignias, gilt-edged angels, and tapestries fill every inch of space, as if Ludwig were afraid of what lay beyond. Open April through September from 9 to 12:15 and 12:45 to 5; off-season, closes at 4.

✤ HOHENSCHWANGAU

From **Linderhof** drive 17 miles through Austria to **Reutte** and 8 miles north to **Füssen.** Follow signs east 2 miles to the castle. It's open April through September from 8:30 to 5:30; off-season, from 10 to 4.

Ludwig's father purchased the ruins of a twelfth-century castle and restored it in 1832–36. Ludwig spent most of his youth here; you can imagine him, a young child, staring up at the murals depicting scenes from medieval legends. What he saw must have encouraged his own romantic inclinations without satisfying them, for the young visionary built an even more fanciful castle of his own. Maximilian's castle, unlike his son's, looks almost livable—which is why visitors prefer Neuschwanstein.

Today, 14 rooms are furnished for public view. The **Authari Room** is where Wagner stayed; he never set foot in Neuschwanstein. The **Music Room** or **Room of the Hohenstaufen** contains the square maplewood piano on which Wagner played his works for Ludwig—who was an accomplished pianist himself. The **bedchamber** ceiling is painted to look like a night sky, with stars that could be made to light up. Through a window the king could watch through a telescope the work progressing at Neuschwanstein. In the **Hall of Heroes** is a bust of Ludwig by an American sculptor; the king posed for it in 1869.

✤ NEUSCHWANSTEIN

Bavarian *Kitsch*—that's how you'd describe Ludwig's castle. Yet in its own tacky, overstated way it has the purity of, say, Versailles, because it remains faithful to a single vision. As a nineteenth-century fortress, its bulwarks and its position on a mountain spur are wonderfully useless—which somehow makes the king's vision even grander.

Maximilian II had thought of building a castle here, too, on the ruins of an ancient family fortress, so in a sense Ludwig was merely carrying out his father's designs. In 1869, influenced by Wagner's operas, Ludwig asked the court stage designer, Christian Jank, to draw up plans. Only later did he consult an architect. What he got, therefore, was a stage set where he could play the role of Lohengrin.

The castle tour takes you through an artificial stalactite **cavern** that recalls Wagner's *Tannhäuser.* The **bedroom** is decorated with a young boy's dreams—fourteen sculptors worked four and a half years to build it. The curtains and coverings are light Bavarian blue—Ludwig's favorite color. Throughout, the upper walls are covered with paintings from a world of fantasy—windows into a world of the mind. There's something sadly appropriate about the **Oriental Throne Room** without a throne. Ludwig lived in his castle only 102 days, and drowned before the gold-and-ivory chair could be completed.

The castle is open April through September from 8:30 to 5:30; off-season, from 10 to 4. After the tour, take an hour's walk (round trip) to the **Pöllat Gorge** and stand on the same bridge *(Marienbrüke)* across the ravine where Ludwig II came at night to look up at his empty castle.

✤ *WIES CHURCH*

Returning to **Garmisch-Partenkirchen** by the northern route, drive north 15 miles on **Route 17**, about 2 miles past **Steingaden**, and look for signs on the right to **Wies**. A 1½-mile side trip (one way) takes you to this Baroque masterpiece. At last word it was closed for restorations—low-flying Air Force planes were weakening its foundations. The pilgrimage church (1746–54) is the work of the celebrated Baroque architect, **Dominikus Zimmerman**. The simple exterior is in marked contrast to the intensely rich interior. There's a similar contrast between the plain lower walls—symbolizing the Earth—and the rich stucco work of the "heavens." The pulpit and organ loft are high points of Rococo art in southern Germany.

✤ *OBERAMMERGAU*

Return to **Route 17** and turn right (east) toward **Echelsbach Bridge** (4 miles), 250-feet above the River Ammer. Head south on **Route 23**, through **Saulgrub** to **Oberammergau** (11 miles), a town famous for its Passion Play. When a devastating plague stopped short of the town in 1636, the villagers vowed to perform the play every ten years. The first took place in 1634. In 1980 some 530,000 visitors watched more than a hundred day-long performances during the summer months, performed by 1,100 local residents—about one villager in five. The next performance is in 1990. When villagers are not acting out the Passion of Christ they are turning out wood-carvings in their colorful painted homes. The **Heimat Museum** has a large collection of handmade Christmas crèches (nativity scenes).

EN ROUTE: From ETTAL to GARMISCH-PARTENKIRCHEN

It's 10 miles on **Route 23** from Ettal back to **Garmisch-Partenkirchen** —where your trip ends. From here, most of you will follow one of four routes:

1. Return to Munich and fly back home.

2. Drive to Salzburg, Austria, and follow the Austrian itinerary described below. (The most scenic route is south from **Garmisch-Partenkirchen** through the lovely village of **Mittenwald** to **Innsbruck.**)

3. Drive to **Zurich** for a tour of Switzerland. (If you're going to Switzerland, don't return to Garmisch-Partenkirchen, but continue from the Royal Castles to **Konstanz.**)

4. Return to Frankfurt through the **Black Forest** and fly home.

Austria

❧ *Salzburg to Vienna*

MAJOR ATTRACTIONS

• The imperial city of Vienna, home of the Spanish Riding School, the world-famous Choir Boys, and a Baroque confection of music and art.

• The Wachau Valley, the most romantic stretch of the Danube, with magnificent abbeys and castles overlooking terraced vineyards and medieval towns.

• Salzburg, a city of historic beauty and natural charm—an ideal stage set for the world-famous music festival.

• The Lake Country, a natural setting of sparkling blue lakes and wooded hills.

INTRODUCTION

The itinerary takes you on the most scenic and historic route from Salzburg to Vienna, with stops in the Lake Country and along the most romantic stretch of the Danube. It's a trip that lets you experience the many sides of Austria—and probably also the many sides of yourself.

Music lovers can hear the best throughout the year, not just in modern concert halls but in Baroque palaces under stucco skies filled with saints and angels. Art and history lovers can trace seven centuries of Habsburg rule in the churches and palaces of Vienna. Photographers and nature lovers can sail the lakes or hike the wooded hills of the Lake Country.

Anyone who appreciates beauty will fall in love with the Wachau, a river valley as enchanting as the Rhine.

You'll begin with the sound of music in Salzburg, where Mozart was born, and then relax in the Lake Country. After exploring the magnificent Baroque abbeys of St. Florian and Melk, you'll wander through the gentle, rolling farmland of the Mühlviertel. From here you'll drive or sail through the romantic Wachau Valley, past crumbling castles, terraced vineyards, and walled medieval towns. After the slow, dreamy pace of the Danube, you'll be ready for Vienna, the most monumental city in the world.

THE MAIN ROUTE (with minimum overnight stays)

3–5 Days

One night: Salzburg
Two nights: Vienna
One night: Dürnstein

5–7 Days

Two nights: Salzburg
Two nights: Dürnstein
Two nights: Lake Country

7–14 Days

Two nights: Vienna
Two nights: Lake Country
Two nights: Dürnstein
Four Nights: Vienna

GETTING AROUND

Getting to Austria

For the 3 to 5-day trip, fly to and from Vienna. **ALIA Royal Jordanian Airlines** (ALIA, 535 Fifth Avenue, New York, N.Y. 10017. Tel. 212/949-0077) flies nonstop to Vienna from New York and Chicago, and direct from Los Angeles. **Pan Am** flies direct to Vienna from New York.

For the 5 to 7- or 7 to 14-day trips, fly to Munich and return home from Vienna. (If you need to arrive and depart from the same European airport, end your trip with a train ride from Vienna back to Munich.) Germany's reliable airline, Lufthansa, flies nonstop from New York and

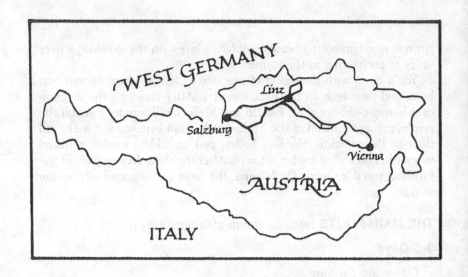

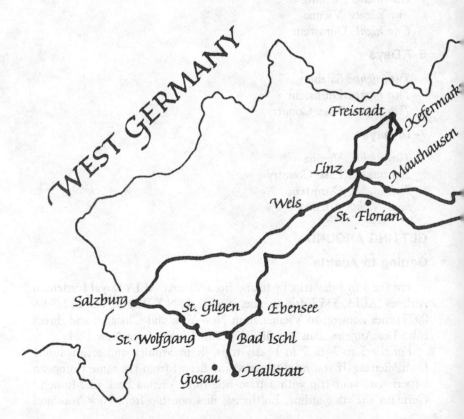

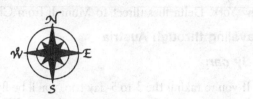

Chicago to Munich. Lufthansa also flies to Munich via Frankfurt from San Francisco, Los Angeles, Dallas, Houston, Philadelphia, Boston, Miami, and Atlanta. Pan Am and TWA fly nonstop to Munich from New York. Delta flies direct to Munich from Chicago.

Traveling through Austria

By car:

If you're taking the 3 to 5-day trip, you'll be flying direct to Vienna. It makes no sense to rent a car here: parking is difficult and public transportation is good. Rent a car only for the visit to Melk and the Wachau Valley—preferably at the end of the trip, when you can return the car to the airport.

If you're taking the 5 to 7- or 7 to 14-day trip, fly direct to Munich and then either rent a car or take the train to Salzburg, where your trip begins. The train from Munich to Salzburg takes 90 minutes. The drive takes 2 to 3 hours. After seeing Salzburg, drive to Vienna and return your car at the Vienna airport on your way home.

Is it better to rent your car in Munich or in Salzburg? If money is no issue and you can pick up the car at the Munich airport and return it at the Vienna airport, do so. Otherwise, catch a train directly from Munich to Salzburg and pick up your car in Salzburg when you're ready to leave. The bus ride from Munich's airport to the city train station takes 30 to 45 minutes.

If you have to pick up and return your car from the same location, fly to Vienna, drive directly to Salzburg on A1 (a 3-hour trip), and then follow the itinerary below back to Vienna. You can also fly to Munich, follow the itinerary to Vienna and then drive directly back to Munich.

By public transportation:

You can follow essentially the same itinerary by car or by a combination of bus, train, and boat. What you'll miss traveling by public transportation are a few towns in the Lake District and the side trip to Mühlviertel.

Austrian Rail Passes, sold at train stations, are good for reduced rates on trains and Danube cruises.

If you're taking the 3 to 5-day trip, which begins in Vienna, you have three ways to reach Melk and the Wachau Valley:

1. Join an escorted tour, which can be arranged through any hotel or

travel agency in Vienna. Make sure the tour includes a boat ride between Melk and Dürnstein.

2. Take a Danube cruise from Vienna to Melk; tour the abbey; take the train back to Dürnstein; spend the night in Dürnstein, and then take a train or boat back to Vienna. You can't take the steamship round trip because it arrives in Melk at 3:50 P.M. and doesn't return until 3:20 the next afternoon. Your nights away from Vienna should be spent not in Melk but in Dürnstein.

3. The third and best alternative is to take the train from Vienna to Melk; visit Melk Abbey; take the steamship back to Dürnstein; spend the night in Dürnstein, and then take either the train or boat back to Vienna.

The evening sail from Dürnstein back to Vienna takes 4 hours. It's not nearly as scenic as the trip along the Wachau, so if you're pressed for time, take the train instead.

Make sure you arrive in Melk in time to tour the Abbey, which closes at 4 or 5 P.M., depending on the season. Melk has two docks, one for the local Wachau ferry, and one for the ship to Vienna. If you want to sail directly back to Vienna, ask a cab driver to take you to the Schiffahrt-Wien. Both ferries stop at Dürnstein, where you'll be spending the night.

The local ferries leave Melk in season at 9, 12:30, 2:30 and 6. The trip from Melk to Dürnstein, along the most beautiful stretch of the Danube, takes under 2 hours. (Check current schedules.)

Combination train/ship tickets can be purchased through travel agencies or directly from the First Danube Steamship Company, DDSG Travel Dept., A-1021 Vienna, Handelskai 265. Tel. 266536-443 or 444.

If you're taking the 5 to 7-day trip, you'll be flying to Munich. Take the 30 to 45-minute bus ride from the airport to the train station. The ride to Salzburg takes 90 minutes. After touring Salzburg, take the 4-hour train ride to Melk. (One train leaves Salzburg at 9:57 A.M. and arrives at Melk at 1:41 P.M.) For the boat and train ride along the Danube, see the 3 to 5-day trip above.

If you're taking the 7 to 14-day trip, you'll also be flying to Munich. It's a 30 to 45-minute bus ride from the airport to the train station, and a 90-minute train trip to Salzburg. After touring Salzburg, take the train or bus to Hallstatt in the Lake Country. Both take about 90 minutes, plus connecting time. A boat meets the train at the northern end of Hallstatt Lake *(Hallstätter See)* and brings you to the village of Hallstatt. If bus or train connections are poor, join an excursion bus direct from Salzburg to Hallstatt. Tickets can be purchased through hotels and tourist offices in Salzburg. From Hallstatt, return by bus or train to Salzburg.

St. Florian is difficult to reach from Salzburg by train, so save the Abbey for another trip, and take the train direct from Salzburg to Melk. If you're determined to visit St. Florian, however, take the train from Salzburg to Linz and then change to a local train to Asten-St. Florian. After visiting St. Florian, return to Linz and continue on the train to Melk. For the boat and train ride from Melk to Vienna, see the 3 to 5-day trip on pages 160–66.

SPECIAL EVENTS

Late July–late August: Salzburg Summer Festival, an international festival of concerts, opera and ballet.

Late May–late June: Vienna Music Festival, with concerts in Baroque palaces and gardens.

A NOTE ON SHOPPING

For purchases over 1,000 schillings (about $60), request a refund on the Value Added Tax (VAT) when you leave the country. Ask for special forms to be filled out at shops where purchases are made.

Things to buy in Salzburg: folk costumes (Lederhosen and dirndls), leather goods, sporting equipment, pottery and candles. *In Vienna:* porcelain, crystal, petit point, leather goods, folk costumes, local handicrafts and antiques.

THINGS TO SEE AND DO WITH CHILDREN

In Salzburg: the Glockenspiel (carillon); the catacombs at St. Peter's; the torture chamber in the fortress; the mummified Ice Age rhinoceros in the Natural History Museum; Hellbrunn, especially the mechanical theater; and above all, the Marionettentheater.

In the Lake District: Windsurfing, swimming, fishing, and boating on the lakes.

In the Abbey of St. Florian: the six thousand skeletons in the crypt.

Along the Wachau: the ramparts of Aggstein Castle; bike riding along the less-traveled southern route (bikes can be rented at train stations in Melk and Krems and returned to these or other stations).

In Vienna: The children's armor collection in the Neue Burg; the Prater amusement park, particularly the Ferris wheel; the zoo; the royal coaches in the Wagenburg coach house outside Schönbrunn Palace; the walk to the top of St. Stephen's; a Sunday morning concert by the Vienna Choir Boys; a training session or performance of the Lippizaner horses at the Spanish Riding School. For babysitters, contact the Austrian Student Service Society, IV, Mühlgasse 20. Tel. 0222-573543 or 573525.

A NOTE ON ART AND ARCHITECTURE

On your trip you'll be seeing the greatest examples of Austrian Baroque: **Salzburg Cathedral** (very early Baroque); the abbeys of **St. Florian** and **Melk**, and the **Karlskirche** in Vienna. The Baroque style was imported from France and Italy, but it expressed architecturally the joy the Austrians felt after their triumph over the Turks in 1683. It was also the art of the Counter-Reformation—a form of visual propaganda to win Catholic Austrians back to the Mother Church by a direct appeal to the senses. It's hard to believe today that a person could get very close to God in such a worldly setting, yet each age approaches God in its own way.

In Austrian Baroque churches, the original Gothic columns direct your eye both upward to God and forward to the altar; but the flowing lines and ornate decorations force your eye to stop along the way, almost as if you were being diverted by this world on your way to the next.

Renaissance architects worked on the Platonic assumption that there was an order in the universe which a building could capture by following certain rules—a certain ideal relationship, say, between the width of a column and its height. What the Baroque artist tried to do was not to satisfy some ideal form of beauty, but to satisfy the direct, emotional needs of the worshipper. Perhaps that's why Renaissance art has always belonged to the cultivated minority, while Baroque belongs to the masses.

Some of you will dismiss these Baroque churches as spiritual ballrooms —as ill suited for repentance as for salvation. But this would miss the essence of Baroque, which is to bring heaven down to earth, and to hold out an image of joy unsullied by guilt or sin. The Baroque church was meant to be God's castle. Created in the spirit of the age, heaven became a dwelling place for God's appointed, the Habsburg kings and queens. Overwhelmed by such splendid surroundings, worshippers became royal, too.

Try to remember the names of the three great Baroque architects— you'll be seeing their major works along the route: **Johann Bernhard Fischer von Erlach** (1656–1723): Karlskirche (Vienna), University Church (Salzburg). **Johann Lukas von Hildebrandt** (1668–1745): Upper and Lower Belvedere (Vienna). **Jakob Prandtauer** (1660–1726): Abbeys of St. Florian and Melk.

A NOTE ON DINING

Restaurants are rated for two: E (expensive, over $65); M (moderate, $25 to $65); I (inexpensive, under $25).

EMERGENCIES

Salzburg. *U.S. Consulate:* Giselakai 51. Tel. 0662-28601. *Ambulance and Police:* Tel. 0662-133.

Vienna. *U.S. Consulate:* Friedrich Schmidtplatz 2. Tel. 0222-1315511. *American Medical Society of Vienna:* Lazarettgasse 13. Tel. 0222-424568. *Ambulance and Police:* Tel. 0222-133.

FOR FURTHER INFORMATION

Austrian National Tourist Office. *New York:* 500 Fifth Avenue, New York, N.Y. 10110. Tel. 212/944-6880. *Los Angeles:* 11610 Wilshire Boulevard, Los Angeles, Cal. 90010. Tel. 213/477-3332. *Houston:* 4800 San Felipe, Houston, Tex. 77056. Tel. 713/850-8888. *Chicago:* 500 North Michigan Avenue, Suite 544, Chicago, Ill. Tel. 312/644-5556.

THE ITINERARY

✤ *SALZBURG*

Vienna absorbs its tourists; Salzburg exists for them. Vienna spreads out; Salzburg nestles. Vienna acknowledges the seasons; Salzburg opens its arms to them. Vienna is ethnically diverse; Salzburg is so homogeneous that Hitler chose it as the headquarters for his Thousand Year Reich.

Like Vienna, Salzburg was redone in Baroque dress. Both cities are monumental, but Salzburg, with its clusters of ancient homes and narrow, cobbled streets, has a much more intimate, medieval feeling to it.

When visitors speak of Salzburg they're referring not to the modern town but to Old Salzburg, nestled between the Salzach River and the cliffs of Mönchsberg and the Hohensalzburg fortress. It's difficult not to love Old Salzburg—its setting is idyllic, its streets safe and clean, its people friendly and polite. It is a show town, a pretty stage set with no apparent purpose but to entertain its paying guests. During the day everything is yours to peek into, buy, listen to and explore—but by 11 at night all the shutters are closed and you can hear your footsteps echoing on the empty squares. There is something unreal about all this, but who needs reality on a vacation?

You'll find yourselves drawn down picturesque alleys, exploring monuments to this world and the next. Most everything is within walking distance: the Baroque churches, the humble house where Mozart was born, the shopping streets with wrought-iron signs as intricate as lacework. Ideally, you should come during the summer music festival, but there are concerts all year long, performed in a Baroque setting as sumptuous as any in the world.

Things to See and Do

• The **cathedral** (Dom) is the physical and spiritual center of the town, so let's begin here. A Romanesque cathedral once stood on this spot, but Archbishop **Wolf Dietrich** either set fire to it or did nothing to stop it from burning down. He wanted the cathedral to be another St. Peter's, but died before its completion. Though its interior is influenced by St. Peter's, particularly in its geometric use of space, it's more closely modeled on Rome's Il Gesù.

Wolf Dietrich was the most notorious of the prince-archbishops who ruled Salzburg and the surrounding territory for over a thousand years, controlling everything from breweries to the salvation of souls. When he became archbishop in 1587, he wasn't yet ordained. Educated in Rome, he shared with Alberti and Palladio the notion that a house of worship should stand isolated on a beautiful square; and so he tore down much of the medieval city and built Italian-style piazzas with lovely fountains, both around the cathedral and around the **Residenz**, where he planned to live.

Living with Wolf Dietrich, probably out of wedlock, was a Jewish woman named Salome Alt, who bore him fifteen children. She tolerated his extravagances more than the townspeople, who rose up and imprisoned him in the **Hohensalzburg**—a fortress built, ironically, to protect archbishops from the people. When Wolf Dietrich died five years later, his only finished project was his mausoleum, which you can see in St. Sebastian's Cemetery, not far from the tombs of Mozart's wife and father.

After Wolf Dietrich came Archbishop **Markus Sittikus**, a man who apparently played as hard as he prayed, building a fun palace called **Hellbrunn** and renaming Salome's castle **Mirabell** after one of his own mistresses.

The last of the three great archbishops who gave Salzburg the face it wears today was **Paris Lodron** (1619–53), who completed the Residenz and a more modest version of the cathedral in Italian Mannerist style. Though he was a more gentle, peace-loving fellow than his predecessors, he was accompanied wherever he went by thirty personal guards, fourteen lords chamberlain carrying enormous gold keys, and a dozen children of the nobility dressed in red velvet.

It was Napoleon who put an end to the line of prince-archbishops; should we be grateful to him? The rulers of Salzburg were often selfish autocrats who led extravagant lives at the expense of their people, yet they loved art and created beauty; can they be forgiven? (Salzburg still has an archbishop, but his domain is limited to matters of the spirit.)

The cathedral's bronze doors and altar are postwar. To the left of the entrance is the baptismal font in which Mozart was christened in 1756. In the crypt is the grave of an early Irish bishop named **Virgil** who created waves twelve centuries ago by insisting that the world was round. In the treasury are Baroque chalices, Romanesque miters, and a traveling flask belonging to the late-seventh-century priest, **Rupert of Worms**. Rupert founded **St. Peter's** Church, which you'll be visiting soon.

• Head south, away from the river, and cross **Kapitelplatz**. The square has an eighteenth-century drinking trough for horses in the shape of a monumental fountain—a reminder that some prince-archbishops may have treated their animals better than their subjects. Walk to the funicular that goes to the **Hohensalzburg**. Buy a one-way ticket. This fortress—one of the best-preserved medieval structures in the world—gets top billing in Salzburg, so go in the morning to beat the lines. (Tours begin at 9 A.M.) The Hohensalzburg was built to protect the prince-archbishops, and was virtually impregnable. The fourth-floor apartments offer fine examples of Late Gothic secular architecture, but there's little else that's memorable on the tour, so if lines are long, pass it up, and admire the breathtaking view of Salzburg.

• Near the fortress is **Nonnberg Convent**, which has a late-fourteenth-century church. It was while staying here that Maria heard the sound of music, or at least the voice of Baron George von Trapp. The real Maria, according to a delightful account in *Salzburg: A Portrait*, lost both parents at age nine and was turned over to an uncle who beat her and put her in an asylum. She escaped to Salzburg and asked to be placed in the strictest convent. While at Nonnberg, she was sent to care for the Baron's children, fell in love with him, and in 1938 escaped with him to the United States. After *The Sound of Music* was released, the Von Trapps bought six hundred acres in Vermont and turned a farmhouse into a

Salzburg-type chalet with a Trapp Family gift shop selling Trapp family postcards. The real Von Trapps lived not in Leopoldskron Castle, as the film suggests, but in a Salzburg suburb. A baroness much sturdier than Julie Andrews married George von Trapp, not in the church in Mondsee but in the convent; and if they had followed the mountain route they took in the movie they would have ended up in Germany. The people of Salzburg don't appreciate songs like "Do Re Mi," which insult their religiously inspired folk melodies; but this doesn't stop them from cheerfully exploiting the film for every tourist dollar they can get—much as they exploit Mozart, who was born here but fled to Vienna.

• Stay on the ridge above the city and enjoy a delightful 30-minute walk through parklands to the **Winkler Café**. (If you make this walk in reverse, starting at the Winkler Café, you'll have a very steep climb to the fortress.) The Winkler terrace is overgrown with tourists, but is still a scenic spot for coffee or lunch. A more peaceful and elegant alternative is the terrace at the **Mönchstein Hotel**, a 10-minute walk farther along the bluff.

• From the Winkler, take the elevator back down to the town and wander along **Getreidegasse**, the main shopping street. Here and on **Judengasse**, the continuation of Getreidegasse, you can buy dirndls, needlework, leather goods, candles, and ski equipment.

• At Getreidegasse 9 is the humble apartment, now a museum, where Johannes Chrysostomus Wolfgangus Theophilus (Amadeus) Mozart was born in 1756. Mozart's clavichord is here; you can imagine his father Leopold standing over him while he played. When Mozart was four, a court musician named Andreas Schatner came here with a friend to play trios with Leopold. Wolfgang begged to play the violin, but Leopold said no: the boy had never taken a lesson in his life. Schatner convinced Leopold to let Wolfgang try. The four-year-old took up the same violin you see on display here and played the piece so perfectly that Schatner could not compete with him, and Leopold was reduced to tears.

At age six, when most children were reading nursery rhymes, Wolfgang was brought to Vienna, where he performed for Maria Theresa at Schönbrunn Palace. Six years later the Emperor commissioned him to write an opera. Mozart's problems with Salzburg began in 1771 when a new archbishop tried to limit what he called Mozart's "begging expeditions" across Europe. What the archbishop really wanted was a less brilliant, less ambitious court musician—someone content to fulfill his obligations at court. Mozart, in turn, felt unappreciated in provincial

Salzburg, where "the audience is all tables and chairs." Eventually he left Salzburg for good.

In 1890 Mozart's fame was sweetened by the arrival of **Mozartkugeln (Mozart balls)**—pistachio-flavored marzipan rolled in nougat cream and dipped in dark chocolate; you can buy them anywhere along Getreidegasse. The factory at Mirabell turns out 150,000 of these tin-wrapped morsels every day; look for the word *echte,* which distinguishes them from the competition.

• Next stop are the **catacombs** of St. Peter's Church. If you want to trace Salzburg's history through its monuments, you should begin not at the cathedral or fortress, but here. A landslide in 1669 killed two hundred people and revealed these crude stone chambers where the early Christians came to pray as early as A.D. 200. On the 20-minute tour you can try to imagine the faith of these early believers, who prayed in secret and died for their beliefs. Some two centuries later a Christian church was built nearby. In the seventh century, **Rupert of Worms** poured the church's profits from salt mining into the monastery and Church of St. Peter. Salzburg (which means "castle of salt") thus began life as a monastic settlement, long before the era of the prince-archbishops. The secular town, where employees of the monastery lived, grew up along the river. You'll get a sense of these early days when you look at the massive Romanesque walls of the church and compare them to the eighteenth-century Baroque interior. It was here in St. Peter's that Mozart first performed his C Minor Mass, with his wife singing solo soprano. Nearby is a peaceful seventeenth-century cemetery where anyone would be happy to spend eternity. The seven old iron crosses belonged to the family of a stonemason named Stumpfegger who died at age seventy-nine after burying six wives.

• You can trace the history of Western architecture in the nearby **Church of the Franciscans** (Franziskanerkirche). Stand near the back and let the massive Romanesque column pull your eyes forward to the Baroque altar. The effect is that of standing in the fourteenth-century and looking toward the eighteenth; of standing in a shaded forest and staring out at a distant sunlit clearing in the woods. The Gothic choir was begun by the Tyrolean wood sculptor **Michael Pacher,** whose work you'll see again in St. Wolfgang. He worked on the High Altar, too; but then **Fischer von Erlach,** the greatest of all Austrian Baroque architects, was called in, and put Pacher's gentle madonna in a Baroque heaven. Von Erlach's other masterpiece in Salzburg is the **University Church** (Kollegienkirche).

• To understand the worldly power of the prince-archbishops, tour the 180-room, Renaissance-style **Residenz**. The staircase, commissioned by Wolf Dietrich, was built to be ascended on horseback. The cathedral, St. Peter's, and the Church of the Franciscans were all so close to the archbishop's home that he could commute from palace to pulpit without stepping outdoors.

• Across the **Residenzplatz** is the **New Building** (Neugebäude), which Wolf Dietrich began in 1590 for visiting royalty. Climb up to see the **Glockenspiel** (carillon) in action. It came broken from Antwerp in 1695 and is still slightly off-key.

• If you've had enough walking for a day, rent a **Fiaker**—a horse-drawn carriage—and clipclop around town.

• In the early evening, cross over the Salzach River, turn left, and enjoy a delightful walk or bike ride along the water.

• The same walk will take you at another time to (1) the **Mozarteum**, (2) **Mirabell**, and (3) the **Marionettentheater**.

The **Mozarteum** has two concert halls and a one-room summer house imported from Vienna where Mozart supposedly wrote *The Magic Flute*.

Mirabell was the palace Wolf Dietrich built for Salome. Because of an early-nineteenth-century fire, little remains of the Baroque alterations except for the **Marble Room** upstairs and the playful white marble staircase, where stubby-legged cherubs ride the waves. The gardens, left as Wolf Dietrich designed them, are a delightful place to doze or sunbathe. Archbishop Franz Anton von Harrach was partial to dwarfs and commissioned the squat, hunchbacked marble figures in the **Dwarf Garden**.

The elegant dining hall of the ninety-year-old Hotel Mirabell is the home of the famous **Salzburger Marionettentheater**. Holography—the art of the laser—creates the illusion of three-dimensional sets for abbreviated, taped performances of *The Magic Flute, Die Fledermaus,* and other famous operas. *The Nutcracker* uses more than a hundred lifelike puppets. Performances are in a sense more realistic than live opera, for there are no actors behind the masks, no real people standing between the characters and our vision of whom they should be.

• A few miles south of town is **Hellbrunn**, the pleasure palace of Archbishop Markus Sittikus. It was apparently built in 1612 for Madame de Mabon, the wife of the captain of the guard; look for her likeness in the **Orpheus Grotto**, wearing a portrait of Sittikus around her neck. The archbishop had a child's fascination with water, and a child's sense of play. The stone dining table, for instance, has a trough down the center to cool wine, and holes in the benches where jets of icy water drenched unsuspecting guests. The warbling in the **Birdsong Grotto** is created by water pressure. In the **Neptune Grotto** is a Groucho Marx-type figure who, when his mouth fills with water, sticks out his tongue and rolls his eyes.

Dining

Alt Salzburg (E, Sigmundsplatz 2. Tel. 0662-41476) has several small, relatively elegant dining rooms. It has one of the best reputations in town, particularly for its Tafelspitz (boiled beef), lamb, and salads, but quality can be uneven.

Salzburg Sheraton Hotel (E, Auerspergstrasse 4. Tel. 0662-793210) has a certain charm and taste, which is carried over into its first-class restaurant, **Mirabell**. There are familiar international dishes for the unadventurous, and delicious local specialties such as Tafelspitz (boiled beef) and Salzburger Nockerl (a kind of sweet soufflé).

If you're staying at the **Österreichischer Hof** (E, Schwarzstrasse 5–7. Tel. 0662-72541), you have a choice of two fine restaurants, the **Salzach Grill** and the **Salzach Keller**, both serving a wonderful Fogosch (a Hungarian fish) and a tasty mixed grill.

Zum Eulenspiegel (M, Hagenauerplatz 2) is a three-story restaurant opposite the house where Mozart was born. It has a fun, tavernlike atmosphere for hungry sightseers.

Peterskeller (M, near the cathedral) and **Moserstuben** (M, around the corner, in the very heart of the old town) are both well known—too well known, some would say. Regional dishes include duckling roasted with fresh mushrooms, and local fish—trout, carp, and pike. A portion of roast suckling pig with Semmelknödel and a warm cabbage-and-bacon salad is always something special. The **Peterskeller** has historic associations and still belongs to the monks.

Mozartkugel (M, also on Schwarzstrasse, near the Österreichischer Hof) is a great place for afternoon coffee and pastries. Ask for a Dobos torte—the best you'll ever have.

For a morning or afternoon coffee break along one of the narrow, winding streets near Getreidegasse, stop at the cozy **Kaffee-Häferl**. Of the other well-known coffeehouses, **Ratzka** (Imbergstrasse 45. Tel. 0662-70919) has the best pastries, including Marillenknödel, petit fours, and tarts with fresh fruits. At **Tomaselli** (M, Alter Markt 9. Tel. 0662-44488) the coffee could be better, the cake fresher, and the waiters more polite, but you haven't been to Salzburg (some say) until you've been here. **Schatz Konditorei** (Schatz Durchhaus, Getreidegasse 3. Tel. 0662-

42792) is a dollhouse of a pastry shop, serving Mozartkugeln, cakes with candied fruit, and Krapferln.

Lodging

Of the expensive, first-class hotels, stay at the **Mönchstein** (E, Mönchsberg 26. Tel. 06222-41363); the **Österreichischer Hof** (E, Schwarzstrasse 5–7. Tel. 06222-72541); or the **Goldener Hirsch** (E, Getreidegasse 7. Tel. 06222-41511). The **Mönchstein** is a castle in a peaceful garden overlooking the city. Filled with serious antiques and softened with dark wood paneling, it has more the atmosphere of a private residence than of a hotel. Some of the 16 rooms are exquisite, others small and tasteless. Room 20 is a good bet; so is 23, if you like pink. Avoid 34. The **Österreichischer Hof** is a tasteful, international-style hotel that makes up in comfort what it lacks in charm. Try for an upstairs room overlooking the river. The **Goldener Hirsch**, an 800-year-old house with rag rugs and old painted chests, is a young American's idea of what a small, charming Austrian inn should be. It's just off the main street, which is a plus or minus, depending on how close to center city you want to be.

A less expensive, four-star hotel is the **Kasererbräu** (E/M, Kaigasse 33. Tel. 06222-42406). Keep your head up so you can ignore the carpets and appreciate the lovely old painted furniture and ornate armoires. Request a room with antiques.

Other friendly hotels include **Weisse Taube** (E/M, Kaigasse 9. Tel. 06222-42406); **Ente** (M, Goldgasse 10. Tel. 06222-45622/23); and **Vier Jahreszeiten** (M, Hubert-Sattlergasse 12. Tel. 06222-72408).

For Further Information

The **Tourist Bureau** (Mozartplatz 5. Tel. 06222-47568) is on the square between the Residenzplatz and the river. To get there, face the Glockenspiel, turn left, and walk to the next square. **American Express** is next door at number 4. There's another **Tourist Office** in the train station *(Hauptbahnhof)*. Tel. 06222-71712.

❧ THE LAKE COUNTRY

East of Salzburg is the **Salzkammergut**, a land of sparkling blue lakes and green mountains, where you can swim, boat, fish, or simply slow down to the pace of the season. This is a popular tourist area, but a short stroll or sail will take you away from the crowds and leave you in the company of birds and whispering pines.

Salt *(Salz)* was mined here for at least 1,500 years before the Romans came, and was the principal source of wealth for the prince-archbishops of Salzburg. Since the managers permitted no visitors, it remained a sealed domain. The situation changed when Emperor Franz Josef (1867–1916) moved his summer court to Bad Ischl. Great families soon moved in and built their estates overlooking the lakes. Painters drew postcards of the Lake Country, and soon the region became one of the most popular resort areas in the country.

◈ LAKE FUSCHL (Fuschlsee)

How to Get There. From Salzburg, take Route 158 15 miles to Lake Fuschl.

Dining and Lodging

Overlooking this delightful lake is an elegant sixteenth-century hotel-castle, **Schloss Fuschl** (E, A-5322 Hof bei Salzburg, Fuschlsee. Tel. 06229-253). This deluxe Relais & Châteaux property has tennis courts, a pool, and a private beach. It's only 15 miles from Salzburg, so consider staying here while touring the city, or stopping for lunch. No luncheon setting could be lovelier than the terrace above the lake.

◈ ST. GILGEN

How to Get There. Continue on Route 158 5 miles to St. Gilgen, where Mozart's mother was born.

Dining

Nannerl (M, St. Gilgen, Tel. 06227-368) is a good café and patisserie for snacks or lunch.

◈ ST. WOLFGANG

How to Get There. Continue south on Route 158 along the southern shore of Lake Wolfgang (Wolfgangsee). Either leave your car at Gschwent, near the eastern end of the lake, and take the ferry; or drive to Strobl, turn left, and head back up the western side of the lake about 3.5 miles. The boat trip is the best part of a visit to St. Wolfgang, so if time permits, take the ferry, checking the schedule the night before.

From the ferry landing at St. Wolfgang, walk to the **Parish Church,** wander down narrow lanes, lunch on a terrace overlooking the lake, rent a rowboat, and then enjoy a peaceful boat ride back to your car. The drawing cards of St. Wolfgang are the lake view and **Michael Pacher's altarpiece** in the sixteenth-century **Parish Church,** one of the most famous Gothic wood carvings in the world. The work is done with such detail that you can see the stitches in the Virgin's robes. Perspective had just been mastered in 1481, and Pacher delights in it like a child who has just learned to walk. Give thanks to the artist who sculpted the Baroque side altar; he was commissioned to update Pacher's work in Baroque style and deliberately made it the wrong size so that the original would not be replaced.

Dining and Lodging

The pilgrims who visited St. Wolfgang seven centuries ago have been replaced by busloads of tourists who during the day saunter in and out of the famous **White Horse Inn** (E/M, Hotel Weisses Rössl. Tel. 06138-2306). Rooms are clean and comfortable, but renovations have eclipsed much of the hotel's natural charm. Request a room with traditional furnishings and a balcony overlooking the lake.

The best restaurant in town is **Lachsen** (M, St. Wolfgang. Tel. 06138-2432).

✤ BAD ISCHL

How to Get There. Continue east about 12 miles on **Route 158** to Bad Ischl.

From May through September take the 60-minute tour of **Kaiservilla,** where Emperor Franz Josef held his summer court. His bedroom, with an iron bedstead, plain pine wardrobe, and uncomfortable armchair, is simplicity itself and reflects the emperor's austere tastes. He was a great hunter who shot selectively, protecting the breeds of deer. His nephew, Franz Ferdinand—the one shot at Sarajevo, precipitating World War I—was not permitted to hunt here because of his passion for indiscriminate slaughter. As you stand in the emperor's bedroom, think of him as a man so set in his Imperial ways that he refused to carry money or speak on the phone—a man who drove in a car only once, as a gesture to Edward VII of England, who came here to offer the emperor an alliance with Britain if Austria-Hungary would agree to break with Germany. If only Edward VII had been more persuasive or Franz Josef less obstinate—"You must not forget that I am a German prince," he said—World War I might have been averted.

Dining

Cafe Zauner (M, Bad Ischl. Tel. 06132-3310 or 3522) is world renowned for its pastries, particularly Zaunerstollen. For a complete meal, try Weinhaus Attwenger (M, Tel. 06132-3327).

❖ HALLSTATT

How to Get There. From Bad Ischl take Route 145 south about 10 miles and make a right turn on Route 166. Hallstatt is about 7 miles farther south along Lake Hallstatt.

The charming village of Hallstatt clings to the side of Dachstein Mountain above the deep blue Hallstatt Lake. Consider spending the night; there are no first-class hotels, but when the daytrippers have left, you'll enjoy one of the loveliest natural settings in the Lake Country. You can rent boats and use the town as a base for excursions. The Parish Church is reached by steps from the center of the village.

Hallstatt is the oldest known settlement in Austria, and many prehistoric graves have been discovered nearby. The cemetery is overcrowded, and skeletons have been periodically dug up and displayed in the charnel house—some inscribed with dates and causes of death. Kids will love it!

Dining and Lodging

Grüner Baun (Tel. 061134-46134) is a terrace restaurant overlooking the lake. For lodging, your best bet is the simple but friendly Gasthof Zauner (I, A-4830 Hallstatt. Tel. 061134-246). Ask for a room with antiques.

❖ EXCURSIONS FROM HALLSTATT

Lake of Gosau: From Hallstatt, turn left on Route 166 to Gosau, and then turn left again to the Lake of Gosau. The surface of this small lake reflects the rock walls and majestic peaks of the nearby mountains. There's no more dramatic setting in the Lake Country, particularly if you arrive in the morning or evening, when the lake is still and the busloads of tourists are gone. The hour-long walk around the lake is a delightful experience.

Salt Mines: From Hallstatt, drive to Lahn, take the funicular to the restaurant, and then a 10-minute walk to the salt mines. You can descend by a staircase or down the same smooth wooden slide used by the miners. A guided walk takes you past an underground lake. The trip ends with a mile-long underground train ride.

The **Ice Caves** and **Mount Krippenstein:** From Hallstatt, drive around the southern end of the lake. Just before **Obertraun** turn right on the road to the **Ice Caves** (Dachsteineishöhle). Take the cable car to the station **Schönbergalpe,** and follow signs to the **Eishöhle.** There are 60-minute guided tours daily from May to mid-October. After the tour, continue up the cable car to **Mount Krippenstein** (6,919 feet) for lunch. The view is breathtaking, particularly from **Pioneer's Cross** (Pionierkreuz), a short walk from the cable car.

✤ EBENSEE

How to Get There. Return to Bad Ischl and take **Route 145** about 11 miles north to Ebensee.

If you're partial to panoramic views, take the cable car to the winter sports area of **Feuerkogel.**

✤ TRAUNKIRCHEN

How to Get There. From Ebensee, continue for about 2.5 miles along the lovely west shore of the **Traunsee** to **Traunkirchen.** The **Parish Church** has ornate Baroque furnishings and a famous **Fisherman's Pulpit** in the form of a boat, representing the Apostle's ship with dripping nets. Overhead is the scene of a lobster returning to St. Francis Xavier a crucifix he lost when shipwrecked near Japan.

✤ GMUNDEN

How to Get There. Continue north about 5 miles.

Gmunden is famous for its ceramics. Stretch your legs on a 1-mile walk under chestnut trees along the shores of the Traunsee. **Ort Chateau** is on an island linked to the mainland. A nephew of the emperor acquired it in 1878. He gave up his title after the death of Franz Josef's son Rudolf, and lived here under the assumed name of Johann Ort.

✤ LINZ

How to Get There. Take **Route 144** north to **A1,** and drive east to Linz.

Dining

The itinerary doesn't have you stopping in Linz, but should you go there, dine at **Allegro** (E, Schillerstrasse 68. Tel. 0732-669800), the best and most expensive restaurant in the old town. The nouvelle menu features lamb, Tafelspitz (boiled beef), and Geschnetzeltes (sliced veal with mushrooms in a cream sauce). The desserts are worth saving room for. But if it's sweets alone you want, or coffee, head for the outdoor terrace of **Traxlmayr** (M, Promenade 16. Tel. 0732-73353), a typical Austrian café where you can read the *International Herald Tribune* for the price of a cup of coffee.

❦ *THE MÜHLVIERTEL*

If you're in a hurry, go directly to the **Abbey of St. Florian**. But if time permits, and the weather cooperates, consider a loop north through the district of **Mühlviertel**. This will take you down back roads, through rolling farmland seldom seen by foreign tourists. There's a Grandma Moses quality to this landscape, with stone barns, milk cans, laundry lines flapping their shadows on lengths of lawn, and everywhere the smells of the good earth.

How to Get There. It's about 50 miles round-trip from **Linz** to **Freistadt**. Leave A1 and follow A7 north toward **Linz**. Continue past **Linz**, following signs to **Route 125** and **Freistadt**. About 7 miles before **Freistadt**, turn right on a small country road to **Kefermarkt**. In the chancel of the Gothic **Church of St. Wolfgang** is a great carved wooden altarpiece about 40 feet high. (If the church is locked, ask in the building behind, number 2, for the key.) Continue north to **Freistadt**. The town has a lovely main square with a **Parish Church** and old, arcaded houses.

Dining

Zum Goldenen Anker (M/I, Freistadt. Tel. 07942-2112) is an informal, reasonably priced hotel-restaurant that's been in the same family for two hundred years. Regional dishes popular with tourists include roast pork with Speckkrautsalat; and Zwiebelrostbraten (roast beef) with Bratkartoffeln. Don't miss the Apfelstrudel or a sweet called Esterhazyschnitte.

Michelin suggests you continue your back-road tour from **Freistadt** to **Bad Leonfelden** on **Route 128**, then south to **Glasau** on **Route 126** and back to **Linz**. Part of this trip takes you through a forest and along a broodingly romantic gorge; but if you've had enough of back roads or need to reach St. Florian before the last tour (4 P.M.), take **Route 125** direct from Freistadt to Linz, and continue to **St. Florian.**

❦ *ST. FLORIAN*

The abbey at Melk, crowning a bluff above the Danube, is more imposing; but St. Florian has a greater variety of things to see, so it would be a mistake to pass it up for Melk. The abbey has been occupied for more than nine hundred years by the Canons of St. Augustine (canons, unlike monks, are not confined to an abbey, but do ministerial work in their district). It was entirely rebuilt under **Carlo Antonio Carlone** and **Jacob Prandtauer** (1686–1751) and is today one of the purest examples of Baroque architecture in Europe.

St. Florian was a Roman administrator who was martyred in 304 and thrown into the nearby river Enns with a millstone around his neck; it was on the site of his grave that the monastery was built. The saint is traditionally invoked against fire with the prayer, "Good St. Florian, spare my house and rather burn my neighbor's." His figure can still be seen in many Austrian houses, dressed as a Roman legionary holding a pail of water to douse the flames.

A great stairway leads to the **Marble Hall,** which has a ceiling depicting Austrian victories over the Turks. Science and Virtue join hands with Religion in allegorical paintings on the **Library** ceiling—a reminder that the Augustines have always regarded the intellect as an ally in their search for spiritual truth.

There were no hotels fit for royalty in those days; hence, the **Imperial Apartments,** lavishly furnished as they were when Empress Maria Theresa and other members of the royal family stayed here. On display, too, is the bed of **Anton Bruckner,** who died here in 1896. Bruckner, the country's greatest nineteenth-century composer of organ music, was accepted into the abbey's choir school at age thirteen, when his father died. Most of his symphonies and masses were composed here after 1845, when he was appointed church organist. He became famous when he went to Linz and Vienna as an organist and teacher, but his roots were here, and he was buried, as he requested, in the crypt beneath the church organ.

Don't miss the exuberant Baroque **Abbey Church** (Stiftskirche). You'll wonder why the architect tried so hard to keep you in this world when you should be thinking of the next—until you realize that he has tried to bring God's kingdom down to you, and overwhelm you with its glory. The organ's 7,343 pipes make music during summer concerts, daily at 4:30. In the crypt below lie Bruckner's coffin and the very un-Baroque bones of some 6,000 early Christians, dug up when the original Gothic church was built, and arranged like so many oranges in a market.

The abbey's most valuable paintings, which you'll see on the tour, are 14 works by **Albrecht Altdorfer** (1480–1538), the master of the early-sixteenth-century Danube School of Painting. The works are noted for their warm, rich colors, their expressiveness, and their use of landscapes not just to provide background, but to influence the total mood of the painting—a technique that foreshadows the Romantics several centuries ahead of its time.

✤ *MELK*

How to Get There. If you're anxious to reach Dürnstein or to make the last tour at Melk (summers at 5; off-season at 4), take A1 direct from **Linz** to **Melk Abbey.** The alternative is to follow A1 only as far as **Enns**, cross the Danube on **Route 123**, take **Route 3** east along the Danube, and then recross the river at **Melk.** This route takes you to **Mauthausen** (16 miles from Linz), the granite quarry used as a concentration camp where nearly 200,000 prisoners were killed. A 90-minute tour takes you to the remaining huts where prisoners waited to be summoned to their deaths.

There's nothing modest about Melk; straddling a rocky bluff 150 feet above the Danube, it is the embodiment of the Church Militant and the Church Triumphant. The **Babenbergs**—the family that ruled Austria for 270 years, before the Habsburgs took over—established their rule here in the late tenth century. The second Babenberg, Heinrich I (994–1018), founded the monastery and turned it over to the Benedictines. The Turks gutted it in 1683, and nineteen years later **Jacob Prandtauer** turned it into what many consider the greatest monument to the Baroque imagination in Austria.

The high points of the tour are the **Library,** one of the richest in Europe, where the light of learning continued to burn during the Middle Ages; and the **Abbey Church.** Leaving the church is like stepping from daylight into a shaded room.

♦ *THE WACHAU VALLEY*

How to Get There. From Melk take Route 3 east along the north shore of the Danube to Krems.

The region along the Danube from Melk to Krems, scarcely 35 miles long, is known as the **Wachau**: one of the dreamiest, most romantic river valleys in the world. Imposing castle ruins loom above as you drive along the wide, silent river, among the terraced orchards and vineyards. In spring, apple, plum, and apricot trees burst into bloom. Medieval vintners' towns with narrow cobbled streets and fortified churches spread along the banks. You're only 90 minutes from Vienna, yet there's little commercial development to mar the beauty of the landscape.

The economy rests on the vineyards, the source of Austria's finest white wines. In 1301 a man named Ritzling, whose vineyards lay along a brook that meets the Danube just west of Dürnstein, developed his own grapes, which were cultivated in Germany's Rhineland and then brought back to Austria under the name Riesling. Today more than 1,000 winegrowers belong to the Wachau cooperative, with headquarters in the 1719 castle outside Dürnstein. Wherever you stay, you'll be able to enjoy these local wines from family-owned vineyards. **Route 3**, the most popular route, takes you through the most historic towns, including **Dürnstein**, where you should spend the night. The other town not to miss is **Weissenkirchen**.

From Melk, cross the Danube and turn right on **Route 3**. Three miles along, on the opposite shore, you'll see an early nineteenth-century castle (closed to the public) called **Schönbühel**. The orchards begin after **Grimsing**. Looming up from the highest point across the river, past the village of **Aggsbach Markt** (7 miles east of Melk) is **Aggstein Fortress**. You'll return here later.

After **Aggsbach Markt** comes **Spitz**, an ancient market town hidden behind apricot and pear trees. **Schlossgasse** is one of its most picturesque streets. The Gothic **Parish Church** has an elegant chancel that is out of line with the nave (the central aisle). If you need to stretch, hike through the vineyards to the **Red Door**, a wall built to keep out the Turks, and enjoy a sweeping view of the valley.

Dining

A delightful spot for lunch or dinner is the **Strand Restaurant** over-looking the river at the far end of town. Try the venison or some fresh Danube fish with a glass of homemade apricot brandy.

Christines Weinlöchl (I, Ottenschlägerstrasse 4, Spitz. Tel. 02713-230) and **Mühlenkeller** (I, Auf der Wehrl, Spitz. Tel. 02713-352) are both cozy wine restaurants in a town that's one of the wine centers of the Wachau. **Christines Weinlöchl** is a historic house with modern paintings, some charcoal-grill specialties, and a great choice of regional wines. The **Mühlenkeller** is in the cellar of an ancient mill. The dishes are better on quantity than quality, but the wines are excellent. The restaurant has some rooms to rent, so you won't have to drink and drive.

Lodging

Two friendly, inexpensive guest houses in Spitz are **Frühstückspen-sionen "Hans Burkhardt"** (Kremserstrasse 19. Tel. 02713-356) and **Früh-stückspensionen "Zur alten Mühle"** (Auf der Wehr 1. Tel. 02713-352).

✦ WEISSENKIRCHEN

This charming medieval village, dominated by a fortified Gothic church, is 9 miles past **Aggsbach**. It's less perfect than Dürnstein, but also less precious and less well known to tourists.

Dining

Florianihof (M/E, Wösendorf. Tel. 02715-3212) is one of the best restaurants along the Danube. The family Mandl takes credit for the friendly service and top cuisine. Popular dishes include fish from the Danube and Vanillerostbraten. For an apéritif, try a dry Dürnsteiner Aus-lese 1977; and with your meal, a Riesling or Veltiner.

Jamek (E, Joching. Tel. 02715-2332) is more expensive than Flori-anihof, but enjoys a somewhat better reputation for its local wines and daily specials, particularly the cream soups, fillet of beef, and pork cutlets with caraway.

Prandtauerhof (M/E, Joching. Tel. 02715-2310) is a perfect choice for an outdoor lunch or dinner of lamb, venison, and excellent wines from the owner's own vineyards.

Lodging

Stay in **Raffelsbergerhof** (Weissenkirchen A-3610. Tel. 02715-2201), the former home of the controller of river traffic. Not even the modern furnishings can destroy the charm of this sixteenth-century manor house.

❧ *DÜRNSTEIN*

Dürnstein, 2½ miles past Weissenkirchen, is the most picturesque village along the Danube. It sits below terraced vineyards, at the most dramatic turn of the river. The main road passes through a tunnel beneath the town, so the modern world—except for the tourists—hardly intrudes. Richard the Lionhearted would probably recognize Dürnstein today, though he might wonder what has happened to the castle where he was imprisoned, since it lies today in ruins.

During the Third Crusade, Richard the Lionhearted, King of England, offended Leopold V, the Duke of Austria, by removing his banner from a tower during the assault on Acre in Palestine. On his way home Richard was shipwrecked off the Yugoslavian coast and had to pass through his rival's lands dressed as a peasant. His royal ring gave him away near Vienna, however, and he was shuttled off to prison in Dürnstein. In the spring of 1193, so the story goes, Richard's faithful servant Blondel was wandering from town to town in search of his master, when Richard, standing in a fortress window, overheard Blondel singing his favorite song, and finished the verse himself. The king was later set free, after paying a king's ransom.

It's only a 10-minute walk from one end of Dürnstein to the other. Wander along the main street *(Hauptstrasse)*, which is lined with turreted sixteenth-century houses dripping with flowers. The fifteenth-century **Parish Church** was redone in Baroque dress—compare the simple Gothic nave to the ornate eighteenth-century pulpit and high altar.

Don't miss the view of Dürnstein from the ruins of the castle above the town. The 20-minute walk should be made in the early morning or at dusk. Also enjoy a mile-long walk along a riverfront promenade, and a 2½-mile walk through the vineyards to Weissenkirchen. Time your trip so you can return by ferry.

If you're partial to boat rides on romantic rivers, take the local ferry round trip from Dürnstein to Melk. You can get off the ferry at Melk if you missed seeing the abbey en route from Salzburg, and then catch another ferry back to Dürnstein later in the day.

The road along the southern bank of the Danube is just as scenic as the one you took (Route 3) along the north shore. The southern route misses the major towns but lets you see them from a distance, framed by vineyards and orchards. To get to the southern route, drive east from **Dürnstein** toward **Krems**, cross the bridge at **Mautern**, and head west along the Danube, back to **Aggstein Fortress**—one of Austria's most romantic castle ruins. The present owner runs a modest restaurant in the old retainer's hall. From the ramparts, 960 feet above the Danube, there's a breathtaking view of the Wachau Valley. Standing at this dizzying height you can decide whether you would rather jump or starve to death —a choice given to prisoners of Schreckenwald ("Terror of the Forest"), the robber baron who stretched a chain across the Danube here and imprisoned those who didn't pay a toll. (Justice was served when an escaped prisoner set the castle on fire, and the Terror was reduced to a wandering beggar.)

Bikes can be rented at train stations in Krems and Melk and returned at other stations along the route. The ferries take bikes (for a fee), so you can bike, say, from Dürnstein to Aggsbach, and then return by ferry. Since most tourists take the north route, the relatively flat south route is ideal for biking. A ferry recrosses the Danube at **Spitz**.

Dining

Schloss Dürnstein (E, Dürnstein. Tel. 02711-212) is the top restaurant in town. It's also the most expensive, but how often do you get to dine in a seventeenth-century castle?

Sänger Blondel (M, Dürnstein. Tel. 02711-253) is more a family restaurant popular with tourists. Meals are less elegantly prepared than at the Schloss, but almost as satisfying, and at half the price. Try the clear soup with liver dumplings; the roasted pork or stuffed brisket of veal; and the house specialty, the Sänger-Blondel Torte.

If you can afford the price, **Restaurant Bacher** (E, Mautern. Tel. 02732-2937) is one of the best in Austria. The owner and chef won the 1983 award as Best Chef in Austria.

Lodging

At **Schloss Dürnstein** (E, Dürnstein. Tel. 02711-212) no pains have been spared to capture the elegance of the original seventeenth-century castle, high on a cliff overlooking the Danube. If you can afford the price, a night in this Relais & Châteaux property will be one of the high points of your trip. There's a swimming pool, a famous gourmet restaurant, and a shaded terrace where you can sip local wines and watch the boats gliding along the river. The vaulted salons are decorated with antique furniture from the family of Count Starhemberg, who kept the Turks from Vienna in 1683. Introduce yourself to the owner/manager, Johann Thiery; he takes a personal interest in the happiness of his guests. The 37 rooms are booked to capacity in season, so make reservations months in advance.

Johann's brother Raimund runs the nearby **Hotel Richard Lowenherz** (Dürnstein A-3601. Tel. 02711-222). This is more a hotel you check into than a castle where you become a privileged guest, and antiques are in the hallways, not in the rooms; yet the hotel does have some character, and rooms are less expensive than at the Schloss.

Budget travelers can enjoy a night in a private home at **Pension Altes Rathaus, "Beate Fürtler"** (Dürnstein 26. Tel. 02711-252).

❧ VIENNA

How to Get There. It's about 60 miles from **Dürnstein** to **Vienna**. As you head east from **Dürnstein** to **Krems**, the mountains recede, and the scenery loses much of its drama. Cross the bridge at **Krems**, and drive south past **Herzogenburg** to **A1**. There's a **Tourist Information Office** on A1 before you reach Vienna.

Vienna says Empire—that's why Americans love it so much. Only a people raised under Jefferson could embrace an imperial city so uncritically and with such longing. We may have left the Old World behind, but not our need for splendor. And splendor, imaginary or not, is what Vienna has to offer.

The people, the palaces—everything about Vienna seems suspended in the eighteenth century, frozen in time. It is a city under glass. The people, born to another age, still hold to courtly forms: addressing each other by titles long abolished; kissing hands; loving food and beauty; ignoring time. It is, literally, a city of dreams—dreams that become your own as you wander through palaces, sip champagne at the opera, or indulge yourself at pastry shops once frequented by Haydn and Mozart, Adler and Freud.

There's a reverse side to this dream, of course. "The Blue Danube," which isn't blue, was written partly to make Austrians forget their humiliating defeat by Prussia, which reduced them to a second-rate power. Coffeehouses thrive in part because of a housing shortage and cramped living conditions. Few cities have been so unkind to their musicians—

while they were alive. The Viennese loved Schubert's pretty songs, but the poignancy of his greatest works escaped them.

Between the Franco-Prussian War and World War I Vienna changed from the center of an empire of 50 million to the capital of a small Alpine nation. It remains today an imperial city without an empire. It is fitting that it is a Baroque city, for Baroque is the art of the façade, the perfect stage set for fantasy. To say that its splendor exists only in the mind's eye, however, makes it no less splendid. Only a shallow person denies the beauty of appearances. If Vienna is a dream, let's dream on.

Things to See and Do

The oldest part of Vienna, bounded by the **Ringstrasse** and the **Danube (Donau) Canal**, is called **District I**. The major sights of District I are described below on the **Walking Tour of Old Vienna and the Ring**. Other sights—**Schönbrunn**, the **Belvedere**, and the **Prater**—are described in the subsequent section called **Outside the Ring**.

The **Hofburg** (the Habsburg Palace) is the number one attraction in Vienna, so visit in the morning, particularly since the **Spanish Riding School** and the **National Library**, both part of the Hofburg, are only open then. In the afternoon either (1) visit museums near the Hofburg (the **Fine Arts Museum** for paintings; the **Neue Burg** for porcelain and silver, arms and armor); or (2) wander the streets of Vienna, shopping and visiting churches and pastry shops. Whichever you choose not to do should be saved for the following day and combined with tours of **Schönbrunn Palace**, the **Belvedere**, and the **Prater**. If any time is left, take a bus ride around the **Ring**. Plan to spend at least one evening dining in Old Vienna and going to a concert or opera. Save another evening for a drive through the **Vienna Woods** and dinner at a **Heuriger** (new wine tavern) at **Grinzing**.

Walking Tour of Old Vienna and the Ring

• Let's begin at the **main tourist office** in the subway station and shopping mall beneath **Opera Square**. Pick up maps and brochures, and listings of weekly events. Be sure to get the latest schedule of opening and closing times, which can vary from building to building; ignoring these times could ruin your trip. Buy a valuable city publication called *Vienna from A to Z*, which describes the major sights by numbers that match numbered plaques on the buildings. Also purchase a money-saving **Three Day Transportation Ticket** valid on all subways, streetcars and buses.

• From the **main tourist office**, cross back inside the **Ring** and head down **Kärntnerstrasse**, past the **State Opera House** (Staatsoper). If you don't plan on going to the opera, take a tour (daily from June through September, depending on rehearsal schedules).

• Continue down Kärntnerstrasse toward **St. Stephen's Cathedral**. Just past the Opera House is **Philharmonikerstrasse**. Turn left. At **Number 4** is one of Vienna's most illustrious hotels, the **Sacher**, where the nobility conducted its affairs, both political and social, during the days of the Empire. Franz Josef's guests used to come here after dining at the Imperial Palace (the Hofburg); etiquette demanded that no one eat after the Emperor finished a course, and Franz Josef, who had Spartan tastes, was a light eater. If the hotel lobby is quiet, a porter may be willing to show you the paneled lounge, private dining rooms, and collection of autographed menus. The **Sacher Torte**, a chocolate-frosted cake topped with whipped cream, was first made here for one of Metternich's banquets. Very overrated, I think, but you'll want to decide for yourself and perhaps ship some home in a hermetically sealed container.

It's said that Franz Josef's son and heir, the **Crown Prince Rudolf**, began his affair here with seventeen-year-old **Mary Vetsera**. Probably because Franz Josef refused to delegate authority to his son, the thirty-one-year-old boy found his own way of growing up by drinking, partying, and associating with liberals and other freethinkers. In late 1888, Rudolf wrote a letter to the Pope. What he said nobody will ever know, but when his father got wind of it, he severely chastised the boy, and the next day Rudolf and Mary were found dead at his hunting lodge at **Mayerling**, about 20 miles southwest of Vienna. Mary had been shot first and covered with flowers. To cover up the scandal, she was spirited away in a rainstorm, sitting up fully dressed in a carriage between two uncles, and buried in a nearby monastery under police supervision. Rudolf left notes for his wife and his mother, but not for his father. That the young couple had a suicide pact seems clear, but that the lovers took their lives because Franz Josef demanded that they part seems doubtful. Rudolf was a man of many affairs—he had, in fact, spent the night before with an actress he had been seeing for some time—so more than likely he was in trouble for his liberal views.

• At the end of Philharmonikerstrasse is a large plaza (**Albertina**). Cross over to the **Capuchin's Crypt**. Three centuries of Habsburgs are buried here—or at least their bodies: their hearts are gathering dust in the crypt of the **Augustinerkirche**, and their entrails are resting in the catacombs of **St. Stephen's**. Maria Theresa used to pay respects to her husband, Franz, here, and an elevator was installed when she got too stout for the trip.

Stuck one day, she cried out, "Look, the dead don't want to let me go"; and a week later she too was dead. Maria and Franz now stare into each other's eyes on the lid of their sarcophagus—an angel waits at their heads with a trumpet to awaken them on Judgment Day. The only non-Habsburg here is **Caroline Fuchs**, governess to Maria Theresa's ten surviving children, including Marie Antoinette. History should note that it was Carolyn Fuchs who made it possible for Maria Theresa to have both a family and a career.

• You are now in the **Hofburg**, the winter residence of the Habsburgs. The palace was begun in the thirteenth century and continued to grow and change for the next seven hundred years. Styles change from one building to the next—the public halls are usually lavish, the private rooms relatively plain and comfortable.

A Brief History of the Habsburgs

Your tour of the Hofburg is a voyage into Austria's past. Let's try to put that past in perspective.

In 976 the Holy Roman Emperor Otto I gave land to a German nobleman named **Leopold of Babenberg** for his help in crushing a Bavarian revolt. The **Babenbergs** ruled Austria for the next 270 years. When the last Babenberg died without an heir, **Count Rudolf of Habsburg** fought his way to power. From this family of minor Swiss nobility came the Habsburg dynasty, the strongest in European history, which ruled continuously from 1278 until 1918. The emperors were brilliant and mad; they wrote music; they built palaces. Their goal was not to win slavish allegiance to Austria but to acquire wealth and land, and they accomplished this less by aggression than by diplomacy, marrying their daughters off to foreign kings. From the **Hofburg** they ruled most of Central Europe, including Spain and Spanish colonies in South America.

Vienna has always been a frontier town on the border between East and West. The Turks attacked in 1529 and were repelled. More than 150 years later, the Turks tried again. While the Emperor and his court fled the city, 24,000 men under **Count Starhemberg** held out for two months against a force of 200,000. With the aid of Polish King John Sobieski, the Turks were finally routed, ending forever the Ottoman threat to Europe. If Vienna had fallen, so might have Christendom. For decades the Viennese had faced outward, bracing themselves for the attack. Victory released a flood of pent-up energy, and with joy, pride and relief the Viennese created the Baroque city you see today.

Before Maria Theresa came the three so-called Baroque emperors:

Leopold I (1658–1705); Josef I (1705–11) and Karl VI (1711–40). Maria Theresa had much in common with Queen Victoria: the long reign (1740 to 1780); the large family (sixteen children); the insistence on duty and morality; the goodness and sincerity; the enlightened despotism. With her death the age of monuments, and, some would say, the glory of the Habsburgs, came to an end.

Her son Josef II (1780–90) tried to continue his mother's reforms, but he pushed too hard and too fast. He reacted against excesses of luxury, but the people loved pomp and splendor. He tried to protect nightingales in the public gardens, but the people preferred keeping songbirds encaged.

When Napoleon's empire fell apart, the crowned heads of Europe gathered in Vienna to pick up the pieces. Vienna was now the center of Europe. The main figure at the **Congress of Vienna** (September 1814 to July 1815) was the Austrian statesman **Prince Metternich**. For centuries, European powers had struggled to dominate by force; what Metternich sought was a balance of power, with Austria as the vital buffer between Russia and France. While Metternich schemed, the Congress danced and dined its way from one wild entertainment to the next. This was the gay, licentious Vienna that lives on in our dreams: Czar Alexander of Russia dancing for forty nights; the fat King of Würtemberg cutting a hole in the dinner table so he could reach his plate; Castlereagh's wife wearing a garter ribbon in her hair. *"Le Congrès danse, mais il ne marche pas"* is the quote to remember; "The Congress dances, but it gets nowhere."

The period from 1815 to 1848 is known as the **Biedermeier Age**, the age of the middle class. Tired of war, the country turned to Schubert songs, pastry, and new wine. Gone was the stately minuet—the dance of the aristocracy; in its place came the rhythms of a Jewish innkeeper's son named Johann Strauss. While twilight fell over Imperial Vienna, Johann Strauss the younger had some 230 musicians working for him in the huge, resplendent ballrooms of Vienna. "Vienna, be gay!" they sang to the strains of the "Blue Danube." "Well, why court sorrow?/ There's still tomorrow,/ So laugh and be merry."

Metternich ruled under a weak emperor. Discontent grew as liberties were repressed, and Metternich was finally forced to flee to London in the Vienna uprising of 1848.

Franz Josef reigned for sixty-eight years, from 1848 to 1916. When he was crowned, James Polk was in the White House; when he died, Woodrow Wilson had been elected to serve a second term.

Until the mid-nineteenth century "Old Vienna" was encircled by the walls that kept the Turks from overrunning Europe. In order for the city to expand, Franz Josef had the walls torn down and replaced by the Ringstrasse—a ring of wide boulevards lined with the monumental, late-nineteenth-century public buildings you see today.

Tearing down the walls was one of Franz Josef's few gestures toward the future. He was a man of simple, austere tastes who hated reform. He was an anachronism—an eighteenth-century figure in a nineteenth-century world; a man who worked long hours, fumbling with documents while the world collapsed around him. His son Rudolf committed suicide at Mayerling; his wife, Elisabeth, was struck down by an assassin's bullet; his nephew Franz Ferdinand was murdered at Sarajevo. Helplessly he watched the growing might of Prussia. It was perhaps a blessing that he died in 1916 and did not live to see his successor, the Emperor Karl, renounce the throne in 1918, bringing to an end more than six centuries of Habsburg rule.

• Bear right on Augustinerstrasse. On your left is the Albertina Gallery. Stop here now, or return another day on your visit to the museums. The Albertina houses one of the largest and best collections of graphic art in the world, including many drawings by Albrecht Dürer. Unfortunately, many works are shown only in facsimile, except during special exhibits.

• Continue down Augustinerstrasse to the fourteenth-century Augustinerkirche. Though remodeled, it gives off an aura of great age and captures the spirit of the early Habsburgs, who came here to pray. They all left their hearts here—buried in urns. Franz Josef gave *his* heart away here to seventeen-year-old Elisabeth. It was here that Napoleon married Marie-Louise, though he decided not to show up and sent someone to marry her by proxy.

Continue a few steps down Augustinerstrasse to a large square (Josefsplatz). On your left is the National Library. The Great Hall is a masterpiece of Baroque decoration.

• Across the Josefsplatz, on the far right, is the Stallburg, the stable for the Spanish Riding School. A passage in front of the Stallburg leads to the Spanish Riding School itself.

The idea of pure or noble thoroughbreds smacks of Empire, which helps explain the lasting appeal of the milk-white Lippizan stallions who perform to capacity crowds in the City of Dreams. Hitler, who, as the world knows, had a fondness for selective breeding, sent the horses to Czechoslovakia to protect them during the war; General Patton, another horse lover, eventually brought them back.

It seems fitting that during the Congress of Vienna, kings and queens danced in the same sumptuous hall where the thoroughbreds performed. As Edward Crankshaw wrote in 1938, "The cabrioling of the pure Lippizaners is, by all our standards, the absolute of uselessness. The horses, fine, beautiful and strong, are utterly divorced from all natural movement, living their lives in an atmosphere of unreality with every step laid down for them and no chance whatsoever of a moment's deviation. And so it was with the 19th-century Habsburgs. The Court, intent on cabrioles and ballotades, was lost to all reality." True as this may be, what visitors seek for and discover at performances today are qualities often missing from our modern world: grace, beauty, and dignity—all born of discipline and self-control.

Most performances are from March through June and then from September through November, Sundays at 10:45 A.M. and Wednesdays at 7 P.M. There are additional shows on some Saturdays at 9 A.M., and training sessions Tuesday through Friday at 10 A.M. Check the latest schedules. To see a Sunday performance, write at least 3 months in advance to the Spanische Reitschule, Hofburg, A 1010 Vienna. You'll get a reservation card and pay when you pick up your tickets. No advance tickets are sold for the 10 A.M. training sessions. Queue up by 9:30.

• Return to **Josefsplatz**. To your right, beside the National Library, is a passageway that leads to the **Swiss Court**, named for the soldiers who once stood here on guard. On the right is the **Imperial Treasury**, where you'll see the crown of the Holy Roman Emperor, Charlemagne's lance, and fabulous fifteenth-century embroidered vestments. Even when the imperial crown was padded it failed to fit most heads, and Maria Theresa had a good silent laugh when it slipped down over the ears of her husband, Franz, at his coronation.

• From the **Treasury**, return to the **Swiss Court**. To your left are steps leading to the beautiful Gothic **Castle Chapel** (Hofburgkapelle), where the **Vienna Choir Boys** sing. The choir, founded in 1498 by Emperor Maximilian, is chosen from some 7,000 applicants every year. See pages 199–200 under The Arts for ticket information.

• Return to the **Swiss Court**, turn left, and pass into the central palace courtyard called **In Der Burg** (Inside the Castle). Turn immediately right and pass beneath a rotunda. On the left is the **Collection of Court Porcelain and Silver**. On the right are the **Imperial Apartments**.

• The **Imperial Apartments** are impressed with the personalities of Franz Josef and his wife, Elisabeth. The emperor's iron bed is as austere as the one he slept in in Bad Ischl. Elisabeth had exercise equipment in the room next to her bedroom because she loved sports and was afraid of getting fat. In the Empire-style Conference Room is a portrait of Elisabeth with the face of both an empress and a playful little girl. What must it have been like for a seventeen-year-old to become an empress with 50 million subjects? According to Rebecca West, it was Elisabeth who convinced her husband to create the Dual Monarchy with Hungary, which permitted the empire to survive into the twentieth century. By 1860, Elisabeth had become a withdrawn, sensitive lady, who hardly ever visited her husband and was seldom at Court. She may have gone a bit mad. If her tyrannical mother-in-law, Sophie, had let her raise her son Rudolf, who knows, the boy might have lived, and Elisabeth with him; and together they might have restrained Austria's imperialist ambitions and avoided World War I. Without them, Franz Josef stood fast against reform. A conscientious but unimaginative man (though liked by his people), he ruled a dying empire. Three years after his son Rudolf took his life at Mayerling, Franz Josef wrote to Elisabeth, "I should like to put into words how very, very deeply I love you, though I am not very good at showing it and I would only bore you if I could." He lived to mourn his wife's senseless death at the hand of an assassin in Geneva. He himself died in 1916, two years before the empire came to an end. The most satisfying and disturbing room on your tour is the **Banquet Hall**, set for a royal feast to which the guests will never come.

• Return to the rotunda and, leaving the Hofburg, turn right to **St. Michael's Church** (Michaelerkirche) on a square called **Michaelerplatz**. The high altar, with angels and saints in a golden heaven, is the essence of Baroque.

• At number 3 Michaelerplatz is the 1910 **Loos House**, considered the first example of modern architecture. Adolf Loos was a New Functionalist who believed that style should be the servant of use. By eliminating meaningless detail and decoration—the essence of Baroque—Loos paved the way for the familiar glass-and-concrete slabs that define our cities today.

• From **St. Michael's**, turn right and take your first right along the pedestrian shopping street called **Kohlmarkt**. Turn right on another shopping street called **Graben**. If you want to see one of the most sumptuous Baroque churches in Vienna, make your first left off Graben to **Peterskirche**.

Halfway up the **Graben** is the **Plague Monument** designed by **Fischer von Erlach** to celebrate the end of a plague in 1679. Though it's not particularly satisfying—it looks like a mound of dirty whipped cream—it does capture the essence of Baroque in the way that the artist completely transforms his material to satisfy his artistic needs.

• The **Graben** ends at **St. Stephen's** (Stephansdom), the spiritual heart and soul of Vienna. This is one of the few Austrian churches whose Gothic austerity has not been retouched with the lightness and color of Baroque. The slender south tower has been hit by lightning and artillery; look for the window where the watchkeeper kept a lookout for Turks. The builder, Hans Puchsbaum, was told not to look down, but did anyway, and fell to his death. For a great view, climb 344 steps up the tower, past the bench where Count von Starhemberg watched the Turkish assault. An elevator takes you to the bell in the northern tower.

The Romanesque (thirteenth-century) main doorway, decorated with stiff apostles, animals, and demons, is the oldest part of the church. In medieval times men and women sat on opposite sides, which is why there are only male saints over the southwest door, where the men entered; and only the Virgin and female saints over the northwest door used by women. Behind the cathedral is a suffering Christ called the "Toothache God."

Immediately on your left as you enter is the **Cross Chapel** (Tirnkapelle). The iron grillwork on the doors is copied from the gates at Belvedere Palace. Look for reliefs (shallow sculptures) depicting scenes from the Turkish wars.

Near the middle of the church, on the left, is the early-sixteenth-century **pulpit** carved from solid blocks of stone. The artist peers through a window near the bottom, looking quite fatigued after so much work. The animals climbing up the railing represent sins.

More beautiful than the black marble main altar is the **Wiener Neustadt altarpiece** (1447) in the chapel to the left. This is one of the most richly carved altarpieces in the world. In the right chapel is the remarkable late-fifteenth-century tomb of Emperor Friedrich III, made from red Salzburg marble. Evil animals try to disturb Friedrich's sleep, while good spirits, in the form of local personages, keep them away.

A 30-minute guided tour of the **catacombs** takes you past the entrails of the Habsburgs preserved in copper jars.

• A block behind the cathedral, at Domgasse 5, is the **Mozart Memorial** (Figarohaus) where Wolfgang lived from 1784 to 1787 and wrote *The Marriage of Figaro*. Haydn came here as a guest and heard the first performance of Mozart's *Haydn Quartets*. Mozart died in 1791 in dire poverty. His body was taken to the cemetery on a cold, snowy day, and no one marked where it was placed. (Freemasons, at that time, advocated extremely simple burials, without markers or tombstones.)

• The choice now is yours: to cross the square (Stephansplatz) and walk up the main shopping street, **Kärntnerstrasse**, back to the **Opera**; or to take a short side trip through the **Old University** district, the oldest part of the city. Let's begin with the Old University District; if your legs refuse to cooperate, skip down to the section below called **Kärntnerstrasse**, and save the old town for another day.

The Old University District

• As you exit through the main door of St. Stephen's, turn right and head down **Rotenturmstrasse**. Turn right on **Lugeckstrasse**, and bear right on **Bäckerstrasse**. You're in the Old University district now (the university has since moved), with lots of narrow lanes and beautiful courtyards. The courtyard at **Number 7** has Renaissance arcades; the French writer Madame de Staël lived in **Number 8** when Napoleon banished her from France. Continue to **Old University Square**. To your left, at the far end of the square, is the dignified **Church of the Jesuits** (Jesuitenkirche). The domed ceiling isn't curved at all—a good example of Baroque *trompe l'oeil* (optical illusion).

• From the church entrance, walk straight on **Sonnenfelsgasse** (behind the Academy) and turn right on **Schönlaterngasse**, which is lined with houses that have not changed much since the days of the Turkish siege. In a niche at **Number 7** is an image of a beast, perhaps 750 years old. Legend has it that a dragon poisoned the water in the well within the courtyard. A hero climbed down with a mirror. When the beast saw himself, he died of fright.

• Just before the street turns right, you'll pass **St. Bernard's Chapel**, which has a peaceful courtyard where you can rest your feet. The monastery was the winter home of monks from the Vienna Woods.

• Leave the courtyard by the far entrance, make your first right, and then a left on **Fleischmarkt** (Meat Market). Turn left again on **Rotenturmstrasse** and a right on **Lugeckstrasse** to the **Hoher Markt**, the old Roman forum, where Vienna began. In the Middle Ages the square was used both as a market and a pillory, where pickpockets and adulteresses got their due. The great personages of Viennese history march from the **Anker Clock** as the hour strikes.

• From the center of the square turn right up **Judengasse** to the Romanesque **Church of St. Rupert** (Ruprechtskirche), the town's oldest church. Though altered, its simplicity provides relief from the bright extravagances of the Baroque, and reminds you that the Viennese must have believed once in guilt and sin. Rupert was the patron saint of the Danube salt merchants, and you can see his salt bucket with his statue outside the church.

• Retrace your steps a short way down **Judengasse** and turn right on a narrow lane called **Sterngasse**. At the **T**, turn left, and then at the **Old Town Hall** (Altes Rathaus), next to St. Salvador Church, turn right down a narrow street to **Maria Am Gestade**. Many consider this the loveliest church in Vienna. Before the Danube was diverted, an arm flowed by the church steps and fishermen moored there to pray. The late eighth-century church was rebuilt in Gothic style in the early fifteenth century and restored since the war. Standing beneath the high narrow nave, many of you will find yourselves thinking, "Here at last is a Viennese church where one can pray!"

• From Maria Am Gestade, turn down the narrow **Schwertgasse**. The first wide street you come to is **Wipplingerstrasse**. Turn left and pass between the **Altes Rathaus** and the old **Chancellery of Bohemia**, which has a Baroque façade by Fischer von Erlach. Turn right around the chancellery, and right again, to a square called **Judenplatz**, the heart of the old ghetto. There was a synagogue here around 1200, but in the fifteenth century the Jews were burned or imprisoned and the synagogue razed. The Jews gradually returned but were again expelled during the Counter-Reformation.

• Cross the square and turn left down another narrow street, **Parisergasse**, which empties into a small square. On your left is the **Vienna Clock Museum** (Uhrenmuseum der Stadt Wien), which has a wonderful collection of timepieces, from medieval sundials to electronic clocks, which perform on the hour. To your right, on the same square, is the **Church of the Nine Choirs of Angels** (Kirche am Hof), a fourteenth-century Gothic church with a simple, early Baroque façade. To the left of the church's entrance is a square called **Am Hof**, surrounded by buildings with Baroque façades. It was here that Franz II announced the end of the Holy Roman Empire in 1804. Turn left as you enter the square and at the corner turn left again on **Bognergasse**. A quick right at the end of the street takes you back to **Kohlmarkt**. Turn left on **Graben** and return to St. Stephen's Cathedral.

Kärntnerstrasse

• From St. Stephen's walk along **Kärntnerstrasse**, the main shopping street, back to the **Opera House** (Staatsoper), where your walk began.

• If your feet are holding up, continue south along **Kärntnerstrasse** past the **Ring** to a large park. To your left, at the far end of the park, standing beneath a magnificent dome, is the **Karlskirche**, one of the most important Baroque churches in Vienna. There's a story that Fischer von Erlach got the idea for it while standing on Pincio, Rome's famous hill, seeing Trajan's column and St. Peter's in a single vision in the setting sun. The **Karlskirche** is a fascinating synthesis of pagan Rome and Christianity; of East and West, of clerical and secular. There's no long nave (central aisle) leading to the altar, so you feel as though you're standing at the center of a cross, or a giant egg, overwhelmed by color and light. It's not surprising that this was the first church built after the victory over the Turks.

• Return to the **Ring** and turn left. The first park you come to on the right is the delightful **Burggarten**. There's a café on the back terrace. The park is bordered by the **Neue Burg**, which has museums of old musical instruments, and of arms and armor.

• Across the Ring is the **Museum of Fine Arts**, which no one who cares about art will want to miss. There are entire galleries devoted to Pieter Bruegel the Elder, Van Dyck, Rubens, and Albrecht Dürer. The paintings come from the collection of the Habsburgs, who must have had a particular fondness for Venetian colors. "One has the feeling," writes Edward Crankshaw, "that to most of the Habsburgs the paintings must have been all one so long as the mixture was *rich.*"

• If you're partial to wide, busy boulevards and monumental mid-nineteenth-century public buildings, continue right around the **Ring** to the **canal**. The Ring that encircles the original, medieval city is a rather ponderous monument to a dying empire that barely survived its completion. The original ramparts, which stood along the Ring until Franz Josef tore them down, were so wide that carriages could ride on top, four horses abreast. Outside the walls was a moat, and then a level area with no buildings, so that enemies could be spotted. The Ring today consists of 8 interlocking boulevards, about 2.5 miles around and 60 yards wide. Though its buildings are not Baroque, they are, in their monumental way, as much a part of Vienna as the Baroque. A village lad, seeing them for the first time, wrote, "The entire Ringstrasse affected me like a fairytale out of the Arabian Nights." The boy's name was Adolf Hitler.

Outside the Ring

The three most popular trips outside the Ring are to the **Belvedere Palace**, **Schönbrunn Palace**, and the **Prater** amusement park.

• **Belvedere Palace**, the summer residence of Prince Eugene of Savoy

(1663–1736), is marked by lightness and grace. You may prefer visiting Schönbrunn because of its historical importance as summer residence of the Court, but you would probably prefer living here. The Prince lived, between campaigns, in the Lower Belvedere; today it houses a museum of Baroque and medieval art. Modern paintings are in the Upper Belvedere. Be sure to enjoy a peaceful stroll through the gardens.

• The grounds of **Schönbrunn Palace**, Austria's answer to Versailles, are rigidly formal. In the gardens of the Belvedere man has tried to cooperate with nature; here he has tried to conquer her. The Belvedere is a graceful tribute to the Baroque in the years of peace following the Turkish defeat; Schönbrunn, in contrast, depends for effect on size and is decorated with all the frivolity of Rococo. Aristocratic, gay, voluptuous in a pale, fleshy sort of way; pleasant rather than strong or spiritual—these are the impressions associated with the Rococo, the last flowering of the Baroque. What is extraordinary is the fact that this world of leaping tendrils and gilded peacocks, this riot of curved and twisted lines, was the choice of **Maria Theresa**—that model of sobriety, that pillar of church and state. Can you imagine Queen Victoria, whom Maria Theresa is often compared to, decorating Schönbrunn? Yet what a pleasant relief it must have been for the empress, with all her awesome responsibilities, to have this opportunity to set her imagination free! And what a pleasure it must have been, staying in Schönbrunn after a winter in the dark and gloomy Hofburg!

It was here in Schönbrunn that Marie-Antoinette, ninth child of Maria Theresa, spent her youth, and here that the six-year-old Mozart amazed Maria Theresa with his skill. (In the white-and-gold **music room** little Mozart slipped on the polished floor, and when Marie-Antoinette, who was about the same age, helped him up, he vowed to marry her.) Here, too, Napoleon established his headquarters from 1805–9; here Franz Josef was born and died; and here the empire came to an end, in 1918, when Franz Josef's successor, Karl I, signed the renunciation papers in the **Chinese salon**.

After touring the **apartments**, stroll through the formal gardens. Don't miss the grand carriages in the old palace coach house *(Wagenburg)*.

• The **Prater** was once the Court game preserve, but Maria Theresa's son Josef II turned it over to the people, and now it's a lovely public park with biking and jogging trails, lakes with rowboats to rent, a golf course, tennis courts, and an amusement park highlighted by a toy train and a giant nineteenth-century Ferris wheel. Bikes can be rented from the **Radfahrverein Prater**, at Böcklinstrasse 2.

The Vienna Woods *(Wienerwald)*

City planners could take a lesson from the Habsburgs who—from a wish to protect their hunting grounds as much as a sense of civic duty—declared that the woods and mountains surrounding Vienna should forever remain inviolate, free from development. Hence, the pastoral charm of the Vienna Woods which encircle the city today. When people speak of the Vienna Woods they're referring to one of two distinct areas—one to the southwest that includes **Baden** and **Mayerling**, where Rudolf took his life; and the other, the **Kahlenberg Heights**, to the west and northwest. If you must choose between the two, go to the Heights: they're closer and offer splendid views of Vienna. A scenic highway takes you from one vantage point to another. It makes sense to combine tours of Schönbrunn and the Heights, and to stop on your way back to Vienna at a new wine tavern in **Grinzing**.

The best approach is from the south. Take the scenic mountain road called the **Höhenstrasse** for 5.5 miles and then drive another 15 miles to **Klosterneuburg Abbey**. There are scenic lookouts, restaurants, and hiking trails along the route. Highlights include:

1. Turn right and follow a winding road to the summit of **Gallitzinberg**, where there's a restaurant.

2. Walk to **Hermannskogel**, one of the less touristy areas.

3. Turn left on **Sieveringerstrasse** toward **Weidlingbach** and drive to the **Jägerwiese Restaurant**. Park and walk to the summit. (If you're using public transportation, take bus 39A to the end, and follow **Sieveringerstrasse**.)

4. Continue to **Kahlenberg**. There's a church, hotel and restaurant near the summit, and the view is impressive. By public transportation, take the streetcar to Grinzing and then a bus. It was on this summit that the Polish King John Sobieski gathered his forces for the attack that routed the Turks.

5. Take a few minutes' drive or a 30-minute walk to **Leopoldsberg**, the mountain with the best view and the biggest crowds.

6. Continue north to **Klosterneuburg** (open from 9:30 to 11, and 1:30 to 4; Sundays, from 1:30 to 4). The eleventh-century monastery wears a Baroque dress. High point of the visit is the famous **Verdun Altar**, which has 51 enameled scenes by a late-twelfth-century goldsmith. From the monastery, either drive 7 miles east along the Danube back to Vienna, or return south on the **Höhenstrasse**, past Leopoldsberg and Kahlenberg, and turn left on **Cobenzlgasse** to the wine town of **Grinzing**.

If you want to Do Vienna, you need to visit a **Heurigen tavern**, many of them in the suburb of Grinzing. Streetcar 38 goes directly there. When the new wine is ready, vintners hang an evergreen branch over their doors. The wine tastes as innocent as soda water—until you stand up. When the weather cooperates, tables are set in outdoor gardens. The Viennese used to bring their own picnic dinners, but most Heurigen now serve meals for the tourist trade. When you're not drinking, you can sing along with the musicians playing old Viennese folk songs on violins, accordions, and zithers. Among the best Heurigen are **Das Alte Haus Rausch-Rohde** (Himmelstrasse 35. Tel. 0222-322321) and **Figlmüller** (Grinzingerstrasse 55. Tel. 0222-324257). Other good bets are **Rohde's Heuriger** (Himmelstrasse 4) and **Rohde's Alte Haus** (Himmelstrasse 37). For additional names, pick up a booklet called *Heuriger in Wien* at any tourist information office.

Shopping

The **Dorotheum** (I, Dorotheergasse 17. Tel. 0222-528565) is the state-run auction house, which has sales almost every day. There's also a flea market (Saturday from 8 to 6) at the end of the Naschmarkt, between Districts V and VI.

The shops listed below are along the streets and squares you'll be visiting in District I. Almost all are on three connecting streets, **Kärntnerstrasse**, **Graben**, and **Kohlmarkt**. Serious shoppers should begin at the **Opera**, stroll down **Kärntnerstrasse** to St. Stephen's, turn left on **Graben**, and left again on **Kohlmarkt**.

Porcelain and Glass: *Lobmeyr*, Kärntnerstrasse 26. **Dirndls and Lederhosen**: *Lanz*, Kärntnerstrasse 10; *Loden-Plankl*, Michaelerplatz 6; *Trachten Schlössl*, Kohlmarkt 2. **Local handicrafts**: *Österreichische Werkstätten*, Kärntnerstrasse 6. **Leather**: *Mädler*, Graben 17. **Watches**: *Wagner*, Kärntnerstrasse 32. **Silverware**: *Rozet & Fischmeister*, Kohlmarkt 11. **Linen**: *Zur Schwäbischen Jungfrau*, Graben 26. **Jewelry**: *A. E. Koechert*, Neuer Markt 15.

Music and the Arts in Vienna

Why did Vienna spawn so many musicians, but so few writers? Perhaps because ideas were censored under the Habsburgs, and one can say most anything in music. Perhaps, too, music is the voice of nostalgia.

Musicians came here in the eighteenth and early nineteenth centuries because the aristocracy maintained small orchestras and groups of performers. A musician who joined a household was treated as a footman and lived and ate with the servants. The intimacy among the Viennese composers is legendary: Mozart and Haydn were friends; Beethoven took lessons from Haydn; Schubert was a pallbearer at Beethoven's funeral; Arnold Schönberg (1874–1951) taught his twelve-tone system here to Alban Berg and Anton von Webern.

The **Haydn Museum** (VI, Haydngasse 19. Open Tuesday to Friday, 10 to 4; Saturdays, 2 to 6; Sundays, 9 to 1) is where Haydn (1732–1809) gave lessons to Beethoven and composed *The Creation*. When Haydn arrived in Vienna at age seventeen he was alone and friendless; at the time of his death, here at this house, he was considered the greatest composer in Europe. He came of peasant stock from a nearby village and was brought to sing in the choir of St. Stephen's. To make ends meet he sang at weddings and funerals. Eventually he was offered the position of Kapellmeister to a prince, at whose estate he composed most of his works.

The **Mozart Monument (Figarohaus)**. See above.

The **Beethoven House** (I, Mölker Bastei. Open Tuesday to Friday, 10 to 4; Saturdays, 2 to 6; Sundays, 9 to 1) is where the composer lived from 1805 to 1815. He came to Vienna from Bonn at age twenty-two and stayed for life. He was a terrible neighbor, playing piano at odd hours, and was forced to move some twenty-five times. It was at this charming house that he composed *Fidelio* and the Fourth, Fifth, and Seventh symphonies. Here too he wrote the Moonlight Sonata, dedicated to an early love of his. It was a walk in the Vienna Woods that may have inspired the Pastoral Symphony. In his house in **Heiligenstadt**, which can be visited on a trip to the Vienna Woods, Beethoven wrote his bitter Heiligenstadt Testament: "What humiliation when someone is standing near me and hears a far-off flute and I cannot hear it, or when someone hears the shepherd singing and I can hear nothing. Such experiences nearly drove me to despair, and it would have taken little to make me end my own life. One thing alone, the art of music, restrained me." When Beethoven conducted the Ninth Symphony in Vienna in 1824, the orchestra watched not him but the concert master. After the second movement there was thunderous applause, but Beethoven didn't hear it; the singer had to turn him around so that he could see the clapping hands and acknowledge the ovation. Beethoven died in Vienna. According to one source, he died saying to his friend Hümmel: "I had a certain talent, hadn't I?"

The **Schubert Museum** (IX, Nussdorferstrasse 54. Open Tuesday to Friday, 10 to 4; Saturdays, 2 to 6; Sundays, 9 to 1) is the birthplace of the only one of the major composers who was actually born here. He was the son of a poor schoolmaster—a small boy with glasses and an angelic voice. When his voice broke, he had to leave the Vienna Choir Boys and find some other way to earn a living. He started teaching in his father's school, but hated it and spent most of his time writing music instead. He was never able to afford his own room (except for a short time), or even his own piano. Many of his songs were written on the backs of menus in neighborhood cafés, where he went with devoted friends. At Beethoven's deathbed he toasted, "To the one of us who is next"; and nineteen months later, at age thirty-one, he himself was dead.

In the **Central Cemetery** (Zentralfriedhof) is "Musician's Square" where you'll find the graves of Schubert, Hugo Wolf, Gluck, Brahms, Beethoven, and Johann Strauss (father and son).

The Arts

The **Vienna Festival** features four weeks of operas and concerts in late May and June. For details, contact any Austrian Tourist Office or write to Wiener Festwochen, Bestellbüro, Rathausstrasse 9, Vienna. Tel. 0222-56-16-70.

The **Summer of Music** (late June through August) is a summer-long festival of daily concerts. Complete programs are available at Tourist Offices or by mail from Wiener Musiksommer, P.O.B. 627, A-1151 Vienna.

The season at the **State Opera** (Staatsoper) runs from September through June. Strauss-type operettas or light operas are performed at the **Volksoper** in summer. It's worth a trip to the Staatsoper just to see the "show" at intermission when the formally dressed Viennese, with their stiff collars and pearly bosoms, sip champagne and nibble on chocolate-dipped strawberries as they promenade up and down the hall. No monument gives you such a sense of living in a City of Dreams. Tickets are sold at box offices and travel agencies.

The tourist office has monthly listings of concerts. The **Vienna Phil-harmonic** performs in the **Musikverein** at Dumbastrasse 3. The **Vienna Symphony** and other groups perform in the **Wiener Konzerthaus** at Lothringerstrasse 20. Concerts are also held in the **Schubert Museum** (Nussdorferstrasse 54). Church music can be heard Sunday mornings at **St. Stephen's, Karlskirche,** and **Augustinerkirche.** Special summer concerts are held in the **Belvedere Garden** and at **Schönbrunn.** Candlelit Baroque concerts, with performers in eighteenth-century dress, are given in the **Palais Pallavicini** at Josefsplatz. To see the **Vienna Choir Boys,** write at least two months in advance to Hofmusikkapelle, Hofburg,

A-1010 Vienna. You'll be sent a reservation card to present at the box office when you pick up your tickets. Additional tickets are sold at travel agencies and at the Burgkappelle (in the Hofburg) every Friday at 5 P.M. Queue up by 4:30.

The two English-speaking theaters are The English Theater (VIII, Josefgasse 12. Tel. 0222-421260 or 428284) and The International Theatre (IX, Porzellangasse 8. Tel. 0222-316272).

Escorted Tours

Try to tour "Old Vienna" (District I) on foot. Bus tours are convenient to the Belvedere, Schönbrunn Palace, and the Vienna Woods.

Two companies offer escorted bus tours: Cityrama Sightseeing Tours and Vienna Sightseeing Tours. Make reservations through hotels or travel agencies. Some leave from the Opera, others from the Main Bus Terminal (Wien Mitte). Look for one that picks you up at your hotel.

A 2½-hour escorted walking tour of "Old Vienna" leaves from the Café Lahdtmann near the Bergtheater on Monday, Wednesday, and Saturday at 9:15 A.M. Ask hotels and travel agencies for details or call 0222-324677.

Private guides are available from Travelpoint Vienna, IX, Boltzmanngasse 19. Tel. 0222-314243.

Dining

Viennese food makes up in heartiness what it lacks in subtlety. A legacy of the Austrian-Hungarian Empire is Hungarian goulash and stuffed cabbage and peppers (gefüllte Paprike and gefülltes Kraut). Soup with dumplings is another specialty, particularly Leberknödelsuppe (liver dumpling soup). Veal is featured on most menus, particular Wiener Schnitzel—veal dipped in egg batter and fried. Other specialties include Backhuhn (fried chicken), Rehfilet (venison), and gebackene Champignons (fried mushrooms). For dessert, try the small wild strawberries from the Vienna Woods, topped, of course, with fresh whipped cream.

Zu Den 3 (Drei) Husaren, "The Three Hussars" (E, Weihburggasse 4. Tel. 0222-521192), located just off Kärntnerstrasse, near St. Stephen's, is an elegant restaurant with an Old World atmosphere. Some 45 hors d'oeuvres are wheeled around on four trollies. The excellent French cuisine features goose-liver pâté, fresh lobster, and, best of all, a saddle of venison for two. Dinner only.

Astoria (M, Führichgasse 1. Tel. 0222-526585) is popular with operagoers after evening performances. The atmosphere in this traditional hotel restaurant is "Old Vienna."

König von Ungarn (M, Schulerstrasse 10. Tel. 0222-525319) is another popular restaurant near the cathedral, known for its service, its intimacy, and its boiled beef. The specialty here is an Italian dish, Bollito misto (boiled meats, chicken, and vegetables). For dessert, try Powidltascherl.

Palais Schwarzenberg (E, Schwarzenbergplatz 9. Tel. 0222-784515) is a real palace with an elegant French menu featuring venison and fresh fish.

Sacher (E, Philharmonikerstrasse 4. Tel. 0222-525575) is a world-famous hotel restaurant. (In 1985 the former U.S. Ambassador married the owner and became Mrs. Sacher.) Famous dishes include Tafelspitz, baked boneless chicken Viennoise, and, of course, homemade Sacher Torte.

Bei Max (I, Landhausgasse 2. Tel. 0222-637359), located on a side street off the Augustinerstrasse, not far from the Opera, is known for its large servings and plain, wholesome meals at reasonable prices.

Oswald & Kalb (M, Bäckerstrasse 14. Tel. 0222-521371), very near the cathedral, is an Old World restaurant with a young crowd. Dinner only. For a lower-priced meal in the same vicinity, try **Figlmuller** (I, Wollzeile 5. Tel. 0222-526177)—a folksy restaurant in a historic courtyard. Popular regional dishes include its own huge Figlmüller Schnitzel (veal cutlet), Tafelspitz, Powidltascherl, and Palatschinken (small crepes with jam), and excellent fruity wines.

Steirereck (E, Rasumofskygasse 2. Tel. 0222-733168), located near the Rotunden Bridge across the Danube Canal, has reopened after long and careful restorations. The menu features fresh, lightly prepared international and regional dishes, including excellent cream soups, ravioli stuffed with Saibling (a fresh-water fish), and wild duck in a juniper cream sauce.

Zum Kuckuck (M, Himmelpfortgasse 15. Tel. 0222-528470), located on a side street between the Opera and the cathedral, is a modern restaurant with a growing reputation for its creative French cuisine.

Chez Rainer (M, Wiedner Hauptstrasse 27. Tel. 0222-6546460) is a unpretentious restaurant in the south part of town catering more to middle-class Austrians than to tourists. The menu features simply prepared, hearty Austrian dishes at reasonable prices.

Coffeehouses

Sitting at a café is not a pastime but a way of life. Each Viennese has his own favorite, where he comes to talk, read, or dream. Here he becomes a man of leisure, a nobleman from the Court. Once your order has been taken, feel free to stay all day; for a waiter to pressure you to move is un-Viennese. When the Turks fled in 1683, they left behind bags of a dark, bitter-tasting bean called coffee. The first coffee shop was opened by a Pole named George Kolschitsky, who was rewarded with some of these beans for having snuck through Turkish lines with messages to relieving troops. The Kipfel or crescent-shaped pastry was conceived at the same time by a baker tasting victory over the Turks (whose symbol is the crescent). Among your choices: **Einspänner** (black coffee with whipped cream); **Kapuziner** (coffee with a little milk: brown in color like the habit of a Capuchin monk); **Mit Schlag** (with whipped cream and milk); **Doppelschlag** (with more whipped cream than coffee); **Schale licht** (with more milk than coffee).

Pastry Shops

Among the best are **Demel's** (Kohlmarkt 14. Tel. 0222-6355160), which also serves a fine lunch; **Sluka** (Rathausplatz 8); **Gerstner** (Kärntnerstrasse 15); **Heiner** (Kärntnerstrasse 21); and **Lehmann** (Graben 12).

Cafés

Don't miss the historic **Café Central** (Freyung) where Trotsky and Stalin used to play chess, and where Trotsky still owes for an unpaid black coffee; **Café Europa** (in the Hotel Europa, Neuer Markt 3), and **Café Hawelka** (Dorotheergasse, just off the Graben). **Reichenberger Griechenbeisl** (Fleischmarkt) is in a sixteenth-century building in the Old University district. At **Café Sacher** (behind the Opera House) you can decide whether the Sacher Torte is worth its reputation. Eduard Sacher, the rebellious son of the owner of the Sacher Hotel, apparently slipped the recipe to the owner of **Demel's** and claimed that his recipe was the original. After ten years of litigation—only a city of dreams could have a ten-year court battle over pastries!—the judge decided that Sacher could claim the original and that Demel's should call its own, "Eduard Sacher Torte." Why not try both?

Wine Cellars

Below the streets are a number of wine cellars with a cavernous, medieval feel to them that students or newcomers to Europe will love. Some serve modest meals. Among the best are **Melkerstiftskeller** (Schottengasse 3) and **Urbanikeller** (Am Hof 12).

Lodging

The hotel classification system employed in most western European countries is also used for Vienna's hotels. Five stars denote luxury-class; four stars, first-class, and so on. All taxes are usually included in the rates; Continental breakfasts are usually included, too. A free booklet, *Hotels in Wien,* is available from government tourist offices in Vienna and abroad. All hotels listed below are within District I.

There are really only four traditional luxury-class hotels—the **Sacher,** the **Bristol,** the **Imperial,** and the **Palais Schwarzenburg.**

For character and tradition, the privately owned **Hotel Sacher** (E, A-1015 Wien 1, Philharmonikerstrasse 4. Tel. 0222-525575), next door to the Opera, is still the place to stay. Bathrooms can be small, but the hotel is truly nineteenth century, with hallowed, paneled lounges regal in crystal and Habsburg maroon. The Sacher attracts a crowd of intellectuals and artists, which makes its appeal perhaps a bit narrower and deeper than that of the equally opulent Bristol.

Hotel Bristol (E, A-1015 Wien, Kärntner Ring 1. Tel. 0222-521642) rivals the Sacher in prestige and tradition. Its location opposite the Opera House, at the head of the main shopping street, is equally convenient. The bedrooms are larger than those at the Sacher, and the black marble bathrooms are more opulent.

Hotel im Palais Schwarzenberg (E, Schwarzenbergplatz, A 1030 Wien. Tel. 0222-784515) occupies part of a palace within 19 acres of gardens. The rooms are decorated with modern French elegance, with great attention to detail. If you want to be in walking distance of the shops and sights, stay at the Sacher or Bristol, if you want a quiet retreat, and the sense of staying in a private palace, stay at the Schwarzenberg, a 10-minute cab ride to center city.

Hotel Imperial (E, Kärntner Ring 16. Tel. 0222-651765) was completely restored after ten years as the Russian headquarters during the Four Power occupation of Vienna (1945–55). Though it is a palatial indulgence (Wagner liked to stay here), it lacks the nostalgic feeling of the Sacher and Bristol. The service is faultless, however, and many consider the Imperial their favorite hotel.

Rooms at the recently renovated **Ambassador** (E, Neuer Markt 6. Tel. 0222-527511) are grouped around a central courtyard. The red plush drapes and upholstery are, well, typically Viennese. If the top four hotels are booked or too expensive, stay here for comfort and Old World charm.

Hotel Kaiserin Elisabeth (M/E, Weihburggasse 3. Tel. 0222-522626) is in a building that dates back to the fourteenth century. Home to Wagner, Liszt, and Grieg, it offers all the creature comforts of the 5-star hotels, without the trappings of luxury, or the expense.

König von Ungarn (M/E, Schulerstrasse 10. Tel. 0222-526520), only a block from St. Stephen's, has a lovely central courtyard. Rooms are comfortable and adequate, at prices about $100 less than at the Sacher.

Wandl (M, Petersplatz 9. Tel. 0222-636317) faces St. Peter's Church (Peterskirche), off Graben. Rooms are comfortable and reasonably priced.

Geissler (I, Postgasse 14. Tel. 0222-632803) is one of the few inexpensive pensions in District I (near the Danube Canal).

For Further Information

The **Central Information Office** (Tel. 0222-431608) is in the Opernpassage, the underground subway station beneath Opera Square. No room reservations are made. If you're driving from Salzburg or Dürnstein, there's an **Auto Information Center** (Tel. 0222-971271) off the Autobahn (A1) as you approach Vienna. Hotel reservations can be made here. There's another information office at the airport (Tel. 0222-777028).

A taped list of events: Tel. 1515. *General train information:* Tel. 7200. *Train information at the West Train Station (Westbahnhof):* Tel. 0222-835185 or 835188. *Airport information:* Tel. 7770. *Information on travel in Austria:* Österreich Information, Margaretenstrasse 1. Tel. 0222-575714.

Wien International (IX, Alserstrasse 20. Tel. 0222-4395840) is an organization set up to help foreigners.

EN ROUTE: From VIENNA

Most of you will fly home from Vienna or Munich. If you're continuing south to Yugoslavia, drive to **Graz**, and take the highway to **Lubljana** and **Rijeka**. See the Yugoslavian itinerary below.

RECOMMENDED READING

Diane Buregwyn, *Salzburg: A Portrait* (sold in local gift shops).

Richard Rickett, *A Brief Survey of Austrian History* (Heinemann, 1983) and *Music and Musicians in Vienna* (Heinemann, 1973); (sold in local gift shops).

Edward Crankshaw, *Vienna: The Image of a Culture in Decline* (MacMillan, 1938).

Vienna from A to Z (Vienna Tourist Bureau).

YUGOSLAVIA

❦ *The Adriatic Coast*

MAJOR ATTRACTIONS

- Walled medieval towns strung along a wild, romantic coast.
- Two thousand years of art and architectural treasures, from the Roman palace of Diocletian—still inhabited today—to the contemporary sculpture of Ivan Meštrović.
- Dubrovnik, a twelfth-century city of ancient white stone—one of the most graceful and dignified cities in the world.
- Summer-long festivals of music and dance performed in medieval courtyards, Gothic churches, and Renaissance palaces.
- An entire medieval village tastefully transformed into a luxury hotel.
- More than 1,200 islands to explore.
- Some of the lowest prices in Europe.

INTRODUCTION

The Yugoslavian itinerary takes you down a wildly beautiful 515-mile stretch of the Adriatic, between the mountains and the sea. One minute you're driving through a moonscape of shattered stone; the next, you're heading through a fertile coastal plain in a balmy Mediterranean world of cypresses, olive groves, and vineyards.

Strung along the coast is a series of medieval towns where visitors stop to swim, dine, shop, and explore. The towns have spread beyond their ancient walls, but the walls remain, and within them little has changed,

YUGOSLAVIA

Rijeka

Opatija

Senj

Rab

Pag

Novigrad

Zadar

Šibenik

Trogir

ADRIATIC SEA

N

W E

S

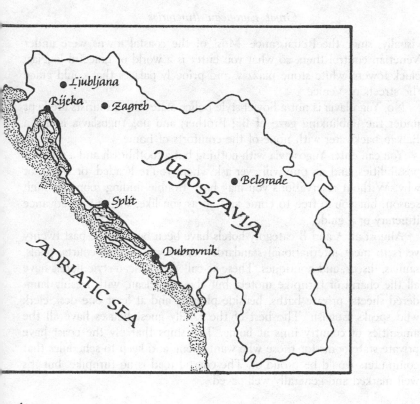

Ljubljana

Rijeka

Zagreb

YUGOSLAVIA

Belgrade

Split

Dubrovnik

ADRIATIC SEA

Split

Hvar Island

Korčula Island

Ston

Trebinje

Hvar

Pelješac

Risan

Korčula

Cavtat

Kotor

Dubrovnik

Herceg Novi

Četinje

Budva

Sveti Stefan

visually, since the Renaissance. Most of the coastal towns were under Venetian control then, so what you enter is a world of graceful loggias, clock towers, white stone piazzas, and princely palaces that could grace the streets of Venice.

No, Yugoslavia is not a Soviet-style police state where tourists are kept under the unblinking gaze of Big Brother; and no, Yugoslavia is not a Balkan backwater with none of the comforts of home.

You can enter Yugoslavia with nothing but a toothbrush and a sense of possibilities, and no one will ever ask where you're headed, or when, or why. Without reservations you may have trouble finding rooms in high season, but you're free to come and go as you like, without an advance itinerary or a guide.

Almost all A and B category hotels have been built in the past twenty years to meet international standards—many with tennis courts, pools, saunas, discos, and boutiques. These so-called American-style hotels have all the charm of turnpike motels, but they *are* clean, with freshly laundered sheets, private baths, bedside phones, and at least one desk clerk who speaks English. The best of the family guest houses have all the amenities of country inns at home. The ships that ply the coast have private staterooms for those who want them, and keep to schedules that commuters would be proud of. The coastal road is no turnpike, but it's well marked and generally well paved.

THE MAIN ROUTE (with minimum overnight stays)

3–5 Days

> *Two nights:* Dubrovnik
> *One night:* Split
> *One night:* Hvar

5–7 Days

> *Two nights:* Dubrovnik
> *Two nights:* Split
> Excursions to Šibenik and Trogir
> *Two nights:* Sveti Stefan

7–14 Days (land route, ending at Dubrovnik or Bar)

> *One night:* Opatija
> *One night:* Rab
> *One night:* Zadar

Two nights: Split
One night: Hvar
Three nights: Dubrovnik
Excursion to Korčula
One night: Sveti Stefan

7–14 Days (land and sea route, ending back at Opatija)

One night: Opatija
One night: Zadar
Two nights: Split
Three nights: Dubrovnik
Two nights: Sveti Stefan
One night: Hvar
One night: Rab

GETTING AROUND

Getting to Yugoslavia

If you're taking the 3–5 or 5–7 day trip, fly to and from **Dubrovnik**. Yugoslav Airlines (JAT) has direct service from New York; Pan American has connecting service from New York. (On *direct* flights you don't change planes, on *connecting* flights you do.)

If you're taking the 7–14 day trip, fly to **Zagreb** or **Ljubljana**, and return from (1) **Zagreb** or **Ljubljana**, (2) **Dubrovnik**, or (3) **Belgrade**. These alternatives are discussed below. When you arrive in Zagreb or Ljubljana, take a bus, train, or rented car to **Rijeka** (near **Opatija**) on the coast, where the itinerary begins. The trip from Ljubljana is shorter. Only Yugoslav Airlines has direct service between New York and Zagreb, Ljubljana, Dubrovnik, and Belgrade. Pan Am has connecting service between New York and Zagreb, Belgrade, and Dubrovnik.

Traveling Through Yugoslavia

By car:

If you're taking the 3–5 or 5–7 day trip, pick up and deliver your rented car at Dubrovnik's airport.

If you're taking the 7–14 day trip, you have three main alternatives:

1. Rent a car at Ljubljana or Zagreb; drive south along the coast, exploring the islands along the way; leave your car at Dubrovnik's airport, and fly home.

2. Rent a car at Ljubljana or Zagreb; drive south along the coast, exploring the islands along the way; continue south, past Dubrovnik, to Bar; either leave your car at Bar and take the train to Belgrade, or drive to Belgrade, and fly home.

3. Rent a car at Ljubljana or Zagreb; drive south along the coast to Dubrovnik; take a car ferry back to Rijeka, stopping at islands along the way; drive back to Ljubljana or Zagreb; leave your car at the airport, and fly home.

The car ferries run both from the mainland to the islands and from one island to another the entire length of the coast. For reservations and schedules, contact the **International Cruise Center** (185 Willis Avenue, Mineola, N.Y. Tel. 516/747-8880 or 800/221-3254). In Yugoslavia, contact any travel agency or **Jadrolinija** (the Yugoslav Adriatic Shipping Co.). They have offices in each port you'll be visiting: Rijeka, Zadar, Šibenik, Split, Dubrovnik, Korčula, Hvar, and Rab.

If you're driving to Yugoslavia from Vienna, take the road from Graz (Austria) to Rijeka, via Ljubljana. The border crossing on the main highway between **Graz** and **Maribor** can be slow in tourist season; if lines are very long, take **Route 69** east about 10 miles to **Mureck**, and cross the border there.

If you're driving from Western Europe, there are car trains from major cities to Rijeka. If you're continuing from Yugoslavia to Italy, there are overnight car ferries from Dubrovnik and Bar to Bari, Italy.

Gas coupons purchased in foreign currency at the border will save you about 5 percent. If you have no visa, you can buy one at border crossings, valid for thirty days.

By public transportation:

If you're taking the 3–5 or 5–7 day trip, you'll arrive in Dubrovnik, where you can take bus excursions to the Gulf of Kotor and ferries to all the major towns and islands along the coast.

If you're taking the 7–14 day trip, fly to Zagreb or Ljubljana and take a train or bus to Rijeka. From here you can take buses or boats anywhere along the coast. Buses are crowded in summer, so coastal ferries are preferable. There's at least one coastal ferry daily in season, and any number of local ferries between islands. The trip from Rijeka to Dubrovnik takes about 24 hours, but you'll want to disembark at Rab, Zadar, Šibenik, Split, Hvar, and Korčula. The **International Cruise Center** can make arrangements, including private staterooms, overnight stays at island hotels, and transportation across the Adriatic to Italy.

SPECIAL EVENTS

Mid-June–mid-August: Split Summer Festival, with music and drama performed within the walls of Diocletian's Palace.

July 10–August 25: Dubrovnik Summer Festival, with music and dance performed against a backdrop of ancient palaces and churches.

July–August: Musical evenings in Zadar, inside the 1,000-year-old Church of St. Donat.

July–August: Korčula Sword Dance, symbolizing Yugoslavia's struggle against oppression. Thursdays and July 27.

A NOTE ON SHOPPING

Art books are top quality and, pricewise, a real steal. For old books with beautiful line drawings, check out the shops on side streets in Dubrovnik. Liqueurs in decorative bottles, such as maraschino and plum brandy (šljivovica) are distilled in Zadar and sold along the coast. The best filigree jewelry is in Montenegro, south of Dubrovnik. The quality of fine lacework varies from shop to shop; the best I saw was sold by peasant women along the benches of the seaside park in Opatija. The best place for antique ceramics is Zadar. For modern art, visit the galleries in Split. Old icons are not for sale, but you can find quality reproductions in Split and Dubrovnik. Inexpensive peasant handicrafts—costumed dolls, embroidered blouses, etc.—are sold everywhere; the best quality is usually in the gift shops in the A-class and Luxury-class hotels. Prices are fixed, except in outdoor markets.

THINGS TO SEE AND DO WITH CHILDREN

Teenagers can join their Yugoslav contemporaries strutting every night along the main street of every town. This daily ritual begins in the early evening and can continue to midnight—the later the hour, the younger the crowd. Medieval buildings along the streets are now ice cream parlors, cafés, and discos, where young people do what young people do.

Kids have a limited tolerance for the past. Spend mornings with them, exploring the ancient cities, and then send them back to the beaches and pools. The resort complexes have tennis courts and can arrange for waterskiing, underwater spear fishing, and windsurfing.

Stay in private homes with English-speaking children the same age as yours. If you have young children, find families willing to baby-sit.

Near Opatija, visit the Postojna Caves. In Split, visit the zoo and aquarium. In Korčula, see the sword dance Moreško on Thursdays in summer.

A NOTE ON SPORTS

Swimming

Most beaches along the Dalmatian coast are pebbly; in many areas you have to clamber over rocks to get wet. Those who can afford the price should stay at hotels with pools. Fortunately, most postwar A-class hotels have them.

Opatija, built as a winter resort, has concrete platforms along its shore. Zadar has a good beach at the Borik Hotel complex. Rab has some great rocky coves; rent a boat to take you there. Beaches on Hvar and Korčula are mostly rocks and pebbles. Dubrovnik's pebbly beach is often crowded; take a boat to the sandy beaches on the nearby islands of Lopud and Lokrum. Near Budva, you'll find good beaches at the Hotel Avala and at Jaz and Beči. There are good sand and pebble beaches along the causeway to Sveti Stefan.

Boating and Fishing

An indented coast with offshore islands is ideal both for saltwater fish —swordfish, mullet, tuna, and sea bass—and fishermen. Deep-sea fishing is popular, so you won't have trouble arranging trips through hotels and travel agencies. Another popular sport is underwater spear fishing, best around the Kvarner Islands and off the seaward coasts of Rab, Cres, and Pag. You can reach these islands from Opatija, Rijeka, and Zadar. From Šibenik, fishermen angle on the River Krka and on Lake Visovačko Jezero for trout, chub, and barbel. From Split, they play the River Jadro for trout.

SOME NOTES ON YUGOSLAVIA

The Country

In the late sixth century, the Roman towns along the coast were invaded by the Avars and the Slavs. The Slavs are still there today. The Slavic nation created after World War II is less one country than a federation of six autonomous republics and two provinces. The republics are Bosnia-Herzegovina, Croatia, Macedonia, Montenegro, Serbia, and

Slovenia. The two provinces (Vojvodina and Kosovo) lie within the borders of Serbia.

In addition to its six republics, Yugoslavia today has two alphabets (Cyrillic, which looks like Russian, and the familiar Latin alphabet used along the coast); four main languages (Slovene, Croatian, Serbian, and Macedonian); and five Slavic nationalities (Slovenes, Croats, Serbs, Macedonians, and Montenegrins).

Most of your trip, as far south as the Gulf of Kotor, lies within the republic of Croatia. (Bosnia-Herzegovina was given a short stretch of land south of Dubrovnik so it would have access to the sea.) South from the Gulf of Kotor to Sveti Stefan, you'll be passing through the republic of Montenegro. The Croats are predominately Roman Catholic; the Montenegrins are predominately Eastern Orthodox.

The Government

The image of Yugoslavia as a grim, Eastern Bloc country is a holdover from the Dulles days. The truth is that Yugoslavia is a nonaligned nation that prides itself on its independence from both the U.S. and the U.S.S.R. Soviet papers are sold in kiosks up and down the coast, but so are *Newsweek* and the *Herald Tribune*.

The socialism practiced in Yugoslavia today is a blend of communism and private enterprise, and has little in common with the top-heavy, state-run system in the U.S.S.R. Workers elect their own managers by secret ballot and help establish company policies by referendum. The billboards you see along the roads are the result of a decentralized system that encourages competition. Private businesses are tolerated so long as they are family run and have no more than five employees. Wherever you go, you can choose between private and state-run restaurants and hotels. The food may come from a state cooperative or from a farmer who cultivates his own fields and sells his produce on the open market.

Language

Where you're going, along the Dalmatian coast, people use the same Latin alphabet you use at home. There are a few different sounds, though, which you should learn:

ć = t as in picture
č = ch as in chuckle
dž = dg as in jungle

j (at the end of a word) = ye as in yeshiva
š = sh as in shenanigan

A NOTE ON ART AND ARCHITECTURE

Let's take a brief look at the architectural styles you'll see along the coast:

Roman. The best example is Diocletian's Palace in Split. Its monumental scale was a form of architectural propaganda, meant to advertise the greatness of the emperor. The Romans were the first city planners, and you can see their ancient street plans—appropriate for a military camp with main thoroughfares crossing at right angles—both in Split and Zadar.

Early Croatian. These Pre-Romanesque churches, strongly influenced by Byzantium (the Eastern Roman Empire), are usually small and circular, and surmounted by a dome. The interiors, like the interiors of Romanesque churches, are based on Roman basilicas: oblong halls with a central corridor (nave), flanked by aisles. The best examples are St. Donat's in Zadar, the Church of the Holy Cross in Nin, and the basilica of St. Barbara in Trogir.

Romanesque. The dominant features are the rounded arch and the stone barrel ceilings (vaults). The best examples are the Cathedral of St. Tryphon in Kotor, the churches of St. Mary and St. Andrew in Rab, and the Cathedral of St. Lawrence in Trogir.

Gothic. The Gothic influence came from Venice and showed a strong continuity with Romanesque forms. In Northern Gothic churches, the high ceilings and delicate columns force you to look upward to God, but in Italian Gothic churches the thrust is still forward to the altar. The best examples of Venetian Gothic are the cathedrals in Šibenik, Korčula, and Split. The master of Late Venetian Gothic was the Croatian sculptor and architect, George of Dalmatia.

Renaissance. Renaissance architecture was almost always mixed with Gothic and Romanesque, as in Trogir, Zadar, Šibenik, and Dubrovnik. Only in the work of Nikola of Florence does the early Florentine Renaissance find expression, notably in the chapel of Ivan Ursini in the Trogir Cathedral and in the dome of the Šibenik Cathedral.

Baroque. The Baroque came via Italy and Austria and can be seen in Dubrovnik, both in the cathedral and in the façades of buildings along the main street (Placa). The Baroque arrived at a time when cities were losing their independence and the great age of building was over.

The Dalmatian painters whose work you should follow are **Blaž of Trogir** (early fifteenth century); **Lovro Dobričenic** (late fifteenth century); **Nikola Božidarević** (the most important Croatian Renaissance painter, early sixteenth century); and **Mihajlo Hamzić** (early sixteenth century).

A NOTE ON DINING

Expect to pay about $20 to $25 per person for a complete meal in the best restaurants. Meals in the small, family-run fish bistros—where most tourists like to eat—run about $10–$12 per person. Restaurants below are rated, for two, E (expensive, over $45), M (moderate, $20–$40), I (inexpensive, under $15).

East meets West in Yugoslavia, not only in architectural styles but in food. In the north, from Opatija to Zadar, the emphasis is Italian and Hungarian, with lots of olive oil and garlic. As you head south, the accent is Greek and Turkish.

The Yugoslavs know that when it comes to restaurants, small is better than big, and privately owned is usually better than state-owned. Hotel food is, as a rule, as bland as the surroundings—what else would you expect from a kitchen that turns out a thousand meals at one sitting? If you must eat at your hotel, avoid the warmed-over specials and have something cooked to order. If you've signed up for a package tour, try not to have your lunches and dinners included, so you can go off on your own.

Room rates usually include a Continental breakfast, but you can order cereal, eggs, etc., for an additional price. The Turkish coffee doesn't have that sweet, muddy sediment you find in real Turkish coffee—it's more like espresso. The regular coffee is terrible; coffee lovers should pack a jar of instant. If you're staying in a private home, find one that serves breakfast.

The floor of the Adriatic dips toward the Yugoslav coast—is that why the fish and crustacea are so delicious? As expected in coastal cities, your best bet is almost always fresh seafood: prawns (škampi), mussels in wine (ostrige), lobster (jastog), baby squid (lignje), red mullet (barbbuni), mackerel (skuše), a bouillabaisse-type fish soup (brodet), oysters, and crabs. The shrimps, remember, come in their shells with little beady eyes that stare at you as you tear them apart. Fish is often sold in restaurants by weight. In the smaller, family restaurants, you'll be shown a platter with the day's catch, from which you choose your very own.

Meat dishes, as a rule, are not exceptional. Best bets are lamb, veal, and mutton. Also tasty are skewered, barbecued lamb, pork, veal (ražnjići), and smoked Dalmatian ham (pršut).

Yugoslavia produces many good, inexpensive, full-bodied wines. Until you find what you like, ask for a two-tenths liter (dva deci) of a local wine —either red *(crno)* or white *(belo)*. Zilavka is a relatively dry white wine. Lighter white wines include Pošip and Vugava. Dingač is a heavy, sweet red wine. Lighter reds are Postup and Plavac. Šljivovica, a fiery plum brandy, used to be the national drink; now it is Loza. Locally made liqueurs include cherry (Maraschino) and walnut (Orahovac).

Fruit juices (voćni sokovi) are special, particularly peach juice (Marelica). Shops that sell juice also sell wonderful ices and sorbets, and delicious pastries such as warm štrudla filled with fruit.

A NOTE ON LODGING

In 1948 Yugoslavia had sixty thousand foreign visitors; in 1980 it had 6.5 million. To deal with this latest invasion, the government has thrown up huge, 600-room, ferro-concrete hotels in complexes several miles outside the main towns. The principle seems to be that one 600-room hotel is more economical than six 100-room hotels. These compounds, complete with pools, shopping arcades, discos, and beauty parlors, were built not to isolate foreigners from the Real Yugoslavia, but to provide them, at minimum cost, with the motel-like comforts of home.

Functional, cavernous, cold—these are words that come to mind to describe these late-twentieth-century Diocletian palaces, built not to awe emissaries from Nicomedia but to accommodate the package-tour trade from Hamburg and Naples. Furnishings, too, are Socialist Modern. On the bright side, there's a certain comfort knowing your room will be relatively new and clean, with the amenities you expect at home. It's nice, too, to have tennis courts, swimming pools, and tour desks with clerks who speak English.

In Yugoslavia, older hotels are usually not more charming but more rundown, so if you want spaciousness and comfort, check into the newest hotel you can find. The country-inn set should do this, too, unless you stay in a private home or in one of the few prewar hotels that has kept its Old World charm.

The Yugoslavs rate their hotels L (luxury), A, B, C, and D. Most Americans will be content with A and B. Bear in mind that a B-class hotel may be as comfortable as an A-class hotel, but gets a lower rating because it lacks, say, a pool. Exchange rates vary from day to day, so the following room rates (for two) are only approximate: *Luxury:* $70–$110; *A-Class:* $60–$100; *B-Class:* $40–$60; *C-Class:* $25; *D-Class:* Under $20.

If you're adventuresome, traveling with kids, or on a tight budget, spend at least one night in a private home. Rooms are as safe and comfortable as bed-and-breakfast houses in Britain, and a hundred times more personal than the big resort complexes. Arrangements can be made through travel agencies at home or through travel bureaus in every major town along the coast. You can also stop at homes with ROOMS FOR RENT signs along the highway, though vacancies are not easy to find in high season near Dubrovnik and Split. The government prefers that you book through them, since families otherwise may not report your visit and pay their taxes; but it's perfectly legal for you to make arrangements on your own.

EMERGENCIES

Police: Tel. 92. *Ambulance:* Tel. 94.

Breakdown service, Yugoslav Automobile Association: Tel. 987.

Doctors: IAMAT (International Association for Medical Assistance to Travelers) has a list of approved English-speaking doctors in major Yugoslavian cities. Contact IAMAT, 736 Center Street, Lewiston, N.Y. 14092.

FOR FURTHER INFORMATION

Yugoslav State Tourist Office, 630 Fifth Avenue, Suite 280, New York, N.Y. 10111. Tel. 212/757-1801.

Make travel arrangements through agencies whose main offices are in the regions you plan to visit: **Opatija:** *Kvarner Express,* Maršala Tita 186, YU-51410 Opatija. Tel. 051-711111. **Split:** *Dalmacijaturist,* Titova Obala 5, YU-58000 Split. Tel. 058-44666. **Dubrovnik:** *Atlas,* Pile 1, YU-50000 Dubrovnik. Tel. 050-27333. **Montenegro:** *Montenegroturist,* YU-81310 Budva. Tel. 082-82008.

THE ITINERARY

✤ *OPATIJA*

If you're partial to middle-class German resort towns with concrete beaches, you'll love Opatija. If you don't—well, there are still reasons to visit.

Opatija was a fishing village until the 1880s, when a Viennese doctor began shipping his patients here to recuperate. The high concentration of ozone in the air was said to work wonders. In the late nineteenth century the resort flourished as a fashionable watering hole for the nobility of Austria and Hungary. Hotels and villas were built in the classical (Roman) style—a form of visual propaganda for the declining Habsburgs. The architecture plays for effect rather than supporting some high intellectual ideals, but it does have a certain opulence that suggests a bygone age.

Today elderly couples come in buses and stroll among the lush, subtropical flowers. They nod at the camellias and promenade along the sea, breathing in the sweet, lime-scented air. Have you stumbled into an octogenarian convention, you may wonder. And yet the experience will put you in a frame of mind to slow down and enjoy life, too.

Mass tourism in a nineteenth-century setting—that's what makes Opatija so compelling, and so off-putting. My favorite image is of a middle-aged Italian couple entering the regal ballroom of the Imperial Hotel, where kings once danced, sitting among the crumbs of an uncleared table, and biting into the uneaten rolls.

Opatija is worth visiting if only to compare a town under Austro-Hungarian influence to all the other Venetian-style cities you'll see along the coast. It's also a convenient place to rest up after a transatlantic flight; it's certainly more attractive than the industrial city of Rijeka. The climate is balmy, and you can offer your face to the sun for a few days before heading down the coast. Built as a winter resort, it has limited beach facilities, so find yourself a hotel with a pool. Hotels can arrange for waterskiing, windsurfing, boat rentals, and tennis.

Excursions

Opatija makes a good base for day trips to Trieste, the Plitvička lakes, and the island of **Rab** (see page 220). Try to overnight on Rab so you can see it when the daytrippers are gone. But if you have only an afternoon to spare, leave your car in Opatija and (in season) take the hydrofoil. It's only an hour's trip. Tours can be arranged through hotels or **Kvarner Express** (Tel. 711070 or 711111).

The **Postojna Caves** are 45 miles north—if you drove from Austria you passed them en route. These are the second-largest underground caverns in the world. A narrow-gauge railroad takes you in, and a guide leads you on a mile-long walk to a chamber that can seat ten thousand. En route you'll pass a pool that contains the eyeless, flesh-colored, pencil-thin *Proteus anguineus*. It must have been such creatures, half-fish, half-mammal, that Thomas Wolfe had in mind when he wrote about the first forms of life crawling out of the primeval mud and then, finding the change unpleasant, crawling back in again. Half-day tours can be arranged through **Kvarner Express** (Tel. 711070 or 711111).

Shopping

Peasant women sell hand-embroidered tablecloths, napkins, and shawls in parks along the harbor.

Dining

Café Jedro (M), has a lovely terrace overlooking the sea. **Ribliji Restoran** (M) has a good reputation for fresh seafood.

Lodging

Furnishings in turn-of-the-century hotels are Early Sears, but rooms have balconies and high ceilings that suggest the elegance of another era. If you're looking for character, best bet is the 60-room **Belvedere II** (B, Tel. 712433), the annex of the Grand Hotel Belvedere. Jan Kubelik, the violinist, once lived in what is today the gambling hall. It has a B rating only because it has no elevator.

Other older hotels with a touch of class include the 95-year-old **Villa Ariston** (A, Tel. 711379 or 711919) on the outskirts of town; the centrally located **Kvarner** (A, Tel. 711211 or 711511), or its annex, **Villa Amalia**.

The 400-bed **Ambassador** (L, Tel. 712111) is the fanciest of the modern high-rise hotels, with indoor and outdoor pools, American bar, and hairdresser. The brochure calls the balconies loggias. Other modern B-class hotels include the **Bellevue** (Tel. 711011), the **Grand Belvedere-Rosalia** (Tel. 712433), the **Astoria** (Tel. 711411), and the **Avala** (Tel. 712411).

For Further Information

Contact **Kvarner Express** (Tel. 711070 or 711111) or the **Tourist Bureau** on the main street, across from the Imperial Hotel.

✤ *RIJEKA* (6 miles from Opatija)

Rijeka is a modern port city with some old buildings—more a point of transit than a place to stay. Rebuilt after heavy damage during the war, it has emerged as Yugoslavia's largest port, the busiest on the Adriatic after Trieste. Only those with more than a passing interest in architecture will want to explore its sights.

Park near the **tourist office** (identified by a large *i)* and walk inland three blocks to the **Old Town** (Stari Grad). One of the few historic buildings that survived the war is the **Cathedral of the Assumption** (Uznesenje Marijini). Here's your first chance to appreciate the sometimes awkward juxtaposition of styles in Yugoslavian churches. The thirteenth-century cathedral preserves both Romanesque and Gothic features but was given a seventeenth-century Baroque face-lift and a nineteenth-century neoclassical façade. Alongside the cathedral is a slightly askew Romanesque bell tower, the upper portion redone in High Gothic.

✥ SENJ

Look out to sea: The channel between the mainland and the island of **Krk** widens to 10 miles here, making a fairway for the north wind. Another channel runs past the south end of Krk, and where the two channels meet, the seas become as violent as anywhere in the world.

In the early sixteenth century, refugees from Turkish-held lands fled to Senj, and, mastering the currents, became the scourge of the Adriatic for almost two hundred years. There were only one thousand of these Uskok buccaneers, but they built a navy with light, quick boats that could leap the waves and lure Turkish and Venetian ships to destruction. Folk songs are still sung of the ferocity of these pirates, who nailed Turkish turbans to Turkish heads, and tore out Turkish hearts and ate them.

There are few signs today of the town's stormy past. If your time is limited, continue on to **Jablanac** and take the ferry to **Rab**. Those with a serious interest in architecture, however, will want to explore some of Senj's notable buildings.

While the Turks were mounting their fiercest attack, a fortress called the **Dreadnaught** (Nehaj) was built above the town. It survives in its original form—ask at the tourist office for a key.

For Further Information

Kvarner Express, Titovo Obala. Tel. 881068.

✥ RAB

At **Jablanac** (23 miles from Senj), a road twists down to the landing for the car ferry to the island of Rab, and the town of the same name. This is the shortest crossing, but lines in season can be long. You may have better luck taking ferries from Opatija, Rijeka, or Senj. Ask local hotels and tourist offices for advice.

If you have time for only one afternoon visit to an island, visit Rab, if only because the town, with its graceful towers and white stone façades, is so distinctive. Try to spend the night so you can experience Rab when the daytrippers are gone and the late afternoon sun turns the stone to gold. (The island of Hvar has a wonderful hotel, and more to see than Rab, so if you have time for only one night on an island, stay on Hvar and visit Rab in an afternoon.)

Rab is a Venetian jewel rising above a blue-green sea. The oldest section (the Kaldanac) sits on a peninsula surrounded by twelfth- and thirteenth-century walls. It was abandoned during a fifteenth-century plague; you can still see houses with windows and doors that were walled up to check the spreading contagion.

Start at the **tourist office** by the harbor. The Sea Gate (Morska Vrara) leads to the main square, which has been the center of town since the fourteenth century, when the population was four times what it is today. There are only three main streets—Lower (Donja Ulica), Middle (Ivo Lola Ribar), and Upper (Gornja Ulica)—all parallel to the harbor and connected to each other by steep narrow steps and passageways. It's only a five-minute walk to the top, where you'll see the four graceful bell towers (campaniles) that give the town its famous skyline.

It's almost impossible to get lost in Rab, but I suggest you try. Wander through this stone citadel as you would stroll through a church, absorbing its atmosphere, stopping to appreciate its elegant Gothic and Renaissance façades. The town has such balance and grace, it really is very much like a single, open-air, white stone church—its four Romanesque bell towers confidently reaching up toward the sky.

Follow Lower Street to the **Dominis-Nimira Palace**, a distinctive secular Gothic building. From the palace climb to Upper Street. In front of you is Trg Slobode *(trg* means "square") and the small twelfth-century **Cathedral of St. Mary Major** (Sveta Marija Velika), also known as **Rab Cathedral**. Though rebuilt in the thirteenth and fifteenth centuries, it's one of the most distinctive Romanesque buildings along the coast. The clumsy but powerful early sixteenth-century pietà over the doorway expresses the tragedy of a subject people. Notice the lightness of the stone canopy; Rebecca West calls it "as weightless as candleflame."

After climbing the **Cathedral Tower**, continue along Upper Street to the Franciscan **Church of St. Anthony the Abbot** (Sveti Antum opat). The convent was founded in 1497 by a princess who sought refuge from the advancing Turks; today it's closed to the public by nuns seeking shelter from advancing tourists.

Retrace your steps past the cathedral, and continue along Upper Street to the **Church of St. Andrew**, which has a resplendent Baroque altar and a twelfth-century bell tower.

Next, you'll come to the almost pure Renaissance **Church of St. Justina** (1573–78), which has an onion-shaped cupola on its bell tower. Farther along is **Komrčar Park**, which contains the Gothic **Church of St. Francis**, redone in Renaissance style, and the ruins of a late-fifteenth-century monastery. Walk down from the park to the **Franciscan Friary of St. Euphemia**, and tour its lovely cloister and garden.

Dining

The former **Nimira Palace** is now a restaurant specializing in lobster.

Lodging

The most comfortable hotels are the 281-bed **Imperial** (B, Tel. 871224) and the newer and smaller **Internacional** (B, Tel. 871224). For a budget hotel, try the **Istra** (C, Tel. 871133) or the smaller **Beograd** (C, Tel. 871266).

For Further Information

The **Tourist Bureau** (Turist Biro Rab) is at Maršala Tita 1, YU-51280 Rab. Tel. 051-871123.

✤ *NOVIGRAD*

If you have a car, it's important at least once to leave the coast and discover a town that hasn't been transformed by tourism. Novigrad is only 6 miles off the coast road, but a trip here is a voyage back in time. The turnoff to **Novigrad** is just past the town of **Ravanjska**. The village preserves a layout typical of medieval Dalmatia, with steep, narrow streets flanked by close-packed rows of stone houses. Park at the harbor. When you're tired of staring at people staring at you, climb to the medieval **Church of St. Catherine**—all that remains of a former abbey.

✤ *ZADAR* (73 miles from Jablanac)

Those who like to put their noses up against the past may be disappointed in Zadar. Heavily bombed during the war, it's less precious, less museum-like than other cities you'll be visiting farther south. The past is less well defined here: The present insinuates itself through broken walls.

But how delightful to find a medieval quarter where local people come to shop: a town that exists not just to be admired.

Gothic styles came to Yugoslavia through Venice; what is uniquely Croatian belongs to the earlier Romanesque and Pre-Romanesque periods. It's in Zadar that you'll discover this early Croatian world, including Dalmatia's outstanding early Christian monument, St. Donat's—a wonderful setting for summer concerts. The hotel complex in Zadar is Motel Modern but includes a pool and private beach where you can relax after a busy day on the road.

• Park at the harbor (Radnička Obala), near the kiosk with the SUN-TURIST sign. Through the **Sea Gate** (Morska vrata) on your left is the almost pure Romanesque **Church of St. Christopher**. One wonders what the saint, executed under Diocletian's orders, would think of the Baroque marble altar covering his bones.

• The street that began at the Sea Gate passes the **Tourist Office**, which has street maps of Zadar and information on obtaining keys to locked churches. The third street beyond the gate, **Ulica Ive Lole Ribara**, is the main street of the medieval town. On your left is a delightful sixteenth-century building containing the **Archeological Museum**. Turn right on the main street to the strong but graceful **Cathedral of St. Anastasia** (Sveta Stošija), which contains some of the country's most beautiful, delicately carved choir stalls. The Romans laid out their towns like military camps, with a series of rectangular blocks and two main streets intersecting at right angles; you'll get a sense of this plan from the top of the cathedral's 184-foot bell tower.

• Turn left from the cathedral and walk one block to the remains of the old **Roman Forum**. The Forum was discovered after houses were razed during air raids in World War II. The 46-foot column, once part of the Forum, was used as a pillory as late as 1840. Cross the Forum and stroll along **Obala Maršala Tita**, at the water's edge, where young people come for their nightly stroll.

• Retrace your steps one block northeast (inland) to **Ulica Borisa**, turn left, and walk to the eastern end of the peninsula. Across a square is the **Franciscan Monastery** and the **Church of St. Francis** (Sveti Frane). This aisleless thirteenth-century church has a treasury with one of the country's few remaining painted, twelfth-century crucifixes. These crucifixes used to be the dominant religious symbol in coastal churches, standing in the center of the chancel screen, on the altar, or in the center of the nave. The image of Christ Triumphant, more a God than a man, must have been painted by an artist under Byzantine influence, for Eastern emperors did not allow Christ to be shown dying or in pain.

• Return to the **Forum** and turn right on **Stomorica** to the Early Croatian **St. Donat's Church** (Sveti Donat), a high stone fortress, one of the oldest-surviving buildings in Dalmatia. Its ninth-century foundations are built entirely of Roman masonry, including fragments of pillars and altar stones dedicated to Jupiter and Juno. Its strength is overwhelming: It's no wonder that of all the buildings in the area it alone survived the air raids in World War II.

• From Sveti Donat, continue down **Stomorica** to the Romanesque **St. Mary's Basilica** (Sveta Marija), once part of a Benedictine convent. Follow **Ulica Ive Lole Ribara** to the city's main square (**Narodni Trg**), where suddenly you're transported from Croatia to sixteenth-century Venice. The **Café Central** is an ideal stop for a glass of local cherry brandy, called **Vishnievacha**.

• Nearby is **St. Simeon's Church** (Sveti Šimun). On the high altar is the saint's sarcophagus borne by two 550-pound Baroque angels. Ask a nun to lift the lid so you can see the saint under glass.

Dining

There are several fish restaurants, all similar and quite good, overlooking the harbor in the old town. If you're staying in the **Borik** complex, don't miss Niko's **Old Fish Tavern**: Ask the desk clerk for directions.

Lodging

The choice is yours—to stay in the modern, motel-like comfort of a high-rise complex 2 miles from the city, complete with hairdressers and pool; or to check into an older hotel with less amenities that is within walking distance of the major sights. The Borik area has 1,420 beds in five A- and B-class hotels. The best is **Barbara** (A, Tel. 24299). Others are **New Park** (B, Tel. 22177); **Slavija** (B, Tel. 23244), and the smaller **Zadar** (B, Tel. 25458).

If you prefer to stay in town, try the 500-bed **Kovolare** (B, Tel. 33022) or the 190-bed **Zagreb** (C, Tel. 24266).

For Further Information

The **Tourist Bureau** (Turist Biro. Tel. 33789) is in the old walled town on the street leading to the Sea Gate. The travel agency **Sunturist** (Tel. 33633 or 33759) is off Narodni Trg, the main square in the old town.

✛ ŠIBENIK (45 miles past Zadar)

Šibenik has been developing into an industrial town, but you should stop at least to see the **Cathedral**, one of the most important along the coast. The road passes through a modern world of high-rises and factories, down to the harbor. Leave your car here. Everything you want to see is within a few blocks' radius.

The **Cathedral of St. James** (Sveti Jakov) took 124 years to build (1431–1555), during which time styles changed from Gothic to Renaissance. The stone roof seems to defy gravity, covering the nave and aisles with no visible support. The satirical portraits around the outer wall of the apse were carved by **George of Dalmatia**. Some say they were George's way of getting even with those who refused to contribute to the building's cost. Turks and Venetians, cooks and warriors—what a colorful and disparate lot! If you want to meet George, there's a statue of him on the square by Ivan Meštrović.

It's worth visiting the Gothic **Church of St. Barbara** (Sveta Barbara) to see the polyptychs by the Venetian-style painter **Nikola Vladanov**. Notice the individuality of the faces of those kneeling below the cloak of the Madonna: each unique yet all joined together by a common faith.

Excursions

If you're into scenic waterfalls, make a short side trip from Šibenik to **Skradin Falls** on the **Krka River**. There's a restaurant on a stone patio under some pines, and steps leading down to a grassy picnic area. It's a lovely spot, but don't expect to be alone. You can sign up here for a boat ride to a Franciscan convent on an island in the Krka.

For Further Information

The **Tourist Bureau** (Turističko Društo. Tel. 22075) borders the Municipal Park, near the Church of St. Francis.

✛ TROGIR

Trogir, surrounded by water, is a beautiful museum town—a place to look at rather than enter into. Yet because it is so well preserved, you get a sense of the past unequaled along the coast. When you cross the bridge you enter a world of glowing stone that has remained essentially unchanged since the Renaissance.

• Above the entrance gate is the lion of St. Mark, the symbol of Venice:

a reminder that Trogir was under Venetian rule for more than 350 years. Make your first left and continue around the island to the **Cathedral of St. Lawrence** (Sveti Lovro). Most memorable of all Trogir's glories is the portal of this thirteenth-century cathedral, a treasury of Romanesque sculpture by the Croatian master **Radovan**. A griffin plucking out the eye of a pig, a centaur, a sea horse, a mermaid, the apostles accompanied by their zodiacal signs—all remind you that, to the early Croatian mind, there were mysteries unanswered by the rituals and dogma of the church —mysteries that were part of their spiritual baggage as they migrated to the Balkans from the east. Pass through Radovan's doorway, flanked by statues of Adam and Eve on their way east of Eden (among the first nudes in medieval art), and you'll find yourself in the dimly lit interior of a Romanesque church. Notable features include the thirteenth-century stone **pulpit**, the fourteenth-century **ciborium** (canopy) over the high altar, the Gothic choir stalls, and the great barrel roof of the **Chapel of John Orsini**. The **treasury** contains works by one of Dalmatia's greatest painters, **Blaž of Trogir**. The play of light and shadow on flesh and fabric is a trademark of the Dalmatian School of painting.

• Stand outside the cathedral and notice how the walls exude the raw, massive power of the Romanesque, while the bell tower—the first two stories Gothic, the third, Renaissance—expresses the grace and elegance of a more refined age.

• The cathedral rises above **National Square** (Narodni Trg), which could be in Venice. Beside the **City Tower** is the oldest of Trogir's churches, the small, tunnel-like **Basilica of St. Barbara** (Sveta Barbara). The ninth-century church (rebuilt in the eleventh) is a rare example of early Croatian architecture.

• In the fourteenth-century **Church of St. Nicholas** (Sveti Nikola) is a crucifix painted against a modest red background—a reminder that gold was not always affordable in this outpost of Christianity. There's no more Byzantine influence here: Both the Virgin's face and the face of St. John (in the right trefoil) are rich with feeling.

• In the fourteenth-century **Church of St. Dominic**, near the quay, is a tomb with an enraged lion, erected by a widow to her husband who was murdered by the Venetians: a reminder that the Venetian occupation was not always a civilizing influence.

Dining

Marijana (M) is a seafood bistro that features the day's catch—usually scampi, langouste, and kingfish—and lots of local white wine and strong Turkish coffee.

Lodging

The itinerary doesn't include Trogir as an overnight stop; but should you want to explore the town when the daytrippers have departed, stay at the 1,126-bed **Medena** (A, Tel. 73788) or the smaller and less expensive Jadran (B, Tel. 73407).

For Further Information

The **Tourist Office** (Turističko Društvo. Tel. 73554) is across the street from the cathedral.

✢ *SALONA*

The road passes through the rich, green **Riviera of the Seven Castles** (Kaštel Riviera), the most fertile region of Dalmatia. About 4 miles before **Split** are the ruins of **Salona**. Stop here only if you have more than a passing interest in antiquity or want to feed your sense of life's mortality. Lizards dart among the broken stones of this first-century Roman town, which is scattered across a hillside. Some seventy thousand people, including the Roman Emperor Diocletian, once lived here—which is more than the present-day population of Dubrovnik. The town was destroyed by the Avars fourteen centuries ago, but you can still see the ruins of the arena, the public baths, the Roman theater, and several early Christian churches. When the town was destroyed, the survivors fled to Split.

✢ *SPLIT*

You'll wonder what the fuss is about as you drive through the sprawling suburbs of Dalmatia's largest town, with its shipyards, cement factories, and ferro-concrete flats. The fuss, you'll discover when you reach the harbor, is the 1,680-year-old palace of Emperor Diocletian—one of the most imposing Roman monuments in the world. Here is an odd twist in the history of urban planning: not a palace built within a town, but a town built within a palace.

The Roman Emperor Diocletian was ruler of all lands from Brittany to Persia, but when he retired in 305 A.D., he chose this spot near his birthplace to build his palace. Some 310 years after his death, survivors from Salona found shelter within its abandoned walls. They waited for peace so they could return home, but peace never came, and so they settled in, partitioning the Emperor's quarters into apartments, building homes in courtyards, up against the palace walls, and within the ancient arcades—turning broad Roman streets into alleyways so narrow that two people had to turn sideways to pass. Centuries later the Venetians came and built grand palaces beside the medieval homes. The medieval and Renaissance town spread beyond the western walls; and beyond that stretches the modern town you see today.

Recent plans to restore the palace to its ancient glory were dropped when it was discovered that the palace would crumble without the medieval and Renaissance homes to support it. What a fine example of architectural symbiosis! The palace was never a great example of Roman architecture, but what a jumble, what a patchwork of styles you'll see in Split today; and what a sense of continuity, as past and present merge in this living testimony to almost seventeen centuries of human history. Laundry lines hang today where imperial banners once unfurled. What was once an emperor's mausoleum is now a cathedral. A Renaissance palace has become a disco, a medieval home, a café. Miraculously, it all holds together, an amalgam of shapes and styles from Roman to Romanesque, Gothic, Renaissance, and Baroque.

The palace has a striking monumentality that visitors tend to overpraise. It is, in fact, one of the most pretentious private residences ever built—the monument of a man not born to wealth; the boast of a local boy made good. It was also the creation of a theocracy in which architecture existed to trumpet the divinity of the emperor to the people. Diocletian, who reigned from 284 to 305, was a true autocrat, an emperor-God, whose concepts of magnificence came not from Rome but from Persia. Jovius was what he called himself—son of Jupiter; subjects had to fall on their knees before they dared to speak.

And yet Diocletian was a sad, lonely man with few friends. His wife converted to Christianity; his daughter was beheaded and thrown into the sea. He spent eleven years building his palace, and when it was complete he abdicated, at age sixty-one. For eight years or so he lived here, cultivating cabbages, watching the decay of the empire which his reforms had merely held in check. His palace must have been—as Monticello was for Jefferson—a brave attempt to give himself the immortality he failed to find in life itself.

The palace was built like a Roman fort, with two main streets intersecting at the central courtyard (peristyle), dividing the palace into four parts. The southern half, facing the sea, was reserved for the imperial apartments and religious buildings; the northern half was for warehouses and for the emperor's bodyguards and staff.

• Begin your tour with a walk along the seafront promenade, beneath the southern wall. In Diocletian's day the sea slapped against this wall, which was fronted by a great portico, and a central hall leading to the emperor's apartments. Houses today cling like barnacles to the façade, but near the southeastern tower you can see how this loggia once appeared to visitors arriving by sea.

Enter through the **Bronze Gate** (Porta Aenea) and descend on the left into the dark, vaulted chambers. This basement floor corresponds roughly to the imperial apartments, which were directly above, but which sadly no longer exist; in fact, there's really very little to see here but the massive walls and some broken columns.

Return to the gate. As you climb the steps to the **central courtyard**, imagine yourself delivering a message to Diocletian some seventeen hundred years ago, perhaps informing him of another barbarian invasion. Pause to admire the columns along the courtyard, which, like the fifteenth-century black granite **sphinx**, were brought here from an Egyptian temple. Walk south (toward the sea) to the **vestibule** (antechamber) of the imperial apartments, where you would have had to prostrate yourself before the Emperor and kiss the hem of his robe.

To the east of this courtyard is **Diocletian's mausoleum**. You have to imagine statues in the niches and mosaics in the dome; otherwise, the octagonal building has kept its original Eastern appearance. As for Diocletian's remains, they disappeared one day; perhaps they'll show up again beneath the basement of some medieval home. In the seventh century the pagan statues were removed and the mausoleum consecrated as the **Cathedral of St. Mary**, commonly known as the **Cathedral of St. Dominius** (Sveti Duje). The conversion included construction of a solid but graceful Romanesque-Gothic bell tower, one of the most graceful you'll see. What a contrast between the refined lines of this bell tower and the rough Roman exterior of the mausoleum. Walk between the two thirteenth-century lions by **Radovan** (you met him in Trogir) and climb the bell tower for a great view of the palace. Of special note in the cathedral are the **doors** by Andrija Buvina of Split (1214) portraying the life and agony of Christ; the thirteenth-century **pulpit** to the left of the entrance; the **Altar of Anastasius** (1428) by our friend George the Dalmatian; and the Romanesque **choir stalls**, which are similar to those you saw in Rab and Zadar.

• When you leave the cathedral, recross the peristyle and follow a narrow street called Kraj Sveti Ivana to the **Imperial Temple**. Though converted during the Middle Ages into St. John's baptistery, it remains one of the world's best examples of a small classical temple. Look closely at the eleventh-century altar screen on the baptismal font: Is that an Adoration of Christ or a portrait of a Croatian king with his subjects?

• Crowded within the palace walls is a maze of medieval streets lined with Romanesque and Gothic buildings. Worth visiting are the eighteenth-century Baroque **Church of St. Philip Neri**, the small Renaissance **Church of St. Roch** (a miniature Šibenik Cathedral), the **Papalic Mansion** (designed by George the Dalmatian, it is the best Late Gothic building in the city), and the seventeenth-century **Cindro Mansion** (a typical Venetian-style patrician palace, the most beautiful Baroque building in Split).

• Medieval Split spreads beyond the western walls of the palace. Among buildings worth visiting here are the ninth-century, Pre-Romanesque **Church of St. Michael** (Sveti Mikula), and, near the harbor, the thirteenth-century **Church of St. Francis** (Sveti Frane), which has a lovely cloister.

• **National Square** (Narodni Trg), once reserved for the upper classes, is directly across from the West Gate. You'll find here the Venetian Gothic **Town Hall** (1433) and the Renaissance **Karepić Mansion**. Follow the western wall south toward the harbor and you'll come to another lovely Venetian square, **Trg Preporoda**.

• The findings at Salona are displayed in the **Archeological Museum** (13 Zrinsko-Frankopanska Street). The most important remains of early Croatian culture are exhibited in the **Museum of Croatian Archeological Monuments** (Šetalište Moše Pijade). The **Art Gallery** (11 Lovretska Street) has paintings from the fourteenth century to the present, and a fine collection of icons.

• From the bus station it's a 4½-mile ride to the high, wooded **Marjan Hill**, the Emperor's former hunting grounds. The road passes the gallery and castle that house some two hundred of Ivan Meštrović's sculptures and reliefs. **Holy Cross Chapel**, 550 yards from the Meštrović Museum, contains his New Testament cycle of bas-relief wood carvings, said to be his best work.

Dining

For people-watching, settle into one of the cafés along the waterfront promenade beneath the southern wall. **Hrudjeva Kula** (E/M), atop the southeast tower of the palace, specializes in grilled meats and lovely views. Try **Adriana** (M, Titova Obala 7) for fresh fish. **Ero** (M, Marmontova 3) has Dalmatian specialties. On special occasions, locals eat at **Mak** (E/M) in the huge, state-run shopping center/sports complex called Koteks. **Sarajevo** (M, Illegaca 6) has Bosnian specialties. **Dioklecijan** (E/M) serves fresh fish on a ship alongside the quay.

Lodging

If you prefer a big modern hotel, stay in the **Lav** complex (A, Tel. 48288) with casino, pool, and beach, 6 miles southeast of town. A smaller complex closer to the old town is **Marjan** (A, Tel. 42866), which also has a beach and pools. My recommendation is the 96-bed **Bellevue** (C, Tel. 47175), not because of the food but because the rooms have some prewar character and the hotel is right on the harbor, a short walk from the palace. Ask for a quiet room. Another good choice is the more luxurious **Park Hotel** (B, Tel. 058555-411).

The **Central Hotel** (C, Tel. 48242), above the **Central Café**, within the palace walls, is acceptable for students or for those who don't mind noise, broken walls, and missing toilet seats. Renovations are scheduled, however; check with a travel agent. For a cheap, clean hotel within the palace, try **Srebrena Urata**. Its ancient shutters open on a courtyard with 1,500-year-old walls. Rooms have sinks but no private baths.

For Further Information

The **Tourist Bureau** (Turist Biro, Tel. 42142) is at the southwest corner of the palace. The **travel agencies** are here, too, including **Dalmacijaturist** (Titova Obala 5. Tel. 44666), **Kompas** (Titova Obala 2. Tel. 42993), and **Kvarner Express** (Titova Obala 17. Tel. 42235). On the square behind the Tourist Bureau is **Atlas** (Trg Preporoda 7. Tel. 43055), which represents American Express.

For information about ships and ferries, contact **Jadroagent** (Marine Terminal. Tel. 48790) or **Jadrolinija** (Marine Terminal. Tel. 43366).

✤ *STON* (104 miles from Split)

If you want to make time between Split and Ston, there's no overwhelming need to stop en route. Desolate 5,000-foot peaks slope down to the sandy beaches of the Makarska Riviera. The island on your right is **Brač**, whose quarries provided the marble for Diocletian's Palace, the White House, and the UN. Beyond **Gradac** the mountains recede and the road winds inland through rocky rolling countryside. The reed beds in the delta near **Ploče** look like Chinese rice paddies. A right turn about 40 miles north of Dubrovnik takes you 5 miles to the fortified Roman and medieval settlement of **Ston**—a side trip worth making if you're interested in early Slavic architecture.

Ston, once the second most important city in the republic of Ragusa, sits on a narrow strip of land connecting the peninsula of **Pelješac** with the mainland. On **Sveti Mihajlo Hill** is the well-preserved Pre-Romanesque **St. Michael's Church** (eleventh or twelfth century). The earliest Croatian kings and bishops worshipped here, as they did in Nin. On the plain below was an ancient settlement with eight churches, two of which still stand: the Romanesque **Church of Our Lady of Lužina** and the small Pre-Romanesque **Church of St. Martin**.

In **Greater Ston**, see the late Romanesque **Church of St. Nicholas** (1347), which preserves a large painted crucifix by **Blaž of Trogir**. Other buildings to see are the Gothic **Chancery of the Republic**; the Gothic **Sorkočević-Djurdjević Mansion**, and the Renaissance **Bishop's Palace**.

✤ HVAR

How to Get There. The 3,000-year-old town of Hvar, on the island of the same name, is reached by car ferry or hydrofoil from Split or Dubrovnik. The passage can be rough, so bring motion-sickness pills. You can depart at 8 A.M. and return at 4:30 P.M., but why not spend the night and experience this most Venetian of Venetian towns when the daytrippers have departed?

Hvar was destroyed by the Turks in 1571, so what you'll see is a late-sixteenth-century town. Within the ancient walls are palaces weathered to the color of gold. Pass through the **Sea Gate** to the main square—the largest in Dalmatia. The town rises on either side: the medieval quarter, with its steep, narrow streets, to the north; the Venetian section to the west. The square is surrounded by notable buildings: the Renaissance **Cathedral of St. Stephen** (Sveti Stefan), which has a bell tower you can climb; the Gothic-Renaissance **Paladini Palace**; the beautiful **Vukašinović Palace**; and the **Arsenal** (1579–1611), which houses the oldest surviving theater (1612) in Yugoslavia.

The dining hall in the mid-fifteenth-century **Franciscan Monastery** (a 5-minute walk along the sea wall) contains one of the best collections of paintings along the coast, and a library that includes a 1524 Ptolemaic atlas and some exquisite sixteenth-century music books. The small garden behind the refectory has a 300-year-old cypress.

For exercise and a great view, follow the cactus-lined walk that zigzags up to the **Spanish Fort**. Fortify yourself with a glass of wine at **Konoba Lepurini** or at one of the other ancient taverns en route.

If you're spending the night, rent a motorboat or rowboat at the harbor and explore the coast. The tiny island of **St. Clement** (Sveti Kliment) has better beaches than Hvar, and a colorful display of tropical plants.

Shopping

Treat yourself to some essence of lavender, which is extensively cultivated on the island for soaps and perfumes.

Tours

Come to Hvar on a guided tour from Split or Dubrovnik—any mainland hotel or tourist office can arrange it—or join a group tour once you reach the island. Arrange for private guides in Dubrovnik or Split.

Dining

Enjoy lunch on the terrace of the **Palace Hotel** (I/E), overlooking the main square. For Dalmatian specialties and fresh fish, try the **Konoba Restaurant** (M), by the harbor. **Luculus** (M/I) and **Zlatha Skolgka** (M/I) also enjoy good reputations for fish and mixed grill.

Lodging

The **Palace** (A, Tel. 74306) is one of the most elegant hotels along the coast. It was built into a Venetian palace with a loggia and clock tower, and was modernized without losing a sense of continuity with the past.

Your second and third choices are **Delfin** (B, Tel. 74168) and **Dalmacija** (B, Tel. 74120). **Bodul** (A, Tel. 74049) is a half mile from the harbor. The 745-bed **Amfora** (A, Tel. 74202) is comfortable but huge. Other choices include the 316-bed **Sirena** (A, Tel. 74144); the 116-bed **Adriatic** (A, Tel. 74024), which has its own beach and an Olympic-size pool; and the small, modest, 68-bed **Galeb** (C, Tel. 74044).

Many houses in the old town rent rooms to visitors.

For Further Information

The **Tourist Office** (Turistički Savez Općine Hvar, Tel. 74058) is on the main square.

Touring the Island of Hvar

If you bring your car to Hvar, you can drive the length of the island to Sućuraj and take the short ferry ride back to the mainland at Drvenik. I drove the 53 miles in 90 minutes, but no sane person should try it in under 2 hours. The road climbs hundreds of feet above the sea, offering breathtaking views of the mountainous coast. Farmers have imposed a semblance of order on this rocky terrain by building stone walls and planting the enclosures with grapevines and lavender. The geometric stone patterns look like hieroglyphics from the dawn of time. From Drvenik, return to Split or head south to Dubrovnik.

♥ KORČULA

How to Get There. There's regular car-ferry service to Korčula from Split and Dubrovnik. You can also take a ferry from Orebić on the Pelješac Peninsula and stop at Ston en route either to or from the coastal highway.

Korčula, like the town of Hvar, sits on an island of the same name. It's similar in size to Hvar but more compact. It's also marked with the same Venetian imprint: the same narrow winding streets opening out on squares surrounded by sixteenth-century palaces and loggias; the same wheat-colored stone that the late afternoon sun turns to gold.

The historical nucleus lies within the fourteenth- to sixteenth-century walls that protected the town from attacks by Turks and pirates. The main street changes directions three times to reduce the impact of the winter wind; the side streets join it at an angle, like veins on a leaf, to reduce the heat of the midday sun. It may have been Greek settlers who thought up this plan in the fourth century B.C.

• A building not to miss is the **Cathedral of St. Mark**. The first masons worked in the Gothic spirit; then came the florid southern Italian influence, and, finally, features of the early Renaissance. Churches were built to teach as well as to provide a sanctuary for prayer; hence, the biblical allegories carved by an itinerant French artist on the cathedral doors. Projecting from a gable above the door is a carving of an old woman with the same questioning, morbid features that you saw in Radovan's work in Trogir. If you're looking for a sensibility that's distinctly Croatian, you'll find it in this face, which, as Rebecca West points out, assumes that all is not known, and that order and proportion may not be the only principles that govern the world. If you want to see what modern Croatian artists have done with these notions, study the twentieth-century works of art on the ground floor of the bell tower. In the cathedral treasury is a polyptych (1421) by Blaž of Trogir.

• From the square you can see the courtyard side of a mansion with a tower. This is reputedly the birthplace of the famous medieval explorer **Marco Polo** (1254–1324). Venice also claims Marco as its own; but what is not contestable is the fact that Polos still live on Korčula and that back in 1298 Marco Polo commanded a Venetian fleet of ten ships within sight of the island and was captured by the Genoese. It was in jail that he dictated to a fellow prisoner the story of his journey to China.

• In the southeast part of the walled town is the renovated, early-fifteenth-century **Church of All Saints** (Svi Sveti), which has another polyptych by Blaž and an impressive collection of Greek icons.

• Come Thursdays in season for the **Moreška**, when armed dancers in magnificent costumes act out a great battle between the Moors and the Turks for possession of a beautiful princess. The dance symbolizes more than a thousand years of Yugoslav history—one dancer representing attack, the other defense.

Dining

Adio Mare (M) and Gradski podrum (M) are both in the old town. Mornar (M) is near the waterfront; Planjak (M) is just outside the walls.

Lodging

The renovated 40-bed **Korčula** (B, Tel. 81004) is the only hotel in the old town. A short stroll along the waterfront takes you to the 230-bed **Marko Polo** (B, Tel. 81100) and the 400-bed **Park** (B, Tel. 81004). If you think that happiness comes in big packages, try the 660-bed **Bon Repos** (B, Tel. 81102), a half mile farther along the shore.

For Further Information

The **Tourist Bureau** (Turist Biro Marko Polo, Tel. 81067) is near the main square.

✤ *DUBROVNIK* (39 miles from Ston)

If you're driving or sailing south, you'll arrive in the suburb of Gruž. The travel agencies are here, along the harbor, and so are most of the large, modern hotels. Don't worry, this is not Dubrovnik. The old walled city is 2.4 miles farther south, sitting on a huge rock formation jutting out into the sea.

The tourist department has billed Dubrovnik as the country's Number One attraction, so you may be surprised by how small it is: only forty thousand people, compared to three hundred thousand in Split. Americans who like to discover new continents may not appreciate the fifty-five thousand fellow tourists, all searching for the Real Yugoslavia; yet the magic of the city somehow survives.

It survives because the city is visually one of the most pleasing in the world. It envelops you. It shelters you within its huge, protective walls. The polished white stone makes everything seem both new and everlasting. Each building has its own decoration, but all were built to conform to strict medieval building codes—the same slant of the roof, the same kind of cornice—and the result is an expression in stone of both the unity and uniqueness people seek in their own lives.

Houses, churches, monasteries, fountains—all are built with the same aristocratic poise and dignity you'll find in the people themselves. Unlike Vienna, where every monument says money, monarchy, and power, Dubrovnik is built to human scale. There is no ostentation here; no building stands out at the expense of another. Despite its Baroque façades, added after a seventeenth-century earthquake, Dubrovnik is still essentially a Gothic-Renaissance city, and when you enter its walls you are whirled back into the sixteenth and seventeenth centuries.

A Brief History

In the twelfth century, Dubrovnik (called Ragusa until World War I) became an independent city-state. It had only forty thousand citizens but was a greater sea power than Britain at that time, and for many decades was Venice's chief rival in the Adriatic. Caravans started from here to Constantinople. Pilgrims visited Ragusa's brothels on their way to Jerusalem—the madam was called "the abbess of the sinners." Goods from the eastern Mediterranean sailed to England in Ragusan ships called *raguisies;* hence, the word *argosy.* In the sixteenth century Ragusa had fifty consulates and more than one hundred and eighty ships sailing the Mediterranean.

Ragusa grew rich on the principle that it's better to negotiate and buy off the enemy than fight him. The people were shrewd businessmen, not fighters, and bought with money what their neighbors, the Montenegrins, bought with their lives. When Constantinople fell to the Turks, the Ragusans sent an annual tribute to the Sultan in return for retaining their trading and maritime rights; they also paid tribute to the Hungarian king and agreed to pray for him in church.

The shipowners were the aristocracy of Ragusa. Under their rule, five hundred years ago, doctors were salaried and forbidden to charge fees except to foreigners—and then only if their remedies did some good. Street sweepers were contracted in 1415 not only to sweep up garbage, but to report those who threw it in the streets. Every shopkeeper and homeowner was required by law to sweep up in front of his own property on Saturday mornings. Europe's first orphanage was established in Ragusa in 1432; unmarried women were allowed to give birth there and then leave their children—in complete secrecy. A person who traded in slaves in 1417 would have been fined and put in jail; fifty years later he would have been sentenced to death. Four hundred and forty-six years before the Emancipation Proclamation (1863), it was written in Ragusa's law-books that "It must be held to be base, wicked and abominable, and to redound to the great disgrace of our city, that the human form, made after the image and similitude of our Creator, should be turned to merce-nary profit, and sold as if it were a beast." This did not stop the Ragusans from holding slaves of their own; but they were not permitted to trade in slaves, an attitude considerably ahead of its time; and in the seventeenth century the Ragusans refused to profit from the slave trade to the Ameri-can colonies.

In 1667 Ragusa was destroyed by an earthquake and rebuilt under strong Venetian influence. Napoleon occupied the city in 1806 and dis-solved the Republic. While the town was under Austrian occupation from 1814 to 1918, the nobility vowed not to have children until they regained their freedom, and many old families disappeared or lived in drafty houses full of cats.

Exploring Dubrovnik

• Enter through the Pile Gate on the west, surmounted by statues of St. Blaise, the city's patron saint. If you're feeling sick, say a prayer to him—he was known for curing diseases, particularly sore throats.

Opening before you is the Placa, a street of glistening white paving stones polished by the feet of merchants and sailors, priests and patricians for more than three hundred years.

Everything in Dubrovnik seems to flow down and meet in the Placa. Whatever is social, whatever is public in human nature seems to find expression here. We have nothing like it in the States, except perhaps the mall—a place where people confirm their connectedness, with each other and with history. Walking here you'll feel part of a noble procession that began hundreds of years before you were born and will continue long after you are gone.

The young people gather along the Placa in the early evening. Up one side of the street they strut, and down the other—a pride of boys and girls, in groups, in pairs, offering themselves to each other's gazes. It's something not to be missed.

Join this pavane, this polonaise, then return to the West Gate (preferably at sunset) and climb the fortifications—among the most remarkable in Europe. From here, 80 feet up, you'll get a fine overview of the town. It's a 45-minute walk around the walls.

• In front of you as you enter the Placa through the West Gate is a fountain by the Neapolitan architect **Onofrio della Cava**, looking much like the dome of a mosque. Onofrio got the contract to build an aqueduct to bring water here, then indulged his Renaissance fancy to build the fountain. It's said that buildings that survived the 1667 earthquake were constructed with fresh water from the aqueduct; those built with mortar diluted with seawater were destroyed.

• To the left of the fountain is the small but beautiful **Church of the Holy Savior** (Sveti Spas). The **Franciscan Church** next door is mostly Baroque (though completed in 1343), and has a noble fifteenth-century pietà over the doorway.

• Don't miss the Romanesque **cloister** in the **Franciscan Friary**. The Roman arcades are supported by graceful double columns crowned with grotesque figures that must have amused or horrified the monks. In the **treasury** is a painting of Dubrovnik before the earthquake and a reliquary said to contain one of St. Blaise's hands. In the **lower cloister** is a fourteenth-century **pharmacy** that is still in use.

• The **Museum of Icons** (Muzej Starih Ikona) near the **Serbian Church** has a great collection of old icons.

On Zudioska Ulica (Jew Street), near the **Eastern** (Ploče) **Gate**, is a fourteenth-century **synagogue**, the third oldest in Europe. Jews came here to escape persecution in Spain and Italy. They were made to draw water from their own fountain, yet some worked as doctors or secretaries to patrician families. Dubrovnik had five thousand Jews before the war; now it hasn't enough to form a congregation.

• Art lovers should make a point of visiting the nearby **Dominican Church**, which has a graceful cloister and paintings by some of Dalmatia's most venerated painters (including a famous model of Dubrovnik by Nikola Božidarević in the **Bundić Chapel**).

• Walk to **Luža Square**, at the far, eastern end of the Placa. The **Column of Orlando (Roland)** was the medieval symbol of a free merchant city. It was here that festivities were announced and laws proclaimed. To your left is the original fourteenth-century **Customs House**, known as the **Sponza Palace**. Dubrovnik in its heyday served as a storage depot between East and West, and packages were stored here on the ground floor. A second floor was added in Venetian Gothic style for literary gatherings; later, a third floor was completed in Renaissance style and the house was faced with a loggia. Inside is a beautiful courtyard.

• To the right of the square is the **Church of St. Blaise** (Sveti Vlaho), a Baroque mass built by a second-rate Venetian architect. The famous sculpture of the saint holding a model of the town now stands on the high altar.

• Across the street, to the right (as you face the harbor), is the two-storied, flowery Gothic **Rector's Palace**, the glory of Dubrovnik, the most beautiful civic building in the city.

• Turn right from the palace and cross to the **Cathedral of Our Lady**, which was given a flashy Baroque dress after the earthquake. The **treasury** has some notable relics, including a hand of St. Blaise, and his skull adorned by an eleventh-century Byzantine crown.

• When you've seen enough sights, make an excursion to the island of **Mljet**. It has three lovely lakes surrounded by pines. In the largest is an islet with a twelfth-century Benedictine convent, now a modest hotel called **Melita** (B, Tel. 89010).

• Unless you have time to spare, don't bother visiting **Trebinje**. It's a popular excursion spot, but there's little to see except two mosques, which will probably be locked.

• A cable car leaves every 30 minutes to the top of **Mount Srdj**, where you'll enjoy a breathtaking view of Dubrovnik.

Dining

Restaurants are very crowded in season between 8 and 10 P.M.; make advance reservations and be prepared to give your order over the phone.

The steep, narrow streets to the north of the Placa (on your left as you face the clock tower) are lined with small, mostly privately owned restaurants, almost all of them specializing in fresh fish. Find a restaurant during the day that suits you and make a reservation for the evening. My favorite—a place where no one pressures you to buy the most expensive meal—is the friendly, state-run **Sirena** (M, Prijeko 34. Tel. 26486). Another friendly spot is the **Domino Steak House** (M, Domino 3. Tel.

32832), located across the Placa. Despite its unfortunate name, it has considerable character and specializes both in beef and fish.

It's worth making an excursion northwest of town to **Ombla** (M/E, Rijeka Dubrovačka, Komolac. Tel. 87713), an old sea captain's house where waiters bring the catch of the day to you on a platter so that you can choose your very own.

Jadran (M, P. Miličevića 1. Tel. 23547) serves Dalmatian food in the cloisters of a former monastery.

On the same street as Sirena are **Prijeko** (M, Prijeko 24. Tel. 24074) and **Wanda** (M, Prijeko 12. Tel. 24934). The latter is more pricey but a better bet for salads and vegetables. In the same area is **Piccolo Mondo** (M), a smart, sophisticated singles bar with Rolling Stones and James Dean posters. Below is a restaurant serving Italian specialties.

Konovoski Dvori (M/E, Tel. 7939) is part of a restored windmill at the mouth of the River Ljuta, about 20 miles east of town. The river cascades by the stone patio, where waitresses serve in native costumes. A waterwheel turns the spit cooking lamb over charcoal; bread is baked in iron pots. It's all a bit hokey, but the setting is idyllic, and hokeyness is a real treat in a socialist country. Konovoski Dvori is a favorite tour bus destination, so your best bet is to go at odd hours (it's open 11 to 11), perhaps on an excursion to or from the Gulf of Kotor.

Lodging

The 90-year-old **Imperial** (A, Tel. 23688) is one of the few hotels along the coast that has retained some Old World character (despite its pedestrian furnishings). It's also one of the few hotels in Dubrovnik that's in walking distance of the walled city. Rooms are both in the original 1897 building (try Number 22) and in a new annex.

On the **Babin Kuk Peninsula**, across the harbor from Gruž, is a huge, modern hotel complex with everything from pools to pizza parlors—even a twentieth-century version of the Placa lined with boutiques. Most luxurious is the **President** (L, Tel. 22999). Others include the 616-bed **Argosy** (A, Tel. 22999), the **Plakir** (A, Tel. 22999), and the **Tirena** (A, Tel. 22999).

Other clean, modern hotels are the 104-bed **Bellevue** (B, Tel. 25076), the 120-bed **Lapad** (B, Tel. 23473), the 400-bed **Libertas** (A, Tel. 27444), and the 600-bed **Dubrovnik Palace** (A, Tel. 28555). **Belvedere** (L, Tel. 23489) is the newest and most luxurious hotel in town.

Argentina (A, Tel. 23855), on the east side of Dubrovnik, is more intimate than the Babin Kuk hotels. It has fewer amenities, but is closer to town. Try Room 194. Next door is the less attractive **Excelsior** (A, Tel. 23566).

Hotels within the old walled city are older and somewhat worse for wear. Best bet is **Dubravka** (C, Tel. 26293). A white stone stairway leads to rooms which are clean but small and basic, some with private showers.

In and around Dubrovnik are many private homes that accept overnight guests. In season, make reservations in advance. **Vera Laklé** (Vladamira Nazora 18. Tel. 25347) is a warm, friendly woman who speaks English. Accommodations are more basic in the home of **A. Baldo** (Solinka 5), where three rooms share a bath. In the home of **Marija** (Ulica N. Tesla. Tel. 26619) three rooms have basins, but share a bath; best bet is the large room with balcony overlooking the harbor.

For Further Information

The **Tourist Information Center** (Turistički Informativi Centar) is near the main gate of the old city. Just outside the West Gate is the travel agency **Atlas** (Tel. 27333), which represents American Express.

✤ *MONTENEGRO*

When you reach **Hercegnovi**, at the entrance to the **Gulf of Kotor**, you'll have left Croatia and entered **Montenegro**. No American loves his country more than the Montenegrin loves his poor, rocky land. Yet no part of Yugoslavia has suffered more from oppression, mostly from the Turks. Wrote Tennyson:

> O smallest among peoples! rough rock-throne
> Of Freedom! Warriors beating back the swarm
> Of Turkish Islam for five hundredyears . . .

The identity of these people comes not from their monuments, but from their struggle. Living in continuous fear, being subjected to massacres and decapitations, has created its own set of moral values: a love of excess, a talent for revenge, a fondness for self-glorification. Fierce and uncompromising in times of war, the Montenegrins also have a reputation for laziness in peacetime. They joke about it themselves. (Why does the Montenegrin sleep with a chair next to his bed? To take a rest after sleeping. Why is the Montenegrin a bad lover? Because he's too proud to get underneath, and too lazy to climb on top.)

The Montenegrins are the only people on the Balkan Peninsula never wholly conquered. Throughout their history they have held to the idea of national independence rising above the temptation of an easier life under the wing of a stronger power. If this is praiseworthy, how should we react to the citizens of Dubrovnik, who said prayers for their enemies and bartered their way to freedom?

✺ THE GULF OF KOTOR

As you drive through **Hercegnovi**, you'll sense a greater Turkish, Byzantine presence. This is the meeting place of East and West—of Roman and Byzantine, Catholic and Orthodox, Christian and Muslim. At the narrows at **Kamenari** you can save time by taking the ferry to **Lepetane**, but don't—not unless the weather is terrible or you plan to explore the Gulf of Kotor on your drive back to Dubrovnik.

✺ RISAN (45 miles from Dubrovnik)

Continue instead around the Gulf to **Risan**. Illyrian tribes lived here around 230 B.C., when Rome was crossing the Adriatic and colonizing Dalmatia. The story of how the Illyrian widow Teuta took up the standard of her fallen warrior husband against the Roman invaders, would wear well on late-night TV, preferably dubbed in English; it would end in the town of Rizon, where Teuta plunged into the gulf rather than acknowledge defeat.

✺ CRKVICE

The road that climbs over a 3,400-foot pass to **Crkvice** offers breathtaking views of the gulf below. The two small islands are **St. George** (Sveti Juraj) and **Our Lady of the Rocks** (Gospa od Škrpjela). The cypress trees on St. George mark a sailors' burial ground and the ruins of a twelfth-century Benedictine monastery. It was this island that inspired Böcklin's painting, *The Island of the Dead*, which in turn inspired Rachmaninoff's music of the same name. **Our Lady of the Rocks** was once a reef to which sailors contributed stones for the foundations of a church.

✺ PERAST

The Gulf of Kotor gave the Adriatic many of its most accomplished seamen, and some of its best came from Perast. Peter the Great sent young Russian noblemen to the naval school founded here in 1698, and they became the nucleus of the Russian fleet in the Baltic. There was probably a shipyard here in the early fourteenth century. In the eighteenth century, Perast had more than fifty cargo vessels sailing the Adriatic and the coast of Greece.

The town today is overgrown with neglect. Lizards dart through the portals of an unfinished church. Wisteria vines hang over balustrades of Venetian Gothic palaces, and Judas trees grow among the broken stones. It's all deliciously melancholy—and worth a visit.

❧ KOTOR

This walled medieval city was badly damaged by the 1979 earthquake, but many monuments are already open to the public. A hidden, inland port which had some six hundred ships in the eighteenth century, it was of great strategic importance to the Venetians, who gave it semi-independence that lasted till it was occupied by Napoleon's forces in 1807. Later it became the base for Austria's Adriatic fleet.

The town has kept its medieval appearance, with churches and patrician mansions from the twelfth through the eighteenth centuries. Most impressive is the twelfth-century Romanesque **Cathedral of St. Tryphon** (Sveti Tripun), flanked by two Renaissance towers added after the earthquake of 1667. Two unusual features are the single wide arch that spans the porch between the towers, and the ninth-century doorway taken from a church that stood on the same site. Legend has it that in 890 a ship carrying sacred relics for sale in Europe found shelter here. Having no patron saint, the people of Kotor bought the head of a Byzantine saint named Tryphon, the patron saint of gardeners. His story is told in reliefs carved in the stone canopy (ciborium) over the high altar. The treasury has several bodys' worth of votive legs and arms, and crosses carried in wars against Turks.

Behind the town is a steep flight of steps leading to the **Gospa od Zdravlja Church** (1500), and, farther up, **Fort St. John** (Sveti Ivan). Walk at least partway for a fascinating view of this devastated town.

❧ THE LOVĆEN PASS

The mountains above the gulf seem to rise forever: How, you wonder, could a road ever be built there? Yet a road there is—one of the most dramatic in Europe. There's a legend, which I hope is true, that an Austrian engineer built the road in the shape of an *M* in honor of a princess named Marija. The stolid Austrians fired him, of course, for squandering good money.

On top of the plateau are the fertile fields of Njeguši, birthplace of Montenegro's poet/ruler, Petar II. There's a restaurant here famous for its smoked ham and cheese, served with a mixture of wine and beer that you may not want to try more than once.

⚓ *CETINJE*

The former capital of Montenegro sits in a fertile valley at the foot of Mount Lovćen. It's a peaceful, unassuming town today, more interesting for its historical associations than for its monuments. The graves of freedom fighters are reminders that Cetinje was the center from which Montenegro organized and waged its battle for independence. When freedom came in 1878, Montenegro was officially recognized as a sovereign state, and Cetinje became its capital—the smallest in Europe. The palace, museum, and banks were all built at the turn of the century.

The railings around the fifteenth-century Vlah Church (Vlaška crkva) were made in 1897 from barrels of 1,550 captured Turkish rifles.

The present monastery, dating from 1785, has a treasury rich in ancient manuscripts, icons, and paintings. Adjoining the monastery is the Biljarda Palace (1837–38), where Njegoš lived. Though he died at thirty-eight (he reigned from 1830 to 1850), he was considered the greatest of the Orthodox bishop-princes to rule Montenegro since the sixteenth century. He was six feet eight, a great poet, and a great billiard player. (The palace is named after the table brought up from the coast by mules.) He knew five foreign languages, and read Shakespeare, French philosophers, and German classical writers in the original. He was a marksman, too, and liked to throw lemons in the air and shoot them, an impressive feat for a bishop.

Colorful Montenegrin costumes are displayed in the palace's Ethnographic Collection. A fascinating relief map of the mountainous terrain will show you why no one ever conquered Montenegro.

A good road climbs 16 miles from Cetinje to the 5,785-foot summit of Mount Lovćen, topped by the Njegoš Mausoleum. The bishop-prince built himself a small chapel here, but the Austrians destroyed it during World War I and brought his remains back to Cetinje. After the war he was reinterred in a mausoleum built by the country's most famous sculptor, Ivan Meštrović. Mount Lovćen is the symbol of Montenegrin independence, the beacon of the homeland, and has inspired many heroic poems, including Njegoš's own famous epic, *The Mountain Wreath*. Here's a verse to recite as you're climbing the 461 steps to Njegoš's tomb.

Some Montenegrin chieftains are talking. Drashko, who has just returned from Venice, says,

> Brother, many a handsome man I saw,
> But ten times more of ugly folk;
> Too ugly much to look upon. . . .
> They like better egg or chicken
> Than sheep's flesh or ball of cheese;
> Untold the quantity of chickens
> That they eat up within a year!
> From this lordly life they die,
> With bellies big and no moustaches,
> Their craniums dusted o'er with powder
> And, like ladies, dangling rings at ear!
> When they reach their thirtieth year,
> They get a face like some old hag,
> Too ugly are they to be seen;
> And even should they climb a stair,
> All pale they grow and linen-white,
> And something rattles in their throat,
> As if had come their dying night!

✤ BUDVA

From Cetinje you'll zigzag down to the coast again, and enjoy breath-taking views along the way. Budva was one of the most attractive walled cities along the coast until it was devastated by the 1969 earthquake. It should be closed to the public until 1988; check with local tourist authorities for details.

Lodging

Within sight of the collapsed walls is the **Avala Hotel** (A, Tel. 82042), which was rebuilt after the earthquake. It's a modern, comfortable hotel with an indoor pool and a sandy beach.

✤ SVETI STEFAN

There's really no reason to come here except to stay in the **Sveti Stefan Hotel**—but what a splendid way to end your trip!

Lodging

After the war, a fortified fifteenth-century settlement, reduced to a sleepy fishing village, was converted into the **Sveti Stefan Hotel** (L, Tel.

41333) and connected to the mainland by a causeway. The luxurious hotel opened in 1960 with a swimming pool hewn from rock and eighty stone houses converted into self-contained apartments and suites. The result is an American's vision of what Yugoslavia is supposed to be like, but who can be cynical in such plush and tasteful surroundings? The rates are high for Yugoslavia, but if you want to be pampered at least once on your trip, here's the place to do it. Rooms 90 and 93 are particularly lovely—and expensive. Entrées on the dinner menu include grouper, lobster, medallions of venison with médoc sauce, wild boar, and braised hare.

A lovely but less expensive alternative is the nearby, 80-bed **Miločer Hotel** (A, Tel. 41013), housed in the former summer residence of the royal family. Tito liked to stay here in Suite 101. Guests can use facilities at Sveti Stefan, including the pool. Rooms facing the sea are worth the small additional fee.

EN ROUTE: From SVETI STEFAN

From Sveti Stefan, you have several choices. (1) Return to Dubrovnik and fly home. (2) Return to Dubrovnik and take the car ferry back to Rijeka. (3) Drive to Belgrade and fly home. (4) Drive to Bar, and take the train to Belgrade. Train buffs will love the dramatic 9-hour, 296-mile train ride, through 154 tunnels and over 234 bridges, including the longest bridge (550 yards) in Europe.

RECOMMENDED READING

Treasures of Yugoslavia: An Encyclopedic Touring Guide, sold in local gift shops, is a passionless but extremely useful compendium of information about virtually every town along the coast.

J. A. Cuddon, *The Companion Guide to Yugoslavia* (Scribner, 1975) is a quirky, witty, passionate description of a journey through Yugoslavia. But beware the dated information on hotels and restaurants!

Rebecca West, *Black Lamb and Grey Falcon: A Journey Through Yugoslavia* (Penguin, 1982) is somewhat dated, but remains the most literate and intelligent book on Yugoslavia.

ITALY

❦ Pompeii, Capri, and the Amalfi Coast

MAJOR ATTRACTIONS

- The most spectacular drive in Italy, along the wild, romantic Amalfi coast.
- Positano—the most popular town on the Amalfi Drive.
- The excavated Roman town of Pompeii—brought back to life as it was almost two thousand years ago.
- The magical island of Capri, with fairytale grottoes, comfortable hotels, dozens of first-class seafood restaurants, and dramatic walks at the edge of the sea.
- Paestum—site of the Greek Temple of Neptune, a building as memorable as the Parthenon.
- The National Museum of Naples, housing the most important collection of classical art in the world.

INTRODUCTION

The Italian itinerary takes you through an extraordinary variety of landscapes and experiences in a minimum amount of traveling time. At no point are you more than 2 hours from Naples, yet you'll be exploring Pompeii and climbing to the heights of Vesuvius, dining on terraces above the spectacular Amalfi coast, and exploring fantastic grottoes on the magical Isle of Capri.

Your trip begins in Naples, only 2 hours south of Rome, with a visit to the world's most important museum of antiquity. Less than an hour from here are the ruins of Pompeii and Herculaneum. Volcanic ash and mud preserved these Roman towns almost exactly as they were on the day Vesuvius erupted in 79 A.D. What you'll see are not just archeological ruins, but living testimony of daily life in the ancient world. You'll walk through the baths and brothels, the bars and bakeries, the sumptuous villas of wealthy patricians and the cramped quarters of the servants. You'll even see the food they ate, the wooden beds they slept in, and the graffiti they wrote on the walls. "Many a calamity has happened in the world," wrote Goethe, "but never one that has caused so much entertainment to posterity as this one."

From Herculaneum, you'll drive or take the funicular to the lip of the volcanic crater that caused so much destruction.

When the ancients imagined the entrance to hell they had a specific place in mind—Lake Avernus—a silent, lonely spot which you will visit on a drive through the Phlegrean Fields just west of Naples. You'll also enter the dark vaulted chamber where the Cumaean Sybil rendered her oracles. This was one of the most venerated sites in antiquity; the writer H. V. Morton calls it the most romantic classical site in Italy today.

Having delved into the past, it's time to indulge in the present along the magnificent Amalfi Drive. The road runs beside deep gorges with fantastically shaped rocks. Sparkling white towns cling to the rocky walls among lemon trees and vineyards. Visitors dine on fresh fish and fall asleep in rooms overlooking the sea.

From here it's less than an hour's trip by hydrofoil to the pleasure island of Capri, famed for its hotels and restaurants, its grottoes, its rich tropical vegetation, and its scenic walks.

Back on the mainland, you'll head south along the coast to Paestum. Though unknown to many tourists, Paestum has three magnificent Greek temples—one of them as wonderful in its own way as the Parthenon in Athens. From Paestum, it's a short drive back to Rome, and the end of a memorable trip through time.

THE MAIN ROUTE (with minimum overnight stays)

3–5 Days

One night: Capri
Day trip to Pompeii and Herculaneum
Two nights: Positano or Ravello
Day trip along the Amalfi Drive

5–7 Days

One night: Naples
Day trip to Pompeii, Herculaneum, and Vesuvius
Two nights: Capri
Day trip along the Amalfi Drive
Two nights: Either Ravello or Positano
One night: Either Ravello or Positano

7–14 Days

Two nights: Naples
Day trips to the Phlegrean Fields, Pompeii, Herculaneum, and Vesu-
vius
Three nights: Capri
Two nights: Ischia
Two nights: Either Ravello or Positano
One night: Either Ravello or Positano
One night: Salerno or Paestum

GETTING AROUND

Getting to Italy

There are no direct flights from the States to Naples, where the trip begins. Your best bet is to fly to Rome, which is a 3-hour drive or a 2-hour train ride to Naples. Three airlines fly nonstop from the States to Rome: TWA (from New York, Boston, St. Louis, and Washington, D.C.), Pan Am (from New York), and Alitalia (from New York). Alitalia has a flight from Los Angeles that stops in Chicago and Milan en route to Rome.

From Rome's airport, you have three ways of getting to Naples: (a) by air, (b) by car, or (c) by train.

(a) Taking a domestic flight is inadvisable for two reasons; first, you may miss your connection; and second, it's a 40-minute trip from the

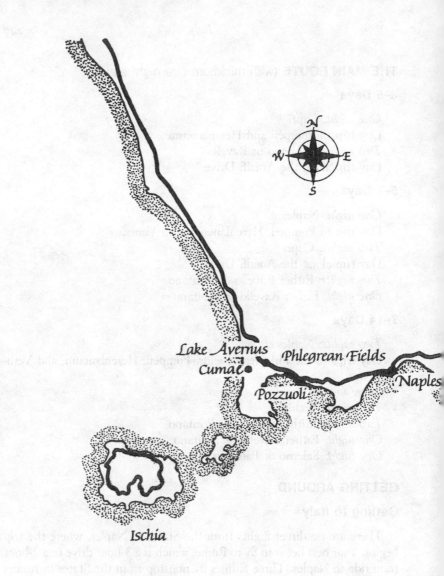

Lake Avernus
Cumae
Phlegrean Fields
Pozzuoli
Naples

Ischia

ITALY

Capri

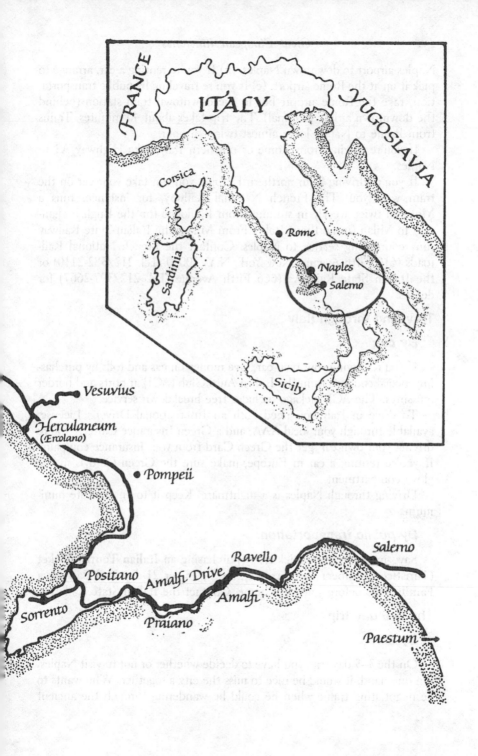

Naples airport to downtown Naples. (b) If you're renting a car, arrange to pick it up at the Rome airport. (c) If you're traveling by public transportation, take the Rome airport bus to the downtown train station (behind the downtown airline terminal). The trip takes about 40 minutes. Trains from Rome to Naples leave almost twice an hour.

If you're driving from Rome or northern Italy, take Highway A2 to Naples.

If you're driving from northern Europe, you can take your car on the train with you. The French National Railway, for instance, runs a Motorail twice weekly in summer from Boulogne (on the English channel) to Milan (in northern Italy). From Milan, the Italian State Railway runs connecting service to Naples. Contact the French National Railroads (610 Fifth Avenue, New York, N.Y. 10020. Tel. 212/582-2110) or the Italian State Railways (666 Fifth Avenue. Tel. 212/397-2667) for details.

Traveling through Italy

By car:

If you're driving your own car, save money on gas and tolls by purchasing special coupons from the Italian Auto Club (ACI) at ports and border crossings. The ACI package includes free breakdown service.

To drive in Italy you need both an International Driver's License, available through your local AAA, and a Green Insurance Card. If you're driving your own car, get the Green Card from your insurance company. If you're renting a car in Europe, make sure the Green Card is in the glove compartment.

Driving through Naples is a nightmare. Keep it to an absolute minimum.

By public transportation:

Save money on train tickets by purchasing an **Italian Tourist Ticket** (Turistico de Libera Circolazione), an 8-, 15- or 21-day **Rail Pass**, or a Family Pass before you leave home. Contact the Italian State Railways.

The 3–5 day trip

By car:

On the 3–5 day trip, you have to decide whether or not to visit Naples. On one hand, it would be nice to miss the city altogether: Who wants to be negotiating traffic when he could be wandering through the ancient streets of Pompeii or floating in a pool on Capri? On the other hand, Naples is home of the San Carlo Opera House, and of the National Archeological Museum, which contains many of the most important discoveries at Pompeii and Herculaneum. A visit to the museum will make your trip to Pompeii and Herculaneum a much more rewarding experience.

If you decide to visit the Archeological Museum (which I recommend): Take **Route A2** from Rome to Naples, check into your hotel, and go directly to the museum, which is open only from 9 to 2 (closed Mondays). You still have the afternoon open to do one of the following: (a) Visit **Herculaneum** (9 miles east of Naples at the Ercolano exit of Route A3); (b) visit **Vesuvius** (the same Ercolano exit off A3); or (c) visit **Pompeii** (the Pompeii exit on A3, 5 miles east of Ercolano). If you can't get to the Herculaneum-Pompeii-Vesuvius area until after 2 P.M., save Pompeii for another day since the excavations take at least a full half day to explore. See Herculaneum instead, which can be toured in about 2 hours, and then if there's any time left over, drive or take the chairlift to the top of Vesuvius (both the road and funicular to the crater begin near Herculaneum). Spend the night either back in Naples or in Sorrento. On your second day, return to Pompeii. After touring the ruins, follow **Route 145** along the Gulf of Naples. Turn off on **Route 163**. This is the beginning of the **Amalfi Drive**. Climb across the Peninsula of Sorrento and down to **Positano**.

If you decide not to visit the Archeological Museum: Avoid Naples altogether. Drive south from Rome on **Highway A2**. Leave A2 on the northern outskirts of Naples, turn east on **Highway A3**, and go directly to Herculaneum, Vesuvius, and Pompeii. It's impossible to do justice to all three in one day, so you'll have to make a choice. I'd vote for Herculaneum for 2 hours in the morning and Pompeii in the afternoon. If you want more time for Pompeii but don't want to backtrack to Naples, spend the night in one of the forgettable hotels in Pompeii or in the resort town of **Sorrento**, with a room overlooking the Bay of Naples.

After a night in **Positano**, leave your car and take the hydrofoil to **Capri**. After either a day trip or an overnight on Capri, return to Positano and continue east along the **Amalfi Drive** to **Amalfi**. Spend a night at **Ravello**. Continue along the coast to **Salerno** and **Paestum**. From Paestum, take A3 back to Naples and Highway A2 back to Rome.

By public transportation:

You'll be arriving at the Central Train Station in Naples. To get from Naples to Herculaneum and Vesuvius, take the Circumversuviana Suburban Railway (Tel. 269.601) from Corso Garibaldi (near the Central Train Station) to the Ercolano Station. Herculaneum is nearby. From the Ercolano Station, it's a 40-minute bus ride to the chairlift (Seggiovia) that goes to the top of Vesuvius. To get to Pompeii from Naples, Herculaneum, or Vesuvius, take the same Circumversuviana Railway. To get to Sorrento from Pompeii, take the narrow-gauge railway. The trip takes less than 30 minutes. To get to the Amalfi Drive (Positano, Amalfi, Sorrento) from Pompeii, take the train to Sorrento, and then a bus along the drive. Buses leave almost every hour. To get to Ravello, which is in the mountains above the drive, you may need to change buses in Amalfi. From Salerno, take the train to Paestum. From Paestum, take the train back to Naples (you may have to change trains in Salerno). From Naples, take the train back to Rome.

The 5–7 day trip

By car or public transportation:

This is essentially the same as the 3–5 day trip, except that it gives you more time at each destination and includes an optional side trip either to the Phlegrean Fields or to the island of Ischia. For the route through the Phlegrean Fields, see the 7–14 day trip below. For the day trip to Ischia, take a ferry from Capri.

The 7–14 day trip

By car:

As with the 3–5 day trip, take Highway A2 south from Rome. You may want to stop en route at Caserta, which is just off A2, about 18 miles north of Naples. Check into a Naples hotel, and visit the National Archeological Museum (open 9 to 2, closed Mondays). Spend a half day visiting the Phlegrean Fields, leaving Naples by the Quattro Giornate Tunnel, then taking Route S7 Quater west toward Pozzuoli. In the Phlegrean Fields, stop at the Solfatara, where sulphurous gasses steam from the ground; then continue west to the Sibyl's Cave at Cumae. Visit Lake Avernus, which the ancients considered the gateway to the Underworld, and the baths at Baia, where Julius Caesar, Nero, and other famous Romans had their villas. The excursion should take 3–4 hours.

After touring the Phlegrean Fields, take the **Tangenziale** back toward Naples. Take A2, then A3 east to **Ercolano (Herculaneum)**, **Vesuvius**, and **Pompeii**. Follow directions under the 3–5 day trip above for visits to these sights. From Pompeii drive south to **Castellammare di Stabia** and continue on Route 145 south to **Sorrento**. Take your car with you on the ferry from Sorrento to **Ischia**.

The itinerary suggests that you save Capri for later—going to the island from Positano. But you could just as easily get to Capri from Ischia. You won't need a car on Capri off-season; and in-season you're not allowed to have one. If you want to go from Ischia to Capri—doing both islands at once—leave your car on Ischia and pick it up on your way back to Sorrento.

As on the 3–5 day trip, drive from **Positano** to **Ravello**. From here, continue along the coast to **Salerno** and on to **Paestum**. For a more leisurely pace, spend your last night in either Salerno or Paestum before returning on A3 to Naples, and then heading north on Route A2 back to Rome.

By public transportation:

Hotels and travel agencies in Naples can arrange for you to join scheduled tours to Caserta, the Phlegrean Fields, Herculaneum, Vesuvius, Pompeii, the Amalfi Drive, and Paestum. Here's some help if you want to do it on your own.

To Caserta from Naples: Buses leave from Piazza Porta Capuana in the old city; best bet is to take a train from the Central Station.

To the Phlegrean Fields from Naples: There are two trains, the Ferrovia **Dello Strato** and the **Circumflegria**, both of which stop in Pozzuoli, where you can visit the **Amphitheater** and (a short cab ride) the **Solfatara**. The **Circumflegria** (Cumana Rail Service) leaves almost every 20 minutes from Piazza Montesanto. It stops not only in Pozzuoli, but also about one mile from **Lake Avernus** and only a short walk from **Cumae**, the site of the **Sibyl's Cave**. **Lake Avernus** and **Cumae** are each less than 4 miles from Pozzuoli, so find a cab in Pozzuoli to take you to both sites.

To Herculaneum, Vesuvius, and Pompeii from Naples: See the 3–5 day trip above.

To Capri: Ferries leave in season from Ischia, Naples, Sorrento, Positano, and Amalfi. The itinerary recommends that you go from Positano.

To Ischia: Ferries leave from Capri, Pozzuoli, Naples, Sorrento,

Positano, and Amalfi. The itinerary recommends that you go from Sorrento or Capri.

To the Amalfi Drive (Positano, Amalfi, Ravello, and Salerno) from Naples, Pompeii, or Sorrento: Take the train from Naples or Pompeii to Salerno. From Salerno there are hourly buses along the Amalfi Drive. To reach Ravello, which is up in the mountains, change buses in Amalfi.

From Salerno to Paestum: Infrequent express trains take about 35 minutes; local trains take about 50 minutes. The station at Paestum is in walking distance of the ruins.

From Paestum back to Naples: The train from Paestum to Salerno takes 35 to 50 minutes. Express trains from Salerno to Naples take about 50 minutes; locals take up to 1¾ hours. Naples has several stations; if you're heading back to Rome, take the train to the Central Station (Napoli Centrale), where you can catch the express train back to Rome.

A NOTE ON SHOPPING

There are good buys on **leather goods, gold jewelry, silk ties, knitwear, ceramics,** and other **handicrafts.** Don't buy **antiques** unless you know the difference between an original and an "authentic reproduction." Buy gold jewelry from a reputable dealer.

Naples. Specialties include **cameos, coral,** and **tortoiseshell.** Combs and other products made from the hawksbill turtle may not be imported into the U.S. For **antiques,** walk from the National Museum up Via Constantinopoli or Via D. Morelli. Fielding recommends **Galleria d'Arte** (Piazza dei Martiri 32).

Pompeii. A great area for **cameos** and **coral** is along the highway from Naples to Pompeii. **M. & G. Donadio** gets busloads of visitors, but the best place for bargains is **Giovanni Apa Co.** (Torre del Greco).

Sorrento. An international center for **inlaid furniture.** Try **Gargiulo Jannuzzi** (on the main square) or the smaller **Notturno.** (Unless you're taking the ferry to Ischia, Sorrento is not on our proposed route. It's only a 3-mile side trip, however.)

Capri. Prices tend to be expensive. For trendsetting **designer clothes,** try **La Parisienne,** on the main square. **Yves Dupris** (Via Canfora) sells men's and women's fashions on opposite sides of the street. For **jewelry,** go to **La Campanina** (Discesa Quisana 18). For good buys in **pottery,** try **Sea Gull** (Via Roma 25).

Positano. Fashionable, handmade **summer clothes** are sold in more than fifty tiny boutiques, many of them near the beach.

The Amalfi Drive. Shops along the eastern end of the drive, particularly around Atrani, sell locally made, hand-painted plates, pitchers, etc.

THINGS TO SEE AND DO WITH CHILDREN

Capri: the Blue Grotto, the hotel pools, the walk to the Natural Arch, the cable car from Anacapri, the 960 steps from Anacapri back down to the harbor.

Pompeii: the casts of bodies and animals exhibited in the Antiquarium. (The more children read beforehand about Pompeii, the more interested they will be.)

The Amalfi Drive: the Emerald Grotto, the hotel tennis courts and pools, the crowded, pebbly beaches, the Italian ices and pizza.

A NOTE ON SWIMMING

Most of the coast is badly polluted, except for the rather crowded, pebbly beaches on Capri and Ischia. There's a decent beach strung with hotels just outside of Paestum. Positano has a small, crowded, pebbly beach. Your best bet is to find hotels with pools.

A NOTE ON DINING

Restaurants on the itinerary are listed for two, E (expensive, over $60), M (moderate, from $30 to $60), or I (inexpensive, under $30).

The region is famous for its seafood, particularly **shellfish soups** and grilled bass. Ask for the fresh fish of the day: **red mullet** (iniglie), **sea bass** (spigola), or **tuna** (tonno). Order **clam** (vongola), **mussel** (cozza), or other seafood sauces on **pasta**, which is the other specialty of the region. Pasta comes in all shapes—not just spaghetti, but also ziti, cannelloni, vermicelli. Most everything is served with local tomatoes; meat dishes are often served **alla pizzaiola** (with tomato sauce and garlic). Naples is said to be the birthplace of the **pizza**, so go ahead and try it, if only to appreciate the Pizza Hut when you get back home. Neapolitan pizza tends to be served lukewarm, with a bit of runny tomato sauce floating on a sea of oil; once I had to pour the oil into a cup and soak up the rest with a napkin.

This is **Mozzarella** (buffalo cheese) country, which puts our own to shame. Other locally produced cheeses are **scamorza** or **fior di latte**, and various types of smoked, fresh, or aged **provolone**.

For wines, try **Falerno**, immortalized by Horace; the **red and white Ischia and Capri wines**; the wines from the volcanic slopes of Vesuvius—

white **Lacrima Christi** (tears of Christ) with fish; red **Gragnano** with meat. Ravello (where you'll be staying) also has its own local wines.

For desserts try the famous **sfogliatelle**, made with two different types of pastry. Happiness is a **profiterole**—a pastry shell filled with vanilla ice cream and topped with hot bittersweet chocolate sauce.

Prices are almost always listed in restaurant windows or just inside the door. Be prepared for a cover charge *(pane e coperto)* for the privilege of sitting down. The additional 15 percent service charge goes only partially to the waiter, so in finer restaurants be prepared to add another 5 percent to the tip.

A NOTE ON LODGING

Hotels in Italy are classified in five categories, Deluxe (L), first (I), second (II), third (III), and fourth (IV). Pensions are rated first (I), second (II), and third (III). The following rates are for two people sharing a room, and include taxes, service charges, and an Added Value Tax of 18 percent for Deluxe hotels and 10 percent for all other hotels and pensions. The value of the American dollar fluctuates against the Italian lira, so be sure to check current rates before leaving home. *Deluxe Hotels:* $130 to $218. *First-Class Hotels:* $48 to $174. *Second-Class Hotels and First-Class Pensions:* $33 to $85. *Third-Class Hotels and Second-Class Pensions:* $19 to $45. *Fourth-Class Hotels and Third-Class Pensions:* $15 to $26.

The most attractive rooms overlook the water—some of them (usually upstairs) with full views, and others (downstairs) with partial views. The better the view, as a rule, the higher the price. Ask for rates and then specify what you want.

Rooms even in better hotels tend to be decorated with a confusion of different brightly colored tiles—the more clashing the better. This busy Moorish-Italian look tends to compete with the naturally lush colors of the landscape. If you come prepared, it may not bother you as much.

Service charges and taxes are usually included in the rates, but it pays to ask in advance. It's a good idea, too, to check the quoted rates against those listed on the back of your hotel door.

Rooms with showers usually cost less than rooms with baths. Specify which you want.

EMERGENCIES

Motoring: Tel. 116 for the Automobile Club of Italy.

Naples: *Emergency:* Tel. 192. *American Consulate:* Piazza della Republica. Tel. 684.615. *First Aid Center:* Tel. 446.221. *24-Hour Pharmacy:* Tel. 192.

FOR FURTHER INFORMATION

Italian Government Travel Tourist Office. *New York:* 630 Fifth Avenue, New York, N.Y. 10111. Tel. 212/245-4822. *Chicago:* 500 North Michigan Avenue, Chicago, Ill. 60611. Tel. 312/644-0990. *San Francisco:* 360 Post Street, Suite 801, San Francisco, Calif. 94108. Tel. 415/ 392-6206.

THE ITINERARY

✤ NAPLES

Is it the sense of doom, living in the shadow of Vesuvius, that makes the people of Naples so volatile, so seemingly blind to everything but the pain and pleasure of the moment? Poverty and overcrowding are the more likely causes; but whatever the reason, Naples is a difficult place for the casual tourist to like. The Committee of Ninety-nine, formed recently to counter Naples's negative image, has its work cut out. If you have the time, and if you're willing to work at it, you'll come to love Naples as a mother loves her reprobate son; but if you're only passing through and hoping to enjoy a hassle-free vacation, spend as little time here as you can.

John Steinbeck must have had Naples in mind when he called Italian traffic "a deafening, screaming, milling, tire-screeching mess." I came to Naples determined to dismiss its noise, dirt, and confusion as so much local color; but after an hour, standing motionless in a traffic jam while a pride of policemen looked indifferently on, I was ready to search for color elsewhere.

Why visit Naples at all? First, Naples is the most sensible base— particularly if you're traveling by public transportation—from which to explore Pompeii, Herculaneum, Vesuvius, and the Phlegrean Fields. Second, it's home of the National Archeological Museum. The most important findings at Pompeii and Herculaneum are on display here—everything from sculpture to carbonized fruit—and seeing them will add to the pleasure of your trip to Pompeii and Herculaneum. Since the museum closes at 2 P.M. (1 P.M. Sunday and all day Monday) spend the morning here, and the afternoon visiting either the Phlegrean Fields or Herculaneum and Vesuvius. Spend the night back in Naples—perhaps at an opera or concert at the world-famous San Carlo Opera House—and the following morning set off on your tour of Pompeii.

• The National Archeological Museum (Museo Archeologico Nazionale, Piazza Museo), was designed as a cavalry barracks in the sixteenth century. The ground floor is devoted to marble sculpture, notably the Farnese Hercules and Bull. On the mezzanine is a collection of ancient frescoes and mosaics, including *Alexander's Battle*, taken from the floor of the House of the Fawn, which you'll see in Pompeii. On the first floor are works from Herculaneum. Don't miss the room with musical and surgical instruments. The collection of erotic art from Pompeii may be open by now.

• The San Carlo Opera House (Via Vittorio Emanuelle III. Tel. 418.266) is famous for its near-perfect acoustics and its sumptuous decoration. The box office is open weekdays from 10 to 1:30, and 4:30 to 6:30.

Dining

The Excelsior (E, Via Partenope 48. Tel. 417.111) is a good choice if you're staying there. Other possibilities include Il Galeone (E, Via Posillip 16. Tel. 684.581), La Sacrestia (E, Via Orazio 116. Tel. 664.186), Giuseppone a Mare (E, Via Russo. Tel. 769.602), Bergantino (M, Via Firenze 86. Tel. 224.380), and La Quercia, a trattoria (I, Vico Quercia. Tel. 323.329).

Lodging

The best—some would say the only—hotel is the Excelsior (L, Via Partenope 48. Tel. 417.111). Get a room overlooking the bay, with a view of Vesuvius and the flickering night lights of Capri. The Jolly Ambassador (I, Via Medina 70. Tel. 416.000) occupies the top floors of a thirty-story skyscraper. What the Jolly lacks in charm it makes up for in cleanliness and comfort.

For a more moderately priced hotel, try the centrally located Torino (II, Via Depretis 123. Tel. 322.410) or the Paradiso (II, Via Catullo 11. Tel. 660.233).

Both airport bus and train leave you near Plaza (Piazza) Garibaldi. If you simply need a place to put your head for the night, stay at one of the nearby hotels: **Terminus** (I, Plaza Garibaldi 19. Tel. 286.011), **Palace** (II, Plaza Garibaldi 9. Tel. 264.575), or **Bristol** (III, Plaza Garibaldi 61. Tel. 281.780).

For Further Information

There are tourist information booths in the Central Train Station, the airport, the Marine Station (Molo Angioino) at the harbor, and at the port of Mergellina, where the hydrofoils leave for Capri.

✤ *CASERTA* (18 miles from Naples)

Visit Caserta, Italy's answer to Versailles, only if you have a special interest in architecture and history or have time to spare. It's off Highway A2, 18 miles north of Naples, so you may want to stop here on the drive from Rome.

The Baroque furnishings and decorations show you how Bourbon royalty lived in the mid-eighteenth century. The Royal Palace was built by Charles III of Spain, the first of the Bourbons to wear the crown of Naples. Charles was in his late thirties when he built this Hollywood-style extravaganza, this monument to megalomania, at Caserta. It was here, in what Eisenhower called "a castle near Naples," that the Allied High Command had its headquarters in World War II; and here that German forces in Italy surrendered in April 1945. Most enjoyable are the gardens and parks, particularly the Cascades, where a life-size Diana and her maidens stand waiting to be photographed.

✤ *THE PHLEGREAN FIELDS*

The **Phlegrean Fields**—the fields of fire—was the name once given to the entire region west of Naples, including the island of Ischia. The whole area floats freely on a mass of molten lava very close to the surface. The fires are still smoldering. Greek and Roman notions of the under world were not the blind imaginings of a primitive people; they were the creations of poets and writers who stood on this very ground—here in the Phlegrean Fields—and wrote down what they saw. The main sights today are (a) the **Solfatara**, the sunken crater of a volcano, where visitors walk among the sulfurous steam jets and pools of bubbling mud; (b) Italy's third-largest and best-preserved **Amphitheater at Pozzuoli**; (c) **Lake Avernus**, which the ancients believed was the entrance to the Under world; (d) **Baia**, the resort town of ancient Rome, where you can see the remains of a spa frequented by Pompey, Julius Caesar, Nero, and Cicero; and (e) the **Cave of the Cumaean Sibyl**, described by Homer and Vergil.

Whether it's worth the half day it takes to tour these sites really depends on your interests. If you've never seen volcanic activity, don't miss the **Solfatara** (it's quite safe, so long as you stick to the path). The **Amphitheater** at Pozzuoli is fascinating because of its well-preserved underground passages and chambers, which give you a good sense of how the wild animals were hoisted up into the arena. At **Lake Avernus** you'll be standing at the very spot which the ancients considered the entrance to Hades. The ruins at **Baia** won't mean too much unless you have more than a passing interest in antiquity. The **Oracle at Cumae** was as famous as the one at Delphi; if you've read *The Aeneid*, you'll want to enter the very cave described in Book VI, where Aeneas sought the Sibyl's aid for his journey to the Underworld.

• The **Solfatara**. From Naples, take Route S7 Quater, "Via Domiziana," west toward **Pozzuoli**. You'll see a sign to the Solfatara on your right, about 1.3 miles before Pozzuoli. The only eruption of this semiextinct volcano was in 1198.

Legends about this smoldering landscape are based on conflicts between the neolithic gods of the soil and the newer Olympian gods brought to Greece by the Achaeans about 1600 B.C. One legend tells of how Zeus hurled a hundred-headed dragon named Typhon—the pre-Olympian god of volcanoes—down the crater of Epomeo on the island of Ischia; and of how every crater in the Phlegrean Fields is one of Typhon's mouths, flashing steam and fire. In a similar legend pitting old values against new, the sulfurous springs of the Solfatara are said to be the poisonous discharges from the wounds the Titans received in their war with Zeus before he hurled them down to hell. Both legends, of course, are efforts to dramatize man's struggle to overcome the mysterious and dangerous forces of nature.

• The **Amphitheater at Pozzuoli** (Anfiteatro Flavio, open 9 A.M. to an hour before sunset; closed Mondays) is slightly more than a mile farther west on S7. It's the third-largest arena in Italy, after the Coliseum and Santa Maria Capua Vetere, and could accommodate forty thousand spectators, who were sometimes treated to mock naval battles when the arena was filled with water.

• You may want to make a short side trip to Pozzuoli's harbor and imagine St. Paul landing here in 61 A.D. en route to Rome. His own ship had been wrecked off Malta, and he was brought here on the *Castor and*

Pollux, a grain ship from Alexandria that was carrying corn from Egypt to Italy only eighteen years before the eruption at Vesuvius.

You could sail from Pozzuoli to Ischia, though the itinerary suggests you wait and go from Sorrento or Capri.

• If time is limited, visit **Lake Avernus** and **Cumae** (the **Sibyl's Cave**) and then return toward Naples on a highway called the **Tangenziale.** A longer route takes you on an 11-mile loop from **Pozzuoli** south to **Baia,** around **Lake Miseno** (a volcanic crater believed by the ancients to be the Styx, across which Charon ferried the souls of the dead), and around **Lake Fusaro.** This 30-minute side trip lets you see the baths at Baia and enjoy some fine views of Pozzuoli Bay and the Phlegrean Fields.

To reach **Lake Avernus** (Lago d'Averno) continue west on S7 toward Cumae and then turn left (south) on the road to Baia. About one mile along this road, turn right and follow signs to Lake Avernus. The best time to visit is at sunset or when the moon is rising. There's a restaurant on the west side, near the tunnel (closed to the public) to Cumae, where you can dine on the terrace. Forested hills rise on three sides; the menacing cone of Monte Nouvo rises on the fourth. The smell of sulfur hangs over this sad, lonely landscape at the very gates of hell. No place evokes Homer, Vergil, and the cult of the Other World better than this silent, mysterious setting.

• The ancient city of **Baia** (3.6 miles from Pozzuoli) is now largely under the sea, but it was once the most opulent and fashionable resort area of the Roman Empire. Sulla, Pompey, Julius Caesar, Tiberius, Nero, Cicero —these are some of the men who built their holiday villas here. Petronius's *Satyricon* is a satire on the corruption and intrigue, the wonderful licentiousness of Roman life at Baia. (Petronius was hired to arrange parties and entertainments for Nero, so he was in a position to know.) It was here at Baia that Emperor Claudius built a great villa for his wife Messalina, who spent her nights indulging herself at public brothels; here that Agrippina poisoned her husband and was in turn murdered by her son Nero; here that Cleopatra was staying when Julius Caesar was murdered on the Ides of March. The famous **baths** are open from 9 A.M. until an hour before sunset; closed Mondays).

• **Cumae** is perhaps the oldest Greek colony in Italy. In the sixth and seventh centuries B.C. it overshadowed the Phlegrean Fields, including Naples. The **Sybil's Cave** (Antro della Sibilla) is here—one of the most venerated sites in antiquity. In the fifth or sixth century A.D., the Greeks hollowed the cave from the rock beneath the present ruins of Cumae's acropolis. Visitors walk through a dark, massive stone tunnel which opens into a vaulted chamber where the Sibyl rendered her oracles. Standing here, imagine yourself having an audience with her, her voice echoing off the dark, damp walls. The sense of mystery, of communication with the Invisible, is overwhelming. "This is the most romantic classical site in Italy," writes H. V. Morton. "I would rather come here than to Pompeii."

Vergil wrote the epic *The Aeneid*, the story of the Trojan prince Aeneas's wanderings, partly to give Rome the historical legitimacy that Homer had given the Greeks. On his journey, Aeneas had to descend to the Underworld to speak to his father, and, to find his way in, he needed the guidance of the Cumaean Sibyl. She told him about the Golden Bough, his ticket through the Stygian swamp to the Underworld.

Vergil did not dream up the Sibil's cave or the entrance to Hades—he must have stood both in her chamber and along the rim of Lake Avernus —as you yourself will stand there. When he wrote, "The way to hell is easy"—*Decensus Averno est facile*—it was because he knew the way. In Book VI of *The Aeneid*, Vergil describes how Aeneas, arriving at Cumae, seeks Apollo's throne (remains of the **Temple of Apollo** can still be seen) and "the deep hidden abode of the dread Sibyl,/An enormous cave. . . ."

The Sibyl was not necessarily a charlatan; she was a medium, a prophetess, an old woman whom the ancients believed could communicate with the Other World. The three most famous Sibyls were at Erythrae, Delphi, and Cumae. Foreign governments consulted the Sibyls before mounting campaigns. Wealthy aristocrats came to consult with their dead relatives. Businessmen came to get their dreams interpreted or to seek favorable omens before entering into financial agreements or setting off on journeys. Farmers came to remove curses on their cows. Love potions were a profitable source of revenue; women from Baia lined up for potions to slip into the wine of handsome charioteers who drove up and down the street in their gold-plated, four-horsepower chariots.

With the coming of the Olympian gods, the earlier gods of the soil were discredited or given new roles and names that reflected the change from a matrilineal to a patrilineal society. Ancient rites, such as those surrounding the Cumaean Sibyl, were carried out in secret and known as the Mysteries. The Romans—like the Soviets—tried in vain to replace these Mysteries by deifying the state in the person of its rulers. Yet even the Caesars appealed to forces of the Other World. And until the fourth century A.D. the Sibyl was consulted by the Christian Bishop of Rome.

EN ROUTE: To HERCULANEUM, VESUVIUS, and POMPEII

From the Phlegrean Fields, take S7 back from Cumae toward Pozzuoli and Naples. Less than 2 miles east of Cumae, turn off on the **Tangenziale**, an expressway that goes along the northern edge of Naples. This will take you to A2, and then to A3 east to the **Ercolano** (Herculaneum) exit.

If you're going directly from Naples to Ercolano (Herculaneum) take A3 to the **Ercolano** exit. The ruins of Herculaneum are here, and also the 8-mile road up the western face of Vesuvius. (There's another road from Pompeii up the south face of Vesuvius, but it's more difficult and requires more walking.)

The road up Vesuvius splits twice. At the first split, a right turn takes you to the observatory. Stay left. At the second split, you can either bear right to the chairlift or bear left to a parking area, where you set off on a stiff, 20-minute climb.

To drive direct from downtown Naples to Pompeii on A3 takes about an hour. To go by train, take the **Circumvesuvia**, which leaves from **Corso Garibaldi**, near the Central Train Station. It's a 30-minute ride to the **Pompeii-Villa dei Misteri Station**. From here it's only a short walk to the **Porta Marina** (Sea Gate), the main entrance to Pompeii.

To drive to **Pompeii** from Herculaneum or Vesuvius, return to A3 and continue east about 7 miles. To go by train, take the **Circumvesuvia** from the Ercolano Station to the **Pompeii-Villa dei Misteri Station**.

After touring Pompeii, you can get a train almost every 20 minutes to **Sorrento**. It's a 30-minute trip. If you're going to return to Pompeii, you can spend the night in Sorrento as an alternative to returning to Naples. From Sorrento, you can catch a boat to Capri or Ischia, or begin your trip along the Amalfi Drive.

An Introduction to Vesuvius, Herculaneum, and Pompeii

Lava is extremely fertile. In less than 20 years it gets covered with greenery which in time becomes luxuriant vegetation. Memories of former eruptions are forgotten. The rich land attracts farmers, and villages are built. Two such towns, Herculaneum and Pompeii, grew up in the shadow of Vesuvius. On the slopes above the town, oaks and chestnuts grew; below were fig and lemon trees, chestnut forests, vineyards, and the yellow blossoms of the mimosa.

In 80 B.C. the Roman General Sulla turned Herculaneum and Pompeii into Roman colonies, where wealthy patricians came to escape the turmoil of city life and relax in the sun. The sea lapped against Herculaneum's walls then, and the citizens were mostly fishermen. Pompeii was a thriving commercial center in a rich agricultural region. If I had written my *Great Weekend Escape Book* then, I would have recommended both Herculaneum and Pompeii as ideal resort towns for overworked Romans seeking a delightful climate and a respite from the frantic pace of everyday Rome.

The towns were laid out on grid patterns, with two main intersecting streets. The wealthiest took a whole block for themselves; those less fortunate built a house and rented out the front rooms, facing the street, as shops. The façades of these houses were relatively plain and seldom hinted at the care and attention lavished on the private rooms within.

When a visitor entered, he passed the shops and entered an open area (atrium). In the back was a receiving room. Behind was another open area called the peristyle, with rows of columns and perhaps a garden with a fountain. Only good friends ever saw this private part of the house, which was surrounded by the bedrooms and the dining area.

How different these homes are from houses today—and how much they say about changing attitudes toward family and society! Today we build homes that face the streets, that look out over the world; in Pompeii and Herculaneum, houses were designed around an inner garden so that families could turn their backs on the world outside. Today we install picture windows that break down visual barriers between ourselves and our neighbors; the people in these Roman towns had few windows, preferring to get their light from the central courtyard—the light within. How pleasant it must have been to come home from the forum or the baths to one's own secluded kingdom with no visual reminders of a life outside one's own.

Not that public life was so intolerable. There were wine shops on almost every corner, and frequent shows at the amphitheater. The public fountains and toilets were fed by huge cisterns connected by lead pipes beneath the sidewalks. Since garbage and rainwater collected in the streets of Pompeii, the sidewalks were raised and huge stepping stones were placed at crossings so pedestrians could keep their feet dry. Herculaneum had better drainage, with an underground sewer that led to the sea.

The ratio of freemen to slaves was about three to two. A small, prosperous family had two or three slaves. Since all manual labor was considered degrading, the slaves did all housework and cooking, including the cutting of meat, which the family ate with spoons or with their hands. Everyone loved grapes, but figs were popular, too. Venison, chicken, and pork were the main dishes. Oranges weren't known, but people used quinces (a good source of Vitamin C) against scurvy. Bread was made from wheat and barley (rye and oats were unknown) and washed down with wine made from grapes from the slopes of Vesuvius.

The government was considered a democracy, but women, children, gladiators, and Jews couldn't vote. They did, however, express their opinions on election day, as you'll see in campaign graffiti left on public walls.

Some fifteen thousand graffiti were found in Pompeii and Herculaneum. Many were political announcements—one person recommending another for office, for example, and spelling out his qualifications. Some were bills announcing upcoming events—a play at the theater, a fight among gladiators at the amphitheater. Others were public notices—that wine was on sale, that an apartment would be vacant on the Ides of March. A good many were personal, and give a human dimension to the disaster that not even the sights can equal. Here are a few:

At the Baths: "What is the use of having a Venus if she's made of marble?"

At a hotel: "I've wet my bed. My sin I bare. But why? you ask. No pot was anywhere."

At the entrance to the front lavatory at a private house: "May I always and everywhere be as potent with women as I was here."

In a back room at the Suburban Baths: "Apelles the waiter dined most pleasantly with Dexter the slave of the emperor, and they had a screw at the same time." (Did they do it with each other, or only at the same time? Homosexuality would not have been uncommon.)

In a house in Herculaneum: "Apollinaris the physician of the Emperor Titus had a good shit here."

"Everyone writes on this wall but me."

"We are as full as wineskins."

"You sell us this watery liquid and drink pure wine yourself."

"Oh, I would rather die than be a god without you."

"Victoria, I greet you, and wherever you are, may your sneeze bring you good luck."

"Lucilla makes money from her lover."

"Virgula to her friend Tertius: Thou art too ugly!"

"Methea loves Chrestus with all her heart. May Venus favor them, and may they ever live in amity."

"Vivius Restitus slept here alone and thought with longing of his Urbana."

"I will knock Venus's ribs to pieces with rods, and I will whip her till she is lame. If she is able to pierce my tender heart, why should I not be able to mash her skull with a cudgel?"

In the year 63 A.D. Vesuvius was considered an extinct volcano. The crater had become a dense forest filled with wild boars. Spartacus and his slaves had lived here during their rebellion against Rome.

An earthquake in 63 A.D. caused so much destruction that the citizens of Pompeii and Herculaneum considered abandoning their towns and settling elsewhere. Nero was in the tenth year of his reign, and the people had to turn to him for help. What was rebuilt was therefore done in Roman style, which was splendid but not always in the best taste—a definite departure from the noble and simple lines of Greek art. Not that everyone minded or even noticed the difference. With so many wealthy visitors, it was only natural that the people in these provincial towns would imitate the manners of the Roman nobility and look to Rome for the latest styles. The Pompeiian artists mostly reproduced famous Greek paintings, not from inspiration but from memory. There were no allegories—just pleasant, agreeable images, mostly mythological love stories—Jupiter carrying off Europa, Apollo pursuing Daphne, Venus in the arms of Mars. False pilasters were painted in fresco, imitating the example of the rich. Artists worked fast and art became an industry.

August 24, 79 A.D., was a hot summer day. On the previous day the annual Festival of Vulcan, the Roman fire god, had been celebrated. At both Herculaneum and Pompeii tremors had been felt for four days. Then came the explosion.

The younger Pliny, age seventeen, was at the house of his uncle, the elder Pliny, at Misenum (which you passed if you drove from Baia to Cumae), when the family's attention was drawn to a cloud of unusual size and appearance. As Pliny reported later in a famous letter to Tacitus:

> It was not clear at that distance from which mountain the cloud was rising (it was afterwards known to be Vesuvius). Its general appearance can best be expressed as being like an umbrella pine, for it rose to a great height on a sort of trunk and then split off into branches. . . . In places it looked white, elsewhere blotched and dirty, according to the amount of soil and ashes carried with it. My uncle's scholarly acumen saw at once that it was important enough for a closer inspection, and he ordered a boat to be made ready, telling me I could come with him if I wished. I replied that I preferred to go on with my studies. . . .

Pliny the elder, both a historian and commander of the naval base at Misenum, was diverted by a note from the wife of a friend, begging him to rescue her husband whose house was at the foot of Vesuvius. And so he ordered the warships launched with the intention of bringing help to those who were trapped. The letter continues:

He [steered] his course straight for the danger zone. He was entirely fearless.
. . . Ashes were already falling, hotter and thicker as the ships drew near, followed by bits of pumice and blackened stones, charred and cracked by the flames: Then suddenly they were in shallow water, and the shore was blocked by the debris from the mountain. For a moment my uncle wondered whether to turn back, but when the helmsman advised this he refused, telling him that Fortune stood by the courageous. . . .

The wind was in my uncle's favor, and he was able to bring his ship in. He embraced his terrified friend, cheered and encouraged him. . . . Meanwhile, on Mount Vesuvius broad sheets of fire and leaping flames blazed at several points, their bright glare emphasized by the darkness of night. My uncle tried to allay the fears of his companions by repeatedly declaring that these were nothing but bonfires left by peasants in their terror, or else empty houses on fire in districts they had abandoned.

Then he went to rest. . . . By this time the courtyard giving access to his room was full of ashes mixed with pumice stones, so that its level had risen, and if he had stayed in the room any longer he would never have got out. He was awakened, came out and joined [his friend] Pomponianus and the rest of the household. They debated whether to stay indoors or take their chances in the open, for the buildings were now shaking with violent shocks, and seemed to be swaying to and fro as if they were torn from their foundations. Outside, on the other hand, there was the danger of falling pumice stones; however, after comparing the risks, they took the latter. As a protection against falling objects they put pillows on their heads tied down with cloths.

Elsewhere there was daylight by this time, but they were still in darkness, blacker and denser than any ordinary night, which they relieved by lighting torches and various kinds of lamps. My uncle decided to go down to the shore and investigate the possibility of escape by sea, but he found the waves still wild and dangerous. A sheet was spread on the ground for him to lie down on.
. . . Then the flames and smell of sulphur which gave warning of the approaching fire drove the others to take flight and roused him to stand up. He stood leaning on two slaves and then suddenly collapsed, I imagine because the dense fumes choked his breathing by blocking his windpipe. . . .

When daylight returned on the sixteenth—two days after the last day he had been seen—his body was found intact and uninjured, still fully clothed and looking more like sleep than death.*

This is the oldest-surviving realistic description of a major natural disaster.

* The younger Pliny, *Letters*, VI, 20, 6, 8–9, 16. Trans. B. Radice.

The eruption actually began at 1 P.M., with flames and a cloud of ashes that whirled with the wind and covered the region in a shroud of darkness. Red-hot boulders were hurled thousands of feet into the air, and rained down on the surrounding countryside. By the following day, Pompeii was covered to a depth of twelve feet by a sudden fall of ashes, pumice, and stones. Later eruptions buried the town another six feet. When excavators uncovered the town, they found six hundred bodies in the streets and the bodies of many others who had tried to flee. An estimated two thousand people—one tenth of the total population—had perished.

What covered Herculaneum was not pumice and ash, but mud. Vesuvius belched forth steam at 2,000 degrees F, which mingled with seawater. Torrents of liquid mud swept down upon the city, leapt the walls, and penetrated into every crevice. The mud moved slowly enough that all but a handful of the five thousand inhabitants escaped. As it solidified, it acted as a prop to the buildings which otherwise would have collapsed. The pressure from this and subsequent eruptions converted the mud into a compact mass of rock (tufa), from 60 to 100 feet deep.

So effective was the covering that eggs and fish were found on a dining room table, and in a bakery eighty-one carbonized loaves were discovered in the half-opened oven. At Herculaneum, the mud scorched papyrus and cloth but did not destroy them. Wooden beds, stairs, cupboards—all were saved and are on view today. In one house excavators found the bread, salad, fruit, and cake that were being served for lunch when the catastrophe struck.

In 1864 Giuseppe Fiorelli, in charge of the excavations at Pompeii, got the idea of forcing liquid plaster into the lava molds that had solidified around the fallen bodies. The plaster forms (which you will see) are so true to life, you can see the pubic hair shaved in semicircles to duplicate the look on certain statues, and the tormented expressions on the faces.

The first deaths at Pompeii must have been caused by the huge stones falling from the sky. Some people hid in their homes; others fled. Many who stayed must have suffocated beneath the falling ash, or, like Pliny the elder, been asphyxiated by fumes. Many who fled must have been struck down by falling pillars and masonry.

At the House of Meander at Pompeii the doorkeeper fled to his room with his little girl, and covered their heads with pillows. That's how they were found eighteen hundred years later. In another house, a mother and daughter escaped through a skylight into a garden. That's where they were found. A woman and her three maids were found with the jewelry and the silver mirror they had squandered time gathering. A man with teeth marks in his flesh was found beside his dog. The Roman sentry at the gate at Herculaneum was found trying to cover his dog with his cloak. Two gladiators with manacled wrists were discovered in the prison cell. Over sixty gladiators were found dead in their barracks; with them was a richly dressed woman: No one will ever know why.

In 1748, when excavators turned over the ashes that for seventeen hundred years had covered Pompeii, they had one objective: to find masterpieces for the king's museums. Excavations were by chance; if nothing was found, the site was abandoned. Litter was thrown back; frescoes not worthy of the museum were left exposed to the influence of the sun and rain; walls cracked and fell. It was only later, in 1863, that the collection of works of art became secondary to the goal of restoring an ancient Roman city. That is why so much of the priceless art is found today in the National Museum in Naples and not where it belongs, in Pompeii. The situation in Herculaneum was somewhat different. Because the town was buried in solidified mud rather than ash, citizens could not return after the disaster, as many did in Pompeii, to recover possessions. Excavations began much later, so much of the art was left where it was found. Though Herculaneum had only one fourth the population of Pompeii, and has only been partially excavated, what has been found is generally better preserved than at Pompeii.

❧ HERCULANEUM

The site is open from 9 A.M. until an hour before sunset.

The best guide is a small red book called *Pompeii-Herculaneum: A Guide with Reconstructions.* Photos are covered with plastic overlays, so you can see how various sites look both today and two thousand years ago. I found a copy at the entrance to Pompeii but not at Herculaneum; pick one up in Naples if you can.

If you want a personal guide, make sure he has certification papers (a booklet with his photo and a stamp). Agree beforehand on the length of the tour and the price. Write the figures down.

Whether you're with a guide or not, be sure to have some small lira notes handy to tip the guards who open the locked houses for you.

You could easily get lost in the streets of Pompeii, but not here. Most important buildings can be seen in about 2 hours. If you feel closer to the past at Herculaneum than at Pompeii, it's in part because there are less hawkers here, and visitors tend to show a certain quiet respect for antiquity that's not always evident in such a famous Tourist Spot as Pompeii. Though there's much less to see here, houses are better preserved, with bright frescoes and mosaics. In some cases, you can even see the original wooden beams, staircases, and furniture. **The following route will help you locate the most important sights:**

1. The sole entrance is at the east corner. You'll walk halfway around the perimeter of the site and enter on **Cardo III**. Only three main streets have been excavated: **Cardo III, Cardo IV,** and **Cardo V**. The two cross streets are **Decumanus Inferior** and **Decumanus Maximus**. As you walk around the excavated site, you can see how it was unearthed like hidden treasure from a pit below the surface of the existing town. Excavations are still going on; the best perhaps is yet to come.

2. On **Cardo III**, make the first right, in front of the badly damaged **Casa dell'Albergo**, and turn left on **Cardo IV**. The first building on the right is the **House of the Mosaic Atrium** (Casa dell'Atrio a mosaico). The entranceway (atrium) is still covered with mosaics. The floors rippled under the weight of the lava. You can still see the wooden window frames in the courtyard (peristyle). Don't miss the bedrooms and the large dining room.

3. Continue up **Cardo IV** (to the right). On your left is the **Wooden Trellis House** (Casa a Graticcio). This is the only surviving example of the use of trellises to make walls—a money-saving technique used by the Romans for shops and secondary rooms.

4. Next door is the **House of the Wooden Partition** (Casa del Tramezzo di legno), which has the charred remains of a bed and a well-preserved façade.

5. Cross **Decumanus Inferior**. The first house on the right is **Casa Sannitica**, which has a beautiful entranceway (atrium) surrounded by Ionic columns. The house retains the simple plan of the Samnites, the race that lived here before the Romans came.

6. A few steps farther along, across the street, is the entrance to the **Baths** (Terme), which have separate rooms for men and women. The dressing room has cubicles for clothing. As in the baths at Pompeii, there's a series of chambers that get progressively hotter, and a sweating room for people with bad livers. The floor is raised on small brick columns. The cavities were filled with hot air from furnaces. The heat was carried through ducts up the walls. The hot rooms had additional pipes in the ceilings. Soap was reserved for medical treatment or hair dye, but bathers brought their own oils, scrapers, and towels. The baths usually opened at noon, when the furnaces were lit. Many bathers came to these

early health and fitness clubs in the evening, after dinner. They sang, bathed, splashed, brawled, got massaged, drank wine, ate pastries and sausages, and sweated off the pressures of the day.

7. Continue (left) up **Cardo IV**. Across the street is the **House with Charred Furniture** (Casa del Mobilio carbonizzato), a small elegant house with an attractive courtyard and the remains of furniture.

8. Next on your left is the **House with the Neptune and Amphitrite Mosaic** (Casa del Mosaico di Nettuno e Anfitrite), the best example of a house whose front room was used as a shop.

9. At the end of **Cardo IV**, turn right on **Decumanus Maximus**. The first entrance on the right is **Casa del Bicentenario**, so called because it was unearthed in 1938, two hundred years after excavations began. The living room has a marble floor and frescoes. In a small upper room (many houses in Herculaneum, unlike those in Pompeii, had two floors) is a small cross in a panel above a wooden altar—the oldest evidence of Christianity in the Roman Empire.

10. Make your first right down **Cardo V**. Halfway down the street, on the left, is the **Bakery** (Pistrinum), which has two original flour mills, an oven, and bread molds.

11. Continue down **Cardo V** and turn left at the first cross street, **Decumanus Inferior**, for a look at the **Palestra**, the sports center, which has a swimming pool in the shape of a cross.

12. Return to **Cardo V** and continue left. On your right is the **House of the Stags or Deer** (Casa dei Cervi), one of the most beautiful patrician houses, which has frescoes of hunting scenes from the time of Nero.

13. Return to **Cardo III** and make your way back to the entrance.

✢ VESUVIUS

You can visit Vesuvius either before or after Herculaneum. The mountain tends to be clearer in the afternoon. If possible, save the mountain till after you've toured the buried city and learned to appreciate the volcano's awesome power. The most important factor is whether the summit is lost in mist—when it is, you'll be lucky to see your hand in front of your face. The volcano is visible from Naples and everywhere else along the Bay of Naples; the best advice is, when you see the summit clearing, head for it. The view then is magnificent, with the curve of the coast and the tiny white houses among the orange and lemon blossoms. The funicular chairlift, which inspired the song "Funiculi! Funicula!" shuts down in inclement weather. If you decide to take the 20-minute walk, wear your hardiest shoes: It's a steep, relentless climb over pulverized ash and lapilli—definitely not for everyone. If the weather's bad and you've never seen a volcano, it's still worth driving to the parking area, past fields of black twisted lava from the 1944 eruption.

When you think of earlier generations being tougher than we are, imagine Goethe in 1787 making his way to the top hanging on to the belt of a guide.

☙ POMPEII

The site is open from 9 A.M. until an hour before sunset.

If your time is limited and you have to choose between Herculaneum and Pompeii, choose Pompeii: The buildings are not as well preserved as at Herculaneum, but the size of the town and the extent of excavations are considerably more impressive. It would be a shame to miss either, however; and since the two towns are so close, there's no reason not to see both. This is one of the few times when it would be preferable to know two things superficially than to know one in somewhat greater depth.

If you want a personal guide, make sure he's registered and that he's standing *inside* the gate. Agree beforehand on the length of the tour and the price.

Many houses will be locked. Ask one of the many guides to open them for you. Be persistent! And have some small lira notes ready if persistence is not enough.

For a self-guided tour, you'll need a map. Most, unfortunately, list only the major streets. The best comes with a useful English guide, *How To Visit Pompeii,* sold at the entrance. Also helpful, particularly for families with children, is the small red guide *Pompeii-Herculaneum: A Guide with Reconstructions,* which includes transparent overlays so you can see the various sites as they looked in 79 A.D.

You'll be spending many hours negotiating rough paving stones; be sure to wear your most comfortable walking shoes.

The following route will help you locate the most interesting sights:

1. Enter through **Porta Marina**, so called because it faces the sea. It is near the **Pompeii-Villa dei Misteri Railroad Station**.

2. On your right is the **Antiquarium**, which contains casts of human bodies and a dog.

3. Past the **Temple of Venus** is the **Basilica**, the law court and the economic center of the city. These oblong buildings ending in a semicir-

cular projection (apse) were the model for early Christian churches, which had a nave (central aisle) and two side aisles separated by rows of columns. Standing in the Basilica you can recognize the continuity between Roman and Christian architecture.

4. The Basilica opens onto the **Forum** (Foro), the public meeting place, surrounded by temples and public buildings. It was here that elections were held and speeches and official announcements made. America's answer to the forum is the village green. The closest we come to it today is the Mall.

5. Turn left. At the far (northern) end of the forum is the **Temple of Jupiter** (Tempio di Giove). Walk around the right side of the temple, cross the street, and continue north on **Via del Foro** (Forum Street). There is a **restaurant** on your left.

6. The next cross street becomes **Via della Fortuna** to your right, and **Via della Terme** to your left. Turn right on **Via della Fortuna**. On your left is **The House of the Fawn** (Casa del Fauno), one of the most impressive examples of a luxurious private house, with wonderful mosaics (originals in the National Museum in Naples).

7. Retrace your steps along **Via della Fortuna** to **Via del Foro**. Cross the street. You're now on **Via della Terme**. The first entrance on the right is the **House of the Tragic Poet** (Casa del Poeta Tragico). This is a typical middle-class house from the last days of Pompeii. Over the door is a mosaic of a chained dog and the inscription, *Cave canem*, "Beware of the dog."

8. Continue west on **Via della Terme** to the end. Turn right and bear left along **Via Consolare**. Pass through the beautiful **Porta Ercolano** (Gate of Herculaneum)—the main gate that led to Herculaneum and Naples.

9. Now outside of Pompeii, walk down **Via dei Sepolcri** (Street of the Tombs), lined with tombs and cypresses. The road makes a sharp left. At the four-way crossing, turn right to the **Villa of the Mysteries** (Villa dei Misteri). This patrician's villa contains what some consider the greatest surviving group of paintings from the ancient world, telling the story of a young bride (Ariadne) being initiated into the mysteries of the cult of Dionysus. Bacchus (Dionysus), the god of wine, was popular in a town so devoted to the pleasures of the flesh. But he also represented the triumph of the irrational—of all those mysterious, chthonic forces that no official state religion could fully suppress. The cult of Dionysus, like the cult of the Cumaean Sybil, gave people a sense of control over Fate, and, in its focus on the Other World, helped pave the way for Christianity.

10. Return along **Via dei Sepolcri** back into Pompeii. Retrace your steps down **Via Consolare**, which joins with **Vicolo di Narcisco**. Make your first left on **Vicolo di Mercurio**. Six blocks down is **Vicolo dei Vettii**. Around the corner, to the left, is the **House of the Vettii** (Casa dei Vetti). This is the best example of a rich middle-class merchant's house, faithfully restored.

11. Return back around the corner to **Vicolo di Mercurio**. Turn left, the direction you took before you turned the corner to visit the House of the Vettii. Continue east one more block. You've now reached **Via Stabiana**, one of the two major intersecting streets of the town. Around the corner to the left is **Casa degli Amorini Dorati** (House of the Gilded Cupids), an elegant, well-preserved home with original marble decorations in the garden.

12. From the door of Casa degli Amorini Dorati, turn right down **Via Stabiana**. Your fourth left should put you on **Via Augustali**. Your first left will take you to the **Lupanare** (the brothel) on **Vicolo del Lupanare**. An uneaten plate of pasta and beans was found here. On the walls are scenes of erotic games which clients could request. The beds have shoe marks left by visitors.

13. Continue south on **Vicolo del Lupanare**. Your first left will put you on **Via dell'Abbondanza**, the other main street of the old town. The first door on your left is the **Stabian Baths**. It was here that people came in the evening to drown the burdens of the day. The baths were heated by underground furnaces. The heat circulated among the stone pillars supporting the floor, rose through flues in the walls, and escaped through chimneys. Water temperature could be set for cold, lukewarm, and hot. Bathers took a lukewarm bath to prepare themselves for the hot room. A tepid bath came next, and then a plunge into cold water to tone up the skin. A vigorous massage with oil was followed by rest, reading, horseplay, and conversation.

14. Continue in the same direction, east on **Via dell'Abbondanza** (a left turn as you leave the baths). Two blocks down on your right is the **Fullonica Stephani**, a house converted into workshops for the cleaning of fabrics. All Roman citizens were required to wear togas in public, which weren't exactly easy to keep clean. It's not hard to imagine why there were more toga-cleaners (fullers) in Pompeii than anything else, except perhaps bakers. The cloth was dunked in a tub full of water and chalk, and stamped upon like so many grapes. Washed, the material was stretched across a wicker cage and exposed to sulphur fumes. The fuller

carded it with a long brush, then placed it under a press. The harder the pressing, the whiter and brighter it became.

15. Go south, completely around the block. Behind the Fullonica Stephani is the entrance to the **Casa di Menandro,** a patrician's villa with many paintings and mosaics.

16. Return to **Via dell'Abbondanza** and turn right. If you've had enough walking, go a few more blocks past the new restorations and then return to the **Porta Marina,** where your tour began.

17. The recommended alternative is to continue east on **Via dell'Abbondanza** seven blocks to **Casa di Octavius**.

18. Two blocks farther is the **Villa di Giulia Felice** (House of Julia Felix), which has a large garden with a lovely portico. The wealthy lady living here had to rent her bath and rooms—no one knows why.

19. Turn right past the villa and continue to the **Amphitheater** (Anfiteatro). The games here were between animals, between gladiators, and between animals and gladiators. There were also Olympic games and chariot races. The crowds rushed in as soon as the gates opened—women and slaves to the bleachers. When the Emperor or some other important person was in attendance, exotic animals—lions and tigers, panthers, elephants, and rhinos—were released. At "halftime," birds of prey were set against hares, or dogs against porcupines—the animals tied to either end of a rope so neither could escape. Most gladiators were slaves or prisoners, but a few were Germans or Syrians who enjoyed fighting. Teams of gladiators worked for impresarios, who hired them out to wealthy citizens, many of whom were running for office and hoping that some gory entertainment would buy them some votes. When a gladiator found himself at another's mercy, he extended a pleading hand to the President of the Games. If the President turned his thumb up, the gladiator lived; if he turned his thumb down, the gladiator's throat was cut. The arena got pretty bloody after a night's entertainment and was sprinkled with red powder to camouflage the carnage. The victorious gladiator got money or a ribbon exempting him from further fights. If he was a slave he was often set free. If the people of Pompeii had had trading cards, they would have collected portraits of gladiators; everyone had his favorite. Says one piece of graffiti: "Petronius Octavus fought thirty-four fights and then died, but Severus, a freedman, was victor in fifty-five fights and still lived; Nasica celebrates sixty victories." Pompeii had a gladiator school (Caserma dei Gladiatori) which you can visit on your way back to Porta Marina.

20. Return to **Porta Marina,** where your walk began, or exit through

the Ingresso Anfiteatro and find a cab for the one-mile trip back to Porta Marina. You could of course begin your trip at Ingresso Anfiteatro, and make the tour in the opposite direction. If you want a personal guide, you may have an easier time finding one here than at Porta Marina.

Lodging

Spend the night in Pompeii only for convenience sake, so that you can tour the city early in the morning. Best bets are Rosario (II, Via Roma. Tel. 863.1002), a large old hotel, and Bristol (II, Piazza Vittorio Veneto. Tel. 863.1625).

For Further Information

AAST, Via Sacra 1. Tel. 863.1041.

EN ROUTE: From POMPEII to the AMALFI DRIVE

As mentioned above, there are frequent trains from the Villa dei Misteri Station at Pompeii (a short walk from Porta Marina) to Sorrento. It's only a 30-minute trip, so if Pompeii closes before you've seen enough, consider spending the night in Sorrento (rather than in Naples) and returning to Pompeii the following morning. The itinerary suggests that if you plan to visit Ischia you should take your car with you on the ferry from Sorrento.

EN ROUTE: From POMPEII to ISCHIA or the AMALFI DRIVE

From Pompeii head south through Castellammare di Stabia. Continue on Route S145 until it intersects with Route S163. From here you have several choices:

By car:

1. Drive 2.5 miles to Sorrento. A very narrow, winding road takes you on a 17-mile loop from Sorrento, around the Sorrento Peninsula, to the Amalfi Drive. Michelin gives this side trip, which offers superb views of the Gulf of Sorrento and the Bay of Naples, three stars. For my money, it's a trip worth taking only if you enjoy endless seascapes framed through a car window.

2. Unless you're (a) going to Ischia or (b) going around the Sorrento Peninsula, there's no need to visit Sorrento. Two and a half miles before Sorrento, turn off on Route S163 and head over the mountains to the Amalfi Drive.

3. If you're going to Ischia, take the car ferry from Sorrento (a 45-

minute trip). As suggested above, you can then leave your car on Ischia and take the ferry to Capri, where cars are either not necessary or not allowed. Return from Ischia to Sorrento, and either take the loop trip around the Sorrento Peninsula, or head directly for the Amalfi Drive on Route S163.

By public transportation:

1. If you're going to Ischia, take the train from Naples or Pompeii to Sorrento, and the boat from Sorrento to Ischia. From Ischia, take a ferry to Capri. From Capri, take a ferry to Positano, and then take buses along the Amalfi Drive.

2. I've recommended that you take buses along the Amalfi Drive because the road is so spectacular. But you should also know that it's possible in summer to take a hydrofoil along the coast. The hydrofoil stops in Sorrento, Positano, Amalfi, and Salerno. The only town it misses is Ravello, which is up in the mountains and can be reached by bus from Amalfi.

3. If you're not going to Ischia, take buses or hydrofoils directly from Sorrento to Positano and other towns along the Amalfi Drive.

✤ SORRENTO (17 miles from Pompeii)

Sorrento is a large, attractive tourist town on the Gulf of Sorrento. Our itinerary has you staying here only as an alternative to Naples if you need an extra day to tour Pompeii. You may also need to stay here if you're headed for the island of Ischia and miss the last ferry.

The most interesting historical site is the Gothic-cum-Baroque **Church of St. Francis** (San Francesco), which has an attractive thirteenth-century cloister. Behind the **Correale Museum** is the **Belvedere**, with orange and lemon trees and a terrace with a beautiful view.

Lodging

Hotel Excelsior Vittoria (I, Piazza Torquato Taso 34. Tel. 878.1900) is a somewhat faded but still romantic old villa overlooking the harbor. **Ambasciatori** (I, Via Califano 16. Tel. 878.2025) is roomy and hugs a cliff above the bay. **Parco dei Principi** (I, Via Roto. Tel. 872.2101) is in an eighteenth-century villa with a modern annex. **Bellevue Syrene** (II, Piazza della Victoria. Tel. 878.1024) is another roomy villa over the sea.

☙ ISCHIA

Since many of you will be going from Sorrento to Ischia, let's discuss the island now. We'll discuss Capri after Positano, since most of you will be going from Positano to Capri.

Capri wows you with its charm and beauty; Ischia takes time to cast its spell. Give Ischia a week and you'll probably grow attached to its special character, its hidden corners and familiar views. But an overnight stay is probably not long enough for the island to get into your blood. It does have its share of white, wine-growing villages beneath the lush volcanic slopes of Monte Epomeo; and, unlike Capri, it enjoys a life of its own that survives when tourists head back home. But there are few signs of antiquity here; the architecture is unremarkable; the beaches are small and pebbly; there's little shopping beyond the high-trash gift shops that attract the German therapeutic trade; and most visitors are either German (off-season) or Italian (in-season). Not that there's anything wrong with Germans or Italians, but many Americans like to be among their own, or at least with people who speak English. On the other hand, some of you will delight in discovering an island not yet overcome with tourists from the States. The mistake you shouldn't make is expecting Ischia to be an unspoiled, undiscovered Capri. When Augustus gave the Neapolitans Ischia for Capri, he knew what he was doing.

Unlike Capri, Ischia is volcanic in origin. From its hidden reservoir of seething molten matter come the thermal springs said to cure whatever ails you. As early as 1580 a doctor named Iosolini published a book about the mineral wells on Ischia. "If your eyebrows fall off," he wrote, "go and try the baths at Piaggia Romano. Are you unhappy about your complexion? You will find the cure in the waters of Santa Maria del Popolo. Are you deaf? Then go to Bagno d'Ulmitello. If you know anyone who is getting bald, anyone who suffers from elephantiasis, or another whose wife yearns for a child, take the three of them immediately to the Bagno di Vitara; they will bless you."

Today the island is covered with thermal baths surrounded by tropical gardens—if you've never been to one before, don't miss the opportunity. Visitors who plan to stay awhile can try the treatments for acne and wrinkles, big breasts and saggy breasts, rheumatism, and premature sexual senility.

The most picturesque part of Ischia today is the port (**Ischia Porto**), with its small shops and charming seafront restaurants. If you're coming for the day, your best bet is to recapture your youth at one of the mineral baths such as **Poseidon Gardens** and then lose it at a harborfront restaurant in **Forio** or **Ischia Porto**.

Ischia also has some lovely hotel-resorts high in the mountains, offering therapeutic programs and rooms with breathtaking views of the sea. If you want to plunk down in the sun for a few days and tune out the world, this is an ideal place to go—remembering, of course, that you're unlikely to find many Americans to talk to.

The **information office** is at the harbor. The best map is in the accommodations guide available at the office. Nearby are two motor launches, *Venus* and *Eros*, which make daily trips to Capri, stopping for passengers at the various communities around Ischia.

It's a 21-mile, two-hour drive around the island. **Poseidon Gardens** and the port of **Forio** are on the opposite side. Take the southern route and you'll come to **Fontana**, the start of an invigorating one-hour climb to the top of **Mount Epomeo**, a huge volcano that last erupted in 1302.

If you don't want to work for your views, take the cable car from Ischia Porto to the top of the volcano.

• **Poseidon Gardens** (south of Forio on the west coast) is a complex of thermal pools, waterfalls, limestone cliffs, and tropical vegetation. There's also a cafeteria and changing rooms. You can sit like a Roman senator on a stone chair recessed in the rock and let the hot water cascade over you. All very campy—and fun. Baths such as **Terme Restituta** on the north coast, near **Casamicciola**, are said to be more formal, with classical façades. I didn't see them, but I take Madame Curie's word for it that the radioactivity of these springs is the highest in the world.

• Near the port is the **Castello** (open 9 A.M. to sunset), which looks the way a fort is supposed to look. It was built by Alphonso V of Aragon in 1450. Best bet is to stroll at sunset in front of the castle, overlooking the Bay of Naples.

Two interesting shops around the harbor are **Perrazzo**, which sells eleven different wines produced on the island, including one that is pizza-flavored; and **Rustica Domus**, an antique shop.

Dining

The port is lined with small family restaurants. Take your pick; the important thing is to order fish. Many consider **Gennaro** (M, Via Porto 66. Tel. 992.917) the best. Also recommended is **Zi Nannina a Mare** (M, Ischia Porto. Tel. 991.350) and **Porticiullo** (M). The harborfront restaurants tend to be a bit dear; if you're looking for a no-nonsense good meal at lower prices, try any of the small family restaurants off the square in the less touristy Ischia Porto area. There are two charming restaurants side by side at the harbor at Forio, on the opposite side of the island, La Bussola (M/I, Via Marina. Tel. 997.645) and La Romancia (M/I, Via Marina. Tel. 997.345). Also at Forio, on San Francisco beach, is the popular La Meridiana (E/M, Tel. 998.464). At Lacco Ameno on the north shore is Padrone del Mare (E/M, Corso Rizzoli 6. Tel. 999.206). As you're driving around the island, stop for drinks or lunch on the terrace of the San Montano Hotel (E, Monte Vico. Tel. 994.033). The atmosphere is expensive and middle-aged, but a more peaceful setting would be hard to find.

Lodging

If you want to be in reach of town, where most of the restaurants and shops are, stay at a hotel in Ischia Porto. Hotels in other communities are for people who want solitude. Be prepared for rooms with lots of clashing tiles. Many hotels require visitors in season to pay for several nights. Many, particularly the pensions, include two meals, and sometimes three. What a shame on an island where half the fun is trying out a different restaurant every night.

In Ischia Porto: Hotel Excelsior Belvedere (I, Via E. Gianturco 3. Tel. 991.020) has a pool, a first-class restaurant, and more American guests than most.

Hotel Punta Molino (I, Lungomare Telese. Tel. 991.544) gets about 10 percent Americans, which is a lot for Ischia. Though close to town, it's quiet, with a pool and lovely views.

Argona Palace (I, Via Porto 12. Tel. 981.383) has some rooms overlooking the harbor and a small round pool. It's conveniently located but has no overwhelming charm.

Hotel Jolly Grande (I, Tel. 991.744) has no particular warmth, but is extremely comfortable and clean. The pool is huge!

Among the less expensive hotels, pensions, and guest houses are Villa Paradiso (III, Tel. 991.501), Villa Diane (Corso V, Colonna 212. Tel. 991.785), and Pensione Villarosa (Tel. 991.316).

In Lacco Ameno: Hotel Regina Isabella (L, Piazza Umberto. Tel. 994.332) has the most formal atmosphere on the island. The Sporting Club is the extra-deluxe part of the hotel. Isolated on the mountain above is San Montano (I, Monte Vico. Tel. 994.033), which belongs to the same hotel chain. Guests are mostly Italians, Germans, and Swiss. A good bet for lunch.

For Further Information

The information booth is at the harbor of Porto Ischia. Tel. 991.146.

✤ THE AMALFI DRIVE

This is the most romantic drive in Italy. The road is gouged from the side of rocky cliffs plunging down into the sea. Small boats lie in sandy coves like so many brightly colored fish. Erosion has contorted the rocks into mythological shapes and hollowed out fairy grottoes where the air is turquoise, and the water, an icy blue. White villages, dripping with flowers, nestle in coves or climb like vines up the steep, terraced hills. The road must have a thousand turns, each with a different view, on its dizzying, 43-mile journey from Sorrento to Salerno.

✤ POSITANO (17 miles from Sorrento)

The most popular town along the drive, particularly among Americans, is Positano, a village of white Moorish-type houses clinging dramatically to slopes around a small sheltered bay. When John Steinbeck lived here in 1953 he wrote that it was difficult to consider tourism an industry because "there are not enough [tourists]." Alas, Positano has since been discovered. The artists came first, and, as happens wherever artists go, the wealthy followed and the artists fled. What Steinbeck wrote, however, still applies:

"Positano bites deep. It is a dream place that isn't quite real when you are there and becomes beckoningly real after you have gone. Its houses climb a hill so steep it would be a cliff except that stairs are cut in it. I believe that whereas most house foundations are vertical, in Positano they are horizontal. The small curving bay of unbelievably blue and green water laps gently on a beach of small pebbles. There is only one narrow street and it does not come down to the water. Everything else is stairs, some of them as steep as ladders. You do not walk to visit a friend, you either climb or slide."

In the tenth century Positano rivaled Venice as an important mercantile city. Its heyday was in the sixteenth and seventeenth centuries, when its ships traded in the Near and Middle East, carrying spices, silks, and precious woods. The coming of the steamship in the mid-nineteenth century led to the town's decline, and some three-fourths of the town's eight thousand citizens emigrated to America, mostly to New York. One major job of Positano's mayor has been to find space in the overcrowded cemetery for New York Positanesi who want to spend eternity here.

What had been reduced to a forgotten fishing village is now the number one attraction on the coast, with hotels for every budget, charming restaurants, and dozens of boutiques. From here you can take hydrofoils to Capri, escorted bus rides to Ravello, and tours of the Emerald Grotto near the town of Amalfi.

Do you see the three islands offshore? They're called **Li Galli** (The Cocks). The local king wanted a castle quick, legend says, and a sorcerer agreed to build one in three days if the king would give him all the roosters in Positano. (The sorcerer had a passion for fowl.) The king ordered them all slaughtered and sent to the sorcerer, but the young daughter of a fisherman hid her rooster under her bed. At dawn the rooster did what a rooster does. The workmen, flying by with rocks for the castle, realized that the king had broken his contract and dropped their loads into the sea.

Positano may not have a castle, but it does have another attraction that's bringing the town considerable wealth: stylish summer clothes. From January to March buyers from all over the world come to Positano to buy the trendsetting handmade clothes that are sold in more than fifty boutiques. One size, loose-fitting cotton dresses; full skirts, plain or covered with lace—some in light pastel colors with handprinted designs, others in bold block colors: bright oranges, pinks, and yellows—the choice is endless, and the prices—well, you're on vacation, and the same dresses would cost twice as much in New York or Rome.

If you're staying in Positano, your hotel will park your car for you; if you're here only for the day, a parking place in summer is almost impossible to find. Best bet for daytrippers is to make a reservation at a hotel-restaurant, which will park your car while you eat, and then try to tip the valet for keeping the car the rest of the day. No matter how much time you spend in Positano, make sure you have some comfortable walking shoes—no heels, please!—and that your back and legs are strong enough to negotiate steps.

A **car service** is available at Via C. Columbo 2. Tel. 875.541.

Dining

Here as elsewhere along the coast, the meal to order is fish, or pasta with clams, mussels, etc. Grilled sea bass is a local speciality.

Buca di Bacco (M/I, Via Marina. Tel. 875.004) is right on the beach, where you can sit under grapevines and look at the colorful fishing boats.

It's larger and less intimate than most restaurants, but the food is considered the best. Reservations are advisable.

Also recommended on the beach, and slightly less expensive, are **Chez Black** (M/I, Via Marina. Tel. 875.036), **Covo dei Saraceni** (M, Via Marina. Tel. 875.059), and **Capurale** (M, Via Marina. Tel. 875.374).

There's nothing exceptional at **Trattoria Vincenzo** (I, Viale Pasitea. Tel. 875.128), but it's inexpensive—particularly the meal of the day—and conveniently located just off the main street, for those who don't want to walk down to the beach.

Lodging

In season you may have trouble finding a room without a reservation; popular hotels are booked months in advance. Since the streets are narrow and winding, and many hotels are accessible only on foot, make sure you get explicit directions on how to reach your hotel. The tourist office is little help because it's down near the beach and inaccessible by car. For reservations and advice, stop at the **AVI Agency** (Tel. 875.555), which you pass as you drive through town.

The town rises up on either side of a cove. Most shops and restaurants are near the beach on the east side (the side away from Sorrento), where you'll find both the domed Parish Church and Le Sirenuse Hotel. Le Sirenuse is in an ideal location: high enough for breezes and dramatic views, yet close enough to restaurants and shops. If you can't afford the steep price of Le Sirenuse, try to find a hotel in the same vicinity.

If you can afford the best, there are only two places to stay, **Le Sirenuse** (I, Via C. Columbo 30. Tel. 875.066) and **Il San Pietro di Positano** (L, 84017 Positano. Tel. 875.454). Le Sirenuse is the older hotel —a converted eighteenth-century villa with seven floors both above and below the road. The more spacious Il San Pietro spreads across a rocky ledge outside of town, an elevator ride down from the road (there's shuttle service to town and back). Because Le Sirenuse is in town, it tends to appeal to a somewhat snappier, younger clientele; but guests at both are well heeled and as a rule on the far side of thirty. A person associated with Le Sirenuse compared the two hotels to two beautiful women. "Here is the elegant, aristocratic, blue-blooded lady," he said, sweeping his arm around a room full of serious old antiques. "There is the young lady showing off." The comparison was quite unfair, but understandable, given all the recent attention lavished on Il San Pietro at Le Sirenuse's expense. Everything at Il San Pietro is in fact tasteful, with natural, pastel fabrics that complement, rather than fight against, the bright colors of the landscape. Nature intrudes everywhere: in the pitchers of wild purple orchids; in the bougainvillea spilling over the terraces and balconies; in the roses and hibiscus growing through the windows and spreading over the lounge and dining room ceilings. For honeymooners or couples trying to slow down and get back in touch, Il San Pietro would be hard to beat.

Albergo L'Ancora (II, Via C. Columbo. Tel. 875.318) is a family-run hotel with the requisite balconies, next door to Le Sirenuse. It doesn't have the panache of Le Sirenuse, but it doesn't have the prices either. Room 21 is a good bet.

Miramere (I, Tel. 875.002) has only 15 simple but adequate rooms with splendid views. Less expensive is the **Pensione Conca d'Oro** (II, Tel. 875.111).

Covo dei Saraceni (II, Tel. 879.059) and **Buca di Bacco** (I, Tel. 875.699) are both down by the beach. The problem here is the absence of panoramic views and the knowledge that everywhere you go is up.

Somewhat higher up is **Palazzo Murat** (II, Via dei Mulino. Tel. 875.177). Some rooms have high, beamed ceilings and antiques. A modern addition is not without charm.

Casa Maresca (III, Viale Pasitea. Tel. 875.140) is a basic budget hotel.

For Further Information

Tourist Office, Via del Saracino 2. Tel. 875.067.

✤ CAPRI

The summer scene on Capri calls to mind the stampeding of bulls through the narrow street of Pamplona: If you can visit in the spring or fall, do. Yet even the crowds are not enough to destroy Capri's very special charm. The town is a Moorish opera set of shiny white houses, tiny squares, and narrow, medieval alleyways hung with flowers. You need to take a funicular to reach the town, which rests on top of rugged limestone cliffs, hundreds of feet above the sea.

The mood is modish but somehow unspoiled. The summer set is made up of smart, wealthy types and college kids. The upper crust bakes in the sun in private villas. The secret is for you, too, to disappear while the daytrippers take over—offering yourself to the sun at your hotel pool, or exploring the hidden corners of the island. Even in the height of summer you can enjoy a degree of privacy on one of the many paved paths that wind around the island hundreds of feet above the sea—if you're willing to walk, you can be as alone here as you've ever wanted to be.

The Blue Grotto is a must, but there are other, lesser-known grottoes to explore at leisure on boat trips around the island. You can also make a day trip to the nearby island of Ischia. When you've seen enough and tanned enough, it's time to go shopping in some trendsetting boutiques or succumb to Capri's cafés, where you'll be watching everything but your waist. As for dinner—there are enough fine restaurants that you can try a different one each night.

In his book *Italian Holiday*, Ludwig Bemelmans offers a fun way to picture Capri. Turn a coffee cup upside down, he says, and next to it invert an oversized cup with a chipped lip. Put a matchbox between them and drape a green handkerchief on top. This is the island of Capri, about 4 miles by 2. The small cup is Mount Tiberio (1,096 feet); the large cup, Mount Solaro (1,920 feet). The matchbox is the saddle between them. On the saddle is the town of Capri. Lean a match against the matchbox —that's the funicular from the harbor (Marina Grande) to town. Put two pieces of limp spaghetti on the other side of the matchbox: These are the roads leading down to the smaller port and beach at Marina Piccola. A strand of spaghetti from the matchbox to the larger cup is the road to the town of Anacapri. Another strand from the matchbox to the top of the smaller cup is the path to Villa Jove, where the Roman Emperor Tiberius spent his declining years. The chip in the cup is, of course, the Blue Grotto.

The boat will disgorge you in a north coast settlement called **Marina Grande**. Here you'll find a few medium-priced restaurants, the tourist information office, boats to the **Blue Grotto**, and the funicular to the town of Capri. If you're staying at one of the larger hotels, a representative will be at the harbor to take your bags. To reach the upper town, take the funicular, mini-bus, or cab (expensive!), or submit to a rigorous 30-minute walk. The funicular lines can be long; if you're coming for the day, it helps to be the first off the boat.

The funicular lets you off at the **Piazzetta (Piazza Umberto I)**, which was probably here when Emperor Tiberius was living on the island in the first century. This open-air drawing room is surrounded by the medieval quarter of the town.

There are three spectacular walks.

1. From the main square of Capri, follow either **Via Longano** or **Via Le Botteghe** to the crossroads. Take **Via Matromania** to the **Natural Arch**, a remarkable phenomenon of geological erosion. Then descend the nearby steps to the **Grotto of Matromania**, a natural cave which was transformed by the ancient Romans into a luxurious Nymphaeum (a

shrine for water nymphs). From here, continue down the steps leading to the **Terrace of Tragara**. Here you'll enjoy views of the famous **Faraglioni**, rocky islets carved into fantastic shapes by the sea. (The best time to see the Faraglioni is in the early evening light.) Follow the picturesque **Via Tragara** amidst sumptuous villas and flowering gardens back to town center. The walk takes about 90 minutes round-trip.

2. From Capri's central plaza, follow either **Via Longano** or **Via Le Botteghe** until you reach a crossroad. Take the road to the left that passes by the little **Church of San Michele**. In 45 minutes you'll reach the summit of **Mount Tiberio** and the ruins of the **Villa Jovis** (open 9 A.M. to an hour before sunset; closed Mondays). This was the largest and most sumptuous of Emperor Tiberius's many villas on Capri. You can imagine him sitting here with Caligula on his 300-foot front porch, planning an orgy in one of the grottoes or watching for imaginary enemies approaching by sea.

3. **Via Krupp** takes you below the beautiful **Augustus Gardens** (Parco Augusto) to the port and beach of **Marina Piccola**. Stop for a drink or pastry here, and then take the 10-minute bus ride back to Capri.

An excursion to the **Blue Grotto** (a 45-minute trip from Marina Grande) is something you have to submit to, if only to have an opinion about one of the most celebrated tourist attractions in the world. The boat ride can be rough; if you have a weak stomach, sit in the back looking forward, rather than on one of the side seats. You can also reach the grotto by cab from Anacapri, but it would be a shame to miss the 10-minute boat ride beneath the towering cliffs. At the entrance to the grotto you'll step from your fourteen-passenger motorboat (expect to get a bit wet) into a tiny rowboat and duck low as you pass through the narrow entrance of the cave on a surge of the sea. The cliff wall doesn't extend to the bottom of the sea, so the sun's rays are refracted about a yard below the surface and indirectly illuminate the cavern from underneath. It's difficult to feel much wonder when it's paid for with a ticket and called for on demand—when in under three minutes you're spewed back out into the world again, among the fleets of boats bobbing at the entrance, waiting for their turn—yet it's worth seeing what all the fuss is about and imagining how wonderful the experience might have been if only you had had this beauty to yourself. To make this wish (almost) come true, rent a boat that follows *your* schedule and visit the less frequented green, yellow, pink, and white grottoes around the island. The trip around the island takes 90 to 120 minutes by motorboat, 3 to 4 hours by rowboat.

Anacapri (about 2.5 miles from Capri) has little to offer the casual visitor, but the ride along the corniche road, gouged from the edge of the cliff, is spectacular. From Anacapri, take the chairlift to the top of Mount Solara for a panoramic view of the whole island, the Bay of Naples, and the Italian coast. Buses run continually from Capri to Anacapri. If you have to catch an afternoon boat back to the mainland, leave plenty of time; lines both in Anacapri for the bus back to Capri and in Capri for the funicular back down to the harbor can be a good 30 minutes long in season. Most people wait for the return bus at the main square in Anacapri; save time by walking away from Capri to an earlier bus stop.

If you need exercise, walk down some 960 steps to the harbor of Marina Grande along the pre-Roman Phoenician Steps (Scala Fenicia). The stairs were probably built by the Greeks in the eighth century B.C. and were restored in the eighteenth and nineteenth centuries. From the bus terminal in Anacapri follow Via San Michele to the Villa San Michele, which was built for a Swedish doctor who lived here until 1910. The steps begin just below the house.

No cars are allowed from June 1 to September 30. For a taxi, call 837.0543.

Dining

In Capri: La Capannina (E, Via delle Botteghe 15. Tel. 837.0732) has 3 rooms and a terrace, and wines from its own vineyards.

Da Augusto a Tiberio (M, Via Tiberio. Tel. 837.7820) is a family-run restaurant.

Aurora (M, Via Fuorlovado. Tel. 837.0181) is a favorite of writers and artists.

Other recommended restaurants include La Savardina (M, Via Lo Capo 8. Tel. 837.6300), serving typical local food, La Pigna (M, Via Lo Palazzo 30. Tel. 837.0280), Da Gelsomina (Via Migliara 6. Tel. 837.1499), and Faraglioni (Via Camarelle 75. Tel. 837.0320). Da Gemma (Via Madre Serafina. Tel. 837.0181) has good pizza.

In Marina Grande (below Capri, where the boats come in): Grotta Verde (M, Marina Grande 69. Tel. 837.0508) is known for its fresh fish at reasonable prices.

In Marina Piccola: Canzone del Mare (Marina Piccola. Tel. 837.0104) is fancy and perhaps a bit overpriced, but good.

In Anacapri: Add'o Riccio (Grotto Azzurra. Tel. 837.1380) is noted for its fresh seafood.

Lodging

When the boat pulls into Marina Grande, the major hotel reps will take your bags; you can follow in a cab, a mini-bus, or the funicular.

As a rule upper rooms get the best breezes and views. Decide whether it's worth the higher price. Most hotels won't rent rooms for less than two or three nights in season. Try not to have meals (except breakfast) included so you can enjoy the local restaurants. If dinners are included, try to trade them in for lunch.

Avoid hotels in the town of Anacapri. They have no particular charm and are a bus ride or an expensive cab ride from Capri, where most of the shops and restaurants are.

Hotel Quisisana (L, Via Camarelle 2. Tel. 837.0788), catering largely to Americans, is the most luxurious and traditional of the in-town hotels.

Hotel La Scalinatella (I, Via Tragara. Tel. 837.0633) is unknown to the American package-tour crowd; but for sophisticates who enjoy an intimate, exclusive, clublike atmosphere, this is the place to stay. All but 4 rooms have exquisite views; ask for one high up. Some rooms have two baths.

Next door to La Scalinatella, with the same views at half the price, is an unpretentious, family-run hotel, **La Pineta** (II, Via Tragara. Tel. 837.0644). The owners are friendly and helpful. This is the best bet for couples on a budget. Ask for a room in the older section with an unobstructed view.

Residence Punta Tragara (I, Porto di Tragara. Tel. 837.0844) is an elegant villa a 10-minute walk from town, with an extremely refined atmosphere. If you like small, old-fashioned hotels that are one of a kind, this is the place to stay. Many of the 20 rooms, each decorated differently, are occupied by long-term guests who appreciate quiet and privacy. (If you're walking down Via Tragara, stop by for drinks; the view from the outdoor terrace is magnificent.)

Other first-class hotels include **Hotel La Palma** (I, Via V. Emanuele. Tel. 837.0133), though rooms with balconies over the street must be noisy; and **Hotel Luna** (I, Via Matteotti 3. Tel. 837.0433), which has striking views, though the heavy furniture needs some help.

Among the small, less expensive pensions, try **Pensione Esperia** or **Pensione Villa Margherita** (II, Tel. 837.0404). Of the third-class hotels, try **Florida** (Tel. 837.0710).

For Further Information

The tourist information booth (Tel. 837.0686) is at the harbor where the ferries dock, below the town.

EN ROUTE: From POSITANO to AMALFI

Since you're heading directly east, it's best to drive in the afternoon, when the sun is behind you.

Drive past the towns of **Véttica Maggiore** and **Praiano**. The 3-mile stretch of the Amalfi Drive between **Praiano** and the **Emerald Grotto** is the most dramatic. The road passes a wild gorge where a waterfall makes its dizzying descent from the plateau above. Wild vegetation clings to the crevices and clambers up the sides. Houses cling to the slopes, and colorful fishing boats are drawn up along the shore. A path goes up one side of the gorge, which you'll see after you pass beneath two tunnels after Praiano. (Trails along the Amalfi Drive are indicated on a blue tourist map [carta turistica] called "Penisola Sorrentina, Costiera Amalfitana," which is sold in tourist shops in Positano.)

✤ THE EMERALD GROTTO

About 3 miles farther along is the **Emerald Grotto** (Grotta dello Smeraldo). An elevator takes you down to a rocky terrace. A small rowboat takes you around a cave with stalactites and an underwater nativity scene. With tourists lined up to Do The Grotto, it's not easy to experience the awe the first visitors must have felt; but the luminescent, emerald-colored water is still magical, and a trip is worthwhile just to be able to enter into the argument over whether the Emerald Grotto is more beautiful than the Blue Grotto on Capri. You can also reach the Emerald Grotto by boat from Amalfi.

✤ AMALFI (8 miles from Positano)

After Positano and Ravello, Amalfi is your third choice of a town to stay at along the Drive. It would have to be a distant third, however, because of the congestion caused by tour buses, which make Amalfi the main stopping point on their excursions. The town is romantically situated at the mouth of a deep gorge and has some quality hotels and restaurants. It's also a convenient base for excursions to Capri and the Emerald Grotto.

During the Middle Ages Amalfi was an independent maritime state—

a little Republic of Venice—with a population of fifty thousand. The ship compass—trivia fans will be pleased to know—was invented here in 1302.

The main historical attraction is the **Duomo** (Cathedral of St. Andrew), which shows an interesting mix of Moorish and early Gothic influences. The interior is a tenth-century Romanesque skeleton in an eighteenth-century Baroque dress. The transept (the transverse arms) and the choir are thirteenth century. The handsome twelfth-century campanile (bell tower) has identical Gothic cupolas (domes), at each corner. Don't miss the beautiful late-thirteenth-century Moorish **cloister**, with its slender double columns. At least one critic has called the cathedral's façade the ugliest piece of serious architecture in Italy—decide for yourself. The same critic snickers at the tourists who fail to note the cathedral's greatest treasure, the eleventh-century bronze doors from Constantinople.

The parking problem here is even worse than in Positano. The small lot in the center of town fills quickly. If you can afford the steep prices, make a luncheon reservation at one of the hotel restaurants and have your car parked for you.

If the sea is calm, you can take a boat back along the coast to the **Emerald Grotto**.

The main street leads back through town from the cathedral to the mountains, and passes **A. Franchini's Ceramic Workshop**. The building in front has a sign, ARTE CERAMICA. The entrance is on the right. Ring the bell. There's no hard sell.

Dining

A local speciality is **Fichi al cioccolato**, chocolate-covered figs with almond filling and lemon or orange flavoring.

The most elegant restaurant is in the **Luna Convento Hotel** (E, Tel. 871.002).

On the Drive, at the entrance to town, is the **Hotel Cappuccini Convento** (E, Tel. 871.008), a twelfth-century monastery on a rocky cliff. The outdoor patio has magnificent views—an ideal spot for drinks or lunch.

Best bet in town, near the cathedral, is **Baracca** (M, Piazza dei Dogi. Tel. 871.285), where local people come on special occasions. **Gemma** (M, Via Cavaliero di Malta. Tel. 871.345) has a terrace overlooking the street and is well known for its fish soup with clams. **Il Tari** (M, Via Capuano. Tel. 871.832) is small and old, with good service. **The Lemon Garden** (M, Valle dei Mullini) is a peaceful retreat in a garden, a 10-minute walk from the cathedral, past A. Franchini's Ceramic Workshop.

Lodging

A lift from the street takes you to what most consider the number one hotel, **Luna Convento** (I, Tel. 871.002), which is built into an old monastery. Public areas show a flashy Moorish influence—clashing tiles again—which works against the building's natural charm. There's a cross over the bed in Room 15, where Ibsen stayed. Room 9 was part of the old cloister. Room 14 is a double overlooking the sea. The beautiful old rooms cost the same as the modern rooms in the new wing.

Hotel Cappuccini Convento (I, Tel. 871.008) should be the top hotel, but the owners have let it fall into disrepair (check to see if renovations have begun), and what should be evidence of character is merely evidence of age. An exterior elevator carries guests 132 feet up to an 800-year-old monastery built into the cliffs above the town. Many rooms are in former monks' cells. The patio is ideal for lunch. The Cappuccini Convento captures the mood of a venerable old monastery much more thoroughly than the Luna Convento, so visitors have to decide between the somewhat worn but genuine ambiance of Cappuccini Convento and the relatively innocuous modernity of the well-tended Luna Convento.

Santa Caterina (I, Tel. 871.012), about a mile from town, has a 150-foot patio and villas among the lemon groves which slope down toward the sea.

Pensione Sole (II, Tel. 871.147) is a clean, family-run house at half the price of the first-class hotels.

For Further Information

The tourist office (Corao Roma 19. Tel. 871.107) is on the Drive, just past the center of town.

❧ *ATRANI*

A few minutes past Amalfi is the less-known but more impressively situated town of Atrani, which is just waiting to be discovered. The valley here is narrower than at Amalfi, and its flanks steeper.

The **Parish Church** is worth a visit.

Porcelain and ceramics are made and sold in Atrani and in nearby towns along the Amalfi Drive. Among the mass-produced turnpikeware are some lovely, simple, hand-painted plates, vases, pillboxes, etc.

Just past Atrani is the road winding up the mountain to **Ravello**. The road heads east, paralleling the coast, then switches back. As it turns again and climbs up the valley, there's a turnoff which ends in a trail climbing 1,000 feet up to Ravello. It's a walk you might want to make going down. Both walk and drive take you up the spectacular Dragon Valley (Valle del Dragone), which is planted with vines, fruit trees, and olives, and offers a breathtaking view of Atrani and the Amalfi coast.

✤ RAVELLO (3 miles from Amalfi)

Envy Gore Vidal for living here in what André Gide calls "a town closer to the sky than to the shore." Because it's a long, steep drive above the sea, tour buses are discouraged and crowds are less overwhelming than at Positano and Amalfi. By early afternoon the daytrippers have departed and Ravello becomes one of the most reposeful settings in the world.

Not that Ravello is everyone's glass of chianti: There's very little to do here except walk through peaceful gardens, admire the view, and exist. Those who need a more active life, with shops and restaurants, should avoid the rarefied air and stick to Positano. But after so much traveling, it's hard to believe many of you wouldn't welcome this excuse to come to a complete stop.

There are two estates to visit, **Villa Cimbrone** and **Villa Rufolo.** Don't miss either, but particularly don't miss Villa Cimbrone.

Villa Cimbrone (open 9 A.M. to sunset) is a scenic 15-minute walk from the main square. The cloister to the left of the entrance looks medieval but was built in 1917. The unusual crypt was finished in 1913. What makes the villa so memorable are its peaceful gardens, with small secluded grottoes and temples hundreds of feet above the sea. The Viale dell'Immensita, a long, straight avenue flanked by oleanders, leads to a belvedere with an unforgettable view of the coast. Few places lend themselves so thoroughly to contemplation. Most construction was carried out in the early twentieth century by the former valet of a British lord. Was the mood of melancholy merely a pose that suited a classical garden? In the Belvedere of Mercury, the god faces away from the view as though tired of running; and on the bench is a quote from D. H. Lawrence:

> Lost to a world in which I crave no part,
> I sit alone and commune with my heart,
> Pleased with my little corner of the earth,
> Glad that I came, not sorry to depart.

Under the cupola of the little temple of Bacchus are verses by Catallus, which say, in translation, "What is sweeter than to return home free of care, and, tired of toiling for others, to repose in one's own bed?"

Villa Rufolo (open 9:30 A.M. to 1:30 P.M. and from 3 to 7:40 P.M. in summer; earlier closing times off-season) is a crumbling eleventh-century palace—the residence of several popes—which has a famous Moorish cloister, ancient trees, and a belvedere with a fantastic view. In 1880, while working on *Parsifal,* Richard Wagner stayed at the Villa Palumbo in Ravello, and on a morning walk he visited Villa Rufolo. In the hotel register he wrote, "The magic garden of Klingstor has been found: May 26, 1880." It's fitting that this beautiful garden-terrace has become the site of summer concerts dedicated to Wagner.

The thirteenth-century **Cathedral** (Duomo di San Pantaleone) was redone five centuries later in Baroque dress and has a notable late-thirteenth-century Byzantine pulpit resting on fantastic beasts.

Dining

The **Palumbo Hotel** (E, Ravello. Tel. 857.244) has the most elegant restaurant in town. Next best is the **Caruso Belvedere Hotel** (M, Ravello. Tel. 857.111), which is famous for its homegrown wines.

Trattoria da Compa (M/I, Via Roma 48) has no view, but good simple food at reasonable prices.

Lodging

Villa Palumbo (I, Family Vuilleumier, 84010 Ravello. Tel. 857.244) is a converted and enlarged twelfth-century palace run by one of two Swiss brothers—the other owns Villa Cimbrone. Wagner, as noted, stayed here; so did Jennifer Jones, Humphrey Bogart, Tennessee Williams, the Kennedys, and a host of other celebrities. Rooms are conversation pieces —a bit cramped for the price (only the very wealthy would ignore the discomfort), but marked by character and good taste. (Ask for a large room and hope for the best.) A pool may be ready by the time we go to press.

Villa Cimbrone (II, 84010 Ravello. Tel. 857.138) rents rooms with magnificent old furniture, but not all with private baths.

Hotel Caruso Belvedere (II, Via Toro 52. Tel. 857.111) has 26 rooms in an eleventh-century palace. Rooms are old-fashioned, but not as lovely as the public areas or the view. Ask for a room with a balcony.

The exterior of **Pensione Villa Maria** (II, Sulla Strada per Villa Cimbrone, 84010 Ravello. Tel. 858.319) is a bit crumbly, but inside is a lovely old house with lots of warmth and charm. Room 3 is huge. For young couples watching their budget, this place is ideal.

Other small, inexpensive pensions include **Parsifal** (I, Ravello. Tel. 857.096) and **Graal** (I, Ravello. Tel. 857.222).

For Further Information

The tourist office is at Piazza Vescovado 13. Tel. 857.096.

◈ *SALERNO* (20 miles from Ravello)

The Amalfi Drive ends at Salerno. There's no overwhelming reason to stay here except to get an early start to **Paestum** the next morning or to catch a morning train back to Naples. Worth seeing before you leave are the **cathedral** and the **Via dei Mercanti**, a picturesque old street with shops selling jewelry and other gift items at less-than-tourist-area prices. Drive along the harborfront, past the port. When you see a wide, grassy seafront promenade on your right, park. **Via dei Mercanti** is a few blocks in from the promenade, depending on where you park. The **cathedral** won't be more than 15 minutes away. Built in 1085 and remodeled in the eighteenth century, it has beautiful Byzantine doors (1099) from Constantinople and an outstanding twelfth-century pulpit. A few blocks away, in the cathedral's **Museum** (open 9:30 to 2; closed Sundays) are the famous Salerno ivories depicting scenes from the Bible.

Lodging

There are two first-class hotels, **Hotel Jolly Delle Palme** (I, Lungomare Trieste 1. Tel. 770.050) and **Lloyd's Baia** (I, Santa Maria degli Geli. Tel. 210.145). **Lloyd's Baia** may have more character; but **Hotel Jolly**, like all hotels in the Jolly chain, is both clean and comfortable, and within walking distance of the main sights. The **Plaza** (II, Piazza Vittorio Veneto 42. Tel. 224.477) is near the train station.

EN ROUTE: From **SALERNO** to **PAESTUM**

Trains run several times daily from Salerno to Paestum. Buses leave about every hour. To drive, take the road along the Salerno harbor and continue south to Paestum.

◈ *PAESTUM* (25 miles from Salerno)

For most visitors, what justifies a trip to Paestum are three classical temples: the **Basilica**, the **Temple of Ceres**, and, above all, the **Temple of Neptune**. (The site is open from 9 A.M. to sunset.) If a building like the Parthenon does nothing for you, don't waste your time here. But if you can be moved by the harmony and proportion of Greek architecture, the trip to Paestum may be the highlight of your trip.

Most of you won't need more than an hour or two. On one side of the main street are the souvenir shops and a museum. On the other are three of the largest and best-preserved Greek temples in the world—surely the greatest Greek buildings in Italy—two of them older than the Parthenon.

The temples were originally part of a sacred area within a Greek colony founded about 600 B.C. by the people of **Sybaris,** which is located on the opposite (eastern) coast of Italy. The Sybarites didn't like the loss of revenues from ships sailing from Greece and Asia Minor through the Straits of Messina (between Sicily and the toe of Italy), so they convinced merchants to unload goods at Sybaris and send them overland to the new town of Paestum, rather than make the dangerous trip through the straits. Eventually Sybaris was razed in a war among competing political parties. Paestum became a Roman colony in 273 B.C. The opening of the Via Appia from Rome to Brindisi in about 22 B.C. spelled the end of Paestum as an important port. Its harbor gradually silted up and inhabitants succumbed to malaria from the marshes. An eleventh-century visitor found the town deserted. Malarial marshes and thick forests hid the temples until road builders came upon them in the eighteenth century. In the nineteenth century, only a few foreigners bothered traveling south of Pompeii; one of them was the poet Shelley. When a train station was built, the stationmaster was given gloves and veils against the mosquitoes (no problem today).

There are very few qualified **guides** at Paestum. The best is **Nunzio Daniele** (Piazza Basilica, Paestum 84063. Tel. 843.282), author of an informative guide to the site. Call him in advance. You can reach him or other guides through the friendly **Salermar Tourist Office** (Via Nazionale 125. Tel. 811.827), a private agency across from the ruins. The agency can also arrange for accommodations.

H. V. Morton points out that the **Temple of Neptune** has "a primitive grandeur that recalls the Great Hall of Karnak rather than the lighter constructions of classical Greece." It may be ruder, less perfect than the Parthenon, but it has a raw, almost animal power that the Parthenon lacks. What makes the Temple of Neptune so extraordinary is its blend of brutal strength and constraint; of defiance and grace. And there it sits, this 2,400-year-old temple, among the rude grasses in a forgotten field. It was called the Temple of Neptune (the Roman name for Poseidon) by some seventeenth-century visitors because the town was named

Poseidonia before it became a Roman colony; but the temple was in fact dedicated to Hera (Juno).

The **Temple of Ceres,** which was originally dedicated to Athena (Minerva), dates from the end of the sixth century B.C. The **Basilica** (so called by some eighteenth-century archeologists who thought it was a secular building) is the oldest of the three temples, dating back to the mid-sixth century B.C. Like the Temple of Neptune, it was dedicated to Hera. Like all Greek temples, it faces east because it is from the east that the sun (the first god of all ancient peoples) rises daily.

The **Museum** (open daily from 9 to 2; Sundays from 9 to 1; closed Mondays) contains bronze vases, unique fifth-century B.C. paintings, and decorated stone slabs from a nearby cemetery depicting details of daily life in the fourth century B.C.

Dining

There are two passable restaurants near the entrance to the temples: **Nettuno** (M, Tel. 811.028) and **Sea Garden** (M, Tel. 811.020). Local specialties include fresh homemade pasta dressed with tomato and cooked with mutton, prawns from the River Sele, spaghetti with fresh fish sauce, and, for dessert, bocconcini alla panna (small cream mozzarella balls).

Lodging

All the hotels listed below are Class II. If you can afford the price, find a hotel with a pool, and/or one that's located on the long stretch of beach 2 to 3 miles from the temples. The **Salermar Tourist Office** (Tel. 811.827), across from the temples, can make reservations. The accommodation booklet includes color photos of the hotels.

Ariston (Laura. Tel. 843.333) is the most lavish, with tennis and pool. **Le Palme** (Via Sterpinina. Tel. 843.036), a relatively large resort hotel, is next in line. Others include **Cerere** (Laura. Tel. 843.170), which has tennis and a small conference center, the newish **Esplanade** (Via Sterpinina. Tel. 843.203), and **San Michele** (Santa Venere. Tel. 811.041).

For Further Information

The tourist office is at Via Aquila. Tel. 811.016. Across from the ruins is the privately run **Salermar Tourist Office** (Via Nazionale 125. Tel. 811.827).

EN ROUTE: From PAESTUM to NAPLES

If you're driving, take **Route SS18** north to **Battippaglia** and pick up Highway **A3** toward Naples. Turn off on Highway **A2** back to Rome. If you're taking the train, there's daily service from Paestum to Naples, with a change in Salerno.

RECOMMENDED READING

H. V. Morton. *A Traveller in Italy* (Dodd, Mead, 1982). Witty and intelligent.

Edward Bulwer-Lytton. *The Last Days of Pompeii* (Buccaneer Books, 1983). The classic 1834 novel that brings Pompeii to life during its final days.

Michael Grant. *Cities of Vesuvius: Pompeii and Herculaneum* (Mac-Millan, 1971). The best unscholary introduction to the two cities.

Vergil. *The Aeneid.* Book VI in particular is essential reading for a trip to the Sibyl's Cave and Lake Avernus in the Phlegrean Fields.

Pompeii-Herculaneum: A Guide with Reconstructions. A guide to both sites with plastic overlays that let you see buildings as they are today and as they were before the eruption.

France

❧ *The Riviera*

MAIN ATTRACTIONS

• The fabulous casino at Monte Carlo. The colorful old town of Nice. Lavish festivals at Cannes. The beach scene at Saint-Tropez. And everywhere, the luminescent light and brilliant sunshine of the Côte d'Azur.

• Historic churches and castles, modern art museums, fortified medieval hill towns where dedicated artists work and sell their wares.

• A bouillabaisse of first-class restaurants, offering the best in classic, nouvelle, and Provençal cuisine.

• Hotels for every taste and budget—from friendly, family-run pensions to some of the most palatial resorts in the world.

INTRODUCTION

In the popular imagination, the Riviera is a golden stretch of beach along the southern coast of France. Life here is a dialogue of sun and flesh, where nothing is meant to be built, just to be burned up. That's one Riviera—but there's another, a few miles inland, where fortified medieval towns are perched on mountaintops, high above the sea. On your trip you'll be traveling both along the coast, from Monte Carlo to Saint-Tropez, and to these so-called perched villages. This makes sense, for until recently the beaches were nothing but extensions of the hill towns.

The Riviera trip, unlike others in this book, won't be taking you from Points A to B, checking off important sights along the way. Happiness, as all travelers know, is staying put whenever possible. Even if you're in southern France for several weeks, there's no need to stay in more than two hotels—three at most. From any of these bases you can make daily excursions to all the places recommended below, and then come back to the same room, the same drawer of underwear and socks.

This itinerary, then, is divided into two main parts:

Part One is a description of the four areas where most visitors prefer to stay: (a) Monte Carlo, (b) the Nice area, including Beaulieu and Cap Ferrat, (c) the Cannes area, including Cap d'Antibes, and (d) Saint-Tropez.

Part Two is a description of the various excursions you can take from any of these four areas. Two of the excursions are to the perched villages of Saint-Paul-de-Vence and Peillon, where you may want to stay, too.

It's important to begin with a realistic sense of Riviera life so you won't spend your holiday nursing wounded expectations. The Riviera conjures up images of fabulous yachts and villas, movie stars and palaces, and budding Bardots sunning themselves on ribbons of golden sand. The truth is that most beaches, at least east of Cannes, are small and pebbly. In summer, hordes of visitors are stuffed into concrete high-rises or road-side campsites—on weekends it can take two hours to drive the last six miles into Saint-Tropez. Yes, the film stars are here—but in their private villas. When the merely wealthy come, they come off-season, in the spring and fall—the best time for you to visit, too.

That said, I can still recommend the Riviera, even in summer, so long as you're selective about the places you choose to visit. Back from the coast, the light that Renoir and Matisse came to capture is as magical as ever. Fields of roses and lavender still send their heady perfume up to the fortified towns, where craftspeople make and sell their wares, as their predecessors did in the Middle Ages. Some resorts are as exclusive as ever, and no one will argue that French chefs have lost their touch.

It's impossible to get bored along the Riviera. You can try a different beach or restaurant every day. When you've had enough of the sun, you can visit pottery towns like Vallauris, where Picasso worked; or perfumeries at Grasse, where three quarters of the world's essences are produced. You can drive along dizzying gorges, one almost as deep as the Grand Canyon. You can disco or gamble the night away in Monte Carlo, and shop for the best Paris has to offer, right in Cannes or Nice. Only minutes from the beaches are some of the world's most famous museums of modern art, featuring the work of Léger, Matisse, Picasso, Renoir, Coc-

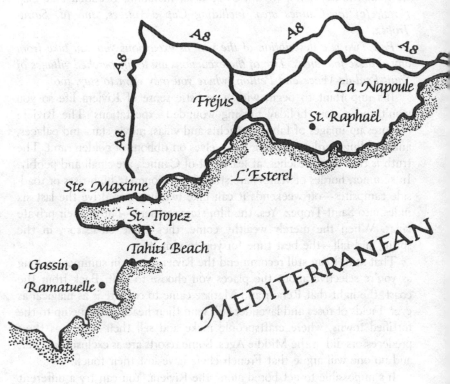

FRANCE

A8   A8   A8

A8

A8

La Napoule

St. Raphaël

Fréjus

L'Esterel

Ste. Maxime

St. Tropez

Tahiti Beach

Gassin

Ramatuelle

MEDITERRANEAN

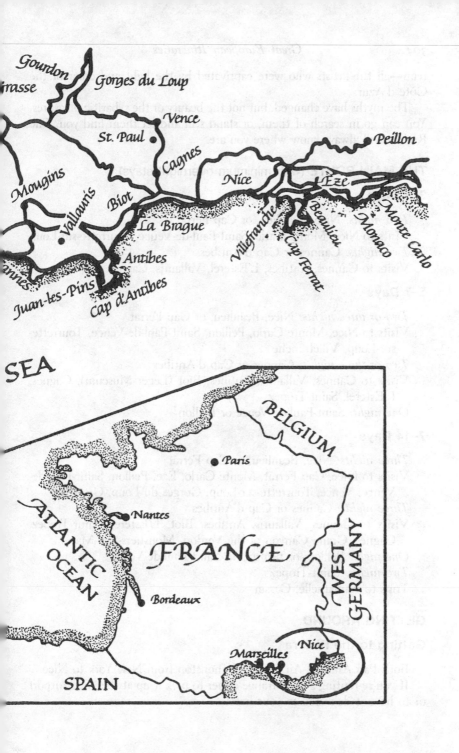

teau—all the artists who were captivated by the light and color of the Côte d'Azur.

The myths have changed, but not the beauty or the sybaritic pleasures. You can go in search of them, or stand still and let them find you. The Riviera will always know where you are.

THE MAIN ROUTE (with minimum overnight stays)

3–5 Days

Two nights: Nice, Beaulieu, or Cap Ferrat
Visits to Nice, Monte Carlo, Saint-Paul-de-Vence, Tourrette-sur-Loup
Two nights: Cannes or Cap d'Antibes
Visits to Cannes, Antibes, L'Esterel, Vallauris, Cagnes.

5–7 Days

Two or three nights: Nice, Beaulieu, or Cap Ferrat
Visits to Nice, Monte Carlo, Peillon, Saint-Paul-de-Vence, Tourrette-sur-Loup, Villefranche
Two or three nights: Cannes or Cap d'Antibes
Visits to Cannes, Vallauris, Antibes, Biot (Léger Museum), Cagnes, L'Esterel, Saint-Tropez
One night: Saint-Paul-de-Vence or Peillon

7–14 Days

Three nights: Nice, Beaulieu, or Cap Ferrat
Visits to Nice, Cap Ferrat, Monte Carlo, Èze, Peillon, Saint-Paul-de-Vence, Vence, Tourrette-sur-Loup, Gorges du Loup, Grasse
Three nights: Cannes or Cap d'Antibes
Visits to Cannes, Vallauris, Antibes, Biot, L'Esterel, Saint-Tropez, Cagnes, Grand Canyon of the Verdon, Moustiers-Ste.-Marie
One night: Peillon, or *two nights:* Saint-Paul-de-Vence
Two nights: Saint-Tropez
Trips to Ramatuelle, Gassin.

GETTING AROUND

Getting to the Riviera

Both Pan Am and Air France fly nonstop from New York to Nice.

If you're renting a car, arrange either to pick it up at the Nice Airport or to have it delivered to your hotel.

If you're arriving in Paris and traveling by train, go by cab, or by bus and subway, from **Charles de Gaulle Airport** to the **Gare de Lyon** train station. The airport bus goes to the RER, which is, in effect, a rural extension of the Paris metro. Take the RER to **Chatelet**. There are about six trains daily from Gare de Lyon to the Riviera. The trip takes slightly under 5 hours to Marseilles (via Lyon), another 2 hours to Cannes, and an additional half hour to Nice. The Paris-Lyon train is the fastest in the world—up to 170 mph. You can also take an overnight sleeper from Paris to Nice (about 11 hours) and save the cost of a hotel. One train, for instance, leaves Paris at 10:36 P.M. and arrives at Marseilles at 7:20 the next morning.

It's advisable to purchase train tickets before leaving home from the **French National Railroads**. First-class or second-class **France-Vacance** tickets are good for unlimited travel, including free round-trip passage from the airport to downtown Paris and free trips on the Paris metro. This and the **Eurailpass**—good for use in sixteen European countries— must be purchased before you leave home. French National Railroads offices are at—*New York:* 610 Fifth Avenue, New York, N.Y. 10020. Tel. 212/582-2110. *Florida:* 2121 Ponce de León Boulevard, Coral Gables, Fla. 33134. Tel. 305/445-8648. *Chicago:* 11 East Adams Street, Chicago, Ill. 90212. Tel. 213/272-7967. *San Francisco:* 360 Post Street, San Francisco, Calif. 94108. Tel. 415/982-1993.

The reduced-rate **Billet Touristique** (Tourist Ticket) and the **Billet de Famille** (Family Ticket) can be purchased at major train stations in France.

If you're driving from Paris, it's 550 miles to Cannes and 570 to Nice. The Autoroute goes from Paris to Lyon and then swings north of Marseilles to Cannes and Nice. You can arrange to have your car transported on the train, but arrangements must be made in France.

Traveling Along the Riviera

Motorcoaches run between Nice Airport and most major towns along the Riviera. There are eleven buses daily, for instance, between the airport and Cannes, and seven between the airport and Monte Carlo. Coaches from Nice Airport to downtown Nice leave every 12 minutes. For information, contact Gare Routière, Boulevard Jean-Jaurès, Nice. Tel. 93.85.61.81.

The **Metrazur** is the local train linking all major towns on the Riviera from Monte Carlo to Saint-Raphaël and Marseilles. The ride from Nice to Monte Carlo takes 24 minutes; from Nice to Cannes, 40 minutes;

from Nice to Saint-Raphaël, 60 minutes; from Nice to Antibes, 24 minutes. For information, contact Gare SNCF, Avenue Thiers, Nice. Tel. 93.87.50.50. For reservations: Tel. 93.88.89.93.

If you want to reach Saint-Tropez by public transportation, take the train to Saint-Raphaël and then the bus or (preferably) the hydrofoil to Saint-Tropez. There's also helicopter service by Heli Air Monaco at Nice Airport. Tel. 93.72.34.62.

There's daily hydrofoil service in season along the coast. It's slower than the train, but can be faster than driving in high season. Check with hotels and travel agencies.

The best regional maps are published by Michelin. If unavailable in local bookstores, order them directly from Michelin Tire Co., Guides and Maps Dept., P.O. Box 1007, Hyde Park, N.Y. 11042. Tel. 516/488-4477 or 212/895-2342. A road map of France isn't detailed enough to help you negotiate the back roads of Provence. Best bet is yellow regional map 245, "Province/Côte d'Azur."

If you're planning to spend at least three weeks in Europe, look into the option of leasing a car from Renault Inc., 650 First Avenue, New York, N.Y. 10016. Tel. 212/532-1221 or 800/221-1052.

If you're traveling by public transportation, the perched towns of Èze and **Saint-Paul-de-Vence** are the most accessible by bus from Nice. To visit other medieval towns in season, sign up for bus excursions at any hotel or travel agency in Cannes or Nice.

Mopeds and motorbikes are ideal for negotiating traffic on crowded beachfront roads, particularly for short distances, such as from Cannes to Cap d'Antibes or from Nice to Cap Ferrat. Contact, *in Nice:* Arnaud, 4 Rue Grimaldi. Tel. 93.87.88.55; or Loca Deux Roues, 29 Rue Gounod. Tel. 93.33.89.75). *In Cannes:* Cycles Remy, 22 Avenue des Hespérides (Tel. 93.43.44.66), or Cannes Location Rent, 5 Rue Alleis. Tel. 93.39.46.15. *In Antibes:* Chenu, Boulevard Dugommier. Tel. 93.33.89.75. *In Beaulieu:* Caneluni, 36 Boulevard Maréchal Leclerc. Tel. 93.01.04.51. Bikes, mopeds, or motorbikes are particularly useful in Saint-Tropez, since the main beaches are several miles from town.

SPECIAL EVENTS

January: Monte Carlo Auto Rally
February: Nice Carnival, for two weeks before Shrove Tuesday
May: Cannes Film Festival, Monaco Grand Prix motor race
June: Nice Festival of Sacred Music

July: Monaco: classical concerts in the palace courtyard
August: Menton Music Festival

A NOTE ON SHOPPING

Jewelry, designer clothing, perfume—whatever you would buy in Paris is sold along the Riviera, particularly in Cannes, Monte Carlo, and Nice. The price and quality are about the same, too. Look for good buys in silk scarves, perfumes, scented soaps, sportswear, and bathing suits (particularly bikinis).

Handmade pottery is sold in Vallauris, some based on original Picasso designs, and in Moustiers-Ste.-Marie (near the Grand Canyon of the Verdon). The town of Biot specializes in handblown glass. Paintings and local crafts—pewter, batik, jewelry, olive-wood carvings, handprinted cotton shoulder bags, etc.—are made and sold in the hilltop villages, particularly in Saint-Paul-de-Vence and Tourrette-sur-Loup. The more commercial villages, such as Èze and Gourdon, also sell scented soaps, candles, herbs, and essences. The town of Grasse is famous for its (not particularly subtle) perfumes. *Poivre d'âne* is a wild savory found only in this region.

There are some first-rate antique shops in Nice and Antibes, and along the road from Cagnes-sur-Mer to Vence. Monaco is the place for stamps.

For refunds of up to 20 percent on purchases exceeding 1,200 francs, fill out a Value-Added-Tax (TVA) form in larger stores and give a copy to customs when leaving the country. A refund will be sent to you. Shops with duty-free signs in windows give this discount on the spot.

THINGS TO SEE AND DO WITH CHILDREN

The Riviera is an ideal vacation spot for children. Every coastal resort has swimming, water sports, and bike rentals. For teenagers, there's a vigorous night life, particularly in Juan-les-Pins, Saint-Tropez, Cannes, and Nice.

Visit the walled medieval towns—the next best thing to sand castles, particularly Peillon. Hike through the Gorge of the Verdon—France's answer to the Grand Canyon. In Monte Carlo, don't miss the Aquarium (on the Rock), which is under the supervision of Jacques-Yves Cousteau, the Anthropological Museum, and the Doll Museum. Cap Ferrat has a zoo with a trained-monkey show. There's a Marineland at the turnoff to Biot on the coastal road between Nice and Cannes.

A NOTE ON SPORTS

Swimming

Beaches between Monte Carlo and Cannes are mostly small and pebbly. Cannes has a sandy beach (with imported sand). The best beach is at Saint-Tropez. Most resorts tend to have a single stretch of sand divided into a public area and a series of private beaches, each with its own distinctive character and clientele. The private beaches charge admission that includes use of a changing room and rental of a sun umbrella and mattress. They also usually serve light lunches. You're free to wander, so find a beach that suits your taste and budget and then go exploring.

Boating

Windsurfers and sailboats are for rent at all major resorts. Waterskiing is also available.

Tennis

Resorts that offer tennis (white outfits only, please!) include *Antibes:* Hotel du Cap and Résidence du Cap. *Cannes:* Hotel Montfleury. *Cap Ferrat:* Grand Hotel du Cap. *Saint-Paul-de-Vence:* Mas d'Artigny. *Vence:* Chateau St. Martin.

Golf

Near Cannes—Golf Bastide du Roy, Biot, Tel. 93.65.08.48; Golf Club de Cannes Mandelieu, Tel. 93.49.55.39; Country Club de Cannes Mougins, Tel. 93.75.79.13; and Golf de Valbonne, Tel. 93.42.00.08 or 93.42.05.29. **Near Monte Carlo**—Monte Carlo Golf Club Mont Agel, Tel. 93.41.09.11.

Biking

In high season bikes can be faster than cars. Two lovely trips on fairly level terrain are (1) around Cap d'Antibes from Nice and (2) around Cap Ferrat from Cannes. Bikes are ideal at Saint-Tropez, since the beach is a few miles from town. Bikes can be rented at train stations in Antibes, Cannes, Juan les Pins, and Nice. They can be taken with you on trains.

A NOTE ON DINING

A set or fixed menu is usually cheaper than à la carte.

The cuisine takes its inspiration from Paris, Provence, and Italy. The closer to the Italian border you are—from Nice eastward—the more pronounced the Italian influence. You'll find essentially three types of meals: classic French, nouvelle cuisine, and regional or Provençale. Classic and nouvelle cuisine are served in the more formal restaurants; regional cuisine, in the small, family-run establishments. The telltale sign of a classic meal is the use of rich, heavy sauces. Nouvelle emphasizes small portions of fresh local produce, cooked simply to enhance natural flavors and attractively arranged. Many meals, of course, are a blend of classic and nouvelle. A dinner served à la Provençale is usually cooked with garlic, tomatoes, and fresh herbs, particularly rosemary or thyme. The emphasis is on simple, robust flavors. A popular local taste is aïoli: mayonnaise with garlic, olive oil, and saffron. The most popular dish is fish—broiled, grilled, cooked in a stew or in a sauce with pasta.

Bouillabaisse is a fish stew with eel, shrimp, crabs, and other fish and shellfish, cooked with olive oil, tomato, garlic, saffron, fennel, and a touch of anise liqueur—all served with garlic toast and a garlic-and-pepper-flavored mayonnaise.

Pistou is a thick vegetable soup with beans, onions, or leeks, fresh herbs (especially basil), garlic, and grated cheese. **Soupe de poisson** is made with tomatoes, saffron, garlic, and onions.

Salade niçoise begins with tomatoes, anchovies, radishes, green peppers, olives, and a vinaigrette dressing. Added to these basics are green beans, tuna, and/or hard-boiled eggs. **Crudités** are raw vegetables.

Loup de mer (sea bass) is a specialty of the Riviera, particularly flambéed with fennel. Less expensive is **daurade** (sea bream), often grilled or baked with onion, tomato, and lemon juice. **Rouget** is red mullet grilled or baked in foil with lemon. Grilled **scampi** is often imported, frozen. **Mussels** (moules) are served in white wine à la marinière or in soup.

Leg of lamb or **brochettes** of skewered lamb are best in the spring. **Daube de boeuf** is a beef stew with a wine-flavored mushroom sauce, popular in Nice.

Chicken is served roasted with herbs (poulet rôti) or with white wine, herbs, tomatoes, and black olives (niçoise). Also popular is **rabbit** (lapin) in a mustard sauce.

As you head east toward Italy, try various kinds of **pasta**, particularly with fresh fish sauce.

Of the various fresh vegetable dishes, the best of all is **ratatouille**—a vegetable stew with tomatoes, onions, eggplant, zucchini, and green peppers. Other local favorites are asparagus and artichokes with herb stuffing.

You can try a different cheese every night for a year without having the same one twice. Be sure to try local goat and sheep cheeses.

For dessert, you can't go wrong with fresh local fruits: particularly melons and strawberries dipped in crème fraîche. Fruit sorbets are special, too.

For quick snacks on the beach, try a simple ham and cheese sandwich on a long thin loaf of french bread, or pan bagnat (a sandwich with tomatoes, hard-boiled eggs, olives, anchovies, onions, olive oil, and sometimes tuna).

Anise-flavored **Pastis** is the Number One drink.

Restaurants on the itinerary below are rated, for two: E (expensive, $60 and up), M (moderate, $30 to $60), and I (inexpensive, under $30).

A NOTE ON LODGING

The French rate their hotels one-star, two-star, three-star, four-star, and four-star-deluxe. Since French hotels can now set their own prices regardless of category, I have rated them, for two, L (luxury, over $100 a night), E (expensive, from $70 to $100), M (moderate, from $30 to $65), I (inexpensive, under $30). Students can usually put up with anything so long as there's a beach nearby; others should, as a rule, take nothing lower than three-star hotels in cities (particularly in Nice, where older hotels can be pretty scuzzy), and two-star hotels in the villages and countryside.

Most but not all hotels include a European breakfast (coffee and croissant) in the price.

A *salle de bain* is a bathroom which may have a shower or a bathtub *(baignoire)*. Specify which you want. A bathtub is more expensive. In less expensive hotels with shared bathrooms, you may have to pay extra each time you take a bath or shower.

Many of the most splendid properties—most of them castles and other historic buildings that have been converted into hotels—belong to an organization called Relais & Châteaux, represented by David Mitchell Co. in New York.

The best of the one-star and two-star hotels are grouped together in an organization called **Logis et Auberges de France** (Country Hotels and

Inns of France). These family hotels are clean and inexpensive, and located in quiet neighborhoods or on back roads. (It helps to have a car to reach them.) About 30 percent of the rooms in the two-star hotels have private baths. Room average $25 a night for two, or $40 a night with three meals. That's the cost of a good bottle of wine in a luxury-class hotel. Most have restaurants which serve fresh, well-prepared family meals. You can recognize these hotels by the distinctive yellow and green signs in front. Members are listed in the *Logis et Auberges de France* guide, which is sold in American bookstores or directly from the American distributor, Faber & Faber, 39 Thompson Street, Winchester, Mass. Tel. 617/721-1427.

Choosing a Place to Stay

A traditional itinerary—moving from place to place—makes no sense on the Riviera. What you should be doing is learning how to relax, not how to pack and unpack every day. Your best bet, therefore, is choosing a limited number of hotels and using them as bases from which to make daily excursions both inland and along the coast.

Begin by answering two important questions: (1) Do you want to spend all your time in one or more seaside resorts, or to split your time between these resorts and one of the walled medieval towns in the interior? (2) Of the time you spend on the coast, do you want to stay in towns where there's lots of activity, or in relatively isolated resorts, or in a combination of the two?

You want to spend all your time in seaside resorts. Stay (a) in or around Cannes and/or (b) in or around Nice. You can also stay in Saint-Tropez and/or Monte Carlo, but Cannes and Nice are more centrally located for excursions. (Picture the Riviera as a straight line along the southern coast of France. Saint-Tropez is at the southwest end, and Monte Carlo is at the northeast end. Cannes is in the middle. Nice is midway between Cannes and Monte Carlo.)

You want to split your time between seaside resorts and perched villages. Stay in one or more of the seaside resorts listed above **and also** in the hill towns of Saint-Paul-de-Vence or Peillon.

You want to stay along the coast, but only in towns with lots of activity. Stay in (a) the city of Nice, (b) the city of Cannes, (c) the village of Saint-Tropez, and/or (d) Monte Carlo.

You want to stay on the coast, but only in quiet, isolated resorts. Stay (a) on Cap d'Antibes near Cannes and/or (b) in Beaulieu or Cap Ferrat, near Nice. The two capes, though different in character, are both off the main coastal road and therefore more tranquil. Village and beach life in Saint-Tropez are pretty frenetic, but there are some peaceful resorts (see the Itinerary below) outside of town.

You want to stay on the coast and experience both quiet resorts and active towns. For a quiet resort, stay either in (a) Beaulieu or Cap Ferrat or (b) Cap d'Antibes. For city life, stay in (a) Cannes, (b) Nice, (c) the village of Saint-Tropez, or (d) Monte Carlo.

Return to these questions after you've read the Itinerary.

EMERGENCIES

U.S. Consulate, 36 Rue Maréchal Joffre, 06000 Nice. Tel. 93.88.89.55.

Police: Dial 17 anywhere in France.

FOR FURTHER INFORMATION

French Government Tourist Office. *New York:* 610 Fifth Avenue, New York, N.Y. 10020. Tel. 212/757-1125. *Chicago:* 645 North Michigan Avenue, Chicago, Ill. Tel. 312/337-6301. *Dallas:* World Trade Center, Section 103, 2050 Stemmons Freeway, Dallas, Tex. 75250. Tel. 214/742-7011. *Beverly Hills:* 9401 Wilshire Boulevard, Beverly Hills, Calif. 90212. Tel. 213/272-2661.

Monaco Tourist and Convention Bureau, 845 Third Avenue, New York, N.Y. 10022. Tel. 212/759-5227.

THE ITINERARY

The first step is to find a place to stay. Let's begin with the most popular areas along the coast—**Monte Carlo**; the **Nice** area, including **Beaulieu** and **Cap Ferrat**; the **Cannes** area, including **Cap d'Antibes**; and **Saint-Tropez**. Then we'll discuss the various excursions, including visits to **Saint-Paul-de-Vence** and **Peillon**—two medieval hill towns where you might want to stay, too.

❧ *MONTE CARLO* and *ÈZE*

How to Get There. Trains run direct from both Cannes and Nice to Monte Carlo. If you're driving, there are three scenic roads at varying heights above the coast between Nice and Monte Carlo, a distance of about 12 miles. All are called "corniches"—literally, a projecting molding along the top of a building or wall. The **Lower Corniche** (Cornice Inférieure) is the busiest and slowest route because it passes through all the coastal towns. The **Middle Corniche** (Moyenne Cornice) is high enough for views and close enough for details. It passes the perched village of Èze, which is discussed below. The **Upper Corniche** (Grande Corniche) winds some 1,300 to 1,600 feet above the sea, offering sweeping views of the coast. The Upper Corniche follows the Via Aurelia, the great Roman military road that brought Roman legions from Italy to Gaul (France). In 1806 Napoleon rebuilt the road and sent Gallic troops into Italy. Best advice is to take the Middle Corniche one way and the Upper Corniche the other. The view from the upper route is best in the early morning or evening.

The Principality of Monaco is 473 acres small and would fit comfortably inside New York's Central Park or a family farm in Iowa. Its five thousand citizens would take up only a small number of seats in the Astrodome. The country is so tiny that residents have to go to another country to play golf.

The present ruler, Rainier III, traces his ancestry back to Otto Canella, who was born in 1070. The Grimaldi dynasty began with Otto's great-great-great-grandson, Francesco Grimaldi, also known as Frank the Rogue. Expelled from Genoa, Frank and his cronies disguised themselves as monks and seized the fortified medieval town known today as the Rock. That was in 1297, almost seven hundred years ago. Except for a short break under Napoleon, the Grimaldis have been there ever since, which makes them the oldest reigning family in Europe. On the Grimaldi coat of arms are two monks holding swords: Look up and you'll see them above the main door as you enter the palace.

Back in the 1850s a Grimaldi named Charles III made a decision that turned the Rock into a giant blue chip. Needing revenues, but not wanting to impose additional taxes on his subjects, he contracted with a company to open a gambling facility. The first spin of the roulette wheel was on December 14, 1856. There was no easy way to reach Monaco then—no carriage roads or railroads—so no one came. Between March 15 and March 20, 1857, one person entered the casino—and won two francs. In 1868, however, the railroad reached Monaco, filled with wheezing Englishmen who came to escape the London fog. The effects were immediate. Profits were so great that Charles eventually abolished all direct taxes.

Almost overnight a threadbare principality became an elegant watering hole for European society. Dukes and their mistresses, duchesses and their gigolos danced and dined their way through a world of spinning roulette wheels and bubbling champagne—preening themselves for nights at the opera, where artists such as Nijinsky, Sarah Bernhardt, and Caruso came to perform.

Monte Carlo—the modern gambling town with elegant shops, man-made beaches, high-rise hotels, and a few Belle Epoque hotels—is actually only one of four parts of Monaco. The second is the medieval town on the Rock ("Old Monaco"), 200 feet above the sea. It's here that Prince Rainier lives. From July through September the Prince goes a-traveling and the Palace is open to the public.

The third area is La Condamine, the commercial harbor area, with apartments and businesses. The fourth is Fontveille, the industrial district on twenty acres of reclaimed land.

Today only about 3 percent of the country's revenues come from gambling; other chips are invested in chemicals, glass, ceramics, plastics, food products, and beer. Monaco may be a handkerchief-size state, a golden ghetto, but it's also a serious country with some ninety-five consulates around the world. Rainier has been adept financially, and citizens still don't have to pay taxes. (If you're thinking of becoming a citizen, there are long residency requirements before you can even apply, and even then it isn't easy: There are no huddled masses here.) Of some thirty-three thousand residents, only about five thousand are citizens. They are called Monégasque, and they are not allowed to gamble.

The principality has the lowest crime rate in Europe, perhaps because it has one security man for every 122 residents. The navy, such as it is, has the fastest boat on the coast—so don't think of robbing the casino and escaping by sea.

When the Monégasques want to expand, they build upward or reclaim land from the sea. The result is a clean, sparkling concrete jewel set in a ring of mountains at the edge of the sea. The climate is the next best to Southern California's. Unlike other towns along the coast, Monaco has a highly defined history and tradition. It is also a town dedicated to conspicuous consumption. The borders with France are open; one moment you're driving through France, the next, through Monaco. The spoken language is French. French money is freely circulated, though there are Monégasque coins stamped with the image of Rainier III.

The casino is worth a visit, even if you don't bet a cent. You might find it fun to count the Jaguars and Rolls-Royces parked outside, and breathe on windows of shops selling $1,200 Saint-Laurent dresses and fabulous jewels. The Oceanographic Museum under Jacques-Yves Cousteau is a treat, and so is the Exotic Garden. Should you decide to stay, there's one hotel straight out of the nineteenth century and a comfortable beach hotel where expensive people offer their oiled bodies to the sun.

Most of the very wealthy stay in their private villas, of course, barricaded behind a wall of old money, and the people you will meet are people like yourself—holidaymakers, sunseekers, coming to Monte Carlo to cloak themselves in the opulence of a world that no longer exists. But no matter. The contrast between yesterday and today is sad and wonderful, funny and obscene—but it's still worth seeing. And while you're mourning what has been lost, miraculously, a bit of the old glamor rubs off, too.

• As you approach Monte Carlo from Nice, you'll see signs on the right to the Jardin Exotique ('Tropical Gardens), the Musé d'Anthropologie Préhistorique (Museum of Prehistoric Anthropology), and the Observatory Caves. All three are worth a visit. The garden (open daily in season from 9 to 7; off-season, daily from 9 to 6) has some nine thousand species of cacti and succulents clinging to a rocky cliff 300 feet above the sea. The view of the palace and the coast is spectacular. Steps take you down to the museum (which has a great collection of skeletons and stone-age tools of interest to the nonspecialist) and to the caves. The caves don't hold a candle to the Carlsbad Caverns in New Mexico or Luray Caverns in Virginia; but you'll still enjoy wandering through an Arthur Rackhamish world of fantastic shapes and shadows. Keep in mind that it's a long, steep walk down to the caves and back again.

• Next stop is Old Monaco—the Rock—to tour the Palace (open daily, July through September, from 9:30 to 12:30 and 1 to 6:30) and the Oceanographic Museum and Aquarium (open daily from 9:30 to 7). Leave your car in the Fontvielle Car Park on your way into town. From Easter to the end of October there is bus service between the car park and the Rock. The walk takes about 30 minutes.

• There's little room on the Rock for anything but official buildings, tourist shops, and restaurants. The marble staircase in the palace was inspired by the one at Fontainebleau. The tour takes you through ornate staterooms filled with priceless antiques and paintings, where you can imagine Princess Grace greeting visiting royalty. The Oceanographic Museum has an aquarium asplash with playful sea lions and turtles.

Families with kids should come early to see the Changing of the Guards in front of the palace, daily at 11:55 A.M.

Also on the Rock is the Cathedral, a neo-Romanesque monstrosity (1875-84) with several important early paintings of the Nice School. This school, led by Louis Bréa—you'll see his work in churches along the coast

—flourished from the mid-fifteenth to the mid-sixteenth century under strong Gothic and Italian Renaissance influence. The simplicity and humanity of Bréa's work have led some critics to call him a Provençal Fra Angelico.

• The **Casino** is a must. Nowhere in the world will you see a more striking contrast between yesterday and today. Wandering through a world of gold-leaf splendor are gamblers looking as though they had just stumbled off the bus to Reno or Atlantic City. Beneath the gilt-edged Rococo ceiling, busloads of women from Dubuque and Jersey City jerk the arms of one-armed bandits. Don't miss it!

The main gambling hall, once called the European Room, has been renamed the American Room and fitted with 150 one-armed bandits from Chicago. Adjoining it is the Pink Salon, now a bar where unclad nymphs float about on the ceiling smoking cigarillos. The private rooms (Salles Privé) are for high rollers. Even if you don't bet, it's worth the price just to see them. The stakes are higher here, so the mood is more sober, and well-wishers are herded farther back from the tables.

On July 17, 1924, black came up seventeen times in a row on Table 5. This was the longest run ever. A dollar left on black would have grown to $131,072. On August 7, 1913, the number 36 came up three times in a row. In those days, if a gamber went broke the casino bought him a ticket home.

The casino opens at 10 A.M. and continues until the last die is thrown. Ties and jackets are required in the back rooms, which open at 4 P.M. Bring your passport.

It seems in the true spirit of Monte Carlo that the Opera House, with its eighteen-ton gilt bronze chandelier, is part of the casino complex. The designer, Charles Garnier, also built the Paris Opera.

• The serious gamblers, some say, play at **Loew's Casino**, nearby. It opens weekdays at 4 P.M. and on weekends at 1 P.M. You may want to try parking here, since parking near the old casino is next to impossible in season.

• The **Museum of Dolls** is in the **National Museum**, a short walk to the left as you exit the casino. Your children will thank you for taking them!

Shopping

The shop windows in Monte Carlo are for many visitors as interesting as the historic sites. Certainly, some of the couturier clothing is as dazzling and, for many, as inaccessible as the furnishings in the palace.

Most of the boutiques—Cartier, Dior, Yves Saint Laurent, and the like—are on streets surrounding the casino: **Place du Casino, Avenue des Beaux-Arts, Boulevard de Moulins,** and **Avenue Princess Grace.** The somewhat younger, trendier boutiques are in the **Park Palace complex** (**Les Allées Lumières**) at the head of the casino gardens.

To help support local artisans, Princess Grace set up two shops called **Boutique du Rocher,** selling handicrafts and goods made from Provençal fabrics. One is at 1 Avenue de Madone in Monte Carlo; the other is on the Rock at 11 Rue Emile de Loth.

Swimming

Plage du Larvotto is a man-made public beach squeezed between two pieces of man-made land. Next door is the private Monte Carlo Sea Club, which has a heated seawater pool free to guests at the Beach Plaza Hotel. If you want to come close to experiencing some of the dazzle that Monte Carlo once knew, the only place to swim is at the exclusive **Monte Carlo Beach** (Tel. 93.78.21.40). A fee of under $10 will admit you to a heated Olympic-size saltwater pool, restaurants, a pebbly beach with cabanas, and a bevy of pretty boys and aspiring Bardots.

Dining

Le Bec Rouge (E, Avenue de Grande-Bretagne. Tel. 93.30.74.91) has the best classic French cuisine in town. Specialties include cold mussels with a mayonnaise of hot pepper and garlic, fresh house foie gras, lobster or prawn gratin, bouillabaisse, Alpine lamb, and fresh bass.

A fashionable and exuberant yachting crowd gathers at **Rampoldi** (E, Avenue Spéluges. Tel. 93.30.70.65) for Italian food in a 1930ish setting. Try Risotto primavera or grilled lamb.

Dominique Le Stanc (E, 18 Boulevard Moulins. Tel. 93.50.63.37) gets top billing from Michelin for its classic dishes, including fresh fish roasted with pistachios. The mood is modern and cheerful. Tables are surrounded by antique toys.

Café de Paris (M, Place du Casino. Tel. 93.50.57.75) is a brasserie-type lunch spot for jet setters who want to see and be seen, and for ladies with poodles and heavy Arpels bracelets.

The budget-minded should head for the **Place d'Armes** in the port below the Rock and munch on hot socca (a thin pancake made with chickpea flour) or a slice of pissaladière (thick pizza with onions) in the open-air market.

Pizzeria Monégasque (M, 4 Rue Terrazzani. Tel. 93.30.16.38) is a chic pizza house. Dinners only.

Pinocchio (M, 30 Rue Compte-Félix-Gastaldi. Tel. 93.30.96.20), featuring French-Italian specialties, is the most popular eaterie on the Rock. Bronzed women and men fighting their age relax in a cozy atmosphere beneath a vaulted ceiling.

Restaurant du Port (M, Quai Albert-ler. Tel. 93.50.77.21) is a popular Italian restaurant with outside tables and efficient service. A large, varied menu includes prawns, pastas, lasagna Bolognese, fettucine, fish risotto, and veal with ham and cheese.

Lodging

Monte Carlo is only a half-hour drive from Nice, so there's no need to stay here unless you're an inveterate gambler or like the idea of waking up in the land of Princess Grace. If you're looking for a luxurious hotel, the Negresco in Nice is as luxurious as the Hotel de Paris in Monte Carlo, and the food is better; if you need a moderately priced or inexpensive hotel, you'll have a better choice in Nice. Don't come to Monte Carlo in season without a reservation, and expect to pay $60 for the cheapest double.

The two places to stay in Monte Carlo, if you can afford the prices, are the **Hotel de Paris** (L, Place du Casino. Tel. 93.50.80.80) and the **Monte Carlo Beach Hotel** (L, Route du Beach. Tel. 93.78.21.40).

The 123-year-old **Hotel de Paris**, located a bone's throw from the casino, is one of the most famous hotels in Europe. Just as the new Loew's Hotel is the offspring of the modern travel world of conventions and gambling junkets, so the ornate Hotel de Paris is the child of a vanishing age of privilege and luxury. It was here in this heavy, Second Empire splendor—this Belle Epoque tour de force—that Escoffier worked his magic for empresses, dowagers, and queens.

Monte Carlo Beach Hotel has 50 small, modern, elegant rooms with balconies overlooking the ocean. It also has the best hotel food in town. It is exactly what its name says—a beach hotel, where guests are given privileges at the exclusive Monte Carlo Beach Club, which occupies the same site. A minibus takes guests to the casino and shops, which are too far to reach by foot.

The 210-room **Hermitage** (E, Square Beaumarchais. Tel. 93.50.67.31) is a grand Belle Epoque palace for people who can't get into (or afford the price of) the Hotel de Paris. The dining room is a tribute to a bygone age, with pink marble columns holding up a gilded, frescoed ceiling. The recently reappointed rooms are comfortable but disappointing after you've seen the lavish public areas.

The **Beach Plaza** (E, 22 Avenue Princesse-Grace. Tel. 93.30.98.80) is part of the respected Trusthouse Forte chain. It is a large modern hotel with 320 rooms and three pools.

Unless restorations have begun, the **Balmoral** (M, 12 Avenue Costa. Tel. 93.50.62.37) is a sad reminder of a lost age. The nicest thing a travel writer can say about it is that it's an old-fashioned family hotel.

The closest thing to a budget hotel is the **Terminus** (I, 9 Avenue Prince Pierre. Tel. 93.30.20.77), near the train station.

For Further Information

The main tourist office is at 2a Boulevard des Moulins, in front of the casino gardens. Tel. 93.30.87.01. Stamp collectors can satisfy their phila-telic fantasies here.

✤ ÈZE

Almost every tour to Monte Carlo includes a visit to the medieval hill town of Èze, which is perched on a rocky spur near the Middle Corniche, some 1,300 feet above the sea. (Don't confuse Èze with the beach town of Èze-sur-Mer, which is down by the water.)

Èze is one of several beautifully preserved medieval towns on moun-taintops behind the coast. It would be a shame to tour the Riviera with-out seeing at least one of these towns, and Èze, directly on the road between Nice and Monte Carlo, is the most accessible. But because of its accessibility it's also the most crowded and commercial. Èze has its share of serious craftspeople, but most of its vendors make their living selling perfumed soaps and postcards to the package-tour trade.

If Èze is your first perched village, you'll be delighted with it, but if you've been to Saint-Paul-de-Vence (also commercial but visually more beautiful), Tourrette-sur-Loup, Peillon, or others, you may be disap-pointed with Èze. If time is limited, certainly, visit Èze, particularly in the early evening when the buses have returned to Nice. But the village really takes second place to others described in the Excursion section below.

Enter through a fortified fourteenth-century gate and wander down narrow, cobbled streets with vaulted passageways and stairs. The **church** is eighteenth century, but the small **Chapel of the White Penitents** dates to 1306 and contains a thirteenth-century gilded wood Spanish Christ and some notable sixteenth-century paintings. Tourist and craft shops line the streets leading to the ruins of a **castle**, which has a scenic belvedere. Some of the most tasteful craft shops are in the hotel/restaurant **Chevre d'Or**.

Near the top of the village is a garden with exotic flowers and cacti. It's worth the admission price, but if you've time for only one exotic garden, visit the one in Monte Carlo.

If you're not going to Grasse, the perfume capital of the world, consider visiting a branch of a Grasse perfumerie called **La Perfumerie Fragonard**, located in front of the public gardens.

Dining

Chevre d'Or (E, Rue Barri. Tel. 93.41.12.12) gets five stars from Fielding and one from Michelin. Classic French cuisine is served in a very restored medieval manor house. Specialties include Saumon mariné, filet de loup (local bass), and pigeon with fresh truffle pâté. The dining area is formal, without much warmth; best bet for daytrippers is the terrace.

Château Eza (E, Tel. 93.41.12.24) is another restored old mansion with a developing reputation.

Lodging

Though Èze has two first-class hotels, you may have the same reservations about staying here as I have about visiting.

Chevre d'Or (E, Rue Barri. Tel. 93.41.12.12) is a restored medieval manor house with 6 well-appointed but smallish rooms and three apartments (number 9 is a good bet). The small pool is surrounded by a terrace: a lovely, peaceful place to take the sun or end the day. The hotel belongs to the prestigious Relais & Châteaux group of hotels.

The newly restored **Château Eza** (L, Tel. 93.41.12.24) is trying hard to match the well-established Chevre d'Or in comfort and class. Rooms here are more spacious, though the atmosphere is a bit "Ye Olde." The hotel occupies the former home of the King of Sweden. The view from the terrace is, as they say, breathtaking.

♦ NICE (including *CAP FERRAT* and *BEAULIEU*)

Near the busy city of Nice is a cape called Cap Ferrat, jutting out into the sea. On the far side of the cape is the coastal village of Beaulieu. A village, a cape, a city—which of these three is right for you? Let's look at the alternatives.

NICE

Nice is less glamorous, less sophisticated, and less expensive than Cannes. It's also older—weathered-old and faded-old, like a wealthy dowager who has seen better days but who still maintains a demeanor of dignity and poise. Nice is a big, sprawling city of 350,000 people—five times as many as Cannes—and has a life and vitality that survive when tourists pack their bags and go home. Cannes, on the contrary, exists for its visitors; it was dreamed up by them and blinked into existence almost overnight.

The glitter has moved to Cannes, but Nice has kept some of the local Marseilles flavor that Marseilles has lost and Cannes never had. Cannes is smart, stylish, and international, like nouvelle cuisine; Nice has the simple robust flavor of a meal cooked à la Provençale, with lots of garlic, tomatoes, and herbs.

It's easy to picture Nice, stretching behind the beautiful blue Baie des Anges: Along a narrow strip of pebbly beach is the Promenade des Anglais, lined with hotels and cafés. If you follow the promenade to the west, you'll come to the fabulous **Hotel Negresco**. If you follow the promenade to the east, you'll reach a hill called the **Château**, crowned with the ruins of an old fortress. Below the fortress are both the **old town** —*la vieille ville*—and the harbor. That's it, essentially, as far as visitors are concerned: After the promenade, the old town, and the museums and ruins in an area called **Cimiez**, you're left with a busy, modern city where nothing goes on but life.

The **old town** of Nice is one of the delights of the Riviera. Cars are forbidden on streets narrow enough for their buildings to crowd out the sky. The winding alleyways are lined with faded seventeenth- and eighteenth-century buildings where families sell their wares. Flowers cascade from window boxes on soft, pastel-colored walls. You wander down cobbled streets, proceeding with the logic of dreams, or sit in an outdoor café on a Venetian-like square bathed in a pool of the purest, most transparent light. At the edge of the old town is the **flower market**, a swirl of colors and smells as intoxicating as wine.

Nice is worth a visit, but should you stay here? On the negative side, its beaches are cramped and pebbly. Except for the luxurious Negresco, most of its hotels are either rundown or being refurbished for the convention crowd. On the positive side, Nice is likely to have hotel space when all other towns are full, and at prices you can afford. It's also a convenient base from which to explore Monte Carlo and the medieval towns in the interior. It does have its share of first-class restaurants and boutiques, and an evening stroll through the old town or along the Promenade des Anglais is not easily forgotten.

• Tourists will spend their time (1) on the Promenade des Anglais, (2) in the old town, or (3) in Cimiez.

1. Nice was "colonized" in the mid-eighteenth century by Englishmen fleeing the harshness of northern winters. The Promenade des Anglais got its name because, in the 1820s, the Reverend Lewis Way got the English colony to pay for widening a 2.5-mile footpath along the Baie des Anges, thus creating jobs for fruit pickers thrown out of work by a terrible frost. The eastern end of the boulevard, bordering the old town, is now called the Quai des États-Unis in deference to changing commercial realities. You can lunch in your bathing suit at any of the private beaches along the promenade.

A few blocks inland, to the west of the Negresco Hotel, is a first-rate **Fine Arts Museum** (Jules Chéret), open 10 to 12, and 2 to 5 or 6. The museum contains paintings by masters of the Belle Epoque and Picasso ceramics created in the pottery village of Vallauris in the 1950s.

The **Masséna Museum**, a few blocks west of the Negresco, has a fine collection of Provençal ceramics, and paintings by the early Nice School, including works by Bréa.

2. At the end of the Quai des États-Unis are steps and an elevator leading to a viewing platform at the top of the 300-foot **Château**. From here, continue inland, down to the old town. At **Place Garibaldi** there's a morning fish market. Walk down **Rue St.-François** and bear left on **Rue Droite**. On your right is the **Palais Lascaris** (open July through September daily except Monday and Tuesday, from 9:30 to 12, and 2:30 to 6:30; off-season, to 6). The mid-seventeenth-century palace has an eighteenth-century pharmacy and a Rococo interior with a grandiose staircase and an interesting trompe l'oeil ceiling.

Continue down **Rue Droite**. On your left is the seventeenth-century **St. Jacques Church**, known as the Gesú, because it was modeled on that church in Rome. Three short blocks in from the bay, and paralleling it, is **Cours Saleya**, once the elegant promenade of Old Nice, now a street lined with shops and restaurants. Depending on the speed of restoration work, the **flower market** will either be here or on **Rue St. François-de-Paule** near the Opera.

3. Cimiez, site of ancient Nice, is now a residential neighborhood on a hill back from the bay. The **Marc Chagall Museum** (open 10:30 to 3 or 4; closed Tuesdays) houses the most important permanent collection of

the painter's work, including the seventeen canvases of the *Biblical Message*.

The Roman ruins of a bath and amphitheater will not be high on your list of musts unless you have a special interest in antiquity. Nearby is the seventeenth-century **Matisse Museum** (Villa des Arènes), which has some thirty examples of the painter's work, drawn from different stages of his life. Also near the ruins is a **Franciscan Monastery** with several masterpieces of the Nice School, including a 1475 *Pietà* by Louis Bréa.

Shopping

Best bet for designer bathing suits is **La Boutique du Méridien**, one flight up in the Hotel Méridien. There are several pricey boutiques in the **Royal Salon of the Hotel Negresco**, some selling designer clothes made exclusively for these shops.

In the old town, the most elegant and trendy boutiques are along **Rue Masséna, Place Magenta**, and **Rue Paradis** (Saint-Laurent at Number 8, Gladys Falk at Number 2, Façonnable at Numbers 7–9). On **Rue de la Liberté** is Dorothee Bis at Number 20, Gigi at Number 10, Caroll, for women and children, at Number 9, and **Trabaud**, for men, at Number 10.

Boulevard Risso has a flea market daily except Sunday.

Excursions

Nice is a good base for half-day or full-day excursions to **Monte Carlo** and **Èze**; to the perched villages of **Peillon** and **Saint-Paul-de-Vence**; to the Léger Museum at **Biot**; and to **Cap Ferrat, Villefranche, Antibes**, and **Cannes**. For descriptions of these excursions, look both under the individual towns and under the Excursions section on pages 344ff.

Dining

Dining in Nice is a mixture of Italian, Provençal, and Parisian. Lunchtime specialties include pissaladière (pizza with black olives, onions, and anchovies), and pan bagnat (French bread soaked in olive oil and filled with tomatoes, radishes, hard-boiled eggs, black olives, and parsley).

Le Chantecler (E, in the Negresco Hotel, 37 Promenade des Anglais. Tel. 93.82.25.25) is the top restaurant for nouvelle cuisine. Eric Newby wrote in the New York *Times* that "this is the best, the most imaginative and the most beautifully presented meal I have ever eaten in my entire life, and am ever likely to eat." The *menu dé gustation* includes tiny, elegant portions of a dozen dishes. Other specialties include Charlotte de

St.-Pierre (a fish dish), lobster salad with asparagus tips, melon and grape-fruit soup with sauterne wine, and lobster ravioli in a shellfish bouillon. Expect to pay about $60 per person.

Of the many harborfront restaurants the best is the well-known **L'Ane Rouge** (E, 7 Quai des Deux-Emmanuel. Tel. 93.89.49.63). Fielding gives it three stars for what many consider the freshest fish in town. Specialties include bourride (a fish stew), lobster, sweetbreads, and chocolate cake.

La Poularde Chez Lucullus (E/M, 9 Rue Gustave-Deloye. Tel. 93.85.22.90) is an old favorite for classical cuisine in a turn-of-the-century setting. Specialties include roast lamb, trout with almonds, and veal kidneys flambéed in champagne.

Los Caracoles (M, 5 Rue St.-François-de-Paule. Tel. 93.80.98.23), located near the flower market and the opera, is a less expensive alternative for fresh fish.

La Mérenda (I, 4 Rue de la Terrasse. No telephone.) is a popular old town bistro near the flower market. Specialties cooked to order include tripes niçoise, pâté au pistou (pasta with garlic and basil sauce), pizza, and stew Provençale. This is your best bet for a first-rate meal at a low price. No reservations are taken, so come early.

For Italian specialties, try **Chez Don Camillo** (M, 5 Rue des Ponchettes. Tel. 93.85.67.95), a tiny, quiet, comfortable restaurant with attentive service and a good but limited menu. Try the fettucine or filet of sole.

Most tourists are directed to restaurants on the eastern side of the harbor, where glass-enclosed terraces muffle the sound of traffic. None has a very strong reputation among locals. Best bet is **Le Scampi** (M, 65 Quai des États-Unis. Tel. 93.85.42.90), serving good simple meals of pastas, fresh fish, and, of course, scampi).

Those who know will tell you it's worth the trip to **Rotisserie de St. Pancrace** (M/I, five miles north of Nice on D914. Tel. 93.84.43.69), a country inn on a mountaintop, 15 minutes from town. The shaded terrace is ideal for lunch on a pleasant day. The inventive nouvelle menu includes duck with morels, sweetbreads en croute, prawn stew, roast pigeon, ravioli with foie gras (goose liver), sole with vegetables, and la coquille St. Jacques.

Nightlife

La Camargue (5 Place Charles-Félix) is the hottest disco. **Au Pizzaiolo** (4 bis. Rue du Pont Vieux), in the old city, is cheaper and less forbidding. **Superstar** (3 Place de l'Armée-du-Rhin) is another disco on the nightly circuit.

Lodging

Except for the Negresco, which has succeeded in maintaining the elegant standards of a bygone age, Nice's major hotels are either fading or undergoing restoration to satisfy the demands of the package-tour trade. The older hotels in all categories have beautifully ornate façades. Dining rooms, hallways, and stairways also have a certain fading charm. But the rooms are almost always a disappointment. It's not that they're uncomfortable or unclean, but that they lack character and fail to live up to the promise of the public areas.

The **Negresco** (L, 37 Promenade des Anglais. Tel. 93.88.39.51), a turn-of-the-century turreted white castle, is the only hotel in France that the government has declared a national monument. Doormen greet you in red-lined capes, knee-high boots, and blue hats with cockades. The massive suites are designed around different periods of French history—Romantic, Louis XIV, Empire, and others. The marble bathrooms are big enough to throw parties in. The lobby is a huge oval rotunda encircled with columns reaching up to a stained-glass dome. Hanging above its center is a gigantic Baccarat crystal chandelier. The hallway carpet, when woven, represented one tenth of the cost of the hotel.

Méridien (L, 1 Promenade des Anglais. Tel. 93.82.25.25) is a modern, impersonal hotel with a rooftop pool.

Sofitel-Splendid (E, 50 Boulevard Victor-Hugo. Tel. 93.88.69.51) is a family-run, in-town hotel with rooftop pool and sun terrace.

Grand Hotel Aston (E, 12 Avenue Félix-Faure. Tel. 93.80.62.52) has a lovely roof garden overlooking the old city.

La Pérouse (E, 11 Quai Rauba Capeu. Tel. 93.62.34.63) is at the eastern end of the Baie des Anges, near the Château. The reception area is tacky, but rooms are clean and the rooftop pool is a quiet oasis with a spectacular view.

Hotel Busby (I/M, 38 Rue Mar-Joffe. Tel. 93.88.19.41) is one of a group of hotels back from the bay that cater heavily to the package-tour trade. If you're stuck for a room, they're likely to come up with something.

Hotel Harvey (I, 18 Avenue de Suède. Tel. 93.16.43.55) is just off the ocean behind the Méridien. There's no lobby, the wallpaper in rooms I saw was peeling, the closets were unpainted, and carpets needed vacuuming. But the location is great and the rooms are cheap.

For Further Information

The main tourist office is at the central train station (Gare Centrale, Avenue Thiers. Tel. 93.87.97.07).

BEAULIEU and CAP FERRAT

The **Beaulieu-Cap Ferrat** area, just east of Nice, is the quietest, most understated, most refined area along the Riviera. People come here not to see and be seen, but to be left alone. Because of the limited night life, the absence of sandy beaches, and the distance from Cannes, guests tend to be families or couples on the far side of thirty—particularly off-season. If a hotel is nothing more to you than a place to put your head after a full day of sightseeing, stay in Nice; but if you want to escape the frenetic pace of summer life along the Riviera and merely exist in the sun for a few days, stay in Beaulieu or on Cap Ferrat. You will want to have a car here and perhaps a rented bike for rides around the cape.

❖ *BEAULIEU*

The one Thing to Do in Beaulieu is visit the **Villa Kérylos** (open daily in July and August from 3 to 7; off-season, from 2 to 6; closed Mondays). In the early part of the century a rich amateur archeologist named Theodore Reinach asked an Italian architect to build him an authentic Greek house. The villa, now open to the public, is a faithful reproduction made from cool Carrara marble, alabaster, and rare fruitwoods. The furniture, made of wood inlaid with ivory, bronze, and leather, is copied from drawings of Greek interiors found on ancient vases and mosaics.

Excursions

See Excursions under NICE.

Dining

Overnight guests in Beaulieu will probably want to eat in their hotels. Both **La Réserve** and the **Métropole** get one star from Michelin for meals far better than the usual hotel fare. Two reasonably priced local restaurants for regional, home-style meals are **Agaves** (M, 4 Rue Maréchal-Foch. Tel. 93.01.12.09) and **Pignatelle** (I, 10 Rue Quincenet. Tel. 93.01.03.37).

Lodging

The two luxury hotels are next-door neighbors at the edge of the sea: La Réserve (L, 5 Boulevard du Maréchal-Leclerc. Tel. 93.01.00.01) and the Métropole (L, 15 Boulevard du Maréchal-Leclerc. Tel. 93.01.00.08). Both have lovely pools on rocky ledges, and steps leading down into the water. Neither has a beach. The Métropole is visually more relaxed, with comfortable couches in the public areas and 2.5 acres of gardens leading to the sea. La Réserve is a bit more reserved, in an elegant sort of way, with a lounge that resembles the reception room in Rome's Farnese Palace.

For Further Information

The tourist office is at Place Gare. Tel. 93.01.02.21.

❦ CAP FERRAT (Saint-Jean-Cap-Ferrat)

Cape Ferrat, originally the southern tip of the cape, now gives its name to the entire peninsula. It resembles Cap d'Antibes, near Nice, in that it's a rocky finger extending into the sea, covered with sumptuous mansions hidden behind walls of lush vegetation. Because of its proximity to Cannes, Cap d'Antibes tends to attract a noisier, more aggressively star-studded clientele; guests on the more inaccessible Cap Ferrat want nothing but privacy, understated elegance, and seclusion. Land values on Cap Ferrat are second only to those in Monaco.

• The cape is a fine, peaceful place to visit, even if you're not staying here. There's a lovely one-hour walk along the coast from **Paloma Beach** around **Pointe St. Hospice**—ask directions to the **Tourist Path** (Sentier Touristique). There's also a **zoo** (open mid-June through mid-September from 9 to 7; off-season, from 9:30 to 6) with a tropical garden and some 350 species of animals and exotic birds, including a condor and a school of chimps who put on a daily show.

• Best of all is the **Ephrussi de Rothschild Foundation**, a seventeen-acre estate with magnificent gardens and a villa-museum called the Musée Ile-de-France (open 3 to 7 in summer; off-season, 2 to 6; closed Mondays). The museum reflects the sensibilities of its former owner, Madame Ephrussi de Rothschild, sister of Baron Edouard de Rothschild. An insatiable collector, she lived surrounded by an eclectic but tasteful collection of Impressionist paintings, Louis XIII furniture, rare Sèvres porcelain, and objets d'art from the Far East.

Excursions

See Excursions under NICE.

Dining

In addition to the hotel dining room of the **Voile d'Or**, the cape has three first-class restaurants. Overlooking the harbor of Saint-Paul-du-Cap are **Provençal** (M/E, Tel. 93.01.30.15) and **Les Hirondelles** (E, 36 Avenue Jean-Mermoz. Tel. 93.01.30.25). Meals at **Petit Trianon** (M/E, Boulevard Général-de-Gaulle. Tel. 93.01.31.68) are served on a flowery terrace. Les Hirondelles is a good bet for fresh fish, bouillabaisse, and grilled lobster, all served on a vine-covered terrace overlooking the harbor.

Lodging

As in Beaulieu, you have a choice of two first-class hotels. The mood between these two, however, is markedly different.

Grand Hotel du Cap Ferrat (L, Boulevard Général-de-Gaulle. Tel. 93.01.04.54) is a grand but modernized resort standing back from the cliffs in isolated splendor at the very southern tip of the cape. A walk across sweeping lawns takes you to the funicular, which leads down to the seaside pool. Anyone can use the pool for a fee (a plus for visitors, a minus for guests), so if you're only passing through, bring your bathing suit and stay for lunch. The restaurant has a good reputation for classical French cuisine.

Voile d'Or (L, Tel. 93.01.13.13) is a smaller, smarter, younger hotel overlooking the pleasure boats in the colorful harbor of Saint-Jean-du-Cap. The Grand Hotel is a large, isolated resort; the Voile d'Or is a small, tasteful hotel with private pool near the boutiques, restaurants, and antique shops of an active but generally unspoiled seaside village. The sophistication of the clientele is reflected in the tasteful furnishings: white marble floors, chenille spreads, soft pastel-colored walls covered with hand-loomed tapestries.

Brise Marine (M, Avenue Jean-Mermoz. Tel. 93.01.30.73) is a clean, friendly, unpretentious villa with lovely views (try Room 3) and reasonable prices—reasonable, that is, for Cap Ferrat.

For Further Information

The **tourist office** is at 59 Avenue Denis Demis-Semeria. Tel. 93.01.36.86.

❧ CANNES

Cosmopolitan, sophisticated, smart—these are words that describe the most lively and flourishing city on the Riviera. It's a resort town—unlike Nice, which is a city—that exists only for the pleasure of its guests. It's a tasteful and expensive breeding ground for yuppies, a sybaritic heaven for those who believe that life is short and that sin has something to do with the absence of a tan.

Whatever you would want to buy in Paris you can find in Cannes, and at about the same price. There are hair-raising salons where trendies get their New Wave cuts, and boutiques for the model man and fashion-page woman. There are frozen kiwi parlors and late-night clubs for Arab princes, playgirls, and pretty boys. Everywhere—along the coast, high up in the hills—are restaurants where chefs make an art of arranging asparagus and peas. The day's catch is swaddled in ice outside bistros where film stars sit at red-checkered tables, trying not to get oyster juice on their black ties. Couples sip wine at open air cafés behind the beach, where coeds display their expensive bodies. There are few historic monuments, but people come here for the present, not the past.

Picture a long, narrow beach. Stretching along it is a broad, elegant promenade called **La Croisette** bordered by palm trees and flowers. At one end of the promenade is the modern Festival Hall, a summer casino, and an old harbor where pleasure boats are moored. At the other end is a winter casino and a modern harbor for some of the most luxurious yachts in the world. All along the promenade are cafés, boutiques, and luxury hotels like the **Carlton** and the **Majestic**. Speedboats and water-skiers glide by; little waves lick the beach, lined with prostrate bodies. Behind the promenade lies the town, filled with shops, restaurants, and hotels; and behind the town are the hills with the villas of the very rich.

The first thing to do is stroll along the Croisette, stopping at cafés and boutiques along the way. Near the eastern end (turning left as you face the water), before you reach the new port, is the **Parc de la Roserie**, where some fourteen thousand roses nod their heads. Walking west takes you past **Festival Hall** (Palais des Festivals), where the famous film festival is held each May. Just past the hall is a square called **Place du Général-de-Gaulle**. On your left is the **old port**, where boats leave for the **Iles de Lérins**. If you continue straight beyond the port on **Allés de la Liberté**, you'll reach a tree-shaded area where flowers are sold in the morning, *boules* is played in the afternoon, and a flea market is held on

Saturday. If instead of continuing straight from the square you turn inland, you'll quickly come to **Rue Meynadier**. Turn left. This is the old main street, which has many eighteenth-century houses—now boutiques and speciality food shops, where you can buy exotic foods and ship them home. (Be sure to stop at **Number 53** for ice cream; best bet is La Marmite du Diable—a "devil's dish" laced with cocoa and nougat.) **Rue Meynadier** leads to a covered market, **Marché Forville**. Ahead of you is **Le Susquet**, the fortress in the center of medieval Cannes, and narrow, steep streets leading to a tower with a lovely view.

Shopping

Rue d'Antibes, a few blocks behind the Croisette, is one of the coast's most glamorous shopping streets. At **Saint Laurent** (Number 21) you can pay $950 for an evening dress. **Clairefontaine-Maiffret** (Number 31) sells chocolates and candied everything. **Rimay** (Number 46 Rue d'Antibes) is well known for perfumes. **Miss Apollinaire** (Number 62) is a popular boutique for Saint Laurent's second line, at affordable prices. Other boutiques are on nearby streets such as **Notre Dame** and **Rue des États-Unis**. Many, such as **Brutus** (13 Rue Notre Dame), are for men. The *Riviera Guide* insists that **Alexandra** (Rond Point Duboys d'Angers) is the Number One boutique.

The most exclusive shops are along the **Croisette**. Some of Paris's most fashionable boutiques have branches in the **Gray d'Albion** (17 La Croisette). **Cartier** is at Number 57; **Van Cleef et Arpels** is at Number 61. If the prices make you dizzy, buzz over to the flea market on Saturday.

Swimming

Of the public beaches, **Plage du Midi**, to the west of the old harbor, is best in the afternoon; **Plage Gazagnaire**, to the east of the new port, is best in the morning. Between the two are private beaches where anyone can swim for under $10—a fee that includes a mattress, a sun umbrella, and waiters who will take your orders for lunch. As elsewhere along the Riviera, each section of the beach has its own character. An older, Middle Eastern crowd, for instance, gathers at the **Plage (Beach) Gray d'Albion**; the prettiest boys, says the *Riviera Guide*, are at **Ondine**.

Sports

For **deep-sea fishing**, call Hotel Sofitel-Méditerranée. Tel. 93.39.00.84. For golf, try the **Golf Club de Cannes-Mandelieu** (Tel. 93.49.55.39) or the **Golf Country Club de Cannes-Mougins** (Tel. 93.75.79.13). Ask your hotel for help.

For **tennis**, ask hotels to reserve a court at **Complexe Sportif Mont-fleury** or the **Gallia Tennis Club**. Lessons are served up at the **Cannes Tennis Club** (11 Rue Lacour. Tel. 93.43.58.85).

Sailboats and **motorboats** are rented at **Sun Way** (Port de la Napoule. Tel. 93.93.03.04). For **windsurfers**, try the **Centre Nautique Municipal** (9 Rue Esprit-Violet. Tel. 93.43.83.48).

The fastest way to get around locally is by moped or motorbike. For rentals try **Cannes Location Rent**, Tel. 93.39.46.15; **Cycles Rémy**, Tel. 93.43.44.46, or **Cycles Corot**, Tel. 93.39.22.82.

Excursions

You, like St. Honorat almost 1,500 years ago, may want to visit the peaceful **Lerins Islands** (Iles de Lérins) to escape the crowds. The ferry takes 15 minutes to **Sainte-Marguerite**, 30 to **Saint-Honorat**.

Sainte-Marguerite, the larger of the two, is an island of wooded hills, with a tiny main street lined with fishermen's houses. Visitors enjoy peaceful walks through a forest of enormous eucalyptus trees and parasol pines. Paths wind through a dense undergrowth of tree heathers, rosemary, and thyme. The main attraction is the dank cell in **Fort Royal** where the Man in the Iron Mask was imprisoned (1687–98) before going to the Bastille, where he died in 1703. The mask which he always wore was in fact made of velvet. Was he the illegitimate brother of Louis XIV or Louis XIII's son-in-law? No one knows.

Saint-Honorat is wilder but more tranquil than its sister island. It was named for a hermit who came to escape his followers; but when he founded a monastery here in 410, his disciples followed and the monastery became one of the most powerful in all Christendom. A pope was among the pilgrims who came to walk barefoot around the island. It's still worth taking this two-hour walk to the old fortified monastery, where noble Gothic arcades are arranged around a central courtyard. Next door to the "new" nineteenth-century monastery (open on request) is a shop where the monks sell handicrafts, lavender scent, and a home-brewed liqueur called Lerina.

Dining

You may have great success with a classical or nouvelle meal, but your best bet, as a rule, is to stick with simply prepared seafood.

Le Royal Gray (E, Gray d'Albion Hotel, 38 Rue des Serbes. Tel.

93.68.54.54) gets two stars from Michelin for an imaginative nouvelle menu that includes rack of lamb with fresh herbs, fresh salmon salad marinated in ginger on a bed of vegetables, prawn salad with orange dressing, and duck aiguillette with apple sauce. For dessert, succumb to the hot walnut cake.

At **La Reine Pedauque** (E, 6 Rue Maréchal-Joffre. Tel. 93.39.40.91) reliable classical meals are served in a room with oil paintings, brassware hanging from the ceiling, and velvet-upholstered chairs. Specialties include pepper-filet in wine or cream sauce, ris de veau in a pastry shell, and filet d'agneau en croute.

The atmosphere at **Le Festival** (E/M, 52 Boulevard Croisette. Tel. 93.38.04.81) is busy and gay—exactly what you'd expect from a restaurant across from the Palais des Festivals. Lunchtime is best. Specialties include salmon à la menthe and pastries.

La Poêle d'Or (M, 23 Rue des États-Unis. Tel. 93.39.77.65) is very plain, perhaps a bit somber, but it has a solid reputation for dishes such as mousseline of trout and chicken in a creamed morelle sauce.

Chez Félix (M, 63 Boulevard Croisette. Tel. 93.94.00.61) is popular with the film folks and with those who don't mind paying for the ambiance of the Croisette.

La Mirabelle (M, 24 Rue Saint-Maxime. Tel. 93.38.72.75) is a popular bistro in the old quarter. The limited menu includes pastas with Saint Pierre fish, salad with foie gras and honey, and homemade sorbets.

Mère Besson (M, 13 Rue Frères-Pradignac. Tel. 93.39.59.24) is a crowded, fashionable Provençal restaurant with regional specialties.

At **Au Bec Fin** (I, 12 Rue 24-Août. Tel. 93.38.35.86), the owner and his son turn out simple, homemade dishes—thick steaks, grilled fish with fennel, salad niçoise, homemade tarts—in a fun, crowded restaurant near the train station.

Birnbaum says **La Pizza** (3 Quai St.-Pierre. Tel. 93.39.22.56), on a terrace overlooking the old harbor, serves the best pizza in town. The *Riviera Guide* says its the worst.

Part of the **Cannes Experience** is to drive out of town for dinner, to the hills or to other resorts along the coast. Here are some possibilities: *In Golfe Juan* (about 15 minutes east of Cannes on the coastal road to Antibes):

Chez Tetou (M, à la plage. Tel. 93.63.71.16) is a friendly, informal restaurant with wooden tables on a lovely terrace. Michelin gives a star for what some consider the best sole meunière and bouillabaisse on the coast.

In La Napoule (about 10 minutes west of Cannes on the coastal road):
L'Oasis (E, Rue Jean-Honoré Carle. Tel. 93.49.95.52) is one of the few restaurants in France to get three stars from Michelin. Specialties include prawn salad with caviar, mint and Iranian yogurt, lobster with Thai herbs (citronella, ginger, curry, and apples), and squid stuffed with truffles and green asparagus.

In Mougins (a hill town about 15 minutes north of Cannes on the road to Grasse):
Le Moulin de Mougins (E, at Notre-Dame-de-Vie, Route D3, 1.5 miles southeast of Moulins. Tel. 93.75.78.24) is another three-star Michelin restaurant—one of the best known in the country, where you can expect patrician treatment—and prices. An inventive nouvelle cuisine is served in a converted olive mill, with such specialties as lobster fricassee, escallop of fresh salmon, and cold, wild-strawberry soufflé.

Le Relais à Mougins (E, Place Marie. Tel. 93.90.03.47) is another favorite (though some say it rests too heavily on its reputation) that has been under the supervision of André Surmain of New York's Lutèce. Mougins is a lovely old town; consider coming here for lunch, when prices are less dear.

The last of the ruling three is **L'Amandier** (E, Place Lamy. Tel. 93.90.00.91), which gets two stars from Michelin. The chef and the old-olive-mill ambiance are the same as at Le Moulin de Mougins, but the prices are lower. The nouvelle menu includes a creamy mussel and oyster soup with saffron, crayfish bisque, sea bass, young rabbit pâté, farm cheeses, and homemade tarts.

Bistro de Mougins (I, Place du Village, Tel. 93.75.78.34) features such regional dishes as beet pie, sardines with mint, stuffed rabbit, guinea hen with cabbage, and a good selection of local cheeses. The low prices keep the restaurant crowded.

Nightlife

If you want to find out what Cannes is all about, splurge with a drink at the **Carlton Hotel Bar** (58 La Croisette) after 9 P.M. The center ring is at the **Studio Circus** (48 Boulevard de la République). Popular discos include the **Jackpot** (at the Palm Beach Casino), **Jane's** (in the Gray d'Albion), and the **Galaxy** (in the Palais des Festivals).

There's gambling at the **Casino of the Palais des Festivals** from November through May, starting at 4 P.M.; and at the **Palm Beach Casino** from June through October, starting at 5 P.M. Bring a jacket and your passport.

Lodging

Since Cannes exists for its tourists, hotels in season aren't cheap; expect to pay $70 to $200 a night for a room for two on or near the Croisette. If you're on a budget, best bets are the smaller hotels closer to the train station.

The **Carlton** (L, 58 Boulevard Croisette. Tel. 93.68.91.68) has been modernized but still retains the feeling of a luxurious Belle Epoque hotel. The west wing is quieter, with the best views.

The **Majestic** (L, 6 Boulevard Croisette. Tel. 93.68.91.00) is another one of the grand old hotels, which people who know put just a notch below the Carlton. There's a great heated seawater pool in a palm grove. Best bets are the renovated rooms.

Montfleury-Intercontinental (L, 24 Avenue Beauséjour. Tel. 93.68.91.50) has 235 rooms, ten tennis courts, two heated pools, an ice-skating rink, and three restaurants on a nine-acre hillside estate with great views. Its remoteness will be a plus or minus, depending on your priorities.

The Middle Eastern owners redid the **Gray d'Albion** (L, 6 Rue États-Unis. Tel. 93.48.54.54) in 1981 with free video, bathroom phones, and other state-of-the-art amenities. The restaurant is one of the best in town.

Palma (M, 77 Boulevard Croisette. Tel. 93.94.22.16) is a small, less expensive hotel near the east end of the promenade. Rooms are small and bright.

Victoria (M/E, 122 Rue d'Antibes. Tel. 93.99.36.36) nestles among the fancy boutiques on the main shopping street. There's a garden with a small pool and 25 stylish rooms with electrically controlled shutters and other amenities.

Beau Séjour (M, 100 Rue Georges-Clemenceau. Tel. 93.39.63.00) has its own pool and garden not far from the beach.

For relatively low-priced hotels back from the beach, try **Roches Fleuries** (I, 92 Rue Georges-Clemenceau. Tel. 93.39.28.78), **Bristol** (I, 14 Rue Hoche. Tel. 93.39.10.66), near the station, or the somewhat more expensive **Cheval Blanc** (I, 3 Rue de-Maupassant. Tel. 93.39.88.60).

For Further Information

The **Information Center** (Services du Tourisme de la Ville de Cannes. Tel. 93.39.24.53) at the Palais des Festivals on the Croisette is open until midnight in season and helps with accommodations. There's a branch at the railroad station. Tel. 93.99.19.77.

✤ *CAP D'ANTIBES* (including *ANTIBES* and *JUAN-LES-PINS)*

Strictly speaking, Cap d'Antibes refers to the southern tip of the cape, but it has come to mean the entire peninsula, including even the resort towns of **Antibes** and **Juan-les-Pins**. Though we'll discuss the three together, be sure to distinguish among them, for each has its own distinctive character and clientele. On the eastern side of the cape is the village of **Antibes**, which boasts a Picasso Museum and, like Nice, a charming old section with restaurants, antique shops, and boutiques. You'll want to visit Antibes but probably not to stay, since it has no memorable hotels. On the western side of the cape, closer to Cannes, is the village of **Juan-les-Pins**, which has a shoreline backed by ferro-concrete high-rises where French families spend their two-week vacations. Visitors under twenty-five will enjoy the crowded public beaches and the neon night life, but others will have little reason to stay. The place to stay is on the cape itself —a lush and peaceful garden with sumptuous villas, guest houses, and hotels. Cannes is perhaps 20 minutes away, so you can take advantage of everything the city has to offer and then return here at night. If you're single or into crowds, stay in Cannes. But if you want to be alone with someone you want to be alone with—look no farther than Cap d'Antibes.

CAP D'ANTIBES

The main reason to visit the cape, even if you're not staying here, is to enjoy the view at **Pointe Bacon**; to walk through the **Thuret Gardens** (open 8 to 12:30 and 2 to 5:30; closed weekends); to have lunch or a swim at the exclusive **Hotel du Cap**; and to imagine yourself living in the palatial estates discreetly hidden behind hedges and trees.

Follow D2559 along the eastern shore to **Pointe Bacon**, where you should be able to see as far east as Nice and Cap Ferrat. Continue south along the eastern shore of the cape on **Boulevard de Bacon**, which merges with **Boulevard de la Garoupe**. At the end of the boulevard turn left to visit the **Hotel du Cap** (see under Lodging below), or turn right on **Boulevard F. Meilland** and right again on **Chemin des Nielles** to the top of the hill, where the road ends. There's a great view here, and a church, **La Garoupe**, which has two aisles, each built at a different time and dedicated to a different saint.

Return down **Chemin des Nielles** and make the first right on **Boulevard du Cap** to the **Thuret Gardens**. Created by a botanist in 1856, it contains exotic cacti, palms, mimosas, and some 141 species of eucalyptus.

Continue straight on **Boulevard du Cap** and make a left on **Chemin des Sables**. Bear right and return to Cannes, about 7 miles west on N7.

Dining

Many daytrippers have their limousines take them to lunch at the **Pavilion Eden Rock** (E, Boulevard Kennedy. Tel. 93.61.39.01), the restaurant of the exclusive **Hotel du Cap**. The cheery but elegant pavilion sits by itself on a grassy ledge, a short walk behind the hotel, at the very edge of the sea. The menu is nouvelle.

Auberge du Bacon (E, Boulevard Bacon. Tel. 93.61.50.02) is near Pointe Bacon, which you'll pass as you drive down the east shore of the cape. The bouillabaisse is, some say, the best on the coast. Seafood dishes are served on a terrace with a lovely view. Specialties include steamed bass, prawn salad, and grilled mullet.

Lodging

The best-known and most expensive resort on the Riviera is the **Hotel du Cap d'Antibes** (L, Boulevard Kennedy. Tel. 93.61.39.01). The elite of the world stay in this baronial, Second Empire-style resort, which is said to have a staff–guest ratio of one-to-one. The room I saw was about to be occupied by Jimmy Stewart; the *Who's Who* list of recent guests includes Henry Kissinger, Dustin Hoffman, and the members of Duran Duran. Charles Graves tells in his book *The Azure Coast* how George Raft walked down from the hotel to the pool with Norma Shearer, passing hairy-legged Charles Boyer. While Marlene Dietrich was checking out, Edward G. Robinson and Erich Maria Remarque were sitting at the bar—Robinson looking at himself, Remarque just looking glum. F. Scott Fitzgerald of course stayed here with Zelda and is said to have used the hotel as his model in *Tender Is the Night*.

That said, it should be added that the atmosphere today is a shade self-conscious. Daytrippers can pay to use the pool—which is great for them, but not for guests. The Pavilion, when I visited in May, was filled with loud Americans writing postcards home about being in such an exclusive place. A child would be an anomaly here—unless he were dressed in white, with knee-high socks. There is no library, no sequestered bar, no place to relax except at the pool and in the privacy of your room.

La Gardiole (I/M, Chemin de la Garoupe, Cap d'Antibes. Tel.

93.61.35.03) has 20 simple, quiet rooms among the pines, away from the sea.

Hotel Levant (M, à la Garoupe. Tel. 93.61.41.33) is a rectangular, motel-like building by the sea. It has no special charm, but is clean and new and very friendly.

✤ ANTIBES

What makes a visit to Antibes worthwhile are the picturesque old streets lined with shops and cafés, and the Picasso Museum.

The **Picasso Museum** (open from 10 to noon and 3 to 7; earlier closings off-season; closed Tuesdays) is housed in a Grimaldi castle overlooking the sea. Picasso had part of the castle at his disposal when he arrived on the Riviera in 1946. His output was extraordinary—some 145 works in six months; and most of what you'll see was produced during his first season here. Particularly noteworthy are his ceramics from Vallauris and his joyful Antibes paintings, inspired by the marine and mythological life of the Mediterranean. Don't miss them!

Just north of the museum is the **Church of the Immaculate Conception**, which has a valuable wooden crucifix (1447) in the choir and an early sixteenth-century altarpiece by Louis Bréa in the south transept.

From either the church or museum walk inland one block and turn left to the colorful marketplace at **Cours Masséna**. Ahead of you is **Rue de la Touraque**. Spend an hour in this area, strolling through the streets of the old town, among the antique and pastry shops.

Antibes is the rose capital of Europe. Some 625 acres of carnations, tulips, and gladioli grow here, too. Anyone who loves color will want to visit the flower market near the **Vauban Bridge** (Pont Vauban).

Dining

La Bonne Auberge (E, north of Antibes on N7—near La Brague. Tel. 93.33.36.65) is very expensive, but is one of the most famous restaurants on the coast. Dinner, a blend of classic and nouvelle, is served either in a Provençal dining room or on a flowery terrace. Specialties include lobster soup, artichoke salad with lobster, and grilled bass (loup).

Les Vieux Murs (M, Promenade Amiral-de-Grasse. Tel. 93.34.06.73) sits on the ramparts close to the sea. The decor—stucco walls, arched ceilings—is regional. The classical menu includes fish soup and lobster thermidor.

L'Oursin (I, 16 Place République. Tel. 93.34.13.46), on the edge of the old town, is a crowded family restaurant with little atmosphere. But it has a solid reputation for fresh seafood and reasonable prices.

Auberge Provençale (M, 61 Place Nationale. Tel. 93.34.13.24) is located on a lovely old square behind the Picasso Museum. Specialties include smoked trout, coq au vin, and beef filet.

La Marguerite (M, 11 Rue Sadi Carnot. Tel. 93.34.08.27) has white-lacquered paneling and lots of flowers. Prices are reasonable, particularly for the fixed menu. Try the veal and rice salad, stuffed chicken, fresh fish, and regional cheeses.

For Further Information

The **tourist office** is at 11 Place Général-de-Gaulle, Antibes. Tel. 93.33.95.64.

✤ JUAN-LES-PINS

Juan-les-Pins splashed into life in the 1920s, thanks to its mile-long beach (an improvement on the man-made beach at Cannes) and its amenities. The ambiance is—with two notable exceptions—strictly fast-food. If you're alone and don't want to be, hang out on the beach and wait for night, when the bar and disco lights outshine the stars.

Dining

Juan-les-Pins is only 10 minutes from Cannes by train—20 by car—so you may want to come for dinner at the **Terrasse Restaurant** (E, Avenue Georges Gallice. Tel. 93.61.20.37) in the **Juana Hotel**. The *Riviera Guide* calls the chef the most gifted young nouvelle chef on the coast. Specialties include crayfish bisque with garlic, lamb casserole with milk, and lobster Saint-Jacques.

For reasonably priced meals try **Girasole** (I, 17 Avenue Maupassant. Tel. 93.61.22.39), which specializes in fresh fish and regional dishes.

Lodging

The two luxury-class hotels in Juan-les-Pins have no trouble filling their rooms in-season, but it's not easy to understand why. What use is elegance in discoland?

Most tasteful of the two is the recently renovated **Juana** (L, Avenue Gallice-la-Pinède. Tel. 93.61.08.70), where men can sit in their rooms and watch the bare-breasted women floating in the heated pool below. Though hidden behind hedges, the pool sits at the very edge of a busy road near the center of town. The restaurant enjoys a first-class reputation.

The other luxury hotel is **Belles Rives** (L, Boulevard Baudoin. Tel. 93.61.02.79). Rooms are rather small and basic, but the location is lovely, with a stone terrace overlooking the harbor.

For a budget hotel, try **Eden** (I, 16 Avenue Gallet. Tel. 93.61.05.20), located between the train station and the beach.

❧ *SAINT-TROPEZ*

How to Get There. There's only one main road from Sainte-Maxime to Saint-Tropez, and in season the 8.5-mile trip can take 2 hours. If you're planning to drive down from Cannes for the day, be sure to leave in the early morning and to return in the early afternoon or late at night. Stick to **Autoroute A8** and avoid the coast as long as possible. The worst time to come is on summer weekends, when you're competing with the rest of France. Best bet is to take a hydrofoil from Cannes or Saint-Raphaël and avoid the road altogether. If you want to combine trips to the **Esterel** (see pages 56–58) and Saint-Tropez, drive southwest along the coast from Cannes to **Saint-Raphaël** and take the hydrofoil from there. Make arrangements through any travel agency or hotel. Cabs in Saint-Tropez are available at 94.97.05.27. For bus information, call 94.97.01.88.

Old money never came to Saint-Tropez, but Brigitte Bardot did. She came with her director Roger Vadim in 1956 to film *And God Created Woman,* and the resort has never been the same. Actually, the village was "discovered" by Maupassant and by the French painter Paul Signac (1863–1935), who came in 1892 and brought his friends—Matisse, Bonnard, and others. What attracted them was the pure, radiant light, and the serenity and colors of the landscape. Colette moved into a villa here between the wars and contributed to its notoriety. When the cinema people staked their claim in the 1950s, Saint-Tropez became Saint-Trop *(trop* in French means "too much").

Anything associated with the past seems either detestable or absurd in Saint-Tropez, so you may not want to hear the story of how it got its name. In 68 A.D. a Roman soldier named Torpes from Pisa was beheaded for professing his Christian faith in the presence of the Emperor Nero. The headless body was put in a boat between a dog and a cock and drifted out to sea. The body eventually floated ashore, perfectly preserved, still watched over by the two animals. The buried remains became a place of pilgrimage, which by the fourth century was called Saint-

Tropez. In the late fifteenth century, under the Genovese, it became a small independent republic.

Today Bardot is middle-aged, and so is Saint-Tropez. Most would say Bardot has aged more gracefully.

Whatever celebrities are here are packed away in villas. The people you'll see are folks like you and me—many beautiful, many balancing precariously on the far edge of youth, many seriously past their prime. The beaches are filled with every imaginable type of human animal: aggressively cheerful volleyball players searching for meaningful one-night relationships, supergirls with Cartier bracelets, golden boys with big dogs, aspiring Bardots, college girls with organic faces, middle-aged men with mirrored shades, bare-breasted mothers with children and dogs. The atmosphere is part Benetton, part Tarzan-and-Jane. In summer the population swells from 7,000 to 64,000.

Off-season is the time to come, but even in summer you can find reasons to stay. The soft, sandy beaches are the best on the coast. Beauty is beauty—even if it wears gold chains. Take an early morning stroll along the harbor or down the narrow medieval streets—the rest of the world will still be comatose from the Night Before—and you'll see just how pretty Saint-Tropez is, with its tiny squares and its rich, pastel-colored houses bathed in light. There's a weekend's worth of trendy boutiques to explore—to be delighted by or shocked at—and many cute cafés where you can sit under colored awnings sipping wine and feeling very French. The restored harbor front has a reputable art museum. Five minutes from town and you're in a green world of vineyards and fields, where you'll see nothing more lascivious than a butterfly fluttering around some chestnut leaves or a grapevine clinging to a farmhouse wall. Above the fertile fields are mountains crowned with medieval villages, where you can come at dusk for wild strawberry tarts and fabulous views. Perhaps it's the soft light, perhaps the rich fields and faded pastels, but nowhere else along the coast will you experience so completely the magic of Provence.

Near the waterfront is the **Chapelle de l'Annonciade** (open from 10 to noon and from 3 to 7 P.M.; to 6 off-season; closed Tuesdays), a well-known museum of works by Impressionist and post-Impressionist painters who loved Saint-Tropez: Vlaminck, Braque, Seurat, Bonnard, Dufy, Rouault, and others.

Shopping

There are many boutiques at the port, in the old town around the **Hôtel de Ville**, and along the narrow streets between **Quai Suffren** and

Place des Lices. Place des Lices has a market for clothing and antiques on Tuesday and Saturday morning. The *Riviera Guide* recommends Façonnable (Passage Gambetta. Tel. 94.97.29.98) for that Italian-English look, with open shirts to show off your chains and hairy chest. For silk lingerie and rubber dresses by Japanese designers, try the trendy boutiques on **Rue Sibilli.**

Beaches

Beaches close to town—**Plage des Greniers** and the **Bouillabaisse**—are great for families; but holiday people snub them, preferring a 6-mile sandy crescent at **Les Salins** and **Pampellone.** These beaches are about 2 miles from town, so it helps to have a car, motorbike, or bicycle (see below for rentals).

The most magnificent stretch of beach is divided into a number of private beaches, each with its own atmosphere and clientele. **Tahiti,** for instance, tends to get a thirty- to thirty-five-year-old singles crowd. According to the *Riviera Guide,* you'll feel out of place at **Club 55** in cutoffs; **Acqua** beach is popular with transvestites; **Blouch** is invaded by middle-aged Germans; and **La Voile Rouge** is a popular hunting ground for morose women over forty. For under $10 you'll get a mattress and sun umbrella—then you're free to wander up and down the beach at will. Each beach has its own lunch area open to the public. The one at Club 55 began as the canteen for the film crew of *And God Created Women.* If you've never tried to eat a tuna sandwich on rye surrounded by a bevy of topless women, you're in for a treat.

Bikes

To prepare yourself for Muscle Beach, rent a bike at **Peretti** (2 Avenue du Général-LeClerc. Tel. 94.97.00.11) and bike to the beach every day.

Windsurfing

Rentals for windsurfing at Tahiti and Pampelonne beaches are available from the **Surfing Shop** (Avenue du Général-LeClerc. Tel. 94.97.40.52) or **Windsurf** (Rue Paul-Roussel. Tel. 94.97.44.02).

Tennis

There are clay courts at **Tennis de Saint-Tropez,** Tel. 94.97.36.39; **Hotel dei Marres,** Tel. 94.97.26.68; and **Tennis-Club des Salins,** Tel. 94.97.44.84.

Excursions

Visitors seem to enjoy a trip through **Port-Grimaud**, a modern architect's idea of a Provençal fishing village-cum-Venice, built out into the gulf for the yachting crowd—each house with its own mooring. Particularly appealing are the harmonious pastel colors, which have weathered nicely, and the graceful bridges over the canals.

From Saint-Tropez take **D93** south about 7 miles to the old Provençal market town of **Ramatuelle**. The ancient houses are huddled together on the slope of a rocky spur 440 feet above the sea. The central square has a seventeenth-century church and a huge three-hundred-year-old elm. Surrounding the square are narrow, twisting streets with medieval archways and vaulted passages.

From Ramatuelle, follow signs to the old village of **Gassin**, which is less than 2 miles away. The ride is lovely, through vineyards and woods, and takes you over the highest point of the peninsula (1,070 feet), where you can stop and enjoy a splendid view. The perched village of Gassin, with its venerable old houses and its twelfth-century Romanesque church, has somehow managed to maintain its medieval appearance. The best time to visit is in the late afternoon, when the shadows deepen and the tourists have gone home. Find yourself a table at an outdoor café, order a fruit tart, and watch the sunlight turn the fields to gold. From Gassin, return to Saint-Tropez or continue back along the coast to Sainte-Maxime and Cannes.

Dining

Saint-Tropez has many charming restaurants, but no great ones. Best bets are restaurants big on atmosphere, that specialize in fresh fish.

If film stars like Catherine Deneuve leave the privacy of their villas, it's to dine in **Le Mas de Chastelas** (E, Route de Gassin. Tel. 94.56.90.11), a restored eighteenth-century manor house. Specialties include vegetable mousse with tomato and basil purée, fish ravioli with saffron in a sea urchin cream sauce, and mullet with red wine.

Many say a meal at **Byblos** (E, Avenue Paul-Signac. Tel. 94.97.00.04) is worth the giddy price. Specialties include sea bream and lamb in basil.

Les Mouscardins (E, Rue Portalet. Tel. 94.97.01.53) is a busy Provençal-type restaurant in the old city, serving such local favorites as bouillabaisse and grilled sea bass.

The busy waterfront is lined with small restaurants where you can sit in tiny back rooms or people-watch in front, beneath colored awnings.

L'Escale (M, Quai Jean-Jaurès. Tel. 94.97.00.63) is the best (try the bouillabaisse) and busiest. Families come at 8, singles at 10. Also near the port is Le Girelier (M, Au Port. Tel. 94.97.03.87), offering fishy fare at reasonable prices. Rascasse (M, Quai Jean-Jaurès. Tel. 94.97.04.47) has a low-priced menu.

Join the locals in the quieter, old part of town at Les Café des Arts (M, Place des Lices. Tel. 94.97.02.05). The one-price menu includes zucchini, stuffed eggplant, veal in wine sauce, grilled fish, and all the wine you can drink.

Ponche (M/E, Rue Remparts. Tel. 94.97.09.29) is a chic but peaceful terrace restaurant with such specialties as saffron mussel soup, giant shrimp in tarragon sauce, lamb stew, and a homemade lemon pie. The fixed menu is reasonably priced.

Pizzeria Romana (M, Chemin des Conquetes. Tel. 94.97.10.50) is a popular eaterie with a more ambitious menu and higher prices than its name implies. The fresh pasta is tops.

After Hours

The back bar at L'Escale, along the harbor, gets the pick of the pack. The mating cries at Ponche (Rue Remparts) are a few decibels lower.

Les Caves du Roy, in the Hotel Byblos, is Saint-Tropez's answer to New York's fashionable Palladium or area discos.

The golden youth gather at L'Aphrodisiaque (Rue Allard)—at least those who are admitted.

Lodging

The most important choice is whether to stay in the village or out in the countryside. The village is fine if you plan to do a lot of partying. Hotels outside of town tend to be small, quiet, and family run—perfect for families or couples, particularly those with cars.

Le Mas de Chastelas (E, Quartier Bertaud, Route de Ramatuelle. Tel. 94.56.09.11) is a renovated seventeenth-century manor house in a rural setting just outside of town, with a heated pool, tennis courts, and sophisticated dining.

Le Byblos (L, Avenue Paul-Signac. Tel. 94.97.00.04) is a smart, flashy hotel-village where the gold-chain set should feel right at home. The look is New York Casbah, with Persian carpets on the dining room ceiling, a genuine leopard-skin bar, raw stone and brick walls, and lots of heavy damask and hammered brass. A real conversation piece, with an imaginative use of space. There's also a sauna, an exercise room, a palm court with a pool, two discos, and a hairdresser. Any wonder the clientele is 30 percent American?

Levant (M/E, Route Salins. Tel. 94.97.33.33), located just out of town, has 28 modern rooms, a heated pool, and a beautiful garden.

La Ponche (M, Place du Révelin. Tel. 94.97.02.53) is a charming old inn in the old part of town, with 23 tasteful rooms, some with balconies. Expect noise till 11 P.M., or ask for a room in back.

L'Ermitage (M, Avenue Paul-Signac. Tel. 94.97.52.33) is next door to Le Byblos, but the ambiance is more subdued. It's one of the few hotels with a view of the town.

Lou Troupelen (M, Chemin Vendanger. Tel. 94.97.44.88) is a modernized farmhouse with gardens, not far from the beach or town.

Tahiti (M, Tahiti Beach. Tel. 94.97.18.02) is right on the beach, near a Polynesian-looking statue of a man with a green, red-tipped penis, looking out to sea.

There are several small, family-run hotels among the farms and vineyards along the road to Tahiti Beach—one of the most tranquil settings on the Riviera. **La Figuière** (M, Route de Tahiti. Tel. 94.97.18.21) is the only one with a restaurant, tennis, and a pool. **Saint-Vincent** (M, Route de Tahiti. Tel. 94.97.36.90) is pleasant and friendly, with a pool, and vineyards outside the door. **La Ferme d'Augustin** (M/I, Route de Tahiti. Tel. 94.97.18.12) has no pool or air conditioning, but the price is right and so is its location—a peaceful oasis just a hundred yards from the commotion on the beach.

For Further Information

The tourist office is on the main road into town at 23 Avenue Général-LeClerc, Saint-Tropez. Tel. 94.97.41.21. There's another office along the harbor (Quai Jean-Jaurès. Tel. 94.97.45.21).

EXCURSIONS

Here are some of the most worthwhile excursions from the Nice area, (including **Beaulieu** and **Cap Ferrat**), and from the **Cannes** area (including **Cap d'Antibes**).

EXCURSION 1

♦ *PEILLON*

How to Get There. Peillon and Monte Carlo are both about 12 miles east of Nice and can be combined in a single excursion from Cannes or Nice. Monte Carlo is along the coast; Peillon is about 6 miles inland. From Nice take D2204. Turn right on D21. Turn right, up the mountain to Peillon. If you're returning to Nice, return the way you came. If you're continuing to Monte Carlo, return to D21. Turn right. Turn right again on D53 to the medieval town of Peille. Continue south on D53 to Monaco.

To picture Peillon, just close your eyes and imagine a fortified medieval town perched on a craggy mountaintop more than 1,000 feet above the sea. Of all the perched villages along the Riviera, Peillon is the most spectacular and the least spoiled. Unchanged since the Middle Ages, the village has only a few narrow streets and many steps and covered alleys. There's really nothing to do here but look—which is why the tour buses stay away. Some fifty families live in Peillon—including professionals from Paris who think it's chic summering in a genuine medieval village and artists who sincerely want to escape the craziness of the world below. Visit the studio of a very talented and well-known French sculptor; visit the **White Penitants' Chapel** (key available at the Auberge); spend a half hour exploring the ancient streets, and be on your way. Stay for lunch or dinner at the charming **Auberge de la Madone** (Peillon 06440, L'Escarene, Alpes-Maritimes. Tel. 93.91.91.17). The ideal arrangement is to arrive in the late afternoon and spend the night at this lovely, family-run *auberge* (inn), far away from the traffic and heat along the coast.

♦ *ROQUEBRUNE*

How to Get There. If you haven't seen enough medieval towns, continue south on D53 (en route from Peillon to Monte Carlo) and then take the **Upper Corniche** road to Roquebrune. From here, head south to Monaco.

The ancient town of Roquebrune is spread out along the slopes. Shops are filled with the wares of painters and artisans. The Carolingian castle was restored in the early sixteenth century by the Grimaldis. The keep is the oldest in Provence, with walls from 6 to 13 feet thick.

Dining

Vistaero (E, Grand Corniche, 2 miles from Roquebrune. Tel. 93.35.01.50) gets five stars from Fielding. A good deal of what you pay for is the fabulous view.

EXCURSION 2

⚜ *VILLEFRANCHE*

How to Get There. Villefranche is on the coastal road (N98, the Lower Corniche), only 2.4 miles east of Nice on the way to Cap Ferrat and Beaulieu.

The harbor town of **Villefranche**, only about 10 minutes from Nice or Cap Ferrat, is a miniature version of old Marseilles, with steep narrow streets—one, **Rue Obscure,** an actual tunnel—winding down to the sea. The town is a stage set of brightly colored houses—orange buildings with lime-green shutters, yellow buildings with ice-blue shutters—the sort of place where *Fanny* could have been filmed. If you're staying in Nice, include Villefranche on a tour of Cap Ferrat. To see the Cocteau Chapel (see below), you'll need to arrive by 4 P.M. If you can skip the chapel, best bet is to come at sundown (for dinner, perhaps) and enjoy an hour's walk around the harbor, when the sun turns the soft pastels to gold.

The seventeenth-century **St. Michael Church** has a strikingly realistic Christ, carved of boxwood by an unknown convict. The **Chapel of Saint-Pierre-des-Pêcheurs,** known as the **Cocteau Chapel** (open in summer from 9 to 12, and 2 to 4:30; off-season, from 9 to 12, and 2:30 to 7) is a small Romanesque chapel once used for storing fishing nets, which the French writer and painter Jean Cocteau decorated in 1957. Visitors walk through the flames of the Apocalypse (represented by staring eyes on either side of the door) and enter a room filled with frescoes of St. Peter, gypsies, and the women of Villefranche.

Dining

Near St. Michael Church is **La Campanette** (I, 2 Rue de Baron de Brès. Tel. 93.80.79.98), an inexpensive bistro with turn-of-the-century decor, serving such meals as fish ravioli in shellfish sauce, mussels in pastry with chicory, and chicken with clementines.

Somewhat more expensive is **Mère Germaine** (M, Quai Corbet. Tel. 93.01.71.39), which overlooks the port.

EXCURSION 3: *Cagnes, Villeneuve-Loubet, Saint-Paul-de-Vence, Tourrette-sur-Loup, Gorges du Loup, Grasse*

How to Get There. From either Cannes or Nice take Autoroute AB to the Cagnes exit. The route is described below.

This is a half-day or full-day trip that takes you to the Renoir Museum, the Escoffier Museum, some world-famous perfumeries, and two beautiful medieval towns where artists and craftsmen sell their wares.

♨ CAGNES

There are actually three "Cagnes"—Le-Gros-de-Cagnes, the seaside resort on the coast; Cagnes Ville, the modern commercial section; and Haut-de-Cagnes, the old town leading up to the castle. From Cagnes Ville follow signs to the Renoir Museum.

The **Renoir Museum** (open mid-April to mid-October from 2:30 to 6:30; off-season, from 2 to 5; closed Tuesdays) is at Les Collettes, the house which Renoir built for himself in 1908 and where he spent the last twelve years of his life. The word "museum" is really misleading. One of his well-known canvases, *Les Collettes Landscape*, is on view on the ground floor, and his bronze statue of *Venus* stands in the garden surrounded by fruit trees. But what you'll remember most are Renoir's studios, preserved just as he left them, and the gardens where he walked and painted. The sense of his presence is overwhelming as you stroll among the olive trees, gazing out across the fields through the most magical, luminescent light at the ancient town of Cagnes, rising in the distance like a fortress in a dream.

If time is limited and you're planning to visit Saint-Paul-de-Vence and Tourrette-sur-Loup, consider seeing Haut-de-Cagnes only from Renoir's house and continuing to the Escoffier Museum. Haut-de-Cagnes is a lovely old medieval village, but it doesn't have the craft shops you'll see in the other villages; and the streets are very steep and look down on a modern town. If you do decide to visit Haut-de-Cagnes—it's only a few minutes' drive from Renoir's house—park near the top of the town, at the Castle Museum.

The **Castle Museum** (open mid-April through September from 10 to 12, and 2 to 6; off-season, to 5; closed Tuesdays) is a feudal castle restored by the Grimaldis when they lived here from the fourteenth century to the French Revolution, at which time it was looted and sold. The marble stairway, inspired by the one at Fontainebleau, leads to staterooms with ornately painted ceilings and notable collections of objets d'art and paintings. The throne room is most sumptuous. In the cellar the olive gets its due in the Museum of the Olive Tree. On the second floor is a Museum of Modern Mediterranean Art.

Dining

Le Cagnard (E, Rue Pontis-Long, Hauts-de-Cagnes. Tel. 93.20.73.21) gets four stars from Fielding for a nouvelle cuisine menu that includes duck liver pâté, crayfish in sauterne au gratin, and veal with mushrooms. The fixed-price lunch is reasonably priced.

Josy-Jo (M, 8 Place Planastel, Hauts-de-Cagnes. Tel. 93.20.68.76) is well-known for its regional cuisine, including duck pâté, calf's liver, mutton, and a dessert of lemon mousse.

Peintres (I, 71 Montée Borgade, Hauts-de-Cagnes. Tel. 93.20.83.08) has lovely views and reasonable prices.

✤ VILLENEUVE-LOUBET

How to Get There. From Cagnes Ville (the modern city below the old town) take Avenue de la Gare and D2085 (Avenue de Grasse) less than 2 miles to the Escoffier Museum. If this doesn't interest you, go directly from Cagnes to Saint-Paul-de-Vence.

The Escoffier Museum (open daily from 2 to 6; closed Mondays) is the birthplace of the king of chefs, Auguste Escoffier (1846–1935). It includes a Provençal kitchen with every sort of cooking utensil imaginable; mementos of his career as head chef of the Carlton in London and as creator of Peach Melba; and some fifteen thousand menus dating back to 1820.

✤ SAINT-PAUL-DE-VENCE

How to Get There. Take D2 north about 7 miles.

The atmosphere in this perfect gem of a town is Medieval Chic. None of the hill towns is better preserved. Not even the hordes of tourists—for which the village now exists—can destroy its ancient charm. You can walk the narrow, cobbled streets in perhaps 15 minutes, but you'll need another hour to explore the shops—mostly galleries selling second-rate landscape paintings, but also a few serious studios and giftshops selling everything from candles to dolls, dresses, and hand-dipped chocolate strawberries. Best bet is to visit in the late afternoon, when the tour buses are gone, and enjoy a drink among the Klees and Picassos in the Colombe D'Or (see Dining below). You'll want to light a candle in the twelfth-century Gothic church to relieve its wonderful gloom. The treasury is rich in twelfth- to fifteenth-century pieces, including processional crosses, reliquaries, and an enamel Virgin and Child.

The Maeght Foundation (open July and August from 10 to 12:30 and 3 to 7; off-season, to 6) is one of the world's most famous small museums of modern art. Founded in 1964 by Aimé Maeght, a Paris art dealer, and his wife, it sits on a grassy hill a 10-minute walk above Saint-Paul-de-Vence. In addition to regular exhibits, the museum has a permanent collection of ceramics by Miró, mobiles by Calder, bronze figures by Giacometti, and stained-glass windows by Braque. Check for concerts in summer.

Dining

You'll be paying for your meals or drinks at the Colombe D'Or (M, Place de Gaulle. Tel. 93.32.80.02) with cash or cards; Picasso, Klee, Dufy, Utrillo, and others—all friends of the former owner—paid with paintings, which hang today on the walls above the tables. What a vast difference there is between seeing a Calder in a museum and lunching on a terrace with a Calder mobile swaying among the lemon trees. So this is what it means to live with art! Unless you like being an Ugly American, don't visit without having a drink or stopping for lunch or dinner. The restaurant has a reputation for simple, adequate meals in an unforgettable setting. The building has great warmth and character, even though it was constructed only after World War II.

Another lovely spot for lunch is Orangers (E, Rue Colle. Tel. 93.32.80.95). Try a shellfish dish served on a peaceful terrace in an olive grove. Less expensive is the Auberge du Soleil (M, Tel. 93.32.80.60) a small inn serving regional cuisine.

Lodging

For a "complete" Riviera experience, spend at least a night or two in or near one of the medieval hill towns, close to nature and away from the frenetic pace along the coast. Peillon (see page 345) is completely isolated; stay there and you'll dine in the hotel, take a walk perhaps, and go to bed. Saint-Paul-de-Vence is more centrally located—a great starting point for excursions to the interior—and surrounded by several first-class restaurants and hotels.

First choice for people who can afford luxury and good taste is Le

Chateau du Domaine St. Martin (L, Route Coursegoules, Vence. Tel. 93.58.02.02). The castle, complete with pool and tennis courts, sits on a 35-acre Relais & Châteaux property overlooking Vence. Rooms are exquisitely decorated with antiques, needlepoint, and brocade. Visitors are not credit card numbers but guests in a private castle. Rooms in the tower are smaller and less expensive, but decorated with the same loving attention to detail. The formal dining room is one of the best along the coast. (At the table next to mine was Frank Perdue—eating fish.)

Colombe D'Or (see Dining, page 349), only steps from the fortified town, is a conversation piece. Young couples, intellectuals, artists—anyone who likes the ambiance of a country inn will feel at home here. The 14 rooms are booked far in advance. Staying here, you can explore Saint-Paul-de-Vence in the early morning, or under a full moon, when the only footfalls are your own.

On a huge wooded estate a short drive from Saint-Paul-de-Vence is another Relais & Châteaux property, **Mas d'Artigny** (L, Chemin Salettes. Tel. 93.32.84.54). There's tennis, tranquility, and peaceful wooded trails; but unfortunately the public areas, though lavish, are more suited for a convention of professionals than for young lovers. It's not that anything is in bad taste but that the ambiance is chain-hotelish. The main reasons to stay are the private swimming pools—one per room— and the bathtubs built for two.

Orangers (E, Rue Colle. Tel. 93.32.80.95) is an old inn in an olive grove. Each of the 10 rooms has its own balcony.

Hotel Marc-Hely (I, 535 Route de Cagnes—D6. Tel. 93.22.64.10) is an inexpensive family hotel in a private house set back from the road that runs between the coast and Saint-Paul-de-Vence. Another reasonably priced hotel is **Le Hameau** (M/I, 528 Route de la Colle. Tel. 93.32.80.24)—four buildings on the grounds of an old farm set among fruit trees. Try Room 11.

For Further Information

The tourist office is at Rue-Grande, Saint-Paul-de-Vence. Tel. 93.32.86.95.

♆ VENCE

How to Get There. From Saint-Paul-de-Vence continue north on D2, which runs directly into the old section *(Vieille Ville)* of Vence at Avenue M. Maurel. If you haven't seen enough medieval towns, park and walk around. In the center is the Romanesque cathedral, which has a nave (central corridor), four aisles, and no transepts (projecting arms). Of special note is a mosaic by Chagall of Moses in the bullrushes and the ornate fifteenth-century carved wooden choir stalls.

From D2, turn left on **Avenue M. Maurel**. Cross **Avenue Foch** and turn right on **Avenue H. Matisse** to the main attraction of Vence, the **Rosaire (Matisse) Chapel**, open only on Tuesdays and Thursdays from 10 to 11:30 and 2:30 to 5:30. "Despite its imperfections I think it is my masterpiece . . . the result of a lifetime devoted to the search for truth," wrote Matisse, who designed and dedicated the chapel in the late 1940s when he was in his eighties and nearly blind.

❧ TOURRETTE-SUR-LOUP

How to Get There. From Vence, drive west about 3 miles on D2210.

There's a limit to how many medieval hill towns you're going to want to see. The three I'd recommend are Peillon, because it's the most uncommercial and the most dramatically situated; Saint-Paul-de-Vence, because it's easy to reach, is surrounded by first-class hotels and restaurants, and is visually a gem; and Tourrette-sur-Loup, because it's less commercial than other towns and its shops are filled not with postcards and scented soaps but with the work of dedicated artisans. (The village of Moustiers-Ste.-Marie is also recommended, should you make the full-day trip to the Grand Canyon of the Verdon, described below.)

The outer houses of **Tourrette-sur-Loup** form a rampart on a rocky plateau, 1,300 feet above a valley full of violets. A rough stone path takes you on a circular route around the rim of the town, past the shops of engravers, weavers, potters, and painters. Ask any artisan for a map of the town that locates each of the shops. Also worth visiting is a single-nave fourteenth-century church, which has a notable wooden altarpiece.

Dining

It would be difficult to find a sweeter, friendlier restaurant than the tiny **Le Petit Manoir** (I, 21 Grand-Rue. Tel. 93.24.19.19). The artisans eat across the street in the equally friendly but less expensive **La Petite Chanson** (I, 22 Grand-Rue. Tel. 93.24.18.38).

❧ GORGES DU LOUP

How to Get There. From Tourrette-sur-Loup, continue west about 5 miles on D2210 to **Pont-du-Loup**. Take D6 north for 4 miles along the east side of the gorge, then head south on D3, past **Gourdon**, to **D2085**, the main road between **Grasse** and **Cagnes**.

This is a very scenic drive up one side of a dramatic gorge and down the other. It's less impressive than the **Grand Canyon of the Verdon**, but a great deal closer to the coast.

If you're afflicted with a sweet tooth, stop in **Pont-du-Loup** at **La Confiserie des Gorges du Loup** and watch the good people making sugared tangerines, chocolate-covered orange peels, and rose-petal jam. Pretty unsubtle stuff from the land of the tarte aux pommes, but good to munch on as you drive around the gorge.

As you head north on D6, park after the third tunnel and walk back for spectacular views into the depths of the gorge.

The road (D3) that takes you south along the west edge of the gorge reaches dizzying heights. **Gourdon** is touted as one of the must stops on the tourist route, which should be enough to dissuade you from stopping there unless you're lathering for scented soaps or lavender toilet water.

✹ GRASSE

How to Get There. From Gourdon, continue south on D3 to D2085. From here, turn left (east), back to **Cagnes** and **Nice**; or turn right and make a short detour to **Grasse**. If you're headed back to **Cannes**, you have to pass through **Grasse** en route to N85.

Grasse is bottled and sold on every escorted tour along the coast. The reason is its accessibility both to Cannes and Nice, and its perfumeries, where tourists spend money. The town is also famous for its preserves and for its crystallized fruits and flowers.

If touring a perfume factory in an attractive modern town is your idea of pleasure, visit Grasse. If you had visited four centuries ago, when the town specialized in leather work, you would have come for gloves. In the sixteenth century, when scented gloves became the rage, the town began cultivating flowers and distilling essences. That was the beginning of the perfume industry. Today some three fourths of the world's essences are made here from wild lavender, jasmine, violets, daffodils, and other sweet-smelling flowers. Five thousand producers supply some twenty factories and six cooperatives. If you've ever wondered why perfume is so expensive, consider that it takes ten thousand flowers to produce 2.2 pounds of jasmine petals, and that nearly one ton of jasmine is needed—nearly seven million flowers—to distill a quart and a half of essence. Sophisticated Paris perfumers mix Grasse essences into their own secret formulas;

perfumes made and sold in Grasse are considerably less subtle. You can of course buy Parisian perfumes in Grasse—at Parisian prices.

Visitors can buy local perfumes and get some sense of how they're made at any of the three **perfumeries: Fragonard** (20 Boulevard Fragonard); **Galimard** (Les 4 Chemins, Route de Cannes), and **Molinard** (60 Boulevard Victor-Hugo). All three are open weekdays during working hours.

From **Grasse** return to **Cannes** on N85, or to **Nice** on N85, D35, and A8.

EXCURSION 4: *Biot and Vallauris*

How to Get There. Biot and Vallauris are just a mile or two inland from the coastal road between **Cannes** and **Nice**. If you're staying in the **Nice** area, visit these two towns as you head south along the coast to **Cannes**. If you're staying in the **Cannes** area, visit them as you drive north along the coast to **Nice**.

♦ *BIOT*

On the road to Biot is the **Léger Museum**, the Musée National Fernand Léger (open July and August daily from 10 to 12, and 2:30 to 6:30; off-season, to 5; closed Tuesdays). Donated to France by Léger's widow in 1959, it offers visitors a good opportunity to trace the artist's development from 1904 until his death in 1955. The building has a 4,000-square-foot mosaic on the outside wall that is strikingly out of keeping with the surroundings.

The houses of **Biot** cling to a hillside above the Braque Valley. The town is a handicraft center, specializing in gold and silver jewelry decorated with precious and semiprecious stones, and glassblowing. Suspended in the heavy, tinted glass are tiny bubbles which sparkle in the sun: You can buy the glass or simply watch the ancient process by which it's blown.

When you return to the coastal road (**Route 7**), you'll pass a **Marineland** with trained-dolphin shows. Performances begin at 2:30 P.M.; in summer, at 2:30 and 9:30 P.M.

♦ *VALLAURIS*

The wares of more than a hundred local potters overflow **Avenue Georges-Clemenceau** and the neighboring streets, such as **Rue Sicard** and **Rue du Plan**—some of it high quality, most of it turned out for the high-volume tourist trade. With luck you'll find some tasteful cups and plates. Also for sale are handmade marionettes and olive-wood sculpture.

Bricks and pottery have been made here since the time of Tiberius from a local seam of clay. Picasso revived the declining industry when he lived here from 1952 to 1959; his ceramics are on display in the sixteenth-century Renaissance castle, and reproductions are for sale in the **Madoura** studio. Also housed in the castle (open 10 to 12 and 2 to 6; off-season, to 5) is an enormous allegorical fresco by Picasso called War and Peace.

EXCURSION 5

✤ *THE GRAND CANYON OF THE VERDON*

How to Get There. Drive from the Nice area or the Cannes area to **Grasse**. Take N85 northwest toward **Castellane**. Pass **Seranon** on your right. Just beyond the small village of **Villaute**, turn left on **D21** to **Comps-sur-Artuby**. Turn right on D71. As you approach the gorge, you'll see the hill town of **Trigance** on your right. Follow directions below.

This trip will take the better part of a day—a full day or overnight if you plan to walk through the canyon. It is an unforgettable trip—the most spectacular you could make on a one-day excursion from the coast. If you like wild gorges and dizzying heights, the Grand Canyon of the Verdon will be an unforgettable experience. For thousands of years the Verdon River has dug a rift in the earth, making a winding corridor up to 2,300 feet deep and in places only 25 feet wide!

The route follows the southern rim of this 13-mile-long gorge to **Moustiers-Ste.-Marie**, one of the loveliest and unspoiled of the medieval hill towns, where you can buy pottery and dine in a charming country restaurant; then returns along the northern rim, with frequent vantage points where you can leave your car and peer down into the swirling depths. Highly recommended are two dramatic walks, neither particularly demanding—one a 2-hour trip down into the gorge and back; the other a 6- to 8-hour trek along the bottom. Should you decide to spend the night, there's a romantic castle-hotel overlooking the gorge at **Trigance**.

The route around the southern rim is the most dramatic. As you approach the gorge, you'll see the medieval town of **Trigance** crowning a hill on your right. The **Chateau de Trigance** (M, Trigance. Tel. 94.76.91.18) is a Relais & Châteaux property with a splendid view of the valley and the surrounding mountains. There are a few small rooms with a medieval feeling to them—an ideal place to spend the night should you spend a full day at the gorge and not want to drive back after dark.

The views along the gorge are awesome, from a height that will make you feel as though you're piloting a plane. Stop when the spirit moves you, and don't leave your camera in the car. As you leave the gorge behind, the road turns into D19. At the town of **Aiguines**, which has a noble seventeeth-century château, you can buy a descriptive guide to the gorge that indicates the trails. At the lake (Lac de Ste. Croix), turn right on D957. In about 4.5 miles, D957 intersects with D952. You can turn right and head back along the northern rim of the canyon, but it's worth a 1.5-mile detour (a left turn on D957) to visit the unspoiled medieval village of **Moustiers-Ste.-Marie**, where serious craftspeople work and sell their wares. There's an attractive Romanesque **church** with a three-tier bell tower, and a **Pottery Museum** (open summers from 9 to 12, and from 2 to 7; earlier closings off-season; closed Tuesdays) displaying the clear, blue-glazed pottery that made the town famous in the seventeenth and eighteenth centuries, when there were twelve active potteries here. Photographers will want to take the path that winds up above the village to the **Notre-Dame-de-Beauvoir Chapel**. The terrace of **Les Santons** (M, Place Église. Tel. 92.74.66.48), a delightful Provençal restaurant, over-looks a mountain torrent flowing through the town. It's a tiny, family-run restaurant, so make reservations.

After resting up in **Moustiers-Ste.-Marie**, return east on D952, along the northern rim of the gorge. Unless you're in a rush to get back, leave D952 at **La Palud-sur-Verdon** and take the circular **Crest Road** (D23) that hugs the edge of the canyon. The **Crest Road** will return you to D952 near where you left it. Turn right on D952 to **Point Sublime** and continue east to **Castellane**. From here, take N85 back to **Grasse**.

Two Spectacular Walks

The shorter, 2-hour walk (round-trip) begins at the parking lot at **Samson Corridor**. Follow the marked route to the right just beyond the first tunnel (Tusset Tunnel) after **Point Sublime**. Walk down to the foot-bridge over the Baou, cross over, and continue through two tunnels to a promontory with a view of the **Trescaïre Chaos**. Bring a flashlight.

The longer, 6- to 8-hour walk begins at the **Chalet de la Maline** (on the Crest Road), and continues for 9.15 miles to **Point Sublime**. Follow the red and white arrows along the footpath. Wear sturdy shoes and carry a flashlight, water, and food. Before setting off, phone 92.74.68.20 to make sure that a taxi is available; then call again when you reach Point

Sublime and arrange to be picked up. (There may not be a phone at the **Chalet de la Maline**, which is why it's important to end your hike at the phone booth at **Point Sublime**.

EXCURSION 6

♦ *THE ESTEREL*

How to Get There. From Nice, take Autoroute A8 south past Cannes to the La Napoule (N98) exit. Continue south along the coast to **St.-Raphaël**. If you're starting in Cannes, take N98 to La Napoule and continue south along the coast to **St.-Raphaël**. See further directions below.

This is a half-day trip from Cannes that takes you away from the crowds, into a silent world of tortured, rust-colored rocks thrusting their jagged claws into the sea. The contrast between the fiery red rocks, the deep green pines, and the blue sea inspired the Belgian writer Maurice Maeterlinck to call this region "closer to fairyland than any place on earth."

The Esterel is made up of volcanic rocks (porphyry) carved by the sea into dreamlike shapes. The harshness of the landscape is softened by patches of lavender, cane apple, and gorse. The deep gorges with sculpted, parasol pines could have inspired Tang and Sung Dynasty landscape painters. The drive south from La Napoule to St.-Raphäel takes you along the coast, past tiny rust-colored beaches and sheer rock faces plunging into the sea. The route back to Cannes takes you through the mountains of the Esterel, which have many trails and dramatic views.

Art lovers will want to stop in **La Napoule** at the **Château de la Napoule Art Foundation** (open daily from 3 to 5 P.M. except Tuesdays) to see the eccentic and eclectic work of the American sculptor Henry Clews. Clews, who saw himself as Don Quixote and his wife as the Virgin of La Mancha, came from a New York banking family. A cynic and sadist, he had, as one critic remarked, a knowledge of anatomy worthy of Michelangelo and the bizarre imagination of Edgar Allan Poe. His work —as tortured as the rocks of the Esterel—shows an infatuation with big bellies and distorted bodies; his nude of a man with a skull between his thighs is not easily forgotten.

On your right, just past **Théoule**, is **Villa Anna Guerguy** (M, Théoule-sur-Mer. Tel. 93.49.96.04), a small hotel laced with vines, built into the red rocks high above the sea. I didn't see the rooms, but the public areas are full of character: a fun place for young-minded couples looking for seclusion in an unusual, dramatic setting. If nothing else, come for drinks on the red-tiled patio encircled by pines.

From **Le Trayas** to **Anthéor** is the most scenic part of the drive, beneath the tormented mountains, with deep ravines and razor-sharp ridges. **Agay** has the best protected anchorage along the coast. It was here that Antoine de Saint Exupéry was shot down in July 1944. He had just flown over his family castle on his last mission.

St.-Raphaël is a family resort with holiday camps, best known to tourists as the railway stop for Saint-Tropez. It was here the Allied forces landed in their offensive against the Germans in August 1944.

Before returning through the Esterel, you can make a short side trip from **St.-Raphaël** to **Fréjus** (the two towns border each other), but I don't recommend it unless you have a special interest in antiquity. The town has not altogether lost the pedestrian character it had as a Roman naval base. It was at Fréjus that Napoleon landed in 1799 on his way back from Egypt, and it was from here that he embarked for Elba.

Caesar made Fréjus a way station on the road between Italy and Gaul. When Emperor Augustus took over, he wanted a powerful fleet and turned the town into a huge naval base—the second largest in the Empire, where galleys were built and men trained for the victory over Mark Antony at Actium. Today there's little sense of the town's former glory. Remains of the 30-mile aqueduct can best be seen at the east end of the town. The forum is gone and the Temple of Jupiter is a hospital. Best bet is the amphitheater (arena), where bullfights are sometimes held. Of greater interest to casual visitors is the **Episcopal Town,** built in the late tenth century, which includes a cathedral, baptistery, cloister, and bishop's palace. The austere fourth-century baptistery, built with black granite columns from the Roman forum, is one of the oldest in France. The present **cathedral** dates back to the tenth century, with twelfth-century vaulting and handsome fifteenth-century carved wooden choir stalls. Ring the bell on the iron gate to see the lovely, graceful cloister and the amusing fourteenth-century carvings of creatures from the Apocalypse on the ceiling of the upper arcade.

From **St.-Raphaël** return to **Cannes** on N7—the mountain route through the Esterel. There's a fine desolation here, with different views around every curve. At the sign **Forêt Domaniale de Esterel,** turn right and drive to the top of **Mount Vinaigre** (2,030 feet). It's all of 100 feet from the parking lot to the summit. Try to come in the late afternoon, when the coastal views are most striking.

Return to N7 and continue east to **Cannes**.

RECOMMENDED READING

What's Hot, What's Not: French Riviera Guide (available in shops along the coast).

SPAIN

❧ Sevilla, Córdoba, Granada, and the Costa del Sol

MAJOR ATTRACTIONS

- Bullfights and flamenco in Sevilla.
- The palace and gardens of the Alhambra—the greatest monument of Islamic Spain.
- The fabulous mosque of Córdoba, with a full-size cathedral inside.
- Tennis, golf, and sun along the fashionable Costa del Sol.
- A back-road adventure to the perched white villages of Andalusia.
- Accommodations in ancient palaces and abbeys converted into first-class hotels.

INTRODUCTION

Your trip takes you through Andalusia, on a voyage through almost eight hundred years of Islamic Spain. It also includes a few happy days of self-indulgence on the beaches of the Costa del Sol.

In Córdoba you'll visit an eighth-century mosque that is so vast, it contains a sixteenth-century Baroque cathedral within its walls. Nearby are the ancient white streets of the Jewish quarter, unchanged from a time when Jews and Arabs lived together in peace.

When people think of romantic Spain—of Carmens and Don Juans—they think of Sevilla. Here you can discover for yourself whether bullfighting is a butchery or art. After visiting the Alcázar—a Moorish palace of gleaming tiles and arabesques—you'll dine in an old Andalusian house and watch flamenco in the Barrio Santa Cruz—a maze of whitewashed streets overflowing with flowers.

Back roads take you south from Sevilla to the shining white villages of Andalusia, rising like castles above the fields of wheat and corn. From the past you move into the present in Marbella, the most tasteful and sophisticated resort along the Costa del Sol. You can lead an active life playing golf and tennis, and enjoying a different restaurant every night—or spend your days lounging at your hotel pool at the edge of the sea.

The trip ends in Granada, where you'll check into a palace hotel and explore the Alhambra—a fabled palace worthy of the Arabian Nights.

THE MAIN ROUTE (with minimum overnight stays)

3–5 Days

Day excursion to Córdoba
Two nights: Sevilla
One night: Marbella
One night: Granada

5–7 Days

Day excursion to Córdoba
Two nights: Sevilla
Two nights: Marbella
Two nights: Granada

7–14 Days

Day excursion to Córdoba
Three nights: Sevilla
One night: Parador of Carmona
Four nights: Marbella
Day excursions to Ronda and the perched white villages of Andalusia
Two nights: Granada
Day excursion to Úbeda and Baeza

GETTING AROUND

Getting to Southern Spain

If you *don't* plan to visit Madrid, fly direct to and from **Málaga**, on the Costa del Sol, only 31 miles east of **Marbella**. **Iberia** is the only airline with direct flights between Málaga and the States (from New York, Chicago, and Los Angeles).

If you *do* plan to visit Madrid, fly direct to Madrid and return from Málaga; or conversely, fly direct to Málaga and return from Madrid.

Iberia also has direct flights in summer between Madrid and New York, Miami, and Los Angeles. **TWA** has direct flights between Madrid and New York.

If your trip begins in Madrid, and you're traveling by car: Stop in **Toledo** on your way south, taking routes **N401** and **N400** to **N IV**. It's a 5-hour drive from Madrid to **Bailén**, and another 1.5 hours to **Córdoba**.

If your trip begins in Madrid and you're taking public transportation: Take the Madrid airport bus downtown to the central Iberia Airline office (30 minutes), and a cab (20 minutes) to the **South Station** (Atocha). Express trains take about 6 hours to Córdoba or 7 to Granada, about 7.5 hours to Sevilla, and about 9.5 hours to Málaga.

Traveling Through Southern Spain

If you're driving, you need a Green Insurance Card. A rented car should have one in the glove compartment. If you're bringing your own car, get the Green Card from your insurance company before you leave home.

Roads marked **A** are turnpikes *(autopista)*. **N** is for national roads, **C** for country roads. You'll be driving mostly on single-lane roads, so expect delays, and leave plenty of time to get where you're going.

Almost all monuments and buildings close from 1:30 to 3 or 4 P.M., and remain open until 7 or 8 P.M. Plan your itinerary accordingly!

If you're taking public transportation, get a Chequetrén—a book of coupons good for 15 percent discounts on trains. They're sold at main stations. When you're buying the actual tickets, get them from travel agents displaying blue and yellow RENFE signs, and avoid ticket lines at stations.

The itinerary follows an oval path from **Córdoba**, to **Sevilla**, the **Perched Villages of Andalusia**, **Marbella** (the Costa del Sol), and **Granada**. This route lets you follow the development of Moorish culture in

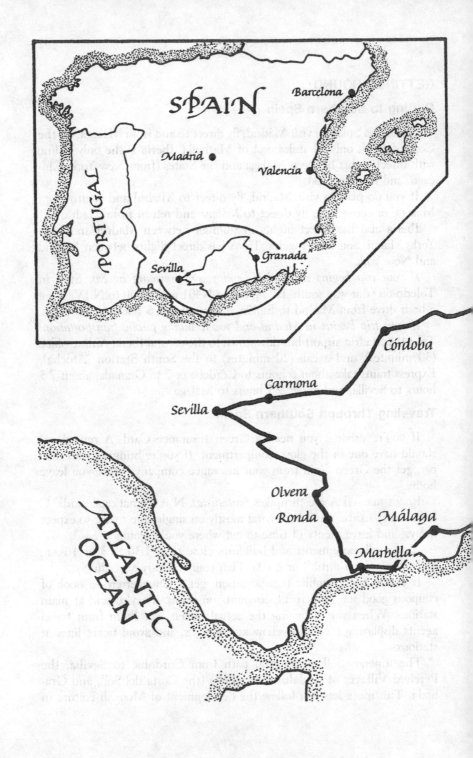

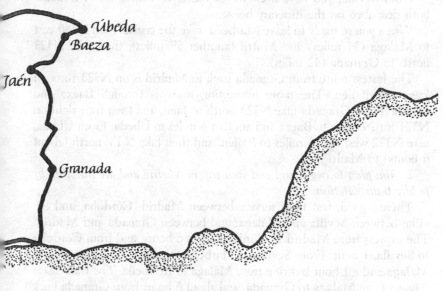

SPAIN

Úbeda

Baeza

Jaén

Granada

MEDITERRANEAN
SEA

Spain from its beginnings in Córdoba to its final flowering in Granada. Here are the roads you'll be taking:

1. *You plan to begin and end your trip in Madrid and are traveling by car:*

Take N IV from Madrid to Bailén (about 6 hours). If you arrive in Madrid after an all-night flight, you may want to stop in Bailén before heading to Córdoba, which is another 66 miles west on N IV. Bailén has a good government-run hotel, Parador Nacional (Tel. 953-67.01.00).

From Córdoba you have a choice of two roads to Sevilla. The fastest is 89 miles on N IV. The slower but more scenic route is on C431 for 49 miles along the Guadalquivir River; south on C432 for 17 miles to Carmona (there's another parador hotel here); and then west for 24 miles on N IV to Sevilla.

From Sevilla, you have a choice of routes to Ronda and Marbella, both described on the itinerary below.

When you're ready to leave Marbella, take the coastal road N340 east to Málaga (34 miles) and Motril (another 57 miles); then take N323 north to Granada (42 miles).

The fastest route from Granada back to Madrid is on N323 through Jaén and Bailén. The more interesting route is through Baeza and Úbeda. From Granada take N323 north to Jaén, and then turn right on N321 for 29 miles to Baeza and another 6 miles to Úbeda. From Úbeda, take N322 west for 25 miles to Bailén, and then take N IV north (about 6 hours) to Madrid.

2. *You plan to begin and end your trip in Madrid and are traveling by public transportation:*

There's good, fast train service between Madrid, Córdoba, and Sevilla; between Sevilla and Málaga; and between Granada and Madrid. The express from Madrid to Córdoba takes 6 hours, and from Córdoba to Sevilla, 1 hour. From Sevilla to Marbella, it's a 3.5-hour train ride to Málaga and a 1-hour bus ride from Málaga to Marbella. The train takes 2 hours from Málaga to Granada, and about 6 hours from Granada back to Madrid.

3. *You plan to begin your trip in Madrid and end it in Málaga and are traveling by car:*

Follow the same route as 1 above, except from Granada return to Málaga by the inland route—west on N342 and south on N321 (78 miles).

4. *You plan to begin your trip in Madrid and end it in Málaga and are traveling by public transportation:*

Follow the same route as 2 above, but instead of taking the train from Granada to Madrid, take the train from **Granada** back to **Málaga**.

5. *You plan to begin and end your trip in Málaga and are traveling by car:*

What you have to decide is whether to (a) do your sightseeing and then reward yourself with a few final days of indolence on the Costa del Sol; to (b) recover from your overnight flight to Spain on the Costa del Sol, and then begin your sightseeing; or to (c) begin and end on the Costa del Sol. The following route lets you do all three. It is essentially the same route described above, but in reverse.

Head west along the coast from **Málaga** to **Marbella**. The drive takes under an hour. You can either save **Marbella** for the end of your trip or stop here now. From **Marbella** continue west on **N340** to **San Pedro de Alcántara**, and turn north on **C339** to **Ronda**. There are two routes from **Ronda** to **Sevilla**, both discussed on the itinerary below. From **Sevilla** there are two roads to **Córdoba**. The fastest is 89 miles on **N IV**. The slower but more scenic route is east for 24 miles on **N IV** to **Carmona**; north on **C432** for 17 miles; and east on **C431** for 49 miles along the Guadalquivir River to **Córdoba**. From **Córdoba**, the shortest route to **Granada** is on **N432**. The more interesting route is on **N IV** to **Bailén**; **N22** to **Úbeda**; **N321** to **Baeza** and **Jaén**; and **N323** to **Granada**. From **Granada**, take **N323** south to **Motril**, and then head west along the coast back to **Málaga**. You can either fly directly home or spend more time in **Marbella**.

6. *You plan to begin and end your trip in Málaga and are traveling by public transportation:*

Buses leave almost every half hour from **Málaga** to **Marbella**. The express trip takes about 1 hour. From **Málaga** take the train to **Sevilla** (3.5 hours). From **Sevilla** take the train to **Córdoba** (1 hour). The bus trip from **Córdoba** to **Granada** takes 3 hours. The train from **Granada** back to **Málaga** takes about 2 hours.

SPECIAL EVENTS

Palm Sunday Through Good Friday: Holy Week festivities in Sevilla
Late April: The Sevilla Fair, with dancing, processions, and bullfights
May 1–12: Córdoba festival of decorated patios
Late June: Sevilla folk-dance competitions
Late June–early July: Granada Festival of Music and Dance, with concerts and ballet in the gardens of the Alhambra

A NOTE ON SHOPPING

Córdoba: filigree silver and embossed leather in the shops of the old Jewish quarter, a short walk from the mosque.

Sevilla: folk costumes and flamenco dresses on the main shopping streets such as Sierpes; pottery, handicrafts, antiques, fine lace, and embroidered cloth in the Barrio Santa Cruz.

Granada: ceramics, marquetry, and woven goods in the shops near the cathedral and on the road to the Alhambra; pottery on Routes N323 and N342, north and east of town.

Marbella: designer clothes (particularly beachwear) in the old Moorish quarter, and in boutiques of individual hotels.

WHAT TO SEE AND DO WITH CHILDREN

Córdoba: the mosque, which looks like a forest of zebras.

Sevilla: a walk through the old quarter to a flamenco show at the Plaza de Santa Cruz; a climb to the top of the Giralda; a horse-drawn carriage ride from the cathedral; a bullfight; the discos across the river near Avenida Republica Argentina.

Granada: the gypsy caves on Sacromonte; a hike from Pico de Veleta.

The Costa del Sol: the pools, beaches, and tennis courts; the Nerja caves; the discos at Puerto Banús.

A NOTE ON HISTORY

The Mosque of Córdoba, the Alcázar of Sevilla, the Alhambra of Granada—these are the three great monuments of Islamic Spain which you'll be visiting on your trip through Andalusia. Let's take a brief look at the history behind them.

When the Visigoths gained control over Spain in the fifth century, they persecuted the Jews and overtaxed everyone else. When the Muslims took over in 711, they were greeted as liberators. There they remained until 1492.

These Muslims are often called Moors, but there really is no such person: The Spaniards used the term merely to designate those people—Arabs, Syrians, Egyptians, Berbers, and others—who settled in their country. To call them Arabs is equally misleading. The first wave of settlers were Berbers—there was not an Arab among them. The Arabs eventually rose to power in Spain, but they were never more than a small minority of the Muslim population, and their power and influence always exceeded their numbers. Since it was the Muslim religion that united these settlers, let's refer to them collectively as Muslims and speak of their kingdom as Islamic Spain.

Islamic Spain

There were three great centers of Muslim culture. Each rose to power, enjoyed a period of glory, and then faded.

Córdoba, 756–1010
Sevilla, 1010–1248
Granada, 1248–1492

The greatest flowering of Moorish culture was during the first 250 years under the Córdoba caliphate. (A caliph is a successor of Muhammed who enjoys both spiritual and temporal power; a caliphate is his office or kingdom.) Undermined by incompetent rulers, the caliphate disintegrated and Islamic Spain broke into twenty-three separate kingdoms *(taifas)*, of which Sevilla became the most important.

In the meantime, the Christians, weakened by squabbles of their own —there was no unified Spain then, only a number of warring kingdoms— banned together in the north, where the Muslims had less control, and began what is called the Reconquest. This struggle to restore Christianity continued for more than four hundred years.

The first major Christian victory was in Toledo in 1085. When Sevilla fell in 1248, Muslim culture moved to Granada, where it survived precariously for 244 years. The marriage of Isabella of Castile and Ferdinand of Aragon brought the two strongest Spanish kingdoms together and unified Catholic Spain against the Moors. Granada finally fell in 1492, about ten months before Columbus sailed for the New World.

Ferdinand and Isabella persecuted the Jews and Moors and hounded them out of Spain. The Spanish Inquisition, which lasted until 1834, was an effort to reestablish a Spanish identity after more than seven hundred years of Muslim rule. Its first victims were not Jews but pure-blood Spaniards who had converted to Islam. By eliminating the Muslims and the Jews, the Inquisition virtually eliminated the Spanish middle class and plunged the country into a decline from which it is still trying to recover.

It's fashionable but unfair to build up Islamic Spain at the expense of the Catholics—to say that whatever is beautiful is the inheritance of Muslim culture. The first invaders, after all, were nomads who lived in tents with no concept of the arts; it was only after many years on Spanish soil that Islamic culture flourished. On the other hand, it's fair to say with Federico García Lorca that "an admirable civilization, a poetry, an architecture, and a delicacy unique in the world—all were lost."

A NOTE ON DINING

Restaurant bills include a 15 percent service charge, but another 5–10 percent is usually expected, particularly in better restaurants.

Ask for water and you'll get bottled mineral water, either *sin qas* (without bubbles) or *con qas* (with). For tap water, which is perfectly safe, ask for *aqua natural.*

The main meal is lunch, which usually doesn't begin until 2 P.M. Dinner often starts at 10 P.M., sometimes as late as midnight. Restaurants open at 1 P.M., so go early if you want quick service.

If you're on a budget, the three-course menu of the day *(menú del día)* is the best bargain, though not usually the best meal. Restaurants are required to have a "menu of the day," but you may have to ask for it.

Spanish food is, as a rule, a food of the people; don't expect gourmet cuisine. The Spaniards usually don't serve their meals steaming hot (extreme heat, they argue, hides the taste), so if you like hot food ask to have it served *muy caliente.* Contrary to what many people think, the Spanish don't like their food highly seasoned; chili is almost never used and pepper is seldom on the table. Most everything is cooked with olive oil, which is not necessarily heavy, and with lots of garlic (al ajillo). Desserts are usually a letdown; best bet are fresh fruits.

The national dish is paella, a base of saffron-flavored rice with anything from mussels to chicken, pimentos, peas, and lobster. If it's properly prepared, you'll taste the separate flavor of each ingredient. It's heavy and takes some 20 minutes to prepare, so it's usually served at lunch, which is the main meal of the day. Best bet near the coast is paella with fresh seafood.

Another universal dish is gazpacho, a cold blend of puréed tomatoes, cucumbers, green peppers, garlic, oil, salt, pepper, onions, and a touch of vinegar. The dominant taste is garlic. Try "white gazpacho" with ground almonds and grapes.

On the Costa del Sol, and to a lesser degree in Sevilla and Granada, you're usually better off with fish than with meat. Specialties include sea bass baked in a shell of salt (lubina al sal) and fritura mixta—a delicate mix of lightly fried fish.

Don't leave Spain without trying some tapas. These tasty tidbits—

potatoes, marinated beef, squid, ham, clams, mussels, fish roe, and so on —are served on counters of bars and cafés, and also as appetizers or main dishes in the paradores (government-run hotels). Like the Spaniards, you can go from bar to bar sharing tapas—a happy alternative to a formal dinner. *Raciones* are larger portions.

Tortilla sacromonte, a potato omelet with diced ham and mixed vegetables, is popular in Granada. ("Tortillas" in Spain are omelets.)

For dessert or for afternoon snacks, try almond-flavored (almendra) ice cream or rum raisin (Málaga-style) ice cream. Granizado de café is iced coffee.

Southern Spain produces sweet apertif and dessert wines, not table wines. Sherry, produced near Jerez de la Frontera (which is not included on the itinerary but is only an hour out of your way) is the most famous Spanish wine. There are three basic types: (1) the light, dry apertifs *(fino)* such as Tío Pepe or La Ina which should be drunk as fresh as possible (don't get the last glass in an open bottle); (2) the fuller-bodied, nutty-tasting *amontillados*—the cheap ones made from blended wines, the better ones from *finos* which have been left to mature; and (3) the darker, fuller-bodied *olorosos*, which have a higher alcohol content. Sherries have a slightly higher alcohol content than other wines because brandy is added while it's being made. You'll find less alcohol content in Spanish sherries than in those you drink at home because extra brandy is added in exported sherries to protect them in transit. There's no such thing as a vintage sherry.

Most restaurants have a cheap, adequate house wine. **Sangria** (a fruit punch with wine, fruit juice, soda, brandy, and slices of oranges and lemons) originated in southern Spain. Brandy and anis (sol y sombra) is another popular drink. Champagne and sorbet (sorbeta de limón) is a great antidote for hot weather.

A NOTE ON LODGING

Hotels are officially rated from one star to five stars, five being the most luxurious. This guide rates rooms, for two: E (expensive, over $60), M (moderate, $30–$60), and I (inexpensive, under $30).

You'll see three signs on Spanish hotels. H means "hotel." HR is a "residential hotel" with no formal restaurant but often a Spanish-style cafeteria. HA designates an "apartment hotel," often with cooking facilities.

Breakfast may or may not be included in the price; ask in advance.

Rooms with bathtubs usually cost more than rooms with showers. On the Costa del Sol, rooms with ocean views often cost more; specify what you want. Many hotels are undergoing restorations; specify whether you want a newer or older room. When possible, ask to see your room before checking in.

The five main hotel chains are **Hotasa** (look for the symbol of two animal heads), **Husa, Meliá, Sol,** and **Entursa.** All tend to be clean and comfortable, but only the **Entursa** hotels have any special character.

Paradores. You would think that government-run hotels would be institutionally bland; but the paradores—some eighty of them—are, as a rule, the most tasteful and interesting hostelries in Spain. Many are restored castles, convents, palaces, and royal hunting lodges that have been modernized but allowed to keep their Old World charm. Most are spacious, with large bathrooms, and decorated with antiques, armor, tapestries, and ceramic tiles. Many are also on high ground with magnificent views or in the old, historic sections of ancient cities. Dining rooms serve regional meals and local wines. The only minus—a plus for some—is the absence of nighttime entertainment and recreation, and a certain lack of warmth in the newer ones. Paradores have only a few rooms, so make reservations in advance. The National Tourist Office of Spain has a brochure that describes "parador vacations," which let you stay in one parador or in a different one every night as you travel. Following the itinerary below, you can stay in paradores in **Bailén** (on the road from Madrid to Córdoba), **Córdoba** (outside the city), **Carmona** (outside of Sevilla), **Granada, Pico de Veleta** (outside of Granada), **Málaga,** and **Úbeda** (may still be closed for restorations).

EMERGENCIES

Police, anywhere in Spain: Tel. 091.

FOR FURTHER INFORMATION

National Tourist Office of Spain. *New York:* 665 Fifth Avenue, New York, N.Y. 10022. Tel. 212/759-8822. *Chicago:* 845 North Michigan Avenue, Chicago, Ill. 60611. Tel. 312/944-0215. *Houston:* 4800 The Galleria, 5085 Westheimer, Houston, Tex. 77056. Tel. 713/491-6674. *Los Angeles:* San Vicente Plaza Building, 8383 Wilshire Boulevard, Suite 960, Beverly Hills, Calif. 90211. Tel. 213/658-7188. *St. Augustine:* Hypolita St. George, Casa Del Hidalgo, Saint Augustine, Fla. 32084. Tel. 904/829-6460.

THE ITINERARY

✤ *CÓRDOBA*

Except for its great mosque and ancient Jewish quarter, the modern city of Córdoba gives little evidence of its former glory. The two sights are a must on any tour of southern Spain, but once you've seen them, you'll probably be content to move on. While the mosque is closed (1:30 to 3:30 P.M.), tour the Jewish quarter and stop for lunch: There are at least two good restaurants nearby.

A Historical Note

As you wander through the mosque and the old Jewish quarter, imagine yourself back in the eighth century, when Córdoba was the first and greatest capital of Islamic Spain.

Your ruler is one-eyed **Abd-er-Rahman I**. His family belonged to a long line of **Umayyads**, who were slaughtered by another branch of Mohammed's family, the **Abbassides**. Abd-er-Rahman escaped and fled to Spain, where he began a dynasty that ruled for three hundred years. It was in 785, under his rule, that the mosque was begun. In 929, his descendent **Abd-er-Rahman III** unmasked the fiction that the Arab world was united and declared himself Caliph. The Arab world was now formally split in two—as the Roman world was split between East and West—one capital in Bagdad, the other in Córdoba.

Americans tend to label Muslims as intolerant, but under the Córdoba caliphate nothing could have been more untrue. For almost fifty years the Muslims shared the Visigoth church with the Christians and made no effort to interfere with their services. When the Muslims decided to build a mosque, they gave the Christians money to build themselves another cathedral. How unlike the intolerance the Christians showed the Muslims after the Reconquest!

For three hundred years the caliphs of Córdoba ruled the most advanced state in Europe. Arabic, the official tongue, was spoken by both Jew and Christian. Córdoba was said to have a population of 500,000—almost twice what it has today. While the rest of Europe was groping through the Dark Ages, Córdoba had illuminated streets. While education in Northern Europe was limited to a few monastic centers, nearly everyone in Córdoba could read and write. Universities flourished. The Renaissance began here with translations of classical learning.

The Spanish Muslims introduced Europe to waterwheel irrigation, peach trees, and dates. They introduced paper and glass, jasmine and the lute. The world's most accomplished mathematicians, they showed the West how to use Arabic digits. Without them we'd still be trying to multiply CCXII times MCLXI.

The caliphate eventually crumbled because of incompetent rulers, and Islamic Spain split into warring states, the most powerful of which was Sevilla. In 1236 Córdoba fell to the Christians. About 100,000 Muslims fled to Granada, where they remained until the last caliph was ousted from power in 1492.

• **The Mosque** (Mezquita), open daily from 10:30 to 1:30, and 3:30 to 7; off-season, closed at 6.

The first experience you'll have is of disorientation—of losing your way in a mysterious forest. Try to remember that in a mosque all paths are supposed to be good, since God is everywhere; that in God's house one can no longer lose his way. How different the feeling from a Christian church, where columns propel the worshipper's gaze forward to the altar, and upward to God.

It's important to realize also that the mosque does not serve the same function as a church. The side facing Mecca has a sanctuary indicating the direction worshippers should face while praying, but the rest of the mosque is a community gathering place—a huge rectangular desert tent where people come to stroll or study. In Islamic times, officials read proclamations here, scholars debated, students attended classes.

The original mosque was not a place of self-abnegation where a worshipper escaped this life in order to find the next: It was a cool oasis (the columns are often compared to palm trees) where people could escape the heat of the sun. Arcaded porticos (rows of columns) kept the mosque open to the outside world. The lines of columns were continued outside in the rows of orange trees in the perfumed courtyard, as if man and nature were working together in the service of God. When the Christians took power they filled in the arcades in order to build shrines against the outer walls. The natural world was locked out and a living mosque became spiritually dead.

Notice how the columns are different shapes and made from different materials: granite, marble, jasper, etc. This is because they were taken by the Muslims from various places they conquered. There are Roman pillars from Gaul, Visigoth pillars with fleur-de-lis designs, Byzantine pillars from Constantinople. The shorter ones are raised on bases; the longer ones are buried beneath the floor.

As the Muslim population increased, the mosque was enlarged three times. Completed, it measured 590 feet by 425 feet, one third of which was the open courtyard.

The horseshoe-shaped arches, a trademark of Early Moorish architecture, were used in the original Visigoth church which the mosque replaced. The double arches—one on top of the other—were added to raise the ceiling and create a sense of airiness and space; the idea may have come from the Roman aqueduct at Segovia. Many of the bronze and copper lamps were made from church bells.

What is mind boggling is the fact that you can wander through this forest of pillars for perhaps 30 minutes without even knowing that within its midst is a full-size cathedral! At first, the Christians merely ripped out some of the pillars to create a space that resembled the nave (central aisle) of a church. This satisfied them for nearly three hundred years, from 1236 to 1520. The local clergy then petitioned Charles V to build a transept, cover it, and close it in from the rest of the mosque. Charles, unaware of the desecration that was to be performed, gave his consent. When, six years later, he saw the results, he exclaimed, "If I had known what you were to do, you would not have done it. For what you have made here may be found in many other places, but what you have destroyed is to be found nowhere else in the world."

Enter through the **Courtyard of the Oranges**. Try to imagine what it was like before it was walled in, when the ornamental fountains were used for ablutions by the faithful as they entered the mosque.

You will enter into the oldest part of the mosque. Head to the right wall, turn left, and walk till you come to a break in the columns. This is where the original cathedral was. Continue to the far wall, turn left, and walk to the **Mihrab**, the sanctuary facing Mecca. This was the holiest part of the mosque. The gold dome is a synthesis of Byzantine and Islamic art—a reminder that the mosque was built by Christian workers loaned by the Christian emperor in Constantinople. Note the paving stones worn smooth by centuries of worshippers kneeling in prayer.

Suddenly, in the midst of this forest, you step into a gilded Baroque cathedral. What, you wonder, is it doing here? From a world of shadows you have stepped suddenly into a radiant clearing. James Michener calls it a monument of "colossal ugliness." Others have called it a worm in a bright red apple and a Jonah in the whale. Still others are content to find it emblematic of southern Spain: the ruins of a Roman basilica incorporated into a Visigoth church, turned into a Muslim mosque with a Christian cathedral inside. Whatever you think of the cathedral, be grateful it was built, for without it the mosque would surely have been torn down.

• Exit through the **Courtyard of the Oranges** and turn right to the famous **Street of the Flowers** (Calleja de las Flores). You can't miss it because it's filled with tourists. On this and adjoining streets are numerous tourist shops, selling leather goods, filigree jewelry, marquetry, fans, and pins. Other, less famous streets are just as beautiful, so walk around.

• Directly behind the mosque is the **Jewish Quarter** (Judería). Like the Barrio in Sevilla, it is an ancient world of narrow, twisted streets, cool courtyards, beautifully wrought window grilles, and whitewashed walls covered with flowers. The fourteenth-century **synagogue** (La Sinagoga) is open from 9:30 to 1:30, and 4:30 to 7:30; off-season, from 9:30 to 1:30 and 3:30 to 6:30. It's no more than a plain, small room with some Mudejar stucco on the upper walls, but it has rich historical associations and is one of three synagogues left in Spain.

For three centuries, under Muslim tolerance, the Jews of Córdoba enjoyed a golden age. They were doctors, philosophers, diplomats, even generals. In the Judería is a statue of **Moses Maimonides** (1135–1204), a Jewish physician and one of the most brilliant men that Spain has ever produced.

Walk from the synagogue to the Zoco, a large courtyard where craftsmen work around a patio, and where you can stop for a light lunch.

Dining

Near the mosque is the highly regarded **El Caballo Rojo** (E/M, "The Red Horse," Cardenal Herrero 28. Tel. 957-22.38.04). The old converted mansion has a terrace, and dining rooms on three levels. Decor is regional. National specialties include cordero a la miel (lamb with honey).

The other top restaurant is **Almudaina** (E/M, Plaza de los Santos Mártires 1. Tel. 957-22.43.36), located in an old converted school at the entrance to the Judería. The specialty is fresh fish.

Castillo de la Albaida (M, about 3 miles from town on the road to Santa María de Trassierra. Tel. 957-27.34.93) is an old Andalusian home with an open terrace and lovely, peaceful views.

Lodging

Parador Nacional de la Arruzafa (Avenida de la Arruzafa. Tel. 957-27.59.00) is a modern, 56-room parador located 2½ miles north of Córdoba, with lovely gardens, a children's dining area, pool, and private terraces overlooking the city.

The 106-room **Meliá Córdoba** (E, Jardines de la Victoria. Tel. 957-29.80.66) is a renovated older hotel with a pool. Accommodations are only fair, but they're the best you'll find in walking distance of the mosque.

The 61-room **Maimónides** (M, Torrijos 4. Tel. 957-47.15.00) is smaller, friendlier, and less expensive than the Meliá. Rooms are a bit worn but clean. The location, in the heart of the historic area next to the mosque, is ideal.

For Further Information

The **National Tourist Office of Spain** is at Avenue Gran Capitán 13. Tel. 957-22.12.05. The **Municipal Tourist Office** is at Plaza de Judás Levi. (Tel. 957-29.07.40), in the Judería, halfway between the mosque and the synagogue.

Train Information: Tel. 957-22.67.94 or 22.16.48.

✤ SEVILLA

When foreigners imagine romantic Spain they think of Sevilla, the largest city in Andalusia. It was here that Velásquez and Murillo were born; here that Don Juan lived; here that Don José first met Carmen. It was Sevilla that inspired *Don Giovanni, The Marriage of Figaro,* and *The Barber of Seville.* Here Cervantes was imprisoned, and here Don Quixote was born.

Things to See and Do

The important sights—the **Cathedral,** the **Giralda,** the **Alcázar,** and the **Barrio Santa Cruz**—are all within walking distance of each other. Not far away are the **bullring** and the **María Luisa Gardens**—among the loveliest in Spain.

• *Sevilla Cathedral* (open summers from 10:30 to 1, and 4 to 6; off-season, to 5:30).

Only St. Peter's in Rome and St. Paul's in London are bigger than the Sevilla Cathedral. When the Christians overran Córdoba, they decided to build their cathedral inside the mosque; here in Sevilla they demolished the mosque and built over it. The Christians were overwhelmed by the beauty of Sevilla and must have felt a need to prove that Christianity could do as well. The size of the cathedral will overwhelm you; walking beneath those massive pillars—the vaults rising 184 feet above the transept crossing—is like strolling through a forest of giant sequoias. The gloom is immense, too—the pillars disappearing upward into darkness. How unlike the Alhambra, where life is seen as something to enjoy, not escape.

To the left of the modern **doors** (Michelin says they harmonize with the whole; another critic says they're "strikingly out of place") is the **Chapel Royal** (Capilla Real), a Renaissance building with an ornamented dome. The **sanctuary** contains some fifteenth- and sixteenth-century **choir stalls**, as rich as the Spanish imagination; and the **Tomb of Christopher Columbus**. There's a school of thought that says Columbus's remains are still in Santo Domingo, but we're in Sevilla now, so let's assume he's here. Besides, Sevilla has been chosen as the site of the 1992 fair to celebrate the five hundredth anniversary of Columbus's discovery of the New World.

The **library** behind the cathedral contains ten books owned by Columbus, including *Marco Polo*, Plutarch's *Lives*, Seneca's *Tragedies*, and Pliny's *History*. Can you imagine Columbus reading Seneca? His marginal notes all have to do with gold, pearls, ivory, pepper—in other words, making money.

The 322-foot **Giralda** (open the same hours as the cathedral) was the only part of the original mosque (other than the **Orange Tree Court**) that the Christians did not destroy. A sixteenth-century Renaissance belfry has been added to the original twelfth-century structure: How typically Andalusian to have a church bell rung from the top of an Arabic minaret!

You'll notice that the Giralda has a solidity, a monumentality not usually associated with Muslim architecture. This is because it was built by the **Almohades**, a fundamentalist dynasty who eschewed all ostentation in an effort to restore the strict religious beliefs and simple lifestyle of the Prophet. Gone are the horseshoe-shaped arches (inspired by the Visigoths) which you saw in the Córdoba mosque; the arches here are more pointed, in the spirit of the Middle East.

Giraldas were built for the muezzin to call the faithful to service. In small mosques he stood at the door; in large ones he climbed the minaret, faced Mecca, put his forefingers in his ears, and cried, "God is most great" (four times) and "Come to salvation" (twice). In the morning he added, "Prayer is better than sleep." The muezzin could not be drunk, insane, or a woman. Climb the gentle ramp—two horses wide—to a platform at 230 feet for a breathtaking view of Sevilla.

• Outside the cathedral are **horse-drawn carriages** *(coche caballos)* waiting to take you for a ride. Be sure to bargain and to agree on a price beforehand. One lovely trip is through **María Luisa Park**.

• On your way from the cathedral and the Alcázar, consider a visit to the **Archives of the Indies** (Archivo General de Indias); guided tours daily, except Sunday, from 10 to 1. Among the documents are signatures of Columbus and Magellan, and a letter Cervantes wrote in 1590, at the age of forty-three, asking for a job in the New World. If accepted, Cervantes would have probably lived out his life as a public accountant and never written *Don Quixote;* but scrawled across his application are the words, "Let him look for something closer to home."

• **The Alcázar** (open 9 to 12:45, and 4:30 to 6; off-season, 9 to 12:45 and 3 to 5:30; closed Sunday afternoons)

The Alcázar is an intricate maze of gleaming tiles, arabesques, carved wood ceilings, and lace-like stucco—a perfect setting, it would seem, for the Arabian Nights. Its stunning profusion of shapes and forms—H. V. Morton calls it "the multiplication table set to music"—will enchant you. Equally fascinating is the fact that this Moorish palace was built for a Catholic king named **Pedro the Cruel** (1333–1369).

When Pedro came to power in 1350, more than seventy years had passed since the Moors had relinquished power, and the palace which the Almohades had built was nearly in ruins. A man as sensuous as he was cruel, Pedro loved the idea of living with his harem in an exotic Moorish palace, and so he hired the finest Muslim craftsmen to emulate the Alhambra in Granada. These craftsmen were called **Mudéjars**, and their art was executed according to Muslim designs and techniques, but under a Christian yoke. Pedro's palace was a hybrid structure, half-Visigoth, half-Moorish; but the fact that it was built at all shows how completely Arabic ideas had infiltrated Spanish thought.

Restorations went on through the nineteenth century, destroying much of the palace's integrity; nonetheless, it remains one of the greatest and purest examples of Mudéjar architecture in the world. As you tour the rooms, have fun trying to distinguish Christian from Muslim elements and comparing the sometimes glaring harshness of the new tiles to the soft, subtle lyricism of the originals.

If you don't see any paintings, it's because the early Muslims, like the Jews, saw the use of idols as a threat to their concept of the One God, and therefore frowned on representational art. Their need for artistic self-expression found its outlet in geometric forms and calligraphy. The greatest mathematicians of the ancient world, they loved logical, coherent lines. Of all the arts, they respected calligraphy the most. In the West we think of the written word as nothing but an abstract symbol; but to the Arabs, language has a visual dimension as well. Words, to them, not only celebrate beauty, they *are* beauty.

A grand sixteenth-century **staircase** takes you to the **Royal Apartments**—the most touched-up part of the palace, some rooms altered as late as the nineteenth century. The lace-like delicacy of some of the work is **Isabeline**—a style named for Isabella, Ferdinand's wife, after they had ousted the Moors from Granada. The need to cover every inch of space with fine designs, like a woman's veil, was inspired by the Moorish love for detail; yet note how the Spanish work is voluptuous for its own sake, while the Moorish work is only the outward expression of a mathematical love of form.

The Moorish **Court of the Maidens** (Patio de las Doncellas) was, sadly, given an upper story in the sixteenth century. Surrounding the court are rooms of finely carved stucco and glazed tiles. The room of **Emperor Charles V**—he was the one who built a Renaissance palace in the Alhambra—has a notable collection of tapestries. Also worth seeing is the domed ceiling (cupola) of the **Hall of the Ambassadors** (Salón de Embajadores). Did Pedro know that the verses on the wall were in praise of Allah?

Also off the **Court of the Maidens** are the apartments of **María de Padilla**, Pedro's mistress. It was she alone who gave beauty to Pedro's life. She was simple and pious and very beautiful. At the advice of the court, he married a French princess, Blanche of Bourbon, but after three days he imprisoned her and fled back to María. He married again, but after one day he was back in María's arms.

Don't miss the terraced **gardens** of the Alcázar, filled with exotic trees, shrubs, and ornamental fountains. You can sit here beneath the magnolia trees and imagine yourself back in the court of Pedro the Cruel.

From the gardens, walk to the **Flag Court** (Patio de las Banderas) and follow a covered passage to the **Barrio Santa Cruz**, the former Jewish quarter, where the Spanish nobility lived in the seventeenth century.

• The **Barrio Santa Cruz** is one of the most picturesque sights in Spain. Narrow white streets open out into tiny squares that could be in North Africa. The sun-bleached walls give no indication of what's within; be sure to peer through the beautiful wrought-iron doors at the tiled courtyards with their gurgling fountains and orange trees. What a contrast between the simplicity of these homes and the Rococo indulgences of the cathedral!

Among the houses are curiosity shops selling everything from old jewelry to mirrors, antique ceramics, and daggers. On several squares are restaurants where you can pause for drinks or lunch. Be sure to return at night when the cafés blast their light and music into the dark streets. At **Plaza de los Venerables** is **Casa Román**, an atmospheric bar with hams hanging from the ceiling. At **Plaza de Santa Cruz** is **Los Gallos**, where you can watch flamenco. The **Plaza de Doña Elvira** has a fountain, and benches for guitarists.

• North of the Barrio is **Pilate's House** (Casa de Pilatos), open 10 to 1, and 3:30 to 7; first floor closed Saturday afternoons and Sundays. This is a smaller, less crowded version of the Alcázar, with carved wooden doors from Lebanon, beautiful old tiles, and a fountain in a central courtyard. A sixteenth-century ancestor of the present owner returned from the Holy Land and built his palace in what he thought was the style of Pontius Pilate's home; yet it's much more Mudéjar than Roman. Upstairs are some lesser-known paintings by Goya, Murillo, and Velásquez.

• **Charity Hospital** (Hospital de la Caridad, Calle Temprado), open from 10 to 1, and 3:30 to 7, is a Baroque almshouse with a single-nave church containing paintings by **Murillo** and **Valdés Leal**. The most well-known work is Leal's morbid *Finis gloriae mundi*, in which a bishop in his coffin is being devoured by cockroaches or worms. Murillo said the painting made him want to hold his nose.

In the crypt below the altar lie the remains of **Miguel de Mañara**. Enscribed on his tomb are the words, "Here lie the ashes of the worst man the world has ever known." **Mañara**, who commissioned Leal's paintings, is often mistaken for the original Don Juan. Actually, he saw a play about Don Juan and was inspired to follow in his footsteps. One story tells of how, after a drunken orgy, he saw a funeral procession with a partially decomposed corpse that was himself. According to another legend he made advances to a beautiful nun, but when she turned her head aside he saw that her face was eaten away by a foul disease more horrible than death. Whatever happened, he was so overwhelmed by a sense of his own mortality that he gave away all his possessions, joined the brotherhood, and spent the rest of his life burying the bodies of executed prisoners. Somerset Maugham describes the chapel he built as "a bed-chamber transformed into a chapel for the administration of the last sacrament."

• After a day of sightseeing, nothing could be lovelier than an early evening stroll along the **Guadalquivir River** between the **San Telmo** and **Isabel II** bridges. The walk takes you past the early thirteenth-century **Golden Tower**, one of the few remaining monuments of Almohade

Spain. Sixty-minute **river cruises** depart from near the tower, usually at 5:45 P.M. For details, contact **Cruceros Sevilla**, Tel. 954-12.19.34.

• To escape the summer heat, stroll through the peaceful **María Luisa Garden**, one of the prettiest in Spain, with pools and fountains and quiet, shaded nooks beneath towering beech trees. On one side of the entrance is the **Tobacco Factory**, where some ten thousand girls worked in the nineteenth century, including Carmen. The building is now part of the University of Sevilla.

Shopping

The main pedestrian shopping street, **Calle de las Sierpes**, will be a disappointment unless you're into Korean castenets, wooden bulls stuck with swords, and imitation Moorish tiles. A few shops sell quality **jewelry**, **pottery**, and **fans**, however, so take a look.

At the **Plaza del Duque** is a department store, **Corte Inglés**, and a daily **craft** and **jewelry** market. Best bet for **antiques** and **ceramics** are the stores in the **Barrio Santa Cruz**. For ceramics in particular, try **Cerámicas Sevilla**. Note how the pottery is more intricate and sophisticated —less rustic and spontaneous—than the pottery made in Granada.

For **lace tablecloths** and **hand-embroidered clothes**, try **Feliciano Foronda**, Alvarez Quintero 52. For **folk costumes** try **Establecimiento Lina** at Plaza Santa Cruz 12, in the Barrio.

Bullfighting

The bullfighting season runs from late-March to mid-October. If you don't know anything about it, you're likely to be confused, repulsed, or bored.

It's usual to divide the bullfight into a prelude and three acts:

The Prelude. There's a roar of applause as the president enters. He signals and the gates swing open. In come the participants, even the man who will drag the dead bulls offstage. The first to enter are the matadors. They are not in step, as they would be in a northern country; each has his own swagger. They're supposed to look grave and unconcerned. The main actor, on the right, will fight the first and fourth bulls. The youngest, in the center, gets to kill the third and sixth. Everyone now leaves the ring. The president signals again.

Act One, scene one. Enter the bull. No one knows how he will perform. Only the young heifers at the bull ranches are tested; if they charge bravely, they are bred; if not they become meat. The bulls are never tested because they would remember. It is assumed that they will inherit bravery from their mothers.

If the bull comes out charging he is a single-minded bull who is easy to handle. This one stops. He thought he was being set free to join the herd, but something is wrong. He sniffs. He has seen the flick of a cape. He has never seen one before; his owners have made sure of that. He charges. Of the three *peones* (assistants) now in the ring, he chooses one victim, who scurries over the stockade. The matador watches. He is not a coward: He wants to see how the bull responds—if his vision is good, if he pulls to the left or to the right.

The matador approaches with his cape, red on one side, yellow on the other. The color really doesn't matter, the bull is color blind. The bull charges and the matador shows off his skill. The first pass of the cape, the *verónica*, is the most basic, deriving from the way in which St. Verónica is said to have held the cloth she used to wipe Christ's face. With each pass the matador gets closer to the bull, as he learns what he can and cannot do. If the bull stakes a territory, it's more dangerous to fight him there, protecting his ground, than when he's headed for it and has nothing on his mind but getting back. Olé! shout the crowds—a word some say comes from the Moorish cry to Allah.

Act One, scene two. Enter the men on horseback, the *picadores*, holdovers from the days when matadors were royal sportsmen who fought bulls from horses. The horses are terrified, but you can't hear them complain because their vocal chords are cut. Their right eyes are bandaged so they won't see the bulls coming to rip them apart. The bull is goaded to attack the right side of the heavily-padded horses while the picadores, in turn, thrust their six-foot lances into his shoulders. The idea is to paralyze the neck muscles so that the head drops and the matador can slay the bull with a sword. The motive is not sadistic; if the picadores pump their pikes or take too long, the audience boos. The bull is encouraged to toss the horses so that he will tire himself out. Much worse than the sight of a dying bull is the sight of a gored horse, writhing in pain, its insides spilling into the ring; pray you don't see this happen. What does happen frequently is that the horse, when tossed, goes down, and with him, the picador, who scurries away while the matadors divert the bull.

Act Two. Enter the *banderillas*, on foot, who dance away from the bull as he charges, thrusting three pairs of 18-inch darts, barbed like fishhooks, into the beast's shoulders. This is the least dangerous part of the show, done not to cause pain but to lower the bull's head so the matador can slay him. The bull stands in pain, trying to lick the pools of blood pouring like paint down his back. "As the wounded bull stands there waiting for the kill," wrote H. V. Morton, "I am reminded of all the tortured Christs in Spain. They wear the same air of spent and hopeless exhaustion. The blood streaks their bodies in the same way."

"No one brought up on Beatrix Potter can understand this," said Morton.

Act Three, scene one. The matador sometimes dedicates the bull to one person; but if he takes off his hat and salutes the whole audience it means he's dedicating the bull to everyone, and we can expect a great performance. With a small red cape, the *muleta*, that hides a sword, he now performs his most dangerous and exciting moves. The matador is judged by his artistry and by his willingness to put himself in danger. He shouldn't move his feet as the bull passes. The bull should avoid him, not he the bull. Arching his body shows less skill than standing straight. Kneeling is dangerous; so is passing the cape over his head (losing sight of the bull), and holding the cape behind his body. What he must do is destroy the bull's will—making the bull do what he wants, rendering him harmless. Getting the bull to perform in slow motion increases the danger.

Act Three, scene two. This is called "The Moment of Truth." The matador returns to the stockade for his sword and then advances toward the bull. He looks along the edge of his blade to the narrow space between the bull's shoulders that leads straight to his heart. This is the most dangerous moment. The matador sweeps the cape in front of the bull to draw his head down; if the head doesn't drop, the horns will rip into the matador. The matador lunges forward. Rarely does he strike true. He thrusts again. The bull totters and begins to cough up blood. If the matador can't make a clean kill, the audience boos loudly to disassociate itself from the butchery. Once the bull is down, he's killed with a final thrust into the brain.

Dining

Since dinners usually don't begin till 9 or 10, consider a drink first at the elegant **Alfonso XIII** (E, San Fernando 2. Tel. 954-22.28.50).

El Rincón de Curro (M, Virgen de Luján 45. Tel. 954-45.02.38) is a 5-minute walk from Alfonso XIII. Regional specialties are formally and graciously presented in what some consider the best restaurant in the city.

Rio Grande (E, Betis 70. Tel. 954-27.39.56) is another top restaurant, serving summer meals alfresco on a scenic terrace above the Guadalquivir River near the west end of San Telmo Bridge. The elegant (as opposed to regional) dining room has globe lamps, oil portraits, and potted plants. If you have only one night in Sevilla, you may prefer a place with more of a barrio atmosphere.

La Albahaca (E, Plaza Santa Cruz 12. Tel. 954-22.07.14) is a small restaurant in an old patrician house in the heart of the barrio. There's a limited menu, but lots of atmosphere.

La Dorada (M/E, Virgen de Aguas Santas 6. Tel. 954-45.51.00) specializes in fresh seafood, such as dorada and lubina baked in a shell of salt. It's near El Rincón de Curro (see above), so check them both out.

Hostería del Laurel (M, Plaza de los Venerables 5. Tel. 954-22.02.95) is in the barrio, with hanging hams, herbs, and a good reputation for fresh fish dishes, such as fritura mixta.

For tapas and regional cooking, try **Hostería del Prado** (M, Prado de San Sabastian), which has a similar "this is the real Spain" ambiance.

Mesón Don Raimundo (E, Argote de Molina. Tel. 954-22.33.55) serves sophisticated regional meals in an old convent near the cathedral. Decor includes a stuffed deer and a suit of armor—just in case you forget you're in Andalusia. A good bet for lunch, particularly for tapas at the bar.

Modesto (M, Cano y Cueto 5. No phone.) is a popular tavern with lots of Spanish snacks on a marbletop bar, and a restaurant upstairs.

Critics seem to agree that **El Burladero** (M, Canalejas 1. Tel. 954-22.29.00), with its bullfighting motif, has been gored by success. It's still popular, though, particularly among el toro fans. The bullring is only an ear's throw away. Try the clams in a sauce of onions, tomatoes, and white wine.

Mesón del Moro (M, Mesón del Moro 6. Tel. 954-21.87.96) is a so-so tourist restaurant with a Moorish ambiance. The arches are said to be fourteenth century. Specialties include sea bass in a spicy sauce, and sea perch with fennel.

Figón del Cabildo (M, Plaza del Cabildo. Tel. 954-22.01.17) is along the pedestrian mall—a good bet for light lunches (salads and desserts).

Los Alcázares (I/M, Miguel de Manara 10. Tel. 954-21.31.03) is a bit travel-posterish but offers good value. It's also conveniently located near the cathedral. Meals are served in a quaint, white-plaster building faced with tiles.

Nightlife

People who know **flamenco dancing** are less than enthusiastic about the tourist shows in Sevilla—but they're the best you're going to find in southern Spain. For under $10 you get a seat at a table for a 60-minute performance. Hostesses serve drinks. Shows begin at 9:30 and 11:30 P.M. The most authentic is at El Arenal (Rodo 7. Tel. 954-21.64.92).

Consider eating dinner in the barrio and then taking in the flamenco show at Los Gallos (Plaza de Santa Cruz 11. Tel. 954-21.69.81). After the show, you can visit some of the quarter's colorful bars, such as Casa Román on the Plaza de los Venerables.

Discos include Turin (Asunción 21), Petrarca (M. Carmelo 10), El Dragon Rojo (Betis 60), El Coto (Luis Montoto 118, Los Bebreros Hotel), and Tukan (Avenida República Argentina 66). Most are in the newer part of the city, across the San Telmo Bridge, on streets such as Calle Fortaleza and Calle del Salado.

Lodging

If you can afford the prices, there are only three memorable places to stay: Alfonso XIII, Doña María, and the Carmona Parador, a 40-minute drive from downtown Sevilla. All three are booked months in advance, so make your reservations early. Luz Sevilla is your best bet for a comfortable, modern hotel with amenities. La Rábida is good for budget travelers.

Alfonso XIII (E, San Fernando 2. Tel. 954-22.28.50) is in a class by itself. It was built to house wealthy guests for an Exhibition in 1929, and has retained the elegance of a stately palace. Some rooms are uninspired, but the courtyard atrium is a museum of Spanish and Moorish tapestries and art. Nonguests will want to come here for predinner cocktails.

Doña María (M/E, Don Remondo 19. Tel. 954-22.49.90) is tucked into a side street only minutes from the barrio and the cathedral. There are 50 doubles, no two alike—some charming with brass, canopied beds, others cramped and plain. There's a top-floor pool and a comfortable Moorish-style lounge with antiques and couches for guests to curl up in. The price is right, too: about half the cost of Alfonso XIII.

The Parador Nacional Alcázar del Rey Don Pedro (Tel. 954-14.10.10) is in Carmona, west of Sevilla. It's a 40-minute drive, but how often do you get to sleep in the ruins of a Moorish fort? You won't want to commute more than once, so stay either the night before you arrive in Sevilla or the night you leave.

La Rábida (M/I, Castelar 24. Tel. 954-22.09.60) is a real find for the budget-minded tourist: an old-fashioned, 87-room hotel on a quietish street near the center of town. Marble hallways lead to basic rooms surrounding an open courtyard. Rooms are unmemorable but clean, with high ceilings. Breakfast is included.

Luz Sevilla (E, Martín Villa 2. Tel. 954-22.29.91) is a five-star, modern hotel with bathroom phones, rooftop barbecue, ground-floor boutiques, children's pool, and beauty parlor. The mood is Spanish International (leather bar with tartan carpets, etc.).

The 262-room **Colón** (E, Canalejas 1. Tel. 954-22.29.00) gets an olé! as one of the better large, modern hotels, popular with bullfight aficionados. The bullring is nearby. Seventh-floor rooms have private balconies.

Pasarela (E, Avenida de la Borbolla 11. Tel. 254-23.19.80) is a relatively new 82-room hotel with sauna.

Nuevo Lar (M/E, Plaza de Carmen Benítez 3. Tel. 954-36.07.00) is a slick, modern hotel a short walk from the barrio. Rooms ending in 18 are best, says Fielding.

Murillo (M/I, Lope de Rueda 7. Tel. 954-21.60.95) is a picturesque hotel on a pedestrian-only street. The owner is the brother of the man who runs Spain's largest chain of antique shops. Front rooms have balconies.

Reyes Católicos (M/I, Gravina 57. Tel. 954-21.12.00) is a small, modern, 26-room annex to the nearby Montecarlo Hotel. If prices are too high, head for the less expensive **Ducal** (I, Plaza de la Encarnación 19. Tel. 954-21.51.07), an adequate, old-fashioned hotel.

In the **Barrio Santa Cruz** are several very basic family-run hotels—**Hostal Toledo** is one of them—in lovely, old, Moorish-style buildings dripping with flowers. Rooms, some of them with bath, but few with air conditioning, cost as little as $10 a night. A great bet for students.

For Further Information

The **National Tourist Office of Spain** is at Avenida de la Constitución 21, a short walk from the cathedral. It's open in summer from 8:30 to 3; off-season, from 9 to 1:30, and 3:30 to 8; closed Saturday afternoons and Sundays.

Train Information: Tel. 954-41.41.11. *Train reservations:* Tel. 954-21.79.98. *U.S. Consulate:* Paseo de las Delicias 7. Tel. 954-23.18.85. *American Express:* c/o Viajes Alhambra, Teniente Coronel Segui 6. Tel. 954-21.29.23. *Iberia Airlines:* Almirante Lobo 3; Information: Tel. 954-22.89.01. *Reservations:* Tel. 954-21.88.00.

EN ROUTE: From SEVILLA to MARBELLA

You have a choice of driving direct from **Sevilla** to **Marbella**, or following back roads through the **perched white villages of Andalusia**.

If you're anxious to see these villages, but have limited time, drive through them en route to Marbella. You'll only see a few of them—but some are better than none. Here's the route to follow: From **Sevilla** take N342 to **Morón**. Continue south to **Pruna** and **Olvera**; then go 2 miles west on N342, and south to **Setenil**, **Arriate**, and **Ronda**. From **Ronda**, drive south on N339 to **San Pedro de Alcántara**, and east on N340 to **Marbella**. The Michelin map of Spain (Number 990) is barely adequate for this trip; pick up the Firestone 1:200,000 Costa del Sol map, Number T-29, at tourist shops in Sevilla.

A better idea, if time permits, is to drive direct from **Sevilla** to **Marbella**, settle into your hotel, and then break the routine one day with a side trip through the perched villages. Two of these excursions are listed below under Marbella.

✤ *MARBELLA*

Marbella is the most fashionable and sedate resort area along the coast. There is a town with both a charming old Moorish quarter and a modern, T-shirt-and-fudge section along the main drag; but when people speak of Marbella they refer both to the town and to the resorts—some more exclusive than others—stretching 10 miles or so on either side of town, between the highway and the beach. If you're vacationing in southern Spain, this is the place to stay. There's championship golf and tennis, fashionable waterfront cafés, and trendy boutiques in the charming, medieval quarter of town.

The "golden bachelor"—the richest catch in Spain—hangs out at the Marbella Club. Petrodollars fill the Arab banks along N340 and underwrite Bjorn Borg's tennis clinic and Regine's nightclub at Puerto Romano. The Arabs, of course, stick to their own wadi (domain); what you'll see are people like yourself, shopping in Marbella and relaxing in one of the resorts surrounded by subtropical foliage at the edge of the sea. Marbella does have a certain Florida land boom feel to it, but development has been controlled, and Marbella, let's hope, will never turn into another Torremolinos.

Most of your time should be devoted to indolence—swimming in the ocean, sunbathing on sandy beaches or by the hotel pool. When you need something to do, visit the old Moorish section of Marbella and wander along the narrow whitewashed lanes radiating from **Plaza de los Naranjos**. Among the trashy souvenir emporia you'll find some tasteful craft shops like El Rey de la Ceramica, selling pottery from Granada; stores such as **Casa Bonet**, selling place mats and tablecloths; boutiques specializing in beachwear; and a choice of charming cafés for lunch or drinks.

Another trip you won't want to miss is to **Puerto Banús**, 5 miles west of Marbella. Less than 20 years ago Puerto Banús was a quiet port with a few bars. Today it has perhaps one hundred restaurants and shops; by the time you get there, it may have another fifty. Blinked into existence by a group of developers with a sense of style and taste, Puerto Banús is an adult fantasyland, a Yuppyland of Benettons and Picasso Pizzerias, quality restaurants and designer boutiques—all stretching along two streets behind the harbor, with a small, sandy beach at one end. Everything is fun and for sale—just as it is in the restored harborfronts of Boston, Newport, and New York. The uniformly whitewashed buildings lend a semblance of order and peacefulness to the profusion of shops—and create an atmosphere more Spanish than Spain. Come for lunch or dinner—restaurants are listed below. Many shops are open till 2 A.M. The young folks take over the piano bars and discos from elevenish, and straggle home at dawn.

Other excursions from Marbella are (1) by car or bus to Gibraltar and Tangier; and (2) to Ronda and the White Villages of Andalusia (see pages 391–94).

Golf

The Costa del Sol has five championship golf courses, all near **Estepona** (17 miles west of Marbella) and **San Pedro de Alcántara** (7 miles west of Marbella): *Aloha*, Tel. 952-78.23.88. *Atalaya Park*, Tel. 952-78.18.94. *Las Brisas*, Tel. 952-78.03.00. *Guadalmina*, Tel. 952-78.13.17. *Nueva Andalucía*, Tel. 952-81.82.00.

Tennis

Most hotels have their own courts. There's also **Bjorn Borg's Tennis Club**, and **Lew Hoad's Tennis Club** in Fuengirola (16 miles east of Marbella).

Fishing

Dozens of fishing boats are docked at Puerto Banús, 5 miles west of Marbella (toward Cadiz), waiting to take you angling for shark.

Nightlife

Marbella has two casinos, **Casino Nueva Andalucía** (Puerto Banús. Tel. 952-81.13.44) and **Casino de Juego de Torrequebrada** (Benalmádena. Tel. 952-44.25.45). The latter also has a nightclub.

Other bright spots, both in the town of Marbella and in Puerto Banús, include **Mau Mau**; **Vic y Peter**, Tel. 952-81.21.03; **Fiesta**, Tel. 952-77.37.43, where you can watch something called flamenco; and the disco **Kiss**, Tel. 952-77-46-94.

Dining: Marbella

La Hacienda Las Chapas (E, 8 miles east of town, toward Málaga. Tel. 952-83.12.67) is a white adobe building with rustic decorations (beamed ceiling, fireplace, tiled floor, wooden tables). Michelin gives it two stars. Specialties include veal cooked in foil, roast partridge in vine leaves, quail flambé, guinea hen, and maize pancakes.

La Fonda (E, Plaza de Fristo 10. Tel. 952-77.25.12) is a small restaurant with tables both inside and on the terrace of an old Andalusian house. Run by one of Madrid's leading restaurateurs, it gets one Michelin star for regional specialties such as Pastel de Trucha Salsa Romos and Pintada en hojaldre.

If you're not staying at the **Marbella Club** (E, N340, 2 miles west of town, toward Cadiz. Tel. 952-77.13.00), make reservations for dinner or come for drinks. The wealthy come down from their private villas to socialize here, creating an intimate, community feeling you won't experience in other Marbella resorts.

Gran Marisquería Santiago (M/E, Paseo Marítimo. Tel. 952-77.00.78) is well known for its fresh seafood: sole meuniere, halibut with mushroom sauce, fresh salmon with herbs, lobster from the tank. The atmosphere is informal—the restaurant is on the busy waterfront, in back of the main town beach—but it enjoys a good reputation.

La Meridiana (E, Camino de la Cruz, Las Lomas, 3 miles west of town, toward Cadiz. Tel. 952-77.61.90) serves meals on the garden terrace of a Bauhaus-type building.

El Balcón de la Vírgen (I, Remedios 2. Tel. 952-77.60.92) is a friendly, low-priced restaurant in a sixteenth-century building in the old quarter of Marbella.

Dining: Puerto Banús, 5 miles west of Marbella

The elegantly decorated **Royale** (E, Muelle Ribera-local. Tel. 952-78.18.98) has the best reputation, particularly for fresh fish.

Cipriano (M/E, Muelle de Levante. Tel. 952-78.10.86) also enjoys a good reputation for fresh fish. Prices are slightly lower than at Royale, and the atmosphere is more casual.

Don Leone (E, Tel. 952-78.17.27) is another local favorite, with such specialties as artichoke soup, fresh homemade pastas, and Merluza fish with mint leaves.

La Poularde (M/E, Ribera 14. Tel. 952-78.15.97) and **Taberna del Alabardero** (M/E, Muelle Benabola. Tel. 952-78.27.94) are both recommended. For good Indian/Pakistani food, try **Shahan** (M, Muelle Benabola. Tel. 952-78.50.44).

Lodging

The only reason to stay in town is if you're on a tight budget and have no car. Students can stay in small, family-run hotels in the old quarter of Marbella for as little as $10 a night. There are a few reasonably priced, package-tour-type high-rise hotels only a block from the busy town beach. For most visitors, air conditioning in summer is a must. The ocean is uninviting at times, thanks to improper pollution controls, so a hotel pool is a plus. Most visitors prefer to stay at one of the sparkling white resorts strung along the beach on either side of town. Finding the right one is critical.

Those who can afford the price will want to stay either at the **Marbella Club** (E, Route N340, 2 miles west of town on the road to Cadiz. Tel. 952-77.13.00) or **Puente Romano** (E, Route N340, 2 miles west of town on the road to Cadiz, just past the Marbella Club. Tel. 952-77.01.00). Though under the same management, each has a different atmosphere. The Marbella Club, the grande dame of Marbella, is smaller, older, more aristocratic, and also more worn. It tends to attract an older, more established clientele, who request the same room year after year. Because the local patricians all belong to the club and come down from their villas for drinks and dinner, the club has a color and class that the more international Puente Romano lacks. Some, of course, will prefer the greater anonymity and the greater number of American guests at Puente Romano.

The bungalow-style rooms at the Marbella Club run from cramped to spacious, and the decor varies from Beach Modern to regional; specify what you want but ask for a room that's been recently renovated. Facilities include a beach and pool. The grounds are exquisite. Breakfast is served on a patio where songbirds flit through the lush, subtropical vegetation. Puente Romano, in comparison, is a very modern hotel/apartment complex of low white stucco buildings on beautifully manicured grounds. There's a beach, two pools, a disco run by Regine, a tennis club, and boutiques. Rooms are more luxurious than at the Marbella Club—and more predictable.

Los Monteros (E, on Route N340, 4 miles east of Marbella, on the road to Malaga. Tel. 952-77.17.00) prides itself on being one of the most expensive hotels in Spain. The 171 rooms are minutes from the famous **Rio Real** golf course (free bus service to the greens). Facilities include three pools, seven tennis courts, and horseback riding. A large pool and lovely lawns separate a modern two-story section from a more old-fashioned, seven-story building. Rooms and views vary; specify what you want. Eighty percent of the guests are English, which may explain the somewhat starched formality of many rooms, and the beach chairs perfectly aligned on manicured lawns, like so many pieces of sculpture.

Stay at the 424-room **Andalucía Plaza** only if you like being surrounded by Americans or don't mind six hundred conventioneers at dinner.

Don Carlos (E, Route N340, 8 miles or 15 minutes east of Marbella, on the road toward Malaga. Tel. 952-83.11.40) is a 232-room, seventeen-story white concrete slab at the edge of the sea. The former Hilton attracts an American crowd. Ask for an upper room facing the ocean. The 13-acre estate has a large pool, tennis courts, lovely gardens, boutiques, and, of course, a hairdresser. The hotel is isolated, so there's no place to go without a car; but you can walk along a lovely natural beach away from the commercial areas.

Golf Hotel (Del Golf) Nueva Andalucía (E, Tel. 952-81.11.45) has only 21 luxurious rooms, mostly for golfers who play on two nearby courses.

Meliá Don Pepe (E, Route 340, Finca Las Marinas, 6 miles west of town on the road toward Cadiz. Tel. 952-77.03.00) is a flairless but comfortable high-rise, which gets perhaps 20 percent Americans, as compared to 80 percent at Don Carlos. Extensive facilities include two tennis courts, a movie theater, private beach, heated pool, water sports, sauna, hairdresser, and shops. The choice is yours: the larger rooms facing the parking lot or the smaller ones facing the sea.

El Fuerte (E/M, Castillo San Luís. Tel. 952-77.15.00) has 146 simple, adequate rooms, in town. There's also a pool, a garden with palm trees, and a certain faded elegance in the public areas which you won't find in other low-priced hotels.

Baviera (I, Camino del Calvaro 2. Tel. 952-77.29.50) is a budget hotel on the main street opposite the bus station.

Skol (M, La Fontanilla. Tel. 952-77.08.00) is one of several serviceable hotels in town which attract an English package-tour trade. Don't expect more than a convenient place to put your head.

Students on a budget can stay in small family-run hotels in the old quarter of Marbella for less than $10 a night. You'll be lucky to find air conditioning or anyone who speaks English, but rooms will be clean and some will have private showers. Best bet is the friendly **Enriqueta**, which has a TV room. Next best is **Hostal el Miro** (Tel. 952-77.00.60).

Emergencies

The **U.S. Consulate** is 16.5 miles east of Marbella, in Fuengirola (Avenida Sáenz de Tejada 1. Tel. 952-47.48.91).

Medical: Clínica Marbella. Tel: (day) 952-77.42.00; (night) 952-77.42.82.

✤ RONDA and THE PERCHED WHITE VILLAGES OF ANDALUSIA

Perhaps it was the light after a late-afternoon storm, but the drive through these hilltop towns was the highlight of my last trip to Spain. There are many such villages, blazing white, clutching the rocky mountainsides above the fields of sunflower and wheat, grape and maize. Strangely, the Michelin guide does not even mention them.

The houses are painted white to ward off the summer heat. Up close, one sees that the streets are dusty and the walls crumbling. But from a distance, the towns seem to rise from the plains like medieval castles. The uniform whiteness gives them an architectural integrity as soothing to the heart as to the eye: Here at last is a world where, visually at least, the individual is subsumed; where everything says "us," not "I." What you'll see is the seasonless, monochromatic world of a Zen landscape painting, where nothing ever seems to blossom or fade. Yet the anonymity is only a façade against a harsh world; the family is still the wellspring of life in these Moorish towns, and the true colors come from the perfumed court-yards within. As the woman is supposed to hide behind her veil, so the

Moorish house turns a plain face to the world. Nothing outside arouses envy. Delights are reserved for guests.

You owe it to yourself at least once to leave the main highways and wander along the back roads, through fields and pastureland, beneath the perched white villages. The roads are as safe as any in Spain, and marked well enough that, with a detailed map, you won't get lost—at least not for long. Listed below are two excursions from Marbella.

EXCURSION 1

Drive west on N340 to **San Pedro de Alcántara** (6.7 miles). Head north on C339 to **Ronda** (27 miles).

✤ *RONDA*

Both the modern district and the old Moorish quarter are split in two by a great gorge. The bridge across it, which has a restaurant in the former prison cell above its central arch, is one of the most spectacular sights in Spain. The only problem with Ronda is its popularity; you have no sense of discovery here as you do in the white villages. The old town lies behind walls built during the Moorish occupation, which lasted until 1485. Because of the high elevation, the houses are low and small, with steep roofs, as they are in the colder regions of the north. Park at the **Collegiate Church**, on your left as you drive through the old town. Of particular note are the Renaissance chancel (where the altar is) and the ornate choir stalls. Walk behind the church (the side away from the road), and turn right to the **Mondragón Palace**, with its twin towers. The terrace overlooks the gorge and the plains below.

The view from the **bridge**, looking down 500 feet, is spectacular. Cross the bridge and enter the new town. On your left is the **bullring**. Built in 1785, it is one of the oldest in Spain. **Francisco Romero**, the father of modern bullfighting—he introduced the cape, the *muleta*, and most of the rituals—was born in Ronda in 1698. His son **Juan Romero** introduced the "supporting team," and his grandson **Pedro Romero** (1754–1839) became one of Spain's greatest bullfighters.

Also on your left, beyond the bullring, are the **Paseo de la Merced Gardens**. Stroll through the gardens and enjoy a dramatic walk along the cliffs.

From Ronda to the Perched Villages

Continue north through the modern section of Ronda on **C339** to **Puerto de Montejaque** (10 miles). Turn left on **C344** to **Grazalema** (8 miles), 2,716 feet up, where you can visit the **Church of the Encarnación** and wander through the white streets, beneath balconies and patios bursting with flowers.

Now you have a decision to make. Fodor calls **Zahara**, which I didn't see, one of the most beautiful of the white villages. The most direct route, which Fodor warns against because of the roughness of the mountain road, is to take **C344** another mile west, and then to turn north (right) on **Route 521** (8 miles), past **Puerto de las Palas**. The longer, less dramatic route is to drive northeast 6 miles from **Grazalema** to **Puerto de Asperilla** on **C339**; then, at the **T**, turn left (north) go about 7 miles, and turn left again on **Route 521** to **Zahara**.

If you're addicted to back roads, follow signs from **Zahara** to the pretty town of **El Gastor** and then head north to the major road, **N342**. If you've seen enough, skip **El Gastor**, and from **Zahara** continue north on **Route 521**, and turn left (north) on **C339**, going 4 miles to **Algodonales**. This town seems even whiter than the other white towns, perhaps because of the striking contrast with the silvery-green olive groves that surround it.

Whether you go to **Algodonales** or **El Gastor**, you'll end up on **N342**. Turn right (east) to **Olvera** (13 miles from Algodonales). The beauty of this village is compromised only by the presence of the main road. From **Olvera**, you can make a side trip northeast to **Pruna** (9 miles round trip).

Drive 2 miles east on **N342**, and head south 7 miles to the perched village of **Setenil**, where the rock forms a natural roof over the streets. This is the most dramatic part of the drive, and should be made in the late afternoon, when the sun is less harsh. From **Setenil** continue south to **Arriate** and **Ronda**, and then take **C339** back south to the coast. The trip will take the better part of a day.

EXCURSION 2

If Excursion 1 hasn't satisfied your wanderlust, try this itinerary to other white villages and a dramatic mountain peak. Drive east along the coast on **Route N340** from **Marbella** to **Fuengirola** (17 miles). Take the beautiful drive north to **Mijas** (5 miles). Continue north, past **Alhaurín** to the white village of **Cartama** (12 miles). Cross the Guadalhorca River

(2 miles) and turn left (north) on C337 to the white village of **Alora** (13 miles). Continue north on another beautiful road to the **Ruinas de Bobastro** (11 miles). Drive to **Las Atalayas**, turn left at the edge of the lake to **Ardales** (4 miles), return to **Alora** via **Carratraca** (14 miles), and retrace your steps back to **Cartama** (15 miles). Take C337 to **Coin** (8 miles), **Monda**, and **Marbella** (17 miles).

EN ROUTE: From MARBELLA to GRANADA

As you approach overdeveloped **Torremolinos**, the traffic increases and so do the real estate and video club signs. What Torremolinos has to offer are high-rise hotels with pools and shops along a highway, and a strip of beach. Life here is geared for the package-tour trade. Fielding calls it a "boom, boom boom town."

Málaga is not a destination, but a point of transit. The only place I'd recommend staying in Málaga is the **Parador de Gibralfaro** (E/M, Tel. 952-22.19.02), which sits on a mountaintop with breathtaking views, about 2 miles from the center of town. The rustic rooms—only a dozen of them—are reasonably priced.

Between **Málaga** and **Salobreña** is the **Nerja Cave** (Cueva de Nerja), open May to mid-September from 9 to 9; off-season, from 10 to 1:30, and 4 to 7. If you're partial to caves or traveling with children, the Nerja Cave is worth an hour of your time. It's not the usual long, dark passageway, but a huge cavern with lots of corners to explore. There's classical music, and, best of all, no guide comparing stalactites to Joe DiMaggio's bat or George Washington's nose. Most thrilling are the **Cascade Chamber**, which hosts an annual festival of music and dance; and a cathedral-like room with a pillar 200 feet long—the longest-known stalactite in the world.

At **Almuñecar**, turn north on N323 for 41 miles to **Granada**. This is a beautiful trip along the western rim of the Sierra Nevadas—a world of wild, red rock, orange and lemon groves, and silver olive trees.

✤ *GRANADA*

The main attraction of Granada—perhaps of all Spain—is a Moorish fort and palace known as the **Alhambra**. You'll want to spend at least a half day here and at the palatial villa called the **Generalife**. The other musts are the **Cathedral** and the adjoining **Royal Chapel**, where Ferdinand and Isabella are buried. You'll also want to wander through the old

Moorish quarter to see the Alhambra at dusk, and journey 29 miles to Pico de Veleta to enjoy the wild mountain views of the Sierra Nevadas.

The Alhambra is open from 9 to 7; off-season, 10 to 6; floodlit visits Saturday nights in summer.

A Historical Note

When Córdoba was at the height of its power, Granada was a mere provincial capital. It was then, in the ninth century, that construction of the Alhambra began—not the palace, but the original fortress that occupies part of the present site.

Granada came to its full glory under the Nasrid dynasty (1232–92), when the rest of Spain had fallen to the Catholics. As many as 100,000 Muslim refugees fled here before the advancing Christian armies. The city was under constant siege, and its existence depended on the payment of tributes, skillful diplomacy, and the whims of the enemy. The situation was worse than precarious; it was just a matter of time before Granada fell into Christian hands.

When Mohammed V began the Alhambra Palace in 1377, he must have known that he was building the last and perhaps most splendid monument of seven hundred years of Moorish culture in Spain. It was the work of an old, dying civilization; the product of a reduced and threatened state. As you tour the palace, try to see it as an oasis of peace and beauty where Mohammed V and other sultans sought to escape impending doom—each room an Arabian tale told to stave off death.

The Alhambra: An Appreciation. Modern Granada is a busy, sprawling town, visually unmemorable. As you climb Alhambra hill, you leave the noise and confusion of modern life behind and enter a green world, where the air is clear and cool. The Alhambra is not one but a series of buildings on a 35-acre plateau, a natural acropolis looming over the modern town of Granada. Think of it as a fortified medieval city with five sections: (1) the **Alcazaba**, the oldest part of the Alhambra (and also the most touched up), dating back to the days when it served as a military fortress; (2) the fourteenth-century **Alhambra Palace**, or Alcázar, where the sultan lived with his harem and entertained important guests; (3) the **Royal City**, which included a college, houses, workshops, and a great mosque—virtually none of which remain; (4) a Christian palace built after the Reconquest by Charles V (grandson of Ferdinand and Isabella); and (5) the **Generalife** (technically outside the walls of the Alhambra), the summer villa of the Sultan and his family.

First impressions. Ask yourself as you walk around: Is the Alhambra the high point of Moslem architecture in Spain, or is it the dying gasp of a decadent culture? One critic calls it "foppish." Another says it looks more like a boudoir than a king's palace. Still another equates the Córdoba mosque to the robustness of early Christian architecture and the Alhambra to the flaccid self-indulgence of Rococo. "No medieval Christian king lived in such feminine exotic surroundings," wrote H. V. Morton in *A Stranger in Spain*. "These pretty vistas, fountains and arcades, designed it seems for eating of rose-petal jam, for tears, for sighs, provoke the thought that the Alhambra is not unlike a woman who has no other quality than beauty."

Size. You will probably be surprised by the smallness of the rooms. No effort has been made to overwhelm you, as, say, at Versailles. Even the Court of Lions is built on an intimate, human scale. The sultans seemed to be seeking an inner peace, not a way of proving their worth in the eyes of the world.

Impermanence. The material of which the Alhambra is made is wonderfully flimsy. Beneath the ornate stuccowork is nothing but bricks, plaster, and rubble. The wood frame is crudely constructed. The ceilings are nothing but carved plaster, which you could break with a hand. The caliphs built schools and mosques to last, but not palaces, which were merely the headquarters of one man who would someday be replaced. That the decorations have survived five hundred years is a miracle.

Style. What you see is not the creation of one man but an accretion of styles over many generations. This explains the seemingly haphazard arrangement of some buildings and the absence of a defined axis. Notice how the builders concealed all solid functional components—walls, arches, ceilings—behind a decorative web of plaster and tile. Lightness was the aim of Moorish architecture as massiveness was for the Egyptians. The goal was worthy of a genii: Not only to fill space with beauty, but to make the walls disappear, to free them of weight; in short, to transcend matter.

Architecture and Decoration. As you walk through the Alhambra, try to think of it as a Moorish heaven: an oasis in a dry desert, with fountains, greenery, and shelter from the sun. Picture the slender columns as tent poles or date palms; the flowery capitals (the heads of columns) as vegetation; the designs on the walls as oriental carpets in a nomad's tent. The desert is empty as a whitewashed wall: Is it any wonder that the Moors would want to fill it with color and life?

Nature. Our own houses shelter us from nature; in the Alhambra, nature is integrated in the design. We admit sunshine from without; the

Alhambra admits it from courtyards within. It's only in recent times that Western architects have begun to catch up with the Arabs—using skylights, and, following the lead of Frank Lloyd Wright, integrating architecture with the natural environment. For this to happen we had to learn what the Moors apparently knew: that man and nature are one, and that happiness comes from experiencing this oneness.

A Tour Through the Alhambra

The Approach. The road to the entrance is lined, inappropriately, with elms: The Spanish King gave Wellington an estate in return for his struggle against Napoleon, and Wellington returned the favor with a decidedly unMoorish gift of elms.

Enter through the **Gate of Justice,** so called because it was here that the sultans held court. In the keystone of the horseshoe-shaped entry arch is a large open hand of Fatima, daughter of Mohammed by his first wife, each finger symbolizing one of the five requirements of the Islamic faith: belief in the oneness of God, prayer, fasting in the month of Ramadan, pilgrimage to Mecca, and the giving of alms.

Turn into the **Place of the Cisterns** (Plaza de los Aljibes), an open area where water was stored in case enemies destroyed the aqueduct. On your right is the fourteenth-century sultan's **palace** (Alcázar), which is where you'll want to spend most of your time. On your left, behind a wall, is the **Alcazaba,** the oldest part of the Alhambra, which contained military headquarters, government offices, a mint, guards' barracks, and apartments for members of court and official guests.

Turn left into the **Alcazaba** and climb the **watchtower** (Torre de la Vela) for a great view of Granada. It was on this terrace that the Catholics placed their first cross in 1492, proclaiming the end of seven hundred years of Muslim rule.

Return to the **Place of the Cisterns.** Ahead of you is **Emperor Charles V's Palace.** It's fashionable to denigrate this Renaissance structure, to dismiss it as a visual obscenity; but not all critics agree. The important thing is to make up your own mind and to see what your verdict says about your own sensibilities. Charles V, the grandson of Ferdinand and Isabella, tore down many Moorish buildings to construct this palace, which was never completed. It's a perfect square with a circular inner court where bullfights were once held. Michener calls its façade "grotesquely ugly, as if someone had set out to burlesque the worst taste of the time." Washington Irving dismissed it as an "arrogant intruder." The Michelin guide, however, praises Charles's work as "one of the most successful creations of the Renaissance in Spain . . . so perfect are its lines, so dignified its appearance, so simple its plan of a circle within a square."

Whatever its architectural virtues, Charles's palace is as inappropriately situated as the cathedral in the Córdoba mosque. Some will be horrified by this tortured juxtaposition of styles; others will be fascinated by the way in which it reflects the double personality of southern Spain.

From Charles V's palace, turn into the **Court of the Myrtle Trees** (Patio de Comares), which has a long pool down the center, bordered by myrtles. This was the reception area for visitors to the **Hall of the Ambassadors**, so try to imagine yourself waiting here for a meeting with the Sultan. Notice how nature is included in this Moorish version of paradise: in the dark green hedges standing out against the gleaming white marble; in the sky sailing across the water. Notice, too, how everything converges on the center: a very Eastern notion, where one looks inward (as opposed to outward, toward the world) to find peace, and where beauty is enclosed within walls as the spirit or soul is encased in the body. The reflections create a playful ambiguity about the nature of reality (which is real, which reflection?). There's a sense of unreality, too, in the narrow columns, which seem too slight to support anything.

At the north end of this court is the **Hall of the Blessing** (Sala de la Barca), which leads into the **Hall of the Ambassadors**. The Sultan met official visitors and held state receptions here. The lavish decoration—the most splendid in the Alhambra—reflects the importance of this hall in a kingdom that depended on diplomacy, not warfare, for its survival.

Turn right down a galley to the **Queen's Dressing Room**, located at the top of a small tower (**Abul Hachach's Tower**). The room has been modernized and painted with arabesques. Washington Irving lived here while writing *The Alhambra*.

Return to the **Court of the Myrtle Trees** and turn left into the famous **Court of Lions** (Patio de los Leones). This fourteenth-century court was the drawing room of the harem, at the heart of the palace. The lions offering their rumps to the fountain are probably Phoenician. The fountain was originally a sundial—at each hour water flowed from the mouth of a different lion.

To your right, off the **Court of Lions**, is the **Hall of the Abencerrajes**. The honeycomb dome is carved from simple plaster: a beehive (one critic writes) whose honey is light. The hall is named after the noble family whose male members were lured here and executed by the last sultan of Granada; guides will insist you can still see their blood.

From the **Hall of the Abencerrajes** return to the **Court of Lions.** Turn right. At the end of the hall is the **Hall of the Kings** (Sala de los Reyes), which houses the portraits of the first ten Nasrid rulers.

Return to the **Court of Lions** and take the passageway to the right. This leads into the **Hall of the Two Sisters,** which many consider the loveliest room in the palace. It would be fun to dream up an Arabian tale about the two sisters, but they are in fact nothing more than the two slabs of flawless white marble. The honeycomb ceiling seems the work of bees. Many compare it to stalactites or icicles—an appropriate sort of wish fulfillment for a people of the desert.

Exit through the **Gate of Justice** and walk left around the walls to the **Generalife,** the summer villa of the sultans. All here is cool and restful, sensual and intimate. The two lines of water jets make visual poetry and remind us again that the Arab heaven is a cool place with water.

Other Sights in Granada

• **Chapel Royal** (Capilla Royal)—open 10:30 to 1 and 4 to 7; off-season, from 10:30 to 1 and 3:30 to 6—is the tomb of the Catholic Monarchs (Los Reyes Católicos), Ferdinand and Isabella. Built in the Isabeline style—a Catholic response to the Moorish love of decoration, but with none of the restraint—is one of the most lavish sepulchres in the world. Isabella's art collection of great Flemish, Spanish, and Italian paintings is in the sacristy.

The Catholic Monarchs wanted to be buried in the city where they won their final victory over the Moors in 1492. Isabella was a year older than Ferdinand. She was a beautiful child, who was pursued at age fourteen by Edward IV of England; had she accepted his advances, she might have become Queen of England! Her modesty went to such extremes that when she was dying she refused to show her bare foot for extreme unction and her silk stocking was annointed instead. She was devoted to Christ's kingdom and thought God approved of the Inquisition and the expulsion of the Jews. It was she, not her husband, who believed in Columbus.

Isabella is looking away from her husband, just as, on another sepulchre, her daughter **Juana the Mad** is looking away from her husband, **Philip the Handsome.**

At age seventeen Juana set sail for Flanders to marry eighteen-year-old Philip of Burgundy. According to H. V. Morton, she was insanely jealous of him and responded to his infidelities with hunger strikes and tantrums. The couple returned to Spain, but Philip hated the stuffiness of the court and fled, leaving Juana alone with her depressions. She tried to flee to him one cold November night, dressed in nothing but her nightgown; and from that time she was known as *Juana la Loca*—Joan the Mad or Crazy Jane. When she was permitted to return to Flanders in 1504, she embarrassed the Spanish court by attacking Philip's lover and cutting off her rival's long hair in public.

When Isabella died, Juana returned to Spain with Philip to claim her inheritance as heir to Castile. Ferdinand acted as her regent, since she was considered unfit to rule. Within a year Philip died. Inconsolable, Juana refused to have him buried and set his corpse on a throne dressed in furs. After the body was embalmed she never left the coffin and had it opened every night so that she could kiss the dead man's face. For several years she wandered about the country, traveling by night with a hearse that carried her husband's body. Her father, Ferdinand, who outlived Isabella by a dozen years, finally convinced Juana to settle in a mansion, still accompanied by Philip's corpse; and there they remained for forty-seven years, until her death at the age of seventy-six. It was the child of Juana and Philip, Charles V, who built his palace in the Alhambra and who approved the construction of the cathedral in the Córdoba Mosque.

A short flight of steps leads down to a vault where the simple coffins of Ferdinand, Isabella, Mad Joan, and Philip lie on a stone slab. On the wall is a crucifix. The reality of death is poignantly brought home in the contrast between the splendid tomb and these four lead boxes.

Next to the Chapel Royal is the **Cathedral** (same opening times as the Chapel Royal), built in the sixteenth and seventeenth centuries. Sit in its dim interior, preferably during one of the daily organ concerts, and contemplate the different values that went into the creation of this church and the Alhambra. What is unusual is the way in which you're made to enter through a rotunda rather than through a nave (the long central aisle).

• One of the highlights of your stay in Granada is the sweeping view of the Alhambra from the terrace of **St. Nicholas Church** in the **Albaicín**, the old Moorish quarter. Come at sunset for a sight you won't forget.

• If you're interested in architecture, visit the **Carthusian Monastery** (open 10 to 1, and 3 to 7; off-season, to 6), which has a lavishly decorated Baroque church, a magnificent late-Baroque sacristy, and a splendid view.

• To escape the heat and enjoy some spectacular mountain scenery, either on foot or from your car, drive 29 miles to **Pico de Veleta**—more than ten thousand feet up in the Sierra Nevadas. You can ski here from mid-December through early May; one of the lifts may be open now in summer. The road to the top is passable only from July to October, but you don't have to reach the summit to appreciate the view. The restaurant **Ruta del Veleta** (M, 44 Cenes de la Vega) is 3 miles from Granada on the road to the mountains, so you may want to stop there for lunch or dinner en route. There's a chalet-style **parador** near the summit, where you can also stop for meals (reserve ahead). Upper rooms are best. You're above timberline, so to take a walk just set off in any direction. Be sure to bring a sweater, even in summer.

Shopping

In the narrow streets such as **Zacatín** and **Angel Ganivet**, between the cathedral and **Reyes Católicos**, is the old Moorish silk market (the **Alcaicería**), which has been turned into a tourist district with some interesting pottery and craft shops. Look for marquetry (chess sets, boxes, music boxes, etc.), ceramics, shoulder bags, rugs, and wall hangings.

Reyes Católicos is the main shopping street leading toward the Alhambra. Other shops are on **Cuesta de Gomérez**, which goes from Reyes Católicos up to the Alhambra.

Dining

There are several good to excellent restaurants in Granada, but none that is consistently first-rate. Several have a great deal of warmth and character.

Top billing goes to **Cunini** (M, Pescadería 9. Tel. 958-22.37.27), located behind the flower market near the cathedral. Downstairs is a tapa bar; the upstairs restaurant is best known for its Basque-style soup-stews and its fresh fish.

Also near the cathedral is the well-established **Sevilla** (M, Oficios 14. Tel. 958-22.12.23). Best bet is not the dining room but the tapa bar.

If you're staying on Alhambra hill, dine at the government-run **Parador** (Recinto de la Alhambra. Tel. 958-22.14.93), perhaps more for its atmosphere than for its cuisine, and **Columbia** (M, Antequeruela Baja 1. Tel. 958-22.74.33), which has live guitar music on a terrace overlooking the city.

Two simple, friendly restaurants with good value are **Casa Salvador** (I, Duende 16. Tel. 958-25.50.09) and the slightly less expensive **Los Leones** (I, José Antonio 10. Tel. 958-25.50.07). Both are a distance from the cathedral, away from the Alhambra.

Los Manueles (I, Zaragoza 2. Tel. 958-22.34.15) is basic, busy, and friendly, with ceramic tiles, and smoked hams hanging from the ceiling.

Nightlife

Nightlife centers on the gypsy caves on **Sacromonte**, the hillside opposite the Generalife. Tourists submit to and sometimes participate in 30-minute flamenco shows, which have been described as "a cosmic low in tourist-racketeering." Two exceptions are **Zincale** (Sacromonte 19) and private shows in the studio of **Mario Maya** from 7 P.M. to 3 A.M., daily except Sunday. If you're seriously interested in flamenco, see it in Sevilla.

The origin of the gypsies is not known, but it's generally believed that they came from northern India and migrated to Persia about 1000 A.D. From there they split into two branches—one heading southwest to Egypt and North Africa, the other moving northwest to Europe and the Balkans. "Gypsy" means "Egyptian." Gypsies from Egypt migrated to Spain in the mid-fifteenth century. They preserved the songs and dances of old Andalusia, but did not create them—being better imitators than creators.

In Granada the gypsies live in caves carved from the hillsides. It's not as primitive as it sounds, for their whitewashed rooms are lit with electricity and heated with tiled stoves. The caves themselves are naturally warm in winter and dry and cool in summer. You may find a passionate or talented dancer here, but most just walk through the steps, clicking their imported castanets, squeezing the myth of Gypsy Spain for every tourist dollar they can get. Go for the experience, expect to be taken, and insist on having a good time.

Lodging

Hotels that claim to be in the Alhambra are not in fact within the walls, but only on Alhambra hill, in walking distance of the palace. Try to stay here: It's quiet and cool, and away from the congestion of the town below. Stay in town only if you need a budget hotel or want to be in walking distance of the nightspots.

The two "Alhambra" hotels where everyone wants to stay are the **Parador Nacional San Francisco** (Recinto de la Alhambra. Tel. 958-22.14.93) and the **Alhambra Palace** (E, Peña Partida 2. Tel. 958-22.14.68). Both are booked up to six months in advance.

The **Parador** is the only hotel that's actually on the grounds of the Alhambra (though not within the walls). The former Arab palace was transformed into a Franciscan convent when Granada was reconquered in 1492. Rooms are simple and restrained; public areas are full of rare icons, rugs, mosaics, and embroideries. The only noise is from the fountains in the gardens, beneath the vine-covered walls. If you want a tastefully subdued environment where you can experience the tranquility of the Alhambra itself, this is the place to stay. (If you can't get a room in the Parador, make reservations for lunch.)

The **Alhambra Palace** is a lavish, Moorish-style palace halfway up the hill to the Alhambra. Since it is located on the main road, with cars and buses constantly pulling into and out of insufficient parking spaces, the mood is more harried than at the more isolated Parador. Despite its busyness, however, the Palace is still a conversation piece, with rich carpets, tapestries, and colorful Moorish tiles. Front rooms are preferable.

Farther up Alhambra hill is the **Washington Irving** (M/E, Paseo del Generalife 2. Tel. 958-22.75.50), where the author of *The Alhambra* once stayed. The hotel is one of a kind, but many rooms are very small and plain. If you stay, ask for a large one.

The most modern hotel near the Alhambra is **Hotel Generalife** (M, Avenida de los Alixares. Tel. 958-22.55.06). Rooms are clean and comfortable but smallish, with little character. The selling point is the terraced pool with a view of the Sierra Nevadas. (If you're not staying here, you may be able to use the pool for a fee.)

Near the Hotel Generalife is **Doña Lupe** (Avenida de los Alixares. Tel. 958-22.14.74), a smaller, functional hotel that's currently undergoing restoration. Check to see whether the pool has been completed. Rooms have a motelish air, but you may find space here when other Alhambra hotels are full.

Of the modern hotels in town, **Luz de Granada** (E, Avenida de Calvo Sotelo 18. Tel. 958-20.40.61) is the best. Rooms, though small, are clean, comfortable, and reasonably priced. The hotel, however, has an impersonal, group-tour ambiance and is inconveniently located northwest of town on the road to Córdoba.

The drawing card of the 221-room **Meliá Granada** (E, Angel Ganivet 7. Tel. 958-22.74.00) is its convenient downtown location near the cathedral. Rooms can be small, noisy, and sometimes shabby; ask for one that's newly renovated.

A grade below the Meliá Granada is the less sophisticated, 205-room **Carmén** (E, José Antonio 62. Tel. 958-25.83.00). The hotel is essentially a high-rise on a busy street not far from the cathedral. Rooms are clean but somewhat basic for a four-star hotel. Inside rooms are quieter—the higher up the better.

The 100-room **Los Angeles** (I/M, Cuesta Escoriaza 17. Tel. 958-22.14.24) caters to tour groups and is away from the center of town. But the surroundings are pleasant and peaceful, the staff is friendly, the price is right, and the hotel is one of the very few with a pool. Stay in the larger rooms added since 1983.

If you just need a place to put your head, there's nothing wrong with the aging **Brasilia** (M, Recogidas 7. Tel. 958-25.84.50)—particularly the seventh-floor rooms with balconies. Prices are about half those of the Melía Granada.

Kenia (M/I, Molinos 65. Tel. 958-22.75.06) is a quiet, unassuming hotel in a residential area.

Carlos V (M/I, 4 Plaza de los Campos 4. Tel. 958-22.15.87) is a quiet, English-style hotel on the fourth floor of a government building in a residential area. A weird location for a hotel, but you'll enjoy talking about it years later. Twin beds only.

América (M, Real de la Alhambra. Tel. 958-22.74.71) is a popular hotel with only 14 simple but friendly rooms near the Alhambra. Good value.

For Further Information

The **National Tourist Office of Spain** (in the Casa de los Tiros, Calle Pavaneras 19. Tel. 958-22.10.22) is located about six blocks from the cathedral. Open 9:30 to 2, and 5 to 7:30; closed Sundays.

⚘ *BAEZA*

How to Get There. If you're driving from **Granada** back to **Madrid** (or from **Granada** to **Córdoba**), consider a short side trip to **Baeza** and **Úbeda**. Take N323 north to **Jaén**, then turn right on N321 for 29 miles to **Baeza** and another 6 miles to **Úbeda**.

Baeza was a former *taifa* capital—one of the feudal kingdoms that developed in Moorish Spain when the Córdoba caliphate collapsed. The **Albaicín**, the old Moorish quarter of Granada, is named for the Baezan Moors who fled to Granada when the Christians reconquered the town in 1227. This was the first reconquered town in Andalusia; the first mass of the Reconquest was held here on a balcony overlooking the **Plaza of the Lions**.

What you'll see in Baeza are some fine examples of early Spanish Renaissance architecture. The casual visitor can expect to spend less than an hour exploring the important sights, which are all within a few minutes' walk of each other.

Park at the lovely **Plaza of the Lions**; the square is on your right as you drive through town on N321. Above the lions is a draped figure said to be Hannibal's wife. The head is new; the old one was decapitated during the Spanish Civil War by Republicans who mistook her for the Virgin.

To the right of the square is the **tourist office**, where you can pick up a walking guide. To the left is the most elegant sixteenth-century **slaughter-house** (abattoir) you ever did see. Stairs lined with sixteenth-century Renaissance-Plateresque buildings lead to the cathedral. (The Plateresque style combines Gothic, Renaissance, and Arabic elements. "Plateresque" comes from *platero*, meaning "silversmith"; the design is so fine, it seems more the work of a silversmith than of a mason. Though this delicate ornamentation is Arab-inspired, the decorative themes and the symmetry and balance of the buildings themselves are inspired by the Italian Renaissance.)

Follow the steps to the **Plaza Santa María**. Turn right to reach the **cathedral**, which was remodeled in the late-sixteenth century and has some outstanding chapels (one of them has a 25-pesata treat; deposit a coin and find out for yourself).

Instead of returning to the lions, cross Plaza Santa María and follow a narrow street to the Romanesque **Church of Santa Cruz**. Next door is the old sixteenth-century university, which had a prison for unruly students. Across from the university is the **Jabalquinto Palace**. The free-flowing, lace-like façade is a great example of the Moorish-inspired Isabeline style, in which every inch of space is covered with intricate designs.

◈ *ÚBEDA*

After the Christians took over in 1234, Úbeda became a stronghold for knights, who continued the fight against the Moors—and amongst themselves.

The focus of your trip has been Moorish Spain; an hour in Úbeda will introduce you to the art and architecture of Catholic Spain during the Renaissance. Those of you with more than a passing interest in the arts will find many notable Renaissance palaces to explore; others will be content visiting the buildings on **Plaza Vázquez de Molina**, and the streets and pottery shops in the **gypsy quarter**.

Stop at the **tourist office** for a map and descriptive booklet. Leave your car here and walk to the **Plaza Vázquez de Molina**. Around the corner from the tourist office, on your way to the square, is a **crafts shop** selling the green glazed pottery for which the town is known. You'll also pass some **antique shops** selling old ceramics.

Plaza Vázquez de Molina, the aristocratic center of the old town, is bordered by several historic buildings. **El Salvador Church,** designed in 1536, has an ornamented sacristy of breathtaking exuberance. The Virgin averts her eyes from the pair of topless Italian Renaissance caryatids (female figures) guarding the door. For the key to the church, walk around the left side—to your left as you're facing the entrance—and down a street of whitewashed buildings. Ring the bell on the first door on the right.

Across the street from the church is a sixteenth-century palace which has been converted into the **Parador Nacional Condestable Dávalos** (Plaza Vázquez de Molina 1. Tel. 953-75.03.45). The parador may still be closed for restorations.

Another church worth visiting is the Gothic **St. Paul's** (San Pablo)— particularly for its chapels.

If you liked the pottery near the tourist office, visit the studios where it's made, along **Calle Valençia** in the **gypsy quarter,** a 10-minute walk from St. Paul's. You step through a Moorish stone archway and enter a monochromatic world of immaculate white walls and angular shadows, where time seems to have stopped. Men crouch in doorways as if waiting for time to begin, and old women huddle in doorways like petals of a black flower. The area is quite safe, and, unlike the ancient quarters of Sevilla and Córdoba, completely unspoiled by the tourist trade.

EN ROUTE: From ÚBEDA to MADRID

From Úbeda, take N322 west for 25 miles to **Bailén** and then take N IV north (about 6 hours) to **Madrid.**

RECOMMENDED READING

John A. Crow, *Spain: The Root and the Flower,* the most readable introduction to Moorish Spain.

Jan Morris. *Spain,* a classic, impressionistic guide.

James Michener. *Iberia,* a wordy and somewhat dated tribute.

Ernest Hemingway. *Death in the Afternoon,* the best book ever written about bullfighting; *The Sun Also Rises,* Spain between the wars; and *For Whom the Bell Tolls,* the Spanish Civil War.

V. S. Pritchett, *The Spanish Temper,* a perceptive, if at times dated, portrait of the Spanish people, with insights into the art of bullfighting.

INDEX